M000279307

The Canonization of Islamic Law

The Canonization of Islamic Law tells the story of the birth of classical Islamic law in the eighth and ninth centuries CE. It shows how an oral normative tradition embedded in communal practice was transformed into a systematic legal science defined by hermeneutic analysis of a clearly demarcated scriptural canon. This transformation was inaugurated by the innovative legal theory of Muḥammad b. Idrīs al-Shāfiʿī (d. 820 CE), and it took place against the background of a crisis of identity and religious authority in ninth-century Egypt. By tracing the formulation, reception, interpretation, and spread of al-Shāfiʿī's ideas, Ahmed El Shamsy demonstrates how the canonization of scripture that lay at the heart of al-Shāfiʿī's theory formed the basis for the emergence of legal hermeneutics, the formation of the Sunni schools of law, and the creation of a shared methodological basis in Muslim thought.

Ahmed El Shamsy is an Assistant Professor of Islamic Thought in the Department of Near Eastern Languages and Civilizations at the University of Chicago.

فلا علم لأحد بسرائر الماضين على حقيقتها فإن علمها عند علام الغيوب و كل ما في أيدينا أن نستدل بالخبر الشاهد على خبر غائب ولكن رب إستدلال وافق صواباً خفياً ولولاه لبطل علم كثير

محمود محمد شاكر

No one truly knows the secrets of those who have gone before us, for only the Knower of the hidden is acquainted with them. All we can do is reason from the known to the unknown. Yet many an inference accords with a hidden truth; were it not so, little could be known.

Maḥmūd Muḥammad Shākir, *Qaḍiyyat al-shiʿr al-jāhilī*, 58

The Canonization of Islamic Law

A Social and Intellectual History

AHMED EL SHAMSY
The University of Chicago

CAMBRIDGE
UNIVERSITY PRESS

CAMBRIDGE
UNIVERSITY PRESS

32 Avenue of the Americas, New York NY 10013-2473, USA

Cambridge University Press is part of the University of Cambridge.

It furthers the University's mission by disseminating knowledge in the pursuit of education, learning and research at the highest international levels of excellence.

www.cambridge.org
Information on this title: www.cambridge.org/9781107546073

First published 2013
First paperback edition 2015

A catalogue record for this publication is available from the British Library

Library of Congress Cataloguing in Publication data
El Shamsy, Ahmed, 1976–
The canonization of Islamic law : a social and intellectual history / Ahmed El Shamsy.
p. cm.
Includes bibliographical references and index.
ISBN 978-1-107-04148-6 (hardback)
1. Islamic law – History. 2. Canonization. I. Title.
KBP50.E4 2013
340.5′9–dc23 2013007633

ISBN 978-1-107-04148-6 Hardback
ISBN 978-1-107-54607-3 Paperback

Contents

Acknowledgments

I never chose this topic. I stumbled upon it quite by accident, via the chance discovery of a manuscript (al-Buwayṭī's *Mukhtaṣar*) that distracted me from the research project on legal maxims that I had been pursuing. What was intended as a semester's digression turned into nearly a decade's exploration of the origins of Islamic law and its institutions. In that time, I have received inspiration, feedback, and support from innumerable people, many of whom I have forgotten to thank here. The questions and hypotheses that animate this book emerged and were refined in conversations with Bilal Aybakan, Murteza Bedir, Eyyüp Said Kaya, Kevin Reinhart, Gregor Schoeler, Himmet Taşkömür, and especially Aron Zysow. In addition, I have benefited from the opportunity to discuss my research at a number of venues, most importantly at the collegial annual gatherings of the American Oriental Society. I gratefully acknowledge the generous advice of Peri Bearman, the developmental guidance of Bud Bynack, the research assistance of Khālid ʿAbduh, and the instruction in Shāfiʿī law given to me by Shaykh Naṣr al-Dīn Shaʿbān, which laid the foundation for everything I have since learned about the subject. Roy Mottahedeh, Aron Zysow, Intisar Rabb, Khaled El-Rouayheb, Andreas Görke, and two anonymous reviewers provided useful comments on drafts of the manuscript or of parts of it. Finally, I thank my wife and editor, Hanna Siurua, for her merciless but constructive prodding, criticism, and suggestions, all of which have immeasurably improved this book in both form and content.

The archival research on which this book is based was made possible by the support of the Social Science Research Council and the Andrew W. Mellon Foundation, the American Research Institute in

Turkey, the Center for Islamic Studies (ISAM) in Istanbul, the Frederick Sheldon Fund at Harvard University, and the Friends of the Princeton University Library. This support allowed me to explore the manuscript collections of the Egyptian National Manuscript Library and the Arab League Manuscript Library in Cairo, the Bibliotheca Alexandrina in Alexandria, the Süleymaniye Library in Istanbul, the Asad National Library in Damascus, the Chester Beatty Library in Dublin, and the Firestone Library at Princeton University. The writing of the book was supported by the Islamic Legal Studies Program at Harvard Law School, the American Council of Learned Societies (with funds provided by the Mellon Foundation), and a book fellowship from the Social Science Research Council (again funded by the Mellon Foundation).

The cover image, of a 1928 painting titled *Courtyard of the Al-Azhar Mosque and University, Cairo* by Ivan Yakovlevich Bilibine (1876–1942), was provided courtesy of MacDougall Auctions. Although Bilibine's painting depicts a scene of scholarly exchange in the early twentieth century, the institutions, texts, and debates that characterized Islamic scholarship at the time of his Cairo visit represent a continuation of the culture of learning whose emergence a thousand years earlier I document in this book.

Note on Dates, Places, and Terms

I give most dates in this book in dual form, with the Hijri date according to the Islamic calendar followed by the Common Era date, separated by a slash. Personal names are transliterated fully; place names and the names of dynasties are not. Nonspecialists should note the small but significant orthographic distinction between "al-Shāfiʿī" (the scholar), "Shāfiʿīs" (the followers of al-Shāfiʿī), and "Shāfiʿī" (one such follower, or the adjective describing al-Shāfiʿī, his ideas, his followers, and the school he founded). I use the anglicized term "Hadith" for reports of the Prophet Muḥammad's sayings and actions in both the singular (orig. *ḥadīth*) and the plural (*aḥādīth*).

Introduction

When Muḥammad died in the year 632 of the Common Era, the community that he had established in Medina a mere ten years earlier seemed unlikely to survive, let alone grow into a world civilization. It is true that two years before his death Muḥammad and his followers had been able to seize control of his native Mecca and subsequently to extend their sphere of influence over the Hejaz and other parts of the Arabian peninsula. But an outside observer in, say, Constantinople would have had little reason to think that the new Muslim state would fare any better than the other short-lived tribal confederations in Arabia that had formed around charismatic leaders only to dissolve at their deaths, leaving few traces beyond ruins in the desert.

Within a century, however, this fledgling community in the backwaters of the ancient Near East had conquered much of the civilized world, bringing under its command an area that reached the Pyrenees in the west and the Indus River in the east. These military successes were made possible by the motivating and unifying force of the new religion, Islam, as well as by the ethnic and cultural cohesion of the Arab tribes that had come together under its banner. The shared values, norms, and traditions of the society in which the Muslims were rooted stood in sharp contrast to the political and religious fragmentation of the Near East of late antiquity.[1] But with the spectacular expansion of a tribal union into an empire that spanned three continents, the hitherto tightly knit community of Muslim

[1] See Richard Lim, "Christian Triumph and Controversy," in *Interpreting Late Antiquity: Essays on the Postclassical World*, ed. G. W. Bowersock, Peter Brown, and Oleg Grabar, 196–218 (Cambridge, MA: Belknap Press of Harvard University Press, 2001).

Arabs found itself scattered across an immense territory, surrounded and outnumbered by non-Muslim and non-Arab native populations. Many of these boasted long and rich histories and a level of cultural sophistication that considerably exceeded that of the conquerors. It would have been natural for the Arabs to become assimilated into the dominant cultures of their new environments, as had the Germanic tribes before them and as would the Mongols after them.

This is not, however, what happened. Instead, around the middle of the second Hijri (eighth Common Era) century, Muslim civilization entered a formative period of intellectual and religious transformations that established an enduring cultural foundation for subsequent Muslim societies.[2] This foundational age, which lasted about a century and a half, gave rise to a stable, distinctively Islamic cultural synthesis that was not defined by ethnicity. Rather, its twin bases were the religion of Islam and the language of Arabic, and upon these foundations grew a characteristic written culture whose myriad genres, incubated in this period of intellectual fermentation, elaborated the former by means of the latter. The formation of this written culture was accompanied by the emergence and consolidation of a class of specialist scholars, who dedicated themselves to the mapping of the world of ideas within the nascent classical disciplines. To claim that this period was formative is not to deny that Muslim civilization continued to evolve in significant ways after it; but what defines this period is the development of the basic cultural vocabulary of Islamic concepts, practices, and institutions. These came to constitute the conceptual building blocks that later Muslim societies then recombined and reinterpreted in historically and geographically specific ways.

Premodern Muslim historians and contemporary scholars alike have recognized that the period between the second/eighth and fourth/tenth centuries witnessed fundamental social and cultural changes with lasting repercussions for Muslim civilization.[3] Both groups identify as the focal point of these changes the discourse of Islamic law, which during this

[2] My focus is primarily, though not exclusively, on Sunnism. Although many of the developments discussed here also had a lasting effect on Twelver and Ismāʿīlī Shiʿism, the institution of the infallible imam shaped Shiʿi perceptions of revelation and religious authority in ways that significantly differentiate the Imāmī Shiʿi tradition from its Sunni counterpart.

[3] For a recent overview of Western studies that acknowledge the formative nature of this period, see Scott C. Lucas, *Constructive Critics, Ḥadīth Literature, and the Articulation of Sunnī Islam: The Legacy of the Generation of Ibn Saʿd, Ibn Maʿīn, and Ibn Ḥanbal* (Leiden: Brill, 2004), 1–21. For the Muslim perspective, see Shāh Walī Allāh al-Dihlawī, *al-Inṣāf fī bayān asbāb al-ikhtilāf*, ed. ʿAbd al-Fattāḥ Abū Ghudda (Beirut: Dār al-Nafāʾis, 1984).

formative age burgeoned into a vast and detailed literature. The reason for the centrality of law lies in its dominant role in defining Muslim identity and culture.

In its classical formulation, Sunni Islamic law is the product of the private efforts of Muslim scholars to capture the divine commands and prohibitions inherent in revelation and to articulate these in the form of detailed legal rulings covering all aspects of a believer's ritual and social life. The process of interpretation is structured by a repertoire of hermeneutic techniques, which are underpinned by theories not only of the sources of the divine law and their interconnections but also of the nature of language, interpretation, and communication. Classical legal theory thus represents the primary site for theorizing the relationship of the Muslim community to revelation and the sacred past, while the voluminous literature on positive law seeks to establish the parameters for ensuring the Islamic identity of individual and communal life in the here and now.

This framework, in its basic form, continued to characterize the discourse of Islamic law into the twentieth century, and it remains influential today. Its foundations, however, were laid in the second/eighth to fourth/tenth centuries, when its essential elements – the classical ideas regarding the sources of the law and their interpretation – first emerged. Yet in spite of its significance, we know very little about how, exactly, Islamic law came to acquire its classical form, and even less about why. This book is my attempt to answer these questions. It tells the story of the transformation of the Islamic normative discourse in the formative age and the consequent birth of the discipline of Islamic law as we have come to know it. By weaving intellectual, sociopolitical, and textual history into an integrated narrative, I draw out the interconnections between developments in different spheres that explain why the transformation happened at this particular juncture in Islamic history, and why the resulting legal system took the form that it did.

The key to this pivotal event, I argue, lies in a process of canonization that took place when the locus of religious authority was transferred from the lived practice of the Muslim community to a written, clearly demarcated canon of sacred sources consisting of the Quran and the body of Hadith (reports concerning Muḥammad's sayings and actions). Canonization does not here refer to the establishment of a definitive textual version of the Quran, which happened earlier, nor to the completion of the so-called canonical collections of Hadith, which took place later. Both of these important developments could be – and have been – described in terms of canonization.[4] This book, however, examines a different kind of transformation, one that is best characterized as a discursive shift vis-à-vis an entire category of texts. Canonization, in the sense employed here, transcends the mere codification of sacred texts in fixed textual form and focuses instead on the relationship of the Muslim community to these texts as sources of religious norms.[5] This relationship, as noted earlier, was mediated by the discourse of Islamic law and by legal scholars, who saw themselves and were seen by others as the guardians of the community's normative tradition.

The effect of canonization on the relationship between Muslims and their sacred texts was profound. Previously, Quran and Hadith (the latter circulating as innumerable individual reports) had represented the "raw material" of religious values, material that was continuously being sifted through the filter of communal experience and scholarly appraisal in order to distill its prescriptive meaning for the community. Canonization anointed these texts as the fount of normativity itself. Scholars recognized a certain category of texts as the uniquely authoritative and hermeneutically self-sufficient statement of God's commandments for humankind. Through this recognition, the canonized sources – and no others – came to constitute the sovereign measuring stick against which the scholars would subsequently evaluate the practices of the community.

The primary societal trigger of this canonization, I demonstrate, was a crisis of identity and authority experienced by the Muslim community, the *umma*, that was caused by the enormous social, cultural, and political changes affecting the *umma* in the second/eighth century. This was not, of course, the first communal crisis to shake the *umma*: the civil wars that followed the murder of the caliph ʿUthmān in 37/656 had bitterly divided the community and prompted deep uncertainty regarding its foundations.

4 See, in particular, A. Al-Azmeh, "The Muslim Canon from Late Antiquity to the Era of Modernism," in *Canonization and Decanonization*, ed. A. van der Kooij and K. van der Toorn, 191–228 (Leiden: Brill, 1998). Al-Azmeh notes (on p. 200) the potential fruitfulness of analyzing the canonization of these sources in relation to Islamic law, suggesting that such a study would constitute "an important vantage point from which one could conceptually review the matter of canonicity in its entirety."

5 The concept of canonization in this sense has been employed by Jonathan A. C. Brown to explain the authoritative status of the two most prominent Hadith collections, and by Hans-Thomas Tillschneider to demonstrate the significance of legal hermeneutics in the canonization of the Quran and Hadith. See Jonathan A. C. Brown, *The Canonization of al-Bukhārī and Muslim: The Formation and Function of the Sunnī Ḥadīth Canon* (Leiden: Brill, 2007), and Hans-Thomas Tillschneider, *Die Entstehung der juristischen Hermeneutik (*uṣūl al-fiqh*) im frühen Islam* (Würzburg: Ergon, 2006). Brown's book contains a useful survey of the literature on canonization (chap. 2).

That crisis, too, had given rise to a radically novel hermeneutic project that sought to provide a solution to the uncertainty and instability created by communal discord. The Khārijīs' approach was starkly literalist: their insistence that only the superficially apparent reading of any Quranic passage was correct necessarily excluded the possibility of legitimate differences of opinion and thus led them to anathemize anyone who disagreed. But although the absolutist Khārijī model was still in circulation in the second and third/eighth and ninth centuries, it remained a marginal phenomenon and eventually died out entirely.[6]

The crisis of the second/eighth century was different in both its causes and its outcome. It was rooted in the changes that accompanied the rapid spread of Islam across much of the known world: the influx and rising prominence of new converts from diverse backgrounds, the emergence of new alliances and localized Muslim subcultures across the empire, and the consequent dissolution of the tribal ties and ethnic homogeneity that had sustained the initial wave of expansion. This social and cultural upheaval undermined confidence in the authenticity of the essentially mimetic normative tradition of the Muslim community, which was predicated on the perception of unbroken continuity with the prophetic age. The resulting anxieties and uncertainties prompted a search for new foundations of religious authority, a way of accessing the authentic message of divine revelation that was more secure than the avenue of communal practice, which seemed increasingly frail and ambiguous. Canonization offered a solution to this dilemma by enshrining revelation in a fixed category of textual sources – the canon – that could then be subjected to systematic analysis by a professionalized group of experts.

The impulse that initiated the process of canonization arose from the work of the jurist Muḥammad b. Idrīs al-Shāfiʿī (d. 204/820). It was al-Shāfiʿī who, having become disillusioned with what he saw as the arbitrariness and even dangerousness of the sacralization of communal tradition, developed the first explicit theorization of revelation as divine communication encapsulated in the textual form of the Quran and its auxiliary, prophetic Hadith. The formulation of this theory was the first step in the process of canonization: it provided a justification for the exclusive status of the sacred texts and for the barring of communal practice from the determination of Islamic law. The second step, then, was the acceptance of al-Shāfiʿī's novel theory by other Sunni Muslim scholars, an

[6] Michael Cook, "ʿAnan and Islam: The Origins of Karaite Scripturalism," *Jerusalem Studies in Arabic and Islam* 9 (1987): 161–82.

acceptance that was facilitated by the confluence of numerous historical developments discussed in this book.

This is not to claim that al-Shāfiʿī was necessarily the first or the sole source of this impulse. The following chapters show clearly that al-Shāfiʿī's ideas were developed in the context of and through engagement with various strands of legal thought in his age, and they formed part of broader cultural and societal trends. Al-Shāfiʿī's work drew together developments that also seem to have been taking place elsewhere – such as the emergence of legal-theoretical thought and epistemological analyses of the authenticity of Hadith – but that found their first systematic and enduring expression in the writings of al-Shāfiʿī.[7]

Al-Shāfiʿī's theory embodied a radical individualism. In sharp contrast to the old communitarian model, al-Shāfiʿī admitted neither communal tradition nor scholarly precedent into the process of interpreting the sacred canon, insisting on the direct and unmediated encounter between the interpreting jurist and the canonized sources. But the ensuing shift from community to canon was not the end of the story. Had it been, the resulting legal discourse would have been very different from the discourse that we actually inherited: a system in which each jurist was forced to redevelop the legal edifice from scratch could not have given rise to the sophisticated discourse and literature that came to characterize Islamic law. Instead, al-Shāfiʿī's canon-centered individualism was tempered by the reintegration of community into Islamic law through a new institution, the school of law (*madhhab*). Whereas the precanonization normative discourse had been embedded in a community of *tradition*, the novel institution of the legal school was first and foremost a community of *interpretation* that defined itself in terms of a shared hermeneutic stance vis-à-vis the canon of sacred sources.

Just as al-Shāfiʿī had set into motion the canonization that prompted the transformation of Islamic legal discourse, so it was al-Shāfiʿī's students who laid the basis for the classical practice of Islamic law within the new framework of interpretive communities. The students interrogated, interpreted, and extended al-Shāfiʿī's ideas; transmitted and popularized his writings; authored their own, secondary works; and established a model of critical adherence to the master's interpretive paradigm. This model

[7] Norman Calder has called into question the authenticity of al-Shāfiʿī's surviving works in *Studies in Early Muslim Jurisprudence* (Oxford: Clarendon, 1993). I offer an extensive refutation of his argument in "Al-Shāfiʿī's Written Corpus: A Source-Critical Study," *Journal of the American Oriental Society* 132 (2012): 199–220, and will take the authenticity of these works for granted in this book.

eventually matured into the classical school of law, while the students' reinterpretations of al-Shāfiʿī's thought formed the bridges over which al-Shāfiʿī's canonization project spread to other schools and fields of scholarship at a remarkable speed. It is thus not an exaggeration to say that the formative history of the Shāfiʿī school is also the formative history of classical Sunni Islamic law.

Examining the transformation of Islamic law in this period through the lens of canonization allows us to make better sense of a phenomenon that has occupied a central place in the modern study of Islamic law. Beginning with Ignaz Goldziher,[8] a number of influential Western scholars have postulated that the corpus of Hadith is mostly the product of deliberate forgery in the second/eighth century. This theory has sought to explain the apparent fact that prior to this time, Muslim jurists disregarded Hadith that later on were widely accepted. In his seminal work on Islamic law, Joseph Schacht argued that the law of the early Muslim community was nothing more than a collection of bureaucratic rules adopted from Roman law. These were then subjected to post hoc islamization through the invention of Hadith that justified them as representing genuine prophetic practice. Al-Shāfiʿī's systematization of legal theory and his theorization of Quran and Hadith as the only real sources of the law were essentially aimed at covering up this process by legitimizing the resulting islamized legal edifice.[9] More recently, Patricia Crone and Martin Hinds have proposed an alternative explanation, which links the emergence of Hadith in Islamic law to a shift in religious authority from the caliphs to the community of scholars. As the victors in this power struggle, the scholars rewrote the history of the law to excise the role of their rivals and to attribute the rules of the law directly to the Prophet.[10] For Crone and Hinds as for Goldziher and Schacht, this post hoc rationalization of the law was carried out by means of large-scale forgery of Hadith reports.[11]

If one accepts the hypothesis that the thousands of Hadith that form the basis of classical Islamic law are the product of deliberate falsification, one can only dismiss wholesale the vast body of Islamic legal and

[8] Ignaz Goldziher, *Introduction to Islamic Theology and Law*, trans. Andras and Ruth Hamori (Princeton, NJ: Princeton University Press, 1981), 38–46.

[9] See, for example, Joseph Schacht, *The Origins of Muhammadan Jurisprudence* (Oxford: Clarendon, 1950), 56.

[10] Patricia Crone and Martin Hinds, *God's Caliph: Religious Authority in the First Centuries of Islam* (Cambridge: Cambridge University Press, 1986).

[11] See also Patricia Crone, *Roman, Provincial, and Islamic Law: The Origins of the Islamic Patronate* (Cambridge: Cambridge University Press, 1987), 24.

historiographical literature that transmits, analyzes, and uses this material as if it were (at least potentially) genuine.[12] From such a perspective, the classical literature embodies a concerted effort to conceal the true nature and origin of "Islamic" law. Far from representing sources for secondary scholarship, therefore, these texts in fact constitute obstacles to earnest inquiry into the history of the law. This is a bold claim, implying as it does that Muslim scholarship is in some fundamental and unique way dishonest and must be decoded by "objective" outsiders.[13] The factual basis of the claim has been challenged by numerous critical studies, which have shown that indiscriminate rejection of the authenticity of the entire Hadith corpus is as misguided as its categorical acceptance.[14] And far from representing an exercise of "imaginative nerve," as Crone called it,[15] interpreting the initial marginality of Hadith in law as evidence of their nonexistence at that time displays a curious lack of imagination: it assumes that Hadith reports, if available, could be used only in the way that classical jurists used them, namely, as one of the primary canonical sources of the law. This approach thus reads an essentialized notion of Islamic law, developed on the basis of later literature, back into the early Islamic period and solves the resulting dissonance by postulating the wholesale invention of prophetic traditions.

Beyond being essentially unimaginative, factually dubious, and methodologically unpalatable, the conclusion that the discourse of Islamic law was born out of the forgery of Hadith is also quite unnecessary. The principle of Occam's razor encourages us to prefer the simplest theory that adequately explains the known facts. The hypothesis that untold hundreds of Muslim scholars over several centuries participated in a vast

[12] Medieval Muslim scholars were, of course, aware that not all Hadith were authentic, and the classical discipline of Hadith study was in large part devoted to the task of assessing the transmission history of individual reports and the reliability of their transmitters.

[13] "There is no way around the fact that we are secularisers: we are secularising history, because we separate the past we are studying from our own and other people's modern convictions; we do not allow the past to be rewritten as mere support of these modern convictions. That's a problem to all traditional believers, and perhaps Muslims more than most." Patricia Crone, "Islam and Religious Freedom" (keynote speech, 30th Deutscher Orientalistentag, Freiburg im Breisgau, Germany, Sept. 24, 2007; available online at http://orient.ruf.uni-freiburg.de/dotpub/crone.pdf).

[14] For a collection of important studies that challenge the a priori dismissal of Hadith and argue convincingly that at least some Hadith predate their putative "invention" in the second/eighth century, see Harald Motzki with Nicolet Boekhoff-Van der Voort and Sean W. Anthony, *Analysing Muslim Traditions: Studies in Legal, Exegetical and Maghāzī Ḥadīth* (Leiden: Brill, 2010).

[15] Crone, *Roman, Provincial, and Islamic Law*, 16.

and successful conspiracy to conceal the real origin and nature of legal discourse does not fare particularly well in this test. The explanation that I propose in this book is far more straightforward and, I believe, convincing: the reason for the "sudden" integration of Hadith into law from the second/eighth century onward lies not in their invention, but rather in their new significance and role – that is, their canonization. This explanation makes no claim as to the authenticity or otherwise of the body of Hadith reports; what matters here is how these reports were seen and used by Muslim scholars, not what their precise provenance in fact is.

Analyzing the history of the law within the wider context of Sunni cultural history not only enables us to identify the phenomenon of canonization and its consequences, including the elevation of Hadith to a position of prominence in legal theory and practice. More broadly, it reveals the deep connections between this development and other shifts that marked this formative period. An ideal conceptual framework for understanding these connections is provided by Aleida and Jan Assmann's theory of cultural memory and its transformation, an approach that links the evolution of cultural and religious discourses to the opportunities and constraints created by specific ways in which collective values are preserved and transmitted.[16] An important contribution of this approach is the observation that cultural upheaval and dislocation prompt societies to seek to safeguard cultural memory through the canonization of texts that possess high symbolic value as carriers of communal identity. The locus of collective memory, hitherto diffused in the realm of oral culture and ritual performance, thus shifts to written texts, whose form becomes fixed and whose content is invested with great authority. Enriching this insight with research done by Gregor Schoeler and Harald Motzki on writing and transmission in early Islam[17] and embedding it in a detailed narrative drawn from primary historical material, this book provides a contextualized account of the transformation of Islamic law from an aural normative tradition to a systematic legal science. As a social and

[16] See, for example, Aleida Assmann and Jan Assmann, eds., *Kanon und Zensur* (Munich: W. Fink, 1987); Jan Assmann, *Religion und kulturelles Gedächtnis* (Munich: C. H. Beck, 2000); and Jan Assmann, *Das kulturelle Gedächtnis: Schrift, Erinnerung und politische Identität in frühen Hochkulturen* (Munich: C. H. Beck, 1992).

[17] Gregor Schoeler, *The Oral and the Written in Early Islam*, ed. James Montgomery, trans. Uwe Vagelpohl (London: Routledge, 2006); Schoeler, *The Genesis of Literature in Islam: From the Aural to the Read*, trans. Shawkat M. Toorawa (Edinburgh: Edinburgh University Press, 2009); and Harald Motzki, *Die Anfänge der islamischen Jurisprudenz: Ihre Entwicklung in Mekka bis zur Mitte des 2./8. Jahrhunderts* (Stuttgart: Deutsche Morgenländische Gesellschaft and F. Steiner, 1991).

intellectual history, it examines early legal discourse as a site where ideas and practices both modify and are modified by social relations and communal identities.

The first part of the book lays out the intellectual milieu of the second/eighth century and shows how al-Shāfiʿī's engagement with other scholars inspired and shaped his revolutionary theory of revelation. To a significant extent, al-Shāfiʿī formulated his theory in response to the work of his teacher Mālik b. Anas (d. 179/796), which in turn reflected the challenge posed by new methods of legal reasoning developed in Iraq. Accordingly, Chapter 1 examines the reasons for and effect of Mālik's attempt to codify in written form the Islamic legal tradition as embodied in the communal tradition of the Prophet's city, Medina. It shows that this innovation laid the basis for the emergence of a legal literature of purposefully authored books, with profound consequences for the nature of legal discourse. Chapter 2 follows al-Shāfiʿī from Medina to Iraq, the intellectual center of the Muslim world in his time, and analyzes his encounters with leading scholars representing the major movements animating Islamic thought in the second/eighth century: dialectical jurisprudence (*ra'y*) and rationalist theology (*kalām*). These "Iraqi debates" had a formative impact on al-Shāfiʿī's thought. In particular, they shaped the development of his ideas about the respective roles of Hadith and communal consensus in jurisprudence and contributed to his gradual estrangement from his erstwhile teacher Mālik. Chapter 3 demonstrates how al-Shāfiʿī's critique of Mālik, expressed in the novel format of an authored work, gave rise to a distinctive and original legal hermeneutic. This was based on the decisive rejection of legal conformism (*taqlīd*) and the canonization of the sacred sources of Quran and Hadith as the uniquely normative basis of the law. Al-Shāfiʿī's project of canonization entailed a reconceptualization of divine revelation as a communicative act between God and humankind, in which the prophetic example, enshrined in Hadith, served the essential function of elucidating the meaning of the Quran.

In order to explain why al-Shāfiʿī's radical theory of the law was able to gain adherents and establish itself in scholarly discourse in spite of the challenge that it embodied to the doctrinal status quo among the dominant elites, the second part of the book reconstructs the sociopolitical history of Egypt from the second/eighth through the third/ninth century and situates it within the broader context of the intellectual and political shifts that were taking place in the Abbasid empire. Chapter 4 shows how the dramatic changes affecting Egyptian society in the second/eighth century created a receptive environment for al-Shāfiʿī's canonization project.

Increasing social heterogeneity and imperial centralization challenged the old Egyptian social order and eroded the basis of the Egyptian elite's vision of a secure and autonomous communal tradition connecting the present-day community to the moment of revelation. The ensuing sense of communal dislocation and uncertainty prepared the ground for al-Shāfiʿī's abandonment of communal practice and the investment of normativity in the sacred texts alone. Chapter 5 pursues the fates of al-Shāfiʿī's immediate successors amid the social and political turmoil of the third/ninth century in order to discover how al-Shāfiʿī's novel theory found its way into the broader scholarly discourse of the time. Shifting currents of political patronage for religious learning played a crucial role in enabling al-Shāfiʿī's students to propagate their master's thought and writings and to achieve their diffusion throughout the Islamic world within a single generation. Two events were particularly significant in driving the trends of persecution, tolerance, and endorsement that shaped the trajectory of early Shāfiʿī scholarship in this period: the Quranic Inquisition (*miḥnat al-Qurʾān*) and the brief but important reign of the Tulunid dynasty in Egypt.

The third and final part of the book investigates how al-Shāfiʿī's teaching, as interpreted and transmitted by his students, was converted into the paradigm that came to form the basis of a common methodology and institutional framework in Sunni legal thought. This achievement enabled both the successful propagation of al-Shāfiʿī's theory of canonization and the reconstitution of Islamic law as a communal venture, albeit one with a character very different from Mālik's concept of sacralized community. Chapter 6 traces the history of al-Shāfiʿī's textual corpus, which was critical to the development of the Shāfiʿī paradigm. It shows that from the very beginning, the scholars of the nascent Shāfiʿī school followed practices of writing and textual transmission that were aimed at safeguarding the integrity, authorial voice, and correct attribution of individual texts. Chapter 7 draws on the sociology of knowledge to shed light on the birth of the legal school as a discursive institution, embodying a shared school doctrine and a secondary literature dedicated to elucidating the writings of the founder. It analyzes the processes of interpretation and extension through which al-Shāfiʿī's students converted his works and ideas into an impersonal Shāfiʿī paradigm. This furnished a set of basic assumptions, methods for expanding these assumptions, and further questions to be explored, which then formed the basis for the scholarly efforts of subsequent generations of Shāfiʿīs. Al-Shāfiʿī's paradigm also had a significant and identifiable influence on Muslim scholars beyond the Shāfiʿī school. Chapter 8 traces this influence through the third/ninth century in order to reveal the diffusion of al-Shāfiʿī's groundbreaking legal theory across the landscape of Sunni thought. A close analysis of the writings and arguments of theologians, Hadith scholars, and jurists belonging to other legal schools who studied al-Shāfiʿī's works with his students demonstrates that many of them internalized the central feature of the Shāfiʿī paradigm – its prioritization of textual evidence rooted in the canonized sacred sources, particularly Hadith – and subsequently employed it in the formulation of their own positions. The influence of al-Shāfiʿī's legal-theoretical doctrine on other schools thus triggered a methodological convergence that eventually gave rise to a shared hermeneutic framework in Sunni religious scholarship.

In dealing with early Islamic history, I inevitably invite questions regarding the reliability of my sources. The general authenticity of the second-/eighth- to fourth-/tenth-century sources, al-Shāfiʿī's own corpus foremost among them, that I use to reconstruct and represent the ideas of that period can be convincingly defended, and I and others have sought to do so.[18] For biographical information I rely most heavily on material that is at least partially corroborated by contemporary sources, such as al-Shāfiʿī's own accounts of his study with Mālik or his debates with Muḥammad b. al-Ḥasan al-Shaybānī (d. 189/804 or 805). Beyond such material, I use my judgment as a historian to steer a course between gullibility and skepticism. For example, in Chapter 6 I quote an account by Abū Zurʿa al-Rāzī (d. 264/878) about his study of al-Shāfiʿī's work with the latter's student al-Rabīʿ b. Sulaymān al-Murādī (d. 270/884). I can think of no plausible reason why Abū Zurʿa would invent such a straightforward account of the nitty-gritty details of student life, nor why the recorder of the extant version of this account, Abū Zurʿa's student Ibn Abī Ḥātim al-Rāzī (d. 327/938), could not be trusted to reproduce it accurately. Much of my historical narrative in Chapters 4 and 5 in particular is based on early chronicles that reproduce further contemporary material in the form of documents and poetry. I also include quite liberally information from later sources that sheds light on the subject matter without being crucial to my core argument. I see no problem in

[18] See my "Al-Shāfiʿī's Written Corpus." See also, e.g., Behnam Sadeghi, "The Authenticity of Two 2nd/8th Century Ḥanafī Legal Texts: The *Kitāb al-āthār* and *al-Muwaṭṭaʾ* of Muḥammad b. al-Ḥasan al-Shaybānī," *Islamic Law and Society* 17 (2010): 291–319, and Andreas Görke, *Das Kitāb al-Amwāl des Abū ʿUbaid al-Qāsim b. Sallām: Entstehung und Überlieferung eines frühislamischen Rechtswerkes* (Princeton, NJ: Darwin Press, 2003).

mentioning what the earliest available sources tell us about important events, and the conclusions drawn by later Muslim historians based on their own research, while naturally not beyond doubt, can often provide valuable insights.

In writing this book, I have sought both to sketch a large-scale historical transformation and to provide a detailed and concrete study of a group of individuals in their historical context. Furthermore, I have tried to present my ideas in a narrative prose that makes it accessible even to those not initiated into the jargon of our field. In a clear-sighted comment, Josef van Ess once pointed out the dangers of such an approach in the field of Islamic studies: given the wealth of available material and the thin coverage that it has received in modern scholarship, attempting a coherent narrative, undisturbed by discussions of scholarly disputes and philological analyses, runs the danger of giving the impression that working hypotheses that still need to be tested and discussed are absolutely valid and accepted.[19] I have taken this statement as a note of caution, rather than as a claim to the impossibility of the task. In order to avoid the pitfalls of such a project, I have striven to indicate points of debate without indulging in a back-and-forth, and to limit my discussion of philological problems to footnotes while avoiding the temptation to compose encyclopedic comments. The kind of detailed *Grundlagenforschung* that a narrative exposition cannot accommodate can be found in three separate articles.[20] I believe that the significance of the events and ideas covered in this book transcends not just Islamic legal studies but Islamic studies as a whole, and I have therefore sought to communicate them in a form that is accessible to a wider readership.

[19] Josef van Ess, review of *Die Festung des Glaubens*, by Tilman Nagel, *Der Islam* 67 (1990): 366–74.

[20] "The First Shāfiʿī: The Traditionalist Legal Thought of Abū Yaʿqūb al-Buwayṭī (d. 231/846)," *Islamic Law and Society* 14 (2007): 301–41; "Rethinking *Taqlīd* in the Early Shāfiʿī School," *Journal of the American Oriental Society* 128 (2008): 1–24; and "Al-Shāfiʿī's Written Corpus." I have drawn on these articles in various chapters of this book.

PART I

CULTURAL REMEMBRANCE TRANSFORMED

Chapter 1

Tradition under Siege

In the 160s of the Islamic era (770s–780s CE), a talented and self-confident young man from a distinguished family traveled from his home in Mecca to Medina, the "city of the Prophet," in order to study the greatest best seller of his time with its author. The author was Mālik b. Anas (d. 179/796), the doyen of Medinan scholarship, to whom students flocked from all over the Muslim world. His book was the *Muwaṭṭa'*, a groundbreaking treatise on Islamic law that was at the time surpassed in popularity and influence only by the Quran.[1] And the young student was Muḥammad b. Idrīs al-Shāfiʿī (d. 204/820), a cosmopolitan prodigy whose innovative ideas about divine revelation and its interpretation would come to transfigure the nature of Islamic law.[2]

Al-Shāfiʿī was a direct descendant of the Prophet Muḥammad's uncle Muṭṭalib – an unusually noble pedigree for a scholar – and thus enjoyed the elevated social status of members of the Prophet's tribe, the Quraysh. He was born most probably in 150/767 in Ashkelon (Palestine), or according to some accounts in Yemen.[3] His father died when the son was still very young, and he subsequently moved with his mother to Mecca, where his youth is said to have been marked by two passions, archery and learning.[4] He also composed poetry and developed a reputation for

[1] Ibn Taymiyya, *Ṣiḥḥat uṣūl ahl al-Madīna,* in *Majmūʿat al-fatāwā*, ed. ʿĀmir al-Jazzār and Anwar al-Bāz, 20 vols., 20:163–219 (Mansura: Dār al-Wafā', 1997), at 20:178.

[2] For an accessible overview of al-Shāfiʿī's life and career, see Kecia Ali, *Imam Shafiʿi: Scholar and Saint* (Oxford: Oneworld, 2011).

[3] Ibn Abī Ḥātim al-Rāzī, *Ādāb al-Shāfiʿī wa-manāqibuh*, ed. ʿAbd al-Ghanī ʿAbd al-Khāliq (Cairo: Maktabat al-Khānjī, 1953), 21–23.

[4] Ibn Abī Ḥātim, *Ādāb al-Shāfiʿī*, 22–23.

eloquence.[5] Al-Shāfiʿī pursued his studies with determination in spite of the family's straitened financial circumstances. In the earliest report about al-Shāfiʿī's education, reproduced in Ibn Abī Ḥātim al-Rāzī's (d. 327/938) *Ādāb al-Shāfiʿī*, al-Shāfiʿī recounts the difficult beginning of his scholarly career:

> I was a [half-]orphan in the care of my mother. She had nothing that she could give to [my] teacher [as payment], but the teacher was content with me replacing him in his absence. When I finished [memorizing] the Quran, I entered the mosque, and I used to sit with the scholars, memorizing Hadith and points of law.... I wrote Hadith and points of law on [bones]. We had a large old jar, and whenever I covered a bone, I put it in the jar.[6]

Given his limited means, al-Shāfiʿī was forced to use animal bones as writing material.[7] He is also reported to have gone to the local government scriptorium (*dīwān*), where official documents were produced, to request discarded writing materials, the backs of which he reused for his studies.[8] In spite of the practical obstacles posed by his circumstances, al-Shāfiʿī received an excellent education, becoming one of the principal students of the Meccan mufti Muslim b. Khālid al-Zanjī (d. 179 or 180/795–97) and the famous traditionist Sufyān b. ʿUyayna (d. 196/811).[9] Al-Zanjī is reported to have authorized al-Shāfiʿī to issue legal responsa (*fatāwā*) when the latter was still in his teens.[10]

In his late teens or early twenties, having already gained some renown as a scholar, al-Shāfiʿī decided to study the legal tradition in greater depth. For this purpose, according to Ibn Abī Ḥātim, he borrowed a copy of Mālik's *Muwaṭṭaʾ* and committed it to memory. Afterward, he wanted to have the text that he had memorized checked and explained by its author.

5 How much of al-Shāfiʿī's *Dīwān* (the collection of poetry assembled and attributed to him by later scholars) is authentic remains to be determined, but there are sufficient examples in the earliest sources to confirm that al-Shāfiʿī did compose poetry. See, for example, *Dīwān al-Imām al-Shāfiʿī*, ed. ʿUmar Fārūq al-Ṭabbāʿ (Beirut: Dār al-Arqam, n.d.); and *Dīwān al-Shāfiʿī*, ed. Mujāhid Bahjat (Damascus: Dār al-Qalam, 1999).

6 Ibn Abī Ḥātim, *Ādāb al-Shāfiʿī*, 24.

7 Evidence of the practice of writing on bones has survived; see Albert Dietrich, "Zwei arabisch beschriftete Knochenstücke aus dem mittelalterlichen Ägypten," *Le Muséon* 65 (1952): 259–70.

8 Abū Bakr al-Bayhaqī, *Manāqib al-Shāfiʿī*, ed. al-Sayyid Aḥmad Ṣaqr, 2 vols. (Cairo: Maktabat Dār al-Turāth, 1971), 1:93.

9 Muḥammad Abū Zahra, *al-Shāfiʿī: Ḥayātuhu wa-ʿaṣruhu, ārāʾuhu wa-fiqhuh* (Cairo: Dār al-Fikr al-ʿArabī, 1948), 15–46.

10 Ibn Abī Ḥātim, *Ādāb al-Shāfiʿī*, 39–40.

Accordingly, he traveled to Medina and approached Mālik, whom he persuaded to hear his recitation of the work:

I said, "I want to hear the *Muwaṭṭa'* from you." He said: "Find someone to read [it] to you." I said: "No, you must hear my recitation, and if you find it agreeable, I will then recite [to the end]." He said: "Find someone to read [it] to you." But I insisted until he said, "Recite." And when he heard my recitation, he said, "Recite [on]," so I recited to him until I had finished it.[11]

This report indicates that in the usual system of instruction in Mālik's Medinan circle a junior student first attended the lessons of advanced students of Mālik. These would recite and explain the text of the *Muwaṭṭa'* to a group of novices, who would follow along (and possibly make supplementary notes) in their own copies of the work. Once the student had mastered the text in this way, he then probably had the opportunity to hear it from the master directly in order to validate the correctness of his written copy.[12] Al-Shāfiʿī, however, insisted on the more exclusive procedure of Mālik listening to him recite the *Muwaṭṭa'* from memory.[13] Clearly, he felt confident enough to skip the lessons with Mālik's senior students and immediately demand the attention of the master.

Mālik was a native of Medina, born in the 80s or 90s (700s or 710s CE). His ancestors seem to have originated in Yemen, but his family had become integrated into the Qurashī clan of Taym b. Murra.[14] This clan could boast of some of the most illustrious Companions of the Prophet Muḥammad, among them his favorite wife, ʿĀ'isha, and her father, the first caliph, Abū Bakr,[15] who had accompanied the Prophet when the latter had left hostile Mecca to migrate to the welcoming Medina. This exodus (*hijra*) had led to the establishment of the first community of Muslims. So momentous was the event of the Hijra that it was taken as the starting point of the Muslim calendar, instead of, for example, the

[11] Ibn Abī Ḥātim, *Ādāb al-Shāfiʿī*, 27–28.

[12] This method of *viva voce* transmission and learning came to be known as *samāʿ*, literally "hearing." See Fuat Sezgin, *Geschichte des arabischen Schrifttums*, 13 vols. (Leiden: E. J. Brill, 1967–), 1:58–60, and Chap. 6 of this volume.

[13] This method of transmission is termed *qirā'a* ("reading"); see Schoeler, *The Oral and the Written*, 32, and Chap. 6 of this volume.

[14] On the issue of Mālik's ancestry, see Muḥammad Abū Zahra, *Mālik: Ḥayātuhu wa-ʿaṣruhu, ārā'uhu wa-fiqhuh* (Cairo: Maktabat al-Anjilū al-Miṣriyya, 1952), 26–27.

[15] Ibn Hishām, *Sīrat Ibn Hishām*, ed. Majdī Fatḥī al-Sayyin, 5 vols. (Cairo: Dār al-Ṣaḥāba, 1995), 2:361; M. Lecker, "Taym b. Murra," in *Encyclopaedia of Islam*, 2nd ed., ed. P. J. Bearman et al., 12 vols. (Leiden: E. J. Brill, 1960–2004) [henceforth *EI2*], 10:401.

first instance of revelation. For Mālik, the Hijra established Medina as the heart of Islam; he believed that the whole oasis was a sacred precinct (*ḥaram*), in contrast to Mecca, where only the ancient temple (*al-bayt al-ʿatīq*, the Kaʿba) was sacred.[16] He argued that Medina had been blessed not only in the past by Muḥammad's residency during his lifetime, but also in the present by the presence of the Prophet's grave, and it would be further blessed in the future, after resurrection, when it would host one of the gardens of paradise.[17]

It is not difficult to imagine how immediate a connection Mālik must have felt to the origins of Islam: he still met and heard Hadith from Nāfiʿ (d. 117–20/735–38), the scholar and client (*mawlā*) of the famous Companion ʿAbd Allāh b. ʿUmar (d. 73/693).[18] Less than ninety years separated Mālik's birth from the death of Muḥammad in 11/632, and only a little more than half a century from the transfer of the capital from Medina to Kufa in Iraq under the fourth caliph, ʿAlī b. Abī Ṭālib (r. 35–40/656–61). Furthermore, in contrast both to recently built towns such as Kufa and to old centers of civilization with their pre-Islamic monuments, such as Damascus and Alexandria, Medina was first and foremost the city of Muḥammad. For Mālik, the landscape of Medina was thus a sacred landscape: to walk in its streets was to walk the same streets the Prophet had trodden after receiving divine revelation.[19] Everyday items that one encountered, such as the measures that the Medinans used to quantify dates and other agricultural produce, were in fact artifacts from the prophetic age.[20] The entire city was a storehouse of memories that led all the way back to the sacred age of revelation.

While on the one hand these memories were woven into everyday communal practice, carried forward by the collective memory of the city's inhabitants, there was also an explicit scholarly discourse that externalized these memories into a normative teaching that was transmitted in circles of learning. The scholars who perpetuated this discourse saw themselves in the role of guardians and preservers of a tradition

[16] Jalāl al-Dīn al-Suyūṭī, *al-Ḥujaj al-mubīna fī al-tafḍīl bayna Makka wa-l-Madīna*, ed. ʿAbd Allāh al-Darwīsh (Damascus: al-Yamāma, 1985), 38.

[17] Al-Qāḍī ʿIyāḍ b. Mūsā al-Yaḥṣūbī, *Tartīb al-madārik wa-taqrīb al-masālik li-maʿrifat aʿlām madhhab Mālik*, ed. Aḥmad Bakīr Maḥmūd, 8 vols. (Rabat: Wizārat al-Awqāf wa-l-Shuʾūn al-Islāmiyya, 1965–83), 1:32–36.

[18] Harald Motzki, "Whither Ḥadīth Studies?," in *Analysing Muslim Traditions*, 47–124.

[19] Al-Qāḍī ʿIyāḍ, *Tartīb al-madārik*, 1:34–35.

[20] Abū Bakr al-Bayhaqī, *al-Sunan al-kubrā*, 10 vols. (Hyderabad: Majlis Dāʾirat al-Maʿārif al-Niẓāmiyya, 1925 or 1926), 4:171.

whose significance reached far beyond the specific locality of Medina. As Mālik, one of the leading figures in this community of scholars, asserted, "everyone ought to follow the people of Medina."[21] For him, the communal practices of the Medinans, safeguarded by their scholars, embodied the authentic memory of the sacred age of revelation as passed down from generation to generation in the hallowed city of the Prophet. The Medinan tradition therefore represented a template of correct behavior for all Muslims, regardless of location.

Such a view had its justification. Unlike the Israelites or the early Christians, the Muslim community had been from its inception autonomous, autonomy literally denoting the capacity to give oneself the law. Indeed, the very name of Medina denotes in Aramaic a "place of jurisdiction."[22] As the constitution (or constitutions) of Medina demonstrates, a legal framework was in fact constitutive of the Muslim polity in Medina under Muḥammad's leadership.[23] Subsequent generations of Muslims were not confronted with the task of conjuring up laws from dead texts; rather, they inherited an ongoing legal tradition that connected each generation back in time to the prophetic past. This continuity allowed legal practices to function as an independent carrier of cultural memory alongside the Quran and the body of Hadith.[24] The law thus possessed its own authority, an authority that was mimetic rather than hermeneutic.

By the mid-second Hijri century, however, a perceptible shift was taking place in the Medinan scholarly discourse. Two of the most prominent jurists of Medina, Mālik and the slightly older ʿAbd al-ʿAzīz b. al-Mājishūn (d. 164/780 or 781),[25] each set out to codify the hitherto aural normative tradition of Medina into authoritative written form. This new development was at least partly triggered by the emergence

[21] "Al-nās tabaʿun li-ahl al-Madīna"; ʿAbd al-Fattāḥ Abū Ghudda, ed., *Namādhij min rasāʾil al-aʾimma al-salaf* (Aleppo: Maktab al-Maṭbūʿāt al-Islāmiyya, 1996), 31.

[22] Charles Torrey, "Medina and ΠΟΛΙΣ, and Luke i. 39," *Harvard Theological Review* 17 (1924): 83–91.

[23] Michael Lecker, *The "Constitution of Medina": Muḥammad's First Legal Document* (Princeton, NJ: Darwin Press, 2004).

[24] Continuity does not, of course, imply immutability. The extent to which Islamic legal practice in the first Hijri century may have reflected borrowing from other legal traditions is a separate issue that lies outside the scope of this book.

[25] Not to be confused with his son, ʿAbd al-Malik (d. 212 or 214/827–30); see Abū ʿUmar Yūsuf b. ʿAbd al-Barr, *al-Intiqāʾ fī faḍāʾil al-aʾimma al-thalātha al-fuqahāʾ*, ed. ʿAbd al-Fattāḥ Abū Ghudda (Aleppo: Maktab al-Maṭbūʿāt al-Islāmiyya, 1997), 104–5. Regarding the short extant fragment of Ibn al-Mājishūn's work, see Miklos Muranyi, *Ein altes Fragment medinensischer Jurisprudenz aus Qairawān* (Stuttgart: F. Steiner, 1985).

of a new type of legal reasoning that was primarily associated with the heartland of the caliphate in Iraq but whose transforming presence began to be felt also in Medina.

THE NATURE OF IRAQI *RA'Y*

Already in the century after the Prophet's death, Iraq had become a hotbed of economic prosperity, political factionalism, theological schisms, and intellectual speculation. Khārijī, Muʿtazilī, and various strands of Shiʿi theologies formed primarily in Iraq, and Basra and Kufa became the cradles of Arabic grammar, lexicography, and related fields. With the Abbasid revolution in 132/750, the center of political power also returned to Iraq, leading to the foundation of the prosperous city of Baghdad and to extensive patronage for Iraqi scholarship. During the early years of Abbasid rule, a number of jurists, most prominently ʿUthmān al-Battī (d. 143/760) in Basra and Abū Ḥanīfa (d. 150/767) in Kufa, formed influential circles in which they elaborated distinctive systems of legal reasoning. Already their contemporaries appear to have recognized that their method was in certain ways revolutionary.[26] It was widely acknowledged that the Companions of the Prophet had engaged in legal reasoning, in the sense both of applying general rules to specific cases and of extending existing rules to cover new situations. Nevertheless, as will be seen, there was an equally clear recognition among second-/eighth-century observers that they were witnessing the emergence of a new kind of reasoning.[27]

This novel approach, one that would prove profoundly unsettling and eventually divide the scholarly community into supporters and opponents, was characterized by the use of *ra'y*. The term *ra'y* has been interpreted variously as common sense,[28] rationalism,[29] or legal opinions;[30] in general, it denotes the exercise and outcome of a jurist's individual reasoning in resolving a legal question. Previous scholarship has analyzed

[26] Al-Khaṭīb al-Baghdādī, *Tārīkh Madīnat al-Salām*, ed. Bashshār ʿAwwād Maʿrūf, 17 vols. (Beirut: Dār al-Gharb al-Islāmī, 2001), 15:543–86.

[27] For an extensive collection of reports on early versions of *ra'y* and their differences, see Ibn al-Qayyim al-Jawziyya's *Iʿlām al-muwaqqiʿīn*, ed. Hānī al-Ḥājj, 4 vols. in 2 (Cairo: al-Maktaba al-Tawfīqiyya, 2013), 1:71–102.

[28] G. H. A. Juynboll, *Muslim Tradition: Studies in Chronology, Provenance, and Authorship of Early Ḥadīth* (Cambridge: Cambridge University Press, 1983), 33; Christopher Melchert, *The Formation of the Sunni Schools of Law, 9th–10th Centuries C.E.* (Leiden: Brill, 1997), 1.

[29] Wael B. Hallaq, *The Origins and Evolution of Islamic Law* (Cambridge: Cambridge University Press, 2005), 74–75.

[30] Jeanette Wakin and Aron Zysow, "Ra'y," in *EI2*, 12:687.

the phenomenon of *ra'y* primarily in juxtaposition to Hadith, identifying *ra'y* with legal reasoning that deals with areas of the law beyond the literal scope of the revealed texts.[31] In this discussion, however, I focus on the dialogic nature of *ra'y* as the crucial characteristic that explains its particular methodology and use of sources, especially Hadith.

The dialectic method of the new *ra'y* movement in Iraq differed markedly from another model of scholarly debate that came to dominate legal discourse later on, namely, the formulation of a coherent statement of an argument and its evidence followed by a similarly complete refutation (*radd*) and, possibly, subsequent counterrefutations. A *ra'y* debate, by contrast, took place through the progressive exchange of propositions (theses) and counterpropositions (antitheses) that did not outline a comprehensive argument but rather probed the details of particular hypothetical situations through questions and assertions that were implicitly juxtaposed with the statements uttered by the opponent. These were often introduced by the interrogatory phrases *a-ra'aita*, *a-fa-ra'aita*, and *a-lā tarā* ("is it not the case that" or, as more generally used, "tell me your opinion about").[32] It is possible that it was the use of these phrases that gave the *ra'y* movement its name, given the common root *r-'-y*, which relates to perception, and the fact that those engaged in *ra'y* were also referred to as the "people of *a-ra'aita, a-ra'aita*."[33]

While the earliest lengthy example of the dialectic method is probably represented by the debates between the illustrious Iraqi jurist Abū Ḥanīfa and his contemporary, the Kufan judge Ibn Abī Laylā (d. 148/765),[34] a more detailed demonstration of the nature of this type of debate – the kind of reasoning that it involved and the types of conclusions that it produced – can be seen in a debate between al-Shāfi'ī and Abū Ḥanīfa's student al-Shaybānī. The discussion is reported by al-Shāfi'ī as follows:

[Al-Shaybānī] said: "What is your opinion about a man who misappropriates (*ghaṣaba*) a log from another man and builds on top of it a building, spending

[31] Beginning with Ignaz Goldziher, *The Ẓāhirīs: Their Doctrine and Their History*, trans. Wolfgang Behn (Leiden: E. J. Brill, 1971), 3, 7.

[32] Heinrich L. Fleischer, "Beiträge zur arabischen Sprachkunde VII," in *Kleinere Schriften*, ed. Anton Huber, Heinrich Thorbecke, and Ferdinand Mühlau, 3 vols. (Leipzig: S. Hirzel, 1885–88), 1:481–87.

[33] See the statement of the Kufan scholar al-Zabarqān (d. 122/739 or 740), as quoted in Muḥammad b. Sa'd, *al-Ṭabaqāt al-kubrā* [partial ed.], 8 vols. (Beirut: Dār Ṣādir, 1957–68), 6:101.

[34] As recorded by Abū Ḥanīfa's student Abū Yūsuf; reproduced by al-Shāfi'ī in *Ikhtilāf al-'Irāqiyyayn* in *al-Umm*, ed. Rif'at Fawzī 'Abd al-Muṭṭalib, 11 vols., 8:219–390 (Mansura: Dār al-Wafā', 2001). I refer to this edition hereafter simply as *Umm*.

in the process one thousand dinars? Then the owner of the log appears, proving through two reliable witnesses that the man has misappropriated his log and built this building upon it. What would you decide in this [case]?" I said: "The value of [the log] is estimated. If [the owner] agrees, he is awarded the value of the log. And if he refuses and only wants his log, the building is taken down and his log is returned." So he said to me: "What is your opinion about a man who misappropriates a silver thread and stitches up his own belly with it [after an injury or operation], then the owner of the thread appears and proves through two reliable witnesses that the man misappropriated the thread with which he stitched up his belly? Would you have the thread removed from his belly?" I said: "No." He said: "God is great; you have abandoned your position!" And his followers exclaimed: "You have abandoned your position!" So I said: "Do not rush. Tell me: what if he had not misappropriated the log from anyone else and wanted to take down the building in order to build another one; would that be permissible or impermissible for him?" They said: "Permissible." I said: "So what is your opinion (*a-fa-raʾaita*) if the thread were his own and he wanted to remove it from his belly [thereby opening the wound again]; would this be permissible or impermissible for him?" They said: "Impermissible." I said: "So how can you draw an analogy between that which is permissible and that which is not?"[35]

The question whether an owner has the right to regain his misappropriated property even if that property has subsequently been integrated into the property of the offender is discussed through sample cases. Once al-Shāfiʿī has committed himself to one position, his opponent brings up an allegedly parallel example that is meant to extend al-Shāfiʿī's position to a point that the latter can no longer accept. Al-Shāfiʿī must then demonstrate that the two cases are not in fact genuinely analogous by identifying a crucial difference (*farq*), in this case the fact that taking down the house is in itself permissible, while the removal of the thread and the ensuing reopening of the wound are impermissible.

The use of the *raʾy* questions (*a-raʾaita*, *a-lā tarā*, etc.) creates a "graded series of cases"[36] in which the discussant moves progressively further

[35] Ibn Abī Ḥātim, *Ādāb al-Shāfiʿī*, 160–61. The substantive content of this debate is already found in al-Shāfiʿī's own work (*Umm*, 4:537–38), and it is presented there in a way that suggests that it did indeed originate in a debate context. Whether the debate actually took place in the extended format provided by Ibn Abī Ḥātim is unimportant here: even if the issue was dramatized in order to glorify the genius of al-Shāfiʿī, it was nonetheless constructed on the model of how a debate should be carried out and therefore allows insights into the mechanics of legal dialectics at an early stage – no later than the direct student generation of al-Shāfiʿī, given that Ibn Abī Ḥātim al-Rāzī gathered his information on al-Shāfiʿī from his students in Egypt. To appreciate the contrast between the *raʾy* style of debate and that characteristic of the *ahl al-ḥadīth*, see al-Shāfiʿī's argument with Isḥāq b. Rāhawayh, reproduced in Yāqūt al-Ḥamawī, *Irshād al-arīb ilā maʿrifat al-adīb [Muʿjam al-udabāʾ]*, ed. Iḥsān ʿAbbās, 9 vols. (Beirut: Dār al-Gharb al-Islāmī, 1993), 6:2399–401.

[36] Joseph Schacht, *An Introduction to Islamic Law* (Oxford: Clarendon, 1964), 205.

away from the original proposition that was accepted by his opponent. As Baber Johansen has shown, in the course of this casuistic movement "cases are discussed in order to show the boundaries of the legal concept's validity and the resistance of the subject matter to its inclusion within the concept."[37] Thus, both al-Shaybānī and al-Shāfiʿī agree that misappropriation is impermissible and that the misappropriated property must be returned. They disagree, however, regarding the limits of this rule, that is, whether the rule should apply in this particular case and to what extent its application is curtailed by other rules. Al-Shaybānī holds that the stolen property itself must be returned only as long as it has not been intermixed with the property of the offender; otherwise, the latter owes only the value of the object. Al-Shaybānī justifies this position by arguing that one cannot consistently hold that all misappropriated objects must be returned, calling upon the case of a thread that prevents the thief's intestines from falling out as a striking example. To create a consistent rule, he thus implicitly suggests that the obligation to return the stolen object itself is dependent on its distinctness from the rightful property of the thief. Al-Shāfiʿī proposes (again implicitly) an alternative rule: all misappropriated objects must be returned if the rightful owner so demands, as long as this does not necessitate a prohibited action – as it would in the thread example. Methodologically, then, the process of *ra'y* begins with an assumption or assumptions that both debaters share; this is progressively extended by one of the debaters through *ra'y* questions in order to show either that his own opinions are consistent or that his opponent's opinions are inconsistent with their common assumptions.

This form of debate is particularly well suited to oral exchanges. Compare the preceding debate with an alternative scenario in which each jurist gives a fifteen-minute paper on the subject: already the expression "giving a paper" suggests that the arguments have been worked out in writing, with evidence for the positions having been marshaled and presented. At the end of such presentations, it would be far more difficult to pronounce a winner without revisiting the arguments in written form. In the dialectic debate, on the other hand, the score of the debate is always clear: had al-Shāfiʿī been unable to respond to al-Shaybānī's claim that he had been defeated, the observer would have concluded that al-Shaybānī had prevailed. If, however, the debate ended after al-Shāfiʿī's rebuttal – as

[37] Baber Johansen, "Casuistry: Between Legal Concept and Social Praxis," *Islamic Law and Society* 2 (1995): 135–56, at 135.

the end of the quotation would have us believe – his position appears more coherent than al-Shaybānī's.

A further advantage of this style of *ra'y* dialectic is its avoidance of the question of authenticity. The search for common assumptions to furnish the starting point ensures a shared basis for reasoning, whether the assumptions stem from commonly accepted legal positions or from texts whose authenticity is recognized by both parties.[38] The actual debate is then about the ramifications and applicability of these shared assumptions. This avoidance of textual evaluation was obviously most useful with regard to Hadith, given that the discipline of Hadith criticism had yet to establish widely accepted criteria for classifying the authenticity of prophetic traditions. Before this point, most traditions could not have provided the argumentative traction to settle such disputes definitively.

The downside of the dialectic method of *ra'y* was its effect of generating countless hypothetical cases (*masā'il*) in the process of reasoning.[39] Since these cases were designed to probe the limits of the original common assumption, they ended up creating many new disputes at their intersection with other concepts or sources. In the preceding debate, for example, the hypothetical case of the lifesaving thread brought out a disagreement between al-Shāfiʿī and al-Shaybānī regarding the relevance of the prohibited nature of the suggested remedy (i.e., the return of the misappropriated thread). The *ra'y* method thus added more and more detail to the existing map of Islamic normativity by plumbing the depths and exploring the boundaries of already established norms.

In the process of elaborating on the most uncontroversial sources, this method by its very nature tended to eradicate the normative implications of more controversial sources, in particular of Hadith whose authenticity or meaning were not universally accepted. For example, Abū Ḥanīfa

[38] Whether this feature of what I call here *ra'y* dialectic has its origins in the Aristotelian sense of dialectic is for the sake of my argument irrelevant; for that debate, see Cornelia Schöck, *Koranexegese, Grammatik und Logik: Zum Verhältnis von arabischer und aristotelischer Urteils-, Konsequenz- und Schlusslehre* (Leiden: Brill, 2006). As I demonstrate, the basic setup of the *ra'y* debate can be explained in terms of the oral nature of the debate and the need to start from common assumptions. Even if we accept Larry Miller's conclusion that from the mid-third/ninth century onward the field of dialectic came to be defined by Aristotelian rules, these rules were most probably accepted because they fitted already established practice. See Larry B. Miller, "Islamic Disputation Theory: A Study of the Development of Dialectic in Islam from the Tenth through Fourteenth Centuries" (PhD diss., Princeton University, 1984).

[39] Abū Ḥanīfa is said to have answered 83,000 individual legal questions (*masā'il*); see Muḥammad Zāhid al-Kawtharī, *Fiqh ahl al-ʿIrāq wa-ḥadīthuhum*, ed. ʿAbd al-Fattāḥ Abū Ghudda (Cairo: Maktab al-Maṭbūʿāt al-Islāmiyya, 1970), 59.

and his students utilized the widely accepted principle, enshrined in a prophetic tradition, that states, "With liability comes [the entitlement to] profit" (*al-kharāj bi-l-ḍamān*).[40] This principle can be used to solve many different legal questions, including the case of a person who buys a cow with full udders but realizes after milking it that it has a defect, which justifies returning the cow for a full refund. The liability-profit principle would grant the buyer the right to keep the milk, given that during the period in which the cow was in his possession, he was liable for it. This conclusion, however, conflicts with another prophetic tradition, which regulates this specific case and obliges the buyer to pay compensation for the milk in the form of a fixed measure of dates.[41] The followers of Abū Ḥanīfa chose to disregard the specific Hadith report in favor of the greater overall consistency afforded by adherence to the liability-profit principle.

Therefore, although the *ra'y* approach was in theory neutral with respect to the substantive basis and content of legal debates, its practical application, particularly by the Ḥanafīs, favored the prioritization of widely accepted reports, especially those that contained maximlike rules (such as the liability-profit principle) that could be extended to a broad set of other, similar cases. In the process, many other transmitted reports dealing with individual cases had to be rejected, whenever these conflicted with the implications of the general rule as applied to those cases. Considering *ra'y* as a dialectic method explains this attitude toward Hadith as a function of the rules of debate. The *ra'y* method provided a reliable basis for reasoning and a reproducible way of extending this basis to cover new issues. To introduce a Hadith that was not generally known into a *ra'y* debate was equivalent to pulling a rabbit out of a hat. Such Hadith reports existed primarily in the oral realm, though they were also written down in note form.[42] There was no reference work for

[40] On the liability-profit principle, see Abū Jaʿfar al-Ṭaḥāwī, *Sharḥ maʿānī al-āthār*, ed. Muḥammad Zuhrī al-Najjār and Muḥammad Jād al-Ḥaqq, 4 vols. (Beirut: ʿĀlam al-Kutub, 1994), 4:17–22; al-Ṭaḥāwī, *Mukhtaṣar al-Ṭaḥāwī*, ed. Abū al-Wafā' al-Afghānī (Hyderabad: Lajnat Iḥyā' al-Maʿārif al-Nuʿmāniyya, n.d.; repr., Cairo: Dār al-Kitāb al-ʿArabī, 1370/1950 or 1951), 79–80; and Ibn al-Qāṣṣ, *al-Talkhīṣ*, ed. ʿĀdil Aḥmad ʿAbd al-Mawjūd and ʿAlī Muʿawwaḍ (Mecca: Maktabat Nizār Muṣṭafā al-Bāz, 1999), 296. For a discussion of this feature of Ḥanafī law, see al-Kawtharī, *Fiqh ahl al-ʿIrāq*, 32–39.

[41] See, for example, al-Shāfiʿī, *al-Risāla*, published as the first volume of the *Umm*, 1:257–59 (paras. 1658–70). Throughout this text, my references to the *Risāla* are to this edition (hereafter simply *Risāla*), but I also give in parentheses the relevant paragraph numbers in the edition of the *Risāla* prepared by Aḥmad Muḥammad Shākir (Cairo: al-Bābī al-Ḥalabī, 1940).

[42] Schoeler, *Genesis of Literature in Islam*, 47–50; Sezgin, *Geschichte des arabischen Schrifttums*, 1:53–84.

Hadith that would have listed them according to either subject or reliability. In contrast to the Quran, whose verses were limited and known to all discussants, the prophetic reports circulating in Kufa in Abū Ḥanīfa's time were too numerous to be known by anyone except the most specialized, who still may have disagreed on their authenticity. Given that a focused *ra'y* debate necessarily had to involve premises and arguments whose value could be reliably evaluated by all participants, the majority of Hadith reports could thus play no role in the dialectic method. However, the sidelining of Hadith led to the emergence of a progressively widening gap between the bulk of transmitted reports and a growing, internally consistent body of legal rulings arrived at through *ra'y*. This phenomenon gave rise to the charge that the proponents of *ra'y* were abandoning the prophetic tradition in favor of their own reasoning.[43]

A second reason for the charge that *ra'y* was inimical to sound Islamic teaching was the contingent and ephemeral nature of its results. Mālik found this feature disturbing. He complained that "whenever *ra'y* is followed, someone else who is stronger in *ra'y* comes along, and then you follow him. So whenever someone comes who defeats you [in debate], you follow him. I see no end to this."[44] As a method of debate, *ra'y* was incompatible with a view of the law as a stable path that one must simply follow. Rather, anyone who engaged in *ra'y* and thereby accepted its ground rules also had to accept that what he considered correct could be overturned by a more skilled dialectician. This fundamental uncertainty contradicted the view held by Mālik and other Medinan scholars of a normative teaching that flowed organically from the past and existed within the community.

RA'Y IN MEDINA

The notion that the systematizing legal reasoning associated with Iraqi jurists was at odds with the established normative tradition of Medina appears already in a report in Mālik's work, the *Muwaṭṭa'*:

Rabīʿa b. Abī ʿAbd al-Raḥmān said, "I asked Saʿīd b. al-Musayyab, 'How much [blood-money must be paid] for the finger of a woman?' He replied, 'Ten camels.' I said, 'How much for two fingers?' He said, 'Twenty camels.' I asked, 'How much

[43] Khalīfa Bā Bakr Ḥasan, *al-Ijtihād bi-l-ra'y fī madrasat al-Ḥijāz al-fiqhiyya* (Cairo: Maktabat al-Zahrā', 1997), 279–90.

[44] Ibn ʿAbd al-Barr, *Jāmiʿ bayān al-ʿilm*, ed. Abū al-Ashbāl al-Zuhayrī, 2 vols. (Dammam: Dār Ibn al-Jawzī, 1994), 2:1085–86.

for three?' He said, 'Thirty camels.' I said, 'How much for four?' He said, 'Twenty camels.' I said, 'Her wound is greater and her affliction more severe, [but] her blood-money is less?' He asked, 'Are you an Iraqi?' I said, 'No; rather, I am a scholar who seeks firm proofs, or an ignorant man who seeks knowledge.' Saʿīd said, 'It is the tradition (*sunna*), my nephew.'"[45]

The "Iraqi" way, then, was to subject the tradition to rigorous reasoning, seeking consistency both within the body of transmitted tradition and among decisions covering new cases. If the report is accurate, this kind of approach was already viewed as typically Iraqi before the end of the first Hijri century, given that Saʿīd b. al-Musayyab, a prominent Medinan jurist, died around 94/712 or 713. Crucially, however, Rabīʿa, the questioner, was not in fact Iraqi but rather hailed from Medina. Rabīʿa b. Abī ʿAbd al-Raḥmān Farrūkh (d. 130 or 136/749–60) also became known as Rabīʿa al-Raʾy, "Rabiʿa the legal reasoner." He was one of Mālik's teachers and counted among the most important Medinan scholars of his generation. The fact that a Medinan of such stature was associated with the new "Iraqi" style of reasoning indicates that the appeal of this trend was not limited to the East but also affected the conservative scholarly circles of Medina. The reactions of Mālik and other Medinans to Rabīʿa, in turn, reveal their apprehension regarding the influence of *raʾy* and their efforts to uphold the unity of the Medinan tradition.

In his statements about Rabīʿa, Mālik displays a great deal of respect for his teacher: in the anecdote quoted, he presents Rabīʿa's questioning of the tradition as a sincere search for knowledge, rather than as the outcome of adherence to an Iraqi intellectual fashion. Nevertheless, Rabīʿa undoubtedly visited Iraq, and it is known that late in his life he was appointed a judge in the Iraqi province of Anbar by the first Abbasid caliph, al-Saffāḥ (r. 132–37/749–54).[46] One report even depicts him in debate with Abū Ḥanīfa.[47] By contrast, Mālik claimed that during his stay in Iraq Rabīʿa remained in his house, refusing any contact with the Iraqis and refraining from issuing legal responsa (*fatāwā*) or transmitting Hadith.[48] It seems likely that Mālik thus sought to distance Rabīʿa from

[45] Mālik b. Anas, *al-Muwaṭṭaʾ* [Yaḥyā al-Laythī's recension], ed. Muḥammad Fuʾād ʿAbd al-Bāqī, 2 vols. (Cairo: Dār Iḥyāʾ al-Turāth al-ʿArabī, 1951), 2:860; see also Mālik b. Anas, *Muwaṭṭaʾ al-Imām Mālik*, ed. Muḥammad Muṣṭafā al-Aʿẓamī, 8 vols. (Abu Dhabi: Muʾassasat Zāyid b. Sulṭān, 2004), 5:1261–62. While the latter is a superior edition that incorporates all extant recensions, the former is most widely available; accordingly, references are to the former unless otherwise specified.

[46] Al-Khaṭīb al-Baghdādī, *Tārīkh Madīnat al-Salām*, 9:414.

[47] Al-Khaṭīb al-Baghdādī, *Tārīkh Madīnat al-Salām*, 9:417.

[48] Al-Khaṭīb al-Baghdādī, *Tārīkh Madīnat al-Salām*, 9:420–21.

association with Iraqi thought. In this effort he was not alone. Mālik's fellow Medinan scholar ʿAbd al-ʿAzīz b. al-Mājishūn replied to Iraqi scholars, who referred to Rabīʿa with the epithet "al-Raʾy," with the retort "You say 'Rabīʿa the legal reasoner'; no, by God, I have never seen anyone keener on protecting the tradition (*sunna*) than him."[49]

However, in spite of their strident public defense of Rabīʿa, Mālik and other Medinan scholars clearly harbored concerns regarding their teacher's intellectual tendencies. A letter written to Mālik by al-Layth b. Saʿd (d. 175/791), the famous Egyptian jurist, hints at the debates and criticisms among the Medinans, making specific reference to Mālik's reservations about Rabīʿa:

> [Already] the Companions of God's Messenger differed after his passing in their normative opinions (*futyā*) with regard to many issues. Were I not certain that you are aware of these [points of difference], I would list them for you. Then the Successors of the Companions of the Messenger of God differed, especially Saʿīd b. al-Musayyab and those like him. Then those who came after them differed [too]; we met them in Medina and other places. Their leaders in legal opinions were Ibn Shihāb[50] and Rabīʿa b. Abī ʿAbd al-Raḥmān, and you know Rabīʿa's divergence from what came before. I heard your opinion about him, and the opinion of the prominent Medinans, such as Yaḥyā b. Saʿīd,[51] ʿUbayd Allāh b. ʿUmar,[52] and Kathīr b. Farqad,[53] and even of some who are older than him, regarding what compelled you to leave his teaching circle. I mentioned to you and ʿAbd al-ʿAzīz b. ʿAbd Allāh [al-Mājishūn] some of the faults that I find in Rabīʿa, and both of you agreed with me regarding what I detest so intensely.[54]

While al-Layth acknowledges the existence of a plurality of opinions within the tradition, a plurality that his letter generally seeks to defend and to justify, it is clear that he considers the opinions of Rabīʿa to fall beyond the scope of acceptable variance. For him, there is a crucial difference between the multivocality of the Companions and Successors and the new interpretations proposed by Rabīʿa and other *raʾy*-minded jurists. The former, argues al-Layth, is legitimate, while the latter is not: "We do

49 Al-Khaṭīb al-Baghdādī, *Tārīkh Madīnat al-Salām*, 9:417.

50 Ibn Shihāb al-Zuhrī, a prominent Medinan Hadith scholar (*muḥaddith*); d. 124/742.

51 Yaḥyā b. Saʿīd al-Qaṭṭān, a Medinan scholar; d. 198/813 or 814.

52 Probably ʿUbayd Allāh b. ʿUmar b. Ḥafṣ b. ʿĀṣim b. ʿUmar b. al-Khaṭṭāb; died in the mid-140s/early 760s.

53 Kathīr b. Farqad al-Madanī, originally from Medina, settled in Egypt; d. unknown. See Ibn Ḥajar al-ʿAsqalānī, *Tahdhīb al-Tahdhīb*, 12 vols. (Hyderabad: Dār al-Maʿārif al-ʿUthmāniyya, 1907–9), 8:424.

54 Abū Ghudda, *Namādhij*, 35–36. For a slightly different version, see Yaḥyā b. Maʿīn, *Tārīkh Yaḥyā b. Maʿīn*, ed. ʿAbd Allāh Aḥmad Ḥasan, 2 vols. (Beirut: Dār al-Qalam, 1990), 2:374.

not consider it permissible for the inhabitants of the Muslims' garrison towns to come up with something new today that was not done by their predecessors among the Companions of the Messenger of God and their Successors; because most of the scholars have passed away, and those who remain do not resemble those of old."[55] Al-Layth thus challenges the right of his contemporaries to disagree with their predecessors by drawing on the motif of the corruption of time.

Rabīʿa and his approach were also viewed unfavorably in the other intellectual center of the Hejaz, Mecca. The great Meccan scholar (and al-Shāfiʿī's teacher) Sufyān b. ʿUyayna analyzed the *ra'y* phenomenon as follows:

Hishām b. ʿUrwa[56] related from his father: "The affairs of the Israelites remained in order until the half-castes (*al-muwalladūn*) – the offspring of foreign captives – appeared in large numbers and began to voice speculative opinions (*ra'y*). They consequently went astray and led others astray." ... Ibn ʿUyayna said: "We looked into this and found that the people's affairs were in order until this was changed by Abū Ḥanīfa in Kufa, al-Battī in Basra, and Rabīʿa in Medina. We looked into this [further] and found that they were [precisely] from the half-castes, the offspring of foreign captives."[57]

Ibn ʿUyayna thus lumps Rabīʿa together with the Iraqi proponents of *ra'y*, accuses them of corrupting religion, and analogizes the influence of *ra'y* to the corruption of the Jewish religion wrought by Jewish proponents of *ra'y*.[58] The rationale for this analogy is his explanation for the phenomenon of *ra'y* in Islam, namely, the influence of foreigners.

THE IMPACT OF *RA'Y* WITHIN THE JUDICIARY

The fluidity of opinions generated by *ra'y* and the ensuing uncertainties also seem to have caused consternation for the Abbasid state bureaucracy.

[55] Abū Ghudda, *Namādhij*, 35.

[56] A well-known scholar of Hadith; d. 146/768. His father, ʿUrwa b. al-Zubayr (d. 93 or 94/711–13), was a grandson of the first caliph, Abū Bakr, and a nephew of the Prophet's wife ʿĀ'isha.

[57] There are various versions of this report with slight differences; see al-Khaṭīb al-Baghdādī, *Tārīkh Madīnat al-Salām*, 15:543, and Ibn Ḥajar al-ʿAsqalānī, *Fatḥ al-bārī*, 13 vols. (Beirut: Dār al-Maʿrifa, n.d.), 13:301. In Abū Yūsuf Yaʿqūb b. Sufyān al-Fasāwī's *al-Maʿrifa wa-l-tārīkh*, ed. Khalīl al-Manṣūr, 3 vols. (Beirut: Dār al-Kutub al-ʿIlmiyya, 1999), 3:134, the original statement ("The affairs of the Israelites ...") is attributed to the Prophet.

[58] The corrupting influence of foreigners on the Israelites is part of an indigenous Jewish exegetical tradition on the story of Solomon. See, for example, the work of the Roman-Jewish historian Titus Flavius Josephus, *The Works of Josephus: Complete and Unabridged*, new ed., trans. William Whiston (Peabody, MA: Hendrickson, 1987), bk. 8, lines 191–93. I am grateful to Jonathan Brown for the reference.

In the well-known letter of the courtier Ibn al-Muqaffaʿ (d. probably 139/756) to the caliph al-Manṣūr (r. 136–58/754–75), the former complained about the rampant inconsistencies in the court system that stemmed from the judges' use of legal reasoning:

> Among the things that the prince of the believers should look into are the affairs of the two cities[59] and other areas, where the differences between contradictory rulings have become a grave problem with regard to punishments, marriage, and financial matters, so that in al-Ḥīra[60] a punishment is meted out and a marriage is valid, while in Kufa neither is the case. Likewise, something is licit in central Kufa, while it is illicit in another part.... The one who engages in speculative legal reasoning (*ra'y*) is so determined to follow his own reasoning that he will come to a decision in a weighty matter affecting the Muslim community – a decision on which not a single other Muslim agrees with him – and then he is not ashamed to be alone in holding this opinion and to enforce this verdict, while acknowledging that it is [the result of] his own reasoning and not based on the Quran or the Sunna.[61]

If we assume that the *ra'y* dialectic and the subsequent casuistry represented the major engines of the new *ra'y* movement,[62] then when Ibn al-Muqaffaʿ complained that "the differences between contradictory rulings have become a grave problem with regard to punishments, marriage, and financial matters," he was not referring to disagreements regarding, for example, whether murder constitutes grounds for execution. Rather, the variance concerned the exact meaning of this rule, especially where it interacts with another accepted rule, such as the imperative to avert punishment by means of doubt (*idra'ū al-ḥudūd bi-l-shubuhāt*). Abū Ḥanīfa, for example, developed an impeccable *ra'y* argument according to which only those killings that were carried out with a lethal weapon (*al-qatl bi-l-muḥaddad*) were punishable by death. If other objects, such as a stick, were used, the killer may have intended only to injure his victim, resulting in accidental manslaughter (*al-qatl bi-l-muthaqqal*). Because the latter crime does not merit the death penalty, this uncertainty activates

[59] Probably Kufa and Basra.

[60] A town not far to the south of Kufa.

[61] Ibn al-Muqaffaʿ, *Risālat al-ṣaḥāba*, in *Rasā'il al-bulaghā'*, ed. Muḥammad Kurd ʿAlī, 120–31 (Cairo: Dār al-Kutub al-ʿArabiyya al-Kubrā, 1913), at 125–26. For an analysis of this epistle, see Muhammad Qasim Zaman, *Religion and Politics under the Early ʿAbbāsids: The Emergence of the Proto-Sunnī Elite* (Leiden: Brill, 1997), 81–85, and Joseph Lowry, "The First Islamic Legal Theory: Ibn al-Muqaffaʿ on Interpretation, Authority, and the Structure of the Law," *Journal of the American Oriental Society* 128 (2008): 25–40.

[62] See Baber Johansen, "Casuistry."

the rule that calls for refraining from the application of corporal punishments[63] where guilt is not certain.[64]

While Abū Ḥanīfa's reasoning shows a high degree of sophistication, the development of such modes of reasoning in a system in which each judge considered himself, at least in principle, entitled to exercise individual legal reasoning unfettered by precedent led inevitably to the Babylonian confusion described by Ibn al-Muqaffaʿ.[65] As a solution, Ibn al-Muqaffaʿ proposed that the caliph codify the law into a single, binding text, enforced throughout the realm, that would put an end to the judicial uncertainties created by *raʾy*. It is tempting to see a direct causal relationship between this recommendation and the reported request made by the same caliph, al-Manṣūr, to Mālik during the pilgrimage of 148 (in 765 or 766).[66] Al-Manṣūr asked Mālik to "gather this knowledge and record it in writing, while avoiding the strictness of ʿAbd Allāh b. ʿUmar, the lenience of Ibn ʿAbbās,[67] and the anomalous [positions] of Ibn Masʿūd.[68] Aim at the middle ground and at what the community and the Companions agreed upon." He, the caliph, would then "compel [the people] to follow it."[69]

If these reports are authentic, the caliph wanted Mālik to record an existing normative tradition, not to add another set of new and original positions to the debate. Specifically, al-Manṣūr wanted to codify the tradition of that center of Muslim learning that had not yet been significantly affected by the confusion caused by *raʾy* in Iraq, and that possessed a natural authority as the original capital of the Islamic community: Medina. Mālik's task was thus to set down the knowledge of the Medinan people, which al-Manṣūr trusted – in sharp contrast to the opinions of the Iraqis.[70] The caliph also indicated an awareness of the

[63] Specifically, penalties falling into the category of *ḥudūd*, fixed criminal sanctions.

[64] Shams al-Dīn al-Sarakhsī, *al-Mabsūṭ*, ed. Khalīl al-Mays, 31 vols. (Beirut: Dār al-Fikr, 2000), 26:122–24.

[65] Indeed, reports about early judges reveal a high degree of improvisation in legal judgments; see Muḥammad b. Khalaf Wakīʿ, *Akhbār al-quḍāt*, ed. ʿAbd al-ʿAzīz Muṣṭafā al-Marāghī, 3 vols. (Cairo: al-Maktaba al-Tijāriyya al-Kubrā, 1947–50), e.g., 1:154, 159, and 279.

[66] The date is given by the twentieth-century scholar Muḥammad Zāhid al-Kawtharī, as quoted in a note by his student, the editor of Ibn ʿAbd al-Barr's *Intiqāʾ*, 81. The Day of Arafat in AH 148 fell on December 29, 765 CE.

[67] A prominent Companion and cousin of the Prophet; d. 68/687 or 688.

[68] A prominent Companion who settled in Kufa; d. 32/652 or 653.

[69] Al-Qāḍī ʿIyāḍ, *Tartīb al-madārik*, 1:92.

[70] Abū Zahra, *Mālik*, 225–28.

differences between the positions transmitted from the Companions and wished Mālik to record the broad consensus, avoiding the exceptional opinions at both the strict and the liberal end of the spectrum.

Mālik was not the only scholar whom al-Manṣūr approached in order to spread Medinan learning. The caliph took several Medinan scholars with him to Iraq, most prominently ʿAbd al-ʿAzīz b. al-Mājishūn, who remained in Iraq until his death.[71] During his stay he not only taught Hadith to Iraqi scholars but also wrote possibly the earliest work that sought to synthesize the normative tradition of Medina into a coherent and univocal teaching.[72] It is conceivable that this work, most of which has been lost, was also composed in response to a request from al-Manṣūr.

Ibn al-Mājishūn's work and Mālik's *Muwaṭṭa'* thus emerged within the context of a threatened local tradition, and possibly the broader context of a centralizing imperial state in search of a unifying and predictable legal code.[73] However, the consequences of writing such a work extended far beyond what either the Medinans or al-Manṣūr could have predicted.

MĀLIK'S *MUWAṬṬA'* AND ITS SIGNIFICANCE

Mālik called his book *al-Muwaṭṭa'*, "the well-trodden path," reflecting the goal of his project: to set down in written form Islamic normativity as enshrined in the traditional practice (*ʿamal*) of Medina as a whole. The *Muwaṭṭa'* not only represents a milestone in the development of Islamic law in that it indicates a certain level of sophistication, but it also functioned as an agent of this development. This fertilizing role of the *Muwaṭṭa'* is based on the effect of writing on tradition in general and on legal thought in particular.

Writing does not simply represent the preservation in written form of something that previously existed in the oral realm. Rather, it entails

[71] Ibn Taymiyya, *Ṣiḥḥat uṣūl ahl al-Madīna*, 20:170: "Abū Jaʿfar [al-Manṣūr] asked the scholars of the Hejaz to travel to Iraq in order to spread knowledge there.... Abū Yūsuf frequented their teaching circles and learned Hadith from them." Al-Shāfiʿī also mentions in the *Umm* that "Muḥammad b. al-Ḥasan [al-Shaybānī] informed me that Ibn al-Mājishūn ʿAbd al-ʿAzīz b. Abī Salama and a group of Medinans were with them in Iraq"; *Umm*, 7:557.

[72] Regarding this work, see Muranyi, *Ein altes Fragment medinensischer Jurisprudenz*.

[73] Benjamin Jokisch has argued, in my view unconvincingly, that the Abbasid caliph Hārūn al-Rashīd commissioned al-Shaybānī to produce a uniform imperial legal code, and that the latter's work was based squarely on Roman law; see Jokisch, *Islamic Imperial Law: Harun-al-Rashid's Codification Project* (Berlin: W. de Gruyter, 2007).

a significant transformation of human thought.[74] As Jack Goody has argued persuasively with regard to East African legal systems, which until the twentieth century remained purely oral, the lack of written forms or bases of legal reasoning prevented legal practitioners from either developing abstract concepts or perceiving inconsistencies in their reasoning.[75] This is so because texts develop a certain degree of autonomy: as "a material object detached from man ... the written word can become the subject of a new kind of critical attention,"[76] since it can be analyzed and critiqued much more thoroughly and in depth than the spoken word. A similar argument has been made by Raymond Tallis in attempting to explain the so-called pre-Socratic awakening in the seventh century BCE, which saw the emergence of philosophical thought. Tallis argues that "sustained passages of writing make greater tracts of general meaning ... available at a given time. It is consequently possible to see new connections, disconnections, consistencies and inconsistencies. This enables thought to develop the ambition ... of encompassing the entire world, a mode of thinking beyond the endless *ad hoc* of the mythologies."[77] I do not intend to suggest that there is only one kind of literacy nor that literacy transforms society without society influencing the form and usage of literacy in return. Nor do I claim that writing is a necessary precondition for history, for a sense of the self, or for rationality – however defined.[78] Rather, what I argue here is that the specific type of literacy that emerged in the second/eighth century enabled systematic engagement with a large body of information in a way that would have been impossible, at least for nonmnemonists, without such literacy. By relieving the burden on memory and by setting ideas down in a materially fixed form, writing fostered the emergence of a kind of reasoning that distanced itself from particulars, searched for universal patterns, and considered higher-level methodological questions.

[74] See Walter J. Ong, *Orality and Literacy: The Technologizing of the Word* (London: Methuen, 1982).

[75] Jack Goody, *The Logic of Writing and the Organization of Society* (Cambridge: Cambridge University Press, 1986), 140–42.

[76] Goody, *Logic of Writing*, 129.

[77] Raymond Tallis, *The Enduring Significance of Parmenides* (London: Continuum, 2008), 122–23.

[78] For a critique of Jack Goody's work, see Brian V. Street, *Literacy in Theory and Practice* (Cambridge: Cambridge University Press, 1984), chap. 2. The importance of recognizing different usages of literacy, as opposed to a simplified dichotomy between literacy and illiteracy, has been demonstrated by Sylvia Scribner and Michael Cole in *The Psychology of Literacy* (Cambridge, MA: Harvard University Press, 1981).

To appreciate the effect of the type of writing that the *Muwaṭṭa'* represented it is important to begin by noting the extent to which writing was used among jurists before Mālik. Until Mālik's generation, normative teaching was expressed and transmitted primarily in aural form: information was *heard* rather than *read*, and the direct, face-to-face encounter between student and teacher was consequently paramount.[79] Writing was used in this process as a mnemonic tool for the transcription of the spoken word, as it had been for centuries among the Arabs, but it did not serve as an expressive device for the development and publication of ideas.

As Gregor Schoeler has shown, there is a fundamental difference between texts of the first type – transcribed speech, written down to produce memory aids (*hypomnēmata*) – and "books properly speaking" (*syngrammata*) that were deliberately composed and published with the aim of conveying ideas to others.[80] *Hypomnēmata* were certainly used much earlier among Muslim scholars than *syngrammata*. The later appearance of the latter is at least in part due to material factors: until the introduction of paper in the Islamic world in the second/eighth century, the available writing materials were either too rudimentary (animal bones, tree bark, stone tablets) or too expensive to produce (parchment, papyrus) to sustain a large-scale book culture.[81] Given that *hypomnēmata* were in most cases simply collections of notes jotted down by students during the oral lectures of a teacher, lacking significant internal ordering and serving the function of private notes for revision, these types of texts rarely survived as independent works. Rather, they were consciously or unconsciously integrated into the teaching of the student who wrote the notes, and who may or may not have credited his ideas to his teacher. The next generation of students again took notes in which they recorded their teacher's ideas either as that teacher's own or as those of the teacher's teacher, and so on. In the passing of generations, the attribution of opinions to a specific scholar thus becomes increasingly problematic. In addition, few quoted texts survive this mode of transmission verbatim.[82] The chain of note taking continues until a student writes a proper book – a *syngramma* – in which he quotes his teacher from his personal notes.

[79] See Schoeler, *Genesis of Literature in Islam*, 8.

[80] See, for example, Schoeler, *The Oral and the Written*, 46–50.

[81] Mohammed Maraqten, "Writing Materials in Pre-Islamic Arabia," *Journal of Semitic Studies* 43 (1998): 287–310.

[82] The exception is those texts that have an explicit codex of transmission, such as was developed at a certain point for prophetic Hadith.

From then on, both the author's and his teacher's opinions become fixed and clearly attributable to their respective originators.[83]

Mālik's *Muwaṭṭa'* straddled the divide between the oral and the written. As the report regarding al-Shāfiʿī's initial encounter with Mālik shows, aurality (perhaps accompanied by note taking) was still the standard in *transmission*, but the *Muwaṭṭa'* itself represented a decisive step toward writing as a mode of *expression*. In contrast to the notes in which Abū Ḥanīfa's students recorded their master's communal debates and that were occasionally rewritten to reflect changes in opinion,[84] Mālik sought to provide a coherent statement of a single authoritative tradition, that of Medina. The *Muwaṭṭa'* was ordered by chapters (*muṣannaf*),[85] beginning with the basic ritual laws (*ʿibādāt*) of purity, prayer, almsgiving, and so on; moving on to the rules of human interaction (*muʿāmalāt*), such as sale, marriage, divorce, and criminal law; and ending with a miscellaneous assortment of ethical, historical, and theological chapters. Instead of being simply a collection of written notes that fixed individual opinions and their justifications on paper, as was the case with Abū Ḥanīfa's *masā'il*, Mālik's *Muwaṭṭa'* drew together the full range of discrete topics in a deliberate and systematic arrangement. By doing this, Mālik opened up the mental possibility of comprising Islamic law as a whole in a single book, not in the sense of laying down every single detail of the law, but of touching upon every relevant area of it.

Dividing the subject matter into chapters represented another important innovation. Far from simply cutting up the law into chunks of equal size, the chaptering itself involved a great degree of legal thought. For example, the separation of ritual law (*ʿibādāt*) from interpersonal law (*muʿāmalāt*) implies the recognition of a significant difference between the two; this might be derived from the widely accepted conclusion that ritual laws, unlike those governing human interactions, are generally based on nonintelligible reasons (*ghayr maʿqūl al-maʿnā*) and therefore cannot serve as the basis of analogy. As another example, placing the chapter on marriage close to the chapter on sales seems to suggest that marriage is theorized as a contractual relationship.

[83] Hossein Modarressi documents these stages in the development of early Shiʿi literature in *Tradition and Survival: A Bibliographical Survey of Early Shīʿite Literature* (Oxford: Oneworld, 2003).

[84] Ibn Abī al-Wafā' al-Qurashī, *al-Jawāhir al-muḍiyya fī ṭabaqāt al-ḥanafiyya*, ed. ʿAbd al-Fattāḥ al-Ḥulw, 5 vols. (Cairo: Dār Iḥyā' al-Kutub al-ʿArabiyya, 1978–88; repr., Giza: Hajr, 1993), 2:285; Melchert, *Formation of the Sunni Schools*, 51–52.

[85] For the difference between a file of notes (*mudawwana*) and a book ordered by subject matter (*muṣannaf*), see Sezgin, *Geschichte des arabischen Schrifttums*, 1:55ff.

Arguably the most significant characteristic of the *Muwaṭṭaʾ* is its fixedness. This contrasts sharply with the fluid notes of Abū Ḥanīfa's students, which recorded only the latest outcomes of the legal debates in his circle. This holds true even though we know that Mālik kept changing his work and publishing altered versions, some of which remain extant in the different recensions (and possibly reworkings) of his students.[86] Behind these differences, a single work is clearly visible, one that speaks with an authority that implies if not an exclamation mark, then a period after each ruling it gives. Compare this with the Iraqi discourses, which – as seen earlier – are structured by the *a-lā tarā/a-raʾayta* formulae that, after all, introduce questions. It seems plausible that Mālik's work was motivated by a desire to put a stop to the rapid proliferation of legal discourse that was caused by the internal logic of the *raʾy* method. Accordingly, the *Muwaṭṭaʾ* sought to capture and present a holistic overview of the Medinan normative tradition as manifested in the practice, *ʿamal*, of the people of Medina.

Even though this practice appears throughout the *Muwaṭṭaʾ* in the actions and sayings of the Prophet, prominent Companions (such as ʿUmar and his son ʿAbd Allāh), and their Successors (such as Saʿīd b. al-Musayyab), the tradition is always bigger and always more than any of the reports about these individuals. In fact, it is tradition that confers normativity on reports about past actions and statements. For Mālik, normativity and authenticity were not the same: a report may be authentic, but it is tradition that informs us whether or not the report conveys an obligation to imitate the described practice. The tradition or practice of the people of Medina (*ʿamal ahl al-Madīna*) thus functions as the *pragmatic context* that demonstrates how the simple semantic meaning of transmitted reports should be translated into communal values and practices.[87]

[86] Miklos Muranyi, "Die frühe Rechtsliteratur zwischen Quellenanalyse und Fiktion," *Islamic Law and Society* 4 (1997): 224–41. For an evaluation of the variance in the recensions, see Muḥammad Muṣṭafā al-Aʿẓamī's introduction to his edition of Mālik's *Muwaṭṭaʾ*, 1:84–118.

[87] My use of the term *pragmatic context* is based on but partially disagrees with Umar Faruq Abd-Allah's concept of Medinan practice as *semantic context* in "Mālik's Concept of *ʿAmal* in Light of Mālikī Legal Theory," 2 vols. (PhD diss., University of Chicago, 1978), 1:379. If *ʿamal* constituted simply a semantic context, it would bring out the meanings of the individual sentences of revelation, but a pragmatic context elucidates the meaning of the sentence as an utterance that is directed at a constituency of hearers. For a discussion of this distinction, see Charles W. Morris, "Foundations of the Theory of Signs," in *Writings on the General Theory of Signs* (The Hague: Mouton, 1971), 17–74.

In addition, tradition provides normative answers to questions regarding which no transmitted reports exist, thus furnishing the skeletal framework of norms derived from transmitted reports with the details, specifics, and procedures necessary to regulate real-life situations.[88] While these answers were originally worked out by individual Medinan scholars and/or officials through legal reasoning, in Mālik's view the "hidden hand" of tradition selected from among these individual opinions those that it would declare normative.[89] The primary instruments of this hidden hand were, in Mālik's opinion, the scholars of Medina. They were the guardians and the carriers of the tradition, representing an unbroken line of learned individuals that reached back to the original Muslim community.[90]

In the *Muwaṭṭa'*, Mālik is keen to mention the sacred sources out of which Medinan practice has grown. In contrast, Mālik's Medinan peer Ibn al-Mājishūn foregrounded legal discussions (*kalām*) and used proof texts, such as prophetic traditions, only secondarily.[91] Mālik is reported to have criticized this method, saying, "But were it I who had done it, I would have begun with reports (*āthār*). Then I would have clarified that by adding the legal discussions."[92] This difference pertains to far more than simply the style of writing. While it is true that Medinan practice was the final arbiter with regard to what was normative in the *Muwaṭṭa'*, the transmitted report (*athar*) was logically prior to practice. By developing his legal discussion out of transmitted reports Mālik emphasized that normativity moves diachronically, connecting the present with the past. For Mālik, Medinan practice presented the portal through which this normative teaching could be accessed: it guaranteed both the authenticity of its sources and the normativity of its content. The collective practice of the Medinan community thus functioned as the site of cultural memory, through which Muslims constructed and perpetuated the remembered connection to their collective past. In other words, it preserved the identity of Medina as a Muslim community by embodying, enshrining, and continuously repeating what it meant to be Muslim.

[88] Abd-Allah, "Mālik's Concept of *'Amal*," 1:398.

[89] The working of the "hidden hand" of tradition will be discussed in more detail in the context of al-Shāfi'ī's critique of Mālik in the following chapter.

[90] Abd-Allah, "Mālik's Concept of *'Amal*," 1:404.

[91] Abd-Allah, "Mālik's Concept of *'Amal*," 1:101; Muranyi, *Ein altes Fragment medinensischer Jurisprudenz*, 35.

[92] Abd-Allah, "Mālik's Concept of *'Amal*," 1:101.

This function is eloquently described in a quotation attributed to the caliph ʿUmar b. ʿAbd al-ʿAzīz (r. 99–101/717–20) that Mālik used as a justification of Medinan practice:

> The Prophet and the holders of authority (*wulāt al-amr*) after him established traditions (*sunan*). To adhere to them means conforming to the book of God, perfecting one's obedience to Him, and strengthening His religion.... Whoever seeks guidance from them will be guided, and whoever seeks success through them will be successful. And whoever contravenes them "follows a path other than that of the believers" (*yattabiʿ ghayra sabīl al-muʾminīn*),[93] and God will turn him over to what he has turned to.[94]

The "path of the believers" mentioned in the Quranic verse cited by the caliph appears to be the same as the "well-trodden path" (*muwaṭṭaʾ*) that Mālik used as the title for his work. The Quran and the prophetic example (Sunna) in this conception are not removed, closed sources that should be followed in the way that a cookbook is followed. Rather, the Quran functions as the ultimate justification for following a continuous tradition (*sunan*, plural of *sunna*) that, though established by the Prophet Muḥammad, was complemented by the leaders of the community who succeeded him. Tradition is thereby cumulative; it is "living."[95] To participate in it means following a path that has been established by the generations that have come before; it means imitating and repeating this model as the way to worship God.

Mālik's concept of Medinan practice as the site of cultural memory represents a transitional stage between the two forms of cultural memory outlined by Jan Assmann: ritual and textual coherence (*rituelle/textuelle Kohärenz*). Ritual coherence is exemplified by the pharaonic religion, which preserved its cultural memory through the cyclical performance of rites; textual coherence was the mode of cultural remembering chosen by the Israelites after the destruction of the temple in 70 CE, an event that transferred the locus of cultural memory from rites to canonized texts, which could no longer be simply repeated and performed, but rather required interpretation.[96] Medinan practice falls between these models. The primary source of normativity – the prophetic tradition – has not been canonized. It is not closed off and demarcated as the Quran is; it has not been captured in an authoritative text whose every letter is

[93] Quran 4:115.

[94] Quoted via Mālik by, e.g., Abū Bakr al-Ājurrī, *Kitāb al-Sharīʿa*, ed. al-Walīd b. Muḥammad b. Nabīh Sayf al-Naṣr, 3 vols. (Cairo: Muʾassasat Qurṭuba, 1996), 1:174.

[95] Schacht, *Introduction to Islamic Law*, 29.

[96] J. Assmann, *Das kulturelle Gedächtnis*, 87ff.

fixed and may not be altered.[97] Reports about the actions and sayings of the Prophet were known to and extensively used by Mālik, but they were not by themselves normative – a key criterion of canonization as used in this book. The true essence of the normative tradition for Mālik was imbued in the place and community in which he lived, in the quotidian "rituals" of daily life as well as in the formal normative discourse of its scholars. It could be found in the tools of common use in Medina (such as the weights and measures); it existed in the call to prayer, in the general customs of the people, and in the judgments of Medinan scholars. The obligation of the individual was simply to follow and repeat these elements, realizing that even such profane actions as buying and selling would take on a ritual character by conforming to and perpetuating tradition.

At this point, however, the paradox in Mālik's project becomes visible: if all that was required was to imitate the practice of Medina, what was the purpose of his project of codifying *'amal* into written form – a step that represents an irrevocable move toward a textual mode of cultural memory? Clearly, Mālik's concept of the practice of Medina did not simply amount to "anything that people in Medina do." The *Muwaṭṭa'* reveals Mālik's careful efforts to match his theory of *'amal* with the multivocal and contested nature of tradition in Medina in his day by drawing distinctions between transmitted norms and norms derived through individual reasoning, as well as between areas that were subject to complete consensus among Medinan scholars and those regarding which only a predominant position could be identified.[98] He pointed out that already at the time of the Companions un-Islamic practices had appeared in Medina, such as usurious speculation on shares in an expected food shipment.[99] However, it was the alliance formed by scholars and government officials that put a stop to this and, for Mālik, to all un-Islamic innovations that raised their heads in Medina. Medinan practice was therefore constantly policed and groomed. However, even the scholars did not represent an undifferentiated class of upholders of the tradition for Mālik. For this reason, Mālik chose his teachers in Medina very carefully – reportedly rejecting the majority.[100]

The task of following the "well-trodden path" does not, therefore, seem to have been a simple one in the eyes of Mālik. Although the

[97] J. Assmann, *Religion und kulturelles Gedächtnis*, 82.
[98] Abd-Allah, "Mālik's Concept of *'Amal*," 2:652–760.
[99] Mālik, *Muwaṭṭa'*, 2:641.
[100] Abd-Allah, "Mālik's Concept of *'Amal*," 1:72–74.

practices that defined it permeated the entire city of Medina, they had to be extracted and separated from practices and opinions that, though present in Medina, did not constitute "normative practice." The authentic tradition thus required constant monitoring in order to prevent disruption of the sacred cycle of repetition that had persisted in Medina since the time of the Prophet. Together with the perception of an impending threat posed by the new method of *ra'y*, this precariousness of the authentic tradition would have contributed to Mālik's sense that the practice of Medina was in danger of being lost and that he needed to build an ark for it in the textual form of his *Muwaṭṭa'*.

The remarkable feature of Mālik's solution to this problem was thus its synthetic nature: his concept of Medinan practice is a patchwork of elements that Mālik himself stitched together, but justified as representing the tradition of Medina. This core rationale validates Joseph Schacht's claim that the earliest, "ancient" Islamic legal schools were primarily regional in nature.[101] This does not mean that the proto-Mālikī school consisted of a unitary doctrine propagated by all Medinan scholars.[102] Rather, the terms "the Medinans" (*al-madaniyyūn*)[103] and "the people of Medina" (*ahl al-Madīna*)[104] refer to scholars who claim to speak in the name of the Medinan tradition – irrespective of whether they form the majority or minority in Medina, or even whether they live in Medina at all. The early legal schools were regional in the sense that they were *justified* in explicitly regional terms: the legitimacy of each school's doctrine was based on the perception that it constituted a genuine representation of the normative tradition of a specific locality. The regional schools of law were thus analogous to the regional schools of Quranic recitation.[105] Each local tradition was rooted in the precedent of the Prophet or of one or more of his prominent Companions, who connected the local tradition directly back to the Prophet himself.

[101] Schacht, *Introduction to Islamic Law*, 28–29.

[102] This is how Wael Hallaq interprets Schacht's argument, in my view inaccurately. See Hallaq, "From Regional to Personal Schools of Law? A Reevaluation," *Islamic Law and Society* 8 (2001): 1–26.

[103] *Umm*, 7:557.

[104] Muḥammad b. al-Ḥasan al-Shaybānī, *al-Ḥujja 'alā ahl al-Madīna*, ed. Mahdī Ḥasan al-Kīlānī al-Qādirī, 5 vols. (Hyderabad: Lajnat Iḥyā' al-Ma'ārif al-Nu'māniyya, 1965–71; repr., Beirut: 'Ālam al-Kutub, 1983).

[105] The variant Quranic readings were justified as based on the copies of the Quran that were sent to the provinces by the caliph 'Uthmān; see Abū 'Amr al-Dānī, *al-Muqni' fī rasm maṣāḥif al-amṣār*, ed. Ḥasan Sirrī (Alexandria: Markaz al-Iskandariyya li-l-Kitāb, 2005), 31. I am grateful to Intisar Rabb for suggesting this analogy.

This framework of a geographically specific Medinan tradition, based on the continuous reenactment of the example of the Prophet and its later accretions as embodied in the "practice of Medina," is what al-Shāfiʿī absorbed from his teacher Mālik during his sojourn in Medina. Though we do not know how long al-Shāfiʿī stayed in Medina, the effect of his studies with Mālik on his later work was formative. The influence of Mālik is clearly visible throughout al-Shāfiʿī's writings, and the Hadith that al-Shāfiʿī learned from Mālik subsequently formed the backbone of his evidentiary material. Why, then, did al-Shāfiʿī eventually turn against his esteemed master? To answer this question, we must follow al-Shāfiʿī to Iraq, where the intellectual potential that he had demonstrated in Medina began to ripen into an independent and radically novel approach.

Chapter 2

Debates on Hadith and Consensus

Around the year 184/800, al-Shāfiʿī traveled to Iraq, the intellectual center of the Muslim world in his time. After the completion of his studies with Mālik in Medina, al-Shāfiʿī had served as a judge in Yemen, and it was in connection with a rebellion in that province that he was summoned to the court of the caliph Hārūn al-Rashīd (r. 170–93/786–809) to answer a charge of conspiracy. Al-Shāfiʿī was acquitted of the charge and stayed on in Iraq for what appears to have been several years.[1] There he encountered leading scholars who represented the major movements animating Islamic thought in the third/ninth century: dialectical jurisprudence (*raʾy*) and rationalist theology (*kalām*). These engagements had a deep impact on al-Shāfiʿī. In particular, they shaped the development of his ideas about the respective roles of Hadith and communal consensus in jurisprudence and contributed to his gradual estrangement from his teacher Mālik in the direction of his own holistic theory of the law.

At the time of al-Shāfiʿī's visit, the caliphal seat had just moved from Baghdad north to the twin cities of Raqqa and Rāfiqa,[2] where Hārūn al-Rashīd's vast palace complex hosted illustrious jurists, great musicians, and scores of renowned poets. The famous grammarian and Quranic scholar al-Kisāʾī (d. 189/805) taught the caliph's children,[3] while the

[1] Abū Zahra, *al-Shāfiʿī*, 22–24; Wilferd Madelung, *Arabic Texts Concerning the History of the Zaydī Imāms of Tabaristān, Daylamān and Gīlān* (Beirut: Deutsches Orient-Institut, 1987), 55.

[2] Stefan Heidemann, "Die Geschichte von ar-Raqqa/ar-Rāfiqa: Ein Überblick," in *Raqqa II: Die islamische Stadt*, ed. Stefan Heidemann and Andrea Becker, 9–56 (Mainz: P. von Zabern, 2003).

[3] Rudolf Sellheim, "al-Kisāʾī," in *EI2*, 5:174–75.

Christian court physician Ibn Māsawayh (d. 243/857) was engaged in translating Greek and Syriac works of medicine into Arabic.[4] But even with the glamour and vitality of the caliphal court, Raqqa and Rāfiqa could not compete with the metropolis of Baghdad, which dwarfed every other city within the Islamic realm; Medina and Mecca were mere villages in comparison. It was a new city, barely three decades old, with a population reaching hundreds of thousands.[5] Under Hārūn al-Rashīd, Baghdad enjoyed its most prosperous period, with taxes and tribute flowing to it from Tunisia in the west and India in the east, and traders converging upon it from as far as northern Europe, China, and East Africa. While Medina might have felt like a landscape of memories, connecting its observer all the way back to the prophetic age, Baghdad was the city of the here and now, irresistibly attracting talent from throughout the empire. Indeed, it provided hospitable ground even for ideas and artistic expressions that were more risqué than was acceptable at the caliph's court. In the protected space of the nobles' courts in Baghdad, unfettered by the conservatism of Hārūn, who harbored a particular distrust of rationalist theology, Muslim theologians of all stripes and colors debated with each other as well as with Magians and Christians.[6]

THE ḤANAFĪS AND HADITH

In the field of law, the most influential scholars in Iraq at this time were Abū Ḥanīfa's students and their students. The grandson of a non-Muslim prisoner of war from today's Afghanistan, Abū Ḥanīfa had grown up and spent his life in Kufa. Although he was trained in the Kufan legal tradition, his systematizing approach to jurisprudence – characterized by the methodology of *ra'y*, of which he was the unrivaled master – had made his name synonymous with Iraqi legal thought. Abū Ḥanīfa himself had refused to accept a judgeship from the Abbasids and eventually died in a Baghdad prison, possibly because he had expressed support for an ʿAlid uprising against the Abbasids.[7] After his death, however, Ḥanafism became the preferred legal doctrine of the Abbasid court, its

[4] Dominique Sourdel, "Ibn Māsawayh," in *EI2*, 3:872–73.

[5] Jacob Lassner, *The Topography of Baghdad in the Early Middle Ages* (Detroit: Wayne State University Press, 1970).

[6] Josef van Ess, *Theologie und Gesellschaft im 2. und 3. Jahrhundert Hidschra: Eine Geschichte des religiösen Denkens im frühen Islam*, 6 vols. (Berlin: W. de Gruyter, 1991–97), 2:31–36.

[7] Joseph Schacht, "Abū Ḥanīfa al-Nuʿmān," in *EI2*, 1:123–24.

preeminence sealed by the appointment of Abū Ḥanīfa's student Abū Yūsuf (d. 182/798) as the judge of Baghdad.[8] By the time of al-Shāfiʿī's arrival in Iraq, Abū Yūsuf had died, leaving Muḥammad b. al-Ḥasan al-Shaybānī, the Iraq-born son of a non-Arab military family from Syria,[9] the most senior surviving disciple of Abū Ḥanīfa. Al-Shāfiʿī attended al-Shaybānī's circle, studied his works, and engaged him in public debates, developing both deep personal respect for al-Shaybānī[10] and a passionate critique of the latter's legal approach. This critique can be reconstructed in considerable detail from the (hitherto ignored) records of al-Shāfiʿī's debates with al-Shaybānī that al-Shāfiʿī included in the text of his magnum opus, *Kitāb al-Umm*.[11]

Both al-Shāfiʿī and al-Shaybānī had studied with Mālik in Medina. While al-Shaybānī nonetheless saw himself squarely within the Iraqi tradition of his primary teacher Abū Ḥanīfa, al-Shāfiʿī arrived in Iraq as a disciple of Mālik. Al-Shāfiʿī's allegiance to Mālik is evident in the following exchange, reported by al-Shāfiʿī and quoted by Ibn Abī Ḥātim:

> **Muḥammad b. al-Ḥasan [al-Shaybānī] said to me:** "Which of the two is more knowledgeable: our master or yours?"
> **I said:** "In all honesty?"
> **He said:** "Yes."
> **I said:** "... Who knows more about the Quran, our master or yours?"
> **He said:** "Your master."
> **I said:** "And who is more knowledgeable about the prophetic tradition, our master or yours?"
> **He said:** "By God, yours."
> **I said:** "... Who is more knowledgeable about the opinions of the Prophet's Companions and the earlier [jurists], our master or yours?"
> **He said:** "Yours."
> **So I said:** "All that is left is analogical reasoning, and such reasoning can only take place on the basis of these things. But on what basis is someone who does not know the sources going to reason?"[12]

[8] Ibn ʿAbd al-Barr, *Intiqāʾ*, 331; Taqī al-Dīn al-Maqrīzī, *al-Mawāʿiẓ wa-l-iʿtibār bi-dhikr al-khiṭaṭ wa-l-āthār* [*al-Khiṭaṭ*], 2 vols., 2:333 (Bulaq: Dār al-Ṭibāʿa al-Miṣriyya, 1853). See also Qasim Zaman, *Religion and Politics under the Early ʿAbbāsids*, 95–101.

[9] Éric Chaumont, "al-Shaybānī," in *EI2*, 9:392–94.

[10] Numerous reports attest to al-Shāfiʿī's high opinion of al-Shaybānī. One of these quotes al-Shāfiʿī addressing al-Shaybānī as "him whose equal has never yet been seen by the eyes of man. But who at the same time gives his observer the impression that he is seeing (in this one person the virtue of) all who were before him"; translated by Franz Rosenthal in "The Technique and Approach of Muslim Scholarship," *Analecta Orientalia* 24 (1947): 1–74, at 9.

[11] Although al-Shāfiʿī does not generally name al-Shaybānī as his opponent in the debates, the latter's identity is noted in the text of the *Umm* by al-Rabīʿ; see *Umm*, 7:417.

[12] Ibn Abī Ḥātim, *al-Jarḥ wa-l-taʿdīl*, 4 vols. in 9 (Beirut: Dār Iḥyāʾ al-Turāth al-ʿArabī, 1952–53), 1:4.

At the beginning of his sojourn in Baghdad, then, al-Shāfiʿī clearly identified with Mālik and seems to have taken it upon himself to defend Mālik against the criticisms that al-Shaybānī leveled at his erstwhile teacher. Al-Shaybānī authored a dedicated critique of Medinan doctrine as represented by Mālik, *al-Ḥujja ʿalā ahl al-Madīna*; al-Shāfiʿī responded with a counterrefutation, *al-Radd ʿalā Muḥammad b. al-Ḥasan*,[13] as well as his own original attack on Ḥanafism, *Ikhtilāf ʿAlī wa-Ibn Masʿūd*.[14] An examination of these works, as well as others composed by Abū Yūsuf and al-Shaybānī, reveals that although Ḥanafī thought already early on took a speculative turn into the hypothetical abstractions of *raʾy*, it, too, retained a regional specificity, rooted in the Kufan legal tradition, that precisely mirrored the Medina-centrism of Mālik. Specifically, the Ḥanafīs continued to anchor their normative positions by linking them to the authoritative precedent of prominent Kufa-based Companions of the Prophet, particularly ʿAlī b. Abī Ṭālib and Ibn Masʿūd.[15] This localized focus is evident, for example, in the two "books of traditions" (*kitāb al-āthār*) authored by Abū Yūsuf and al-Shaybānī, respectively: beyond a handful of prophetic Hadith, these list exclusively reports from Kufan Companions as well as later Iraqi jurists, such as al-Nakhaʿī (d. 96/715), Ḥammād (d. 120/737), and Abū Ḥanīfa.[16] It is also demonstrated by al-Shaybānī's efforts (in his *Ḥujja* as well as in his *Muwaṭṭaʾ*)[17] to promote the opinions of Abū Ḥanīfa by stressing their concordance with the positions of the Kufan Companions, while accusing Mālik of contravening the positions held by those normative forebears on whose precedent the

[13] Included in the *Umm*, 9:85–169.

[14] Included in the *Umm*, 8:391–521.

[15] This notion of a continuous chain of scholars stretching back to the Prophet's time was observed among the Ḥanafīs by Brannon Wheeler in *Applying the Canon in Islam: The Authorization and Maintenance of Interpretive Reasoning in Ḥanafī Scholarship* (Albany: State University of New York Press, 1996), 164–70.

[16] Abū Yūsuf, *Kitāb al-Āthār*, ed. Abū al-Wafāʾ al-Afghānī (Hyderabad: Lajnat Iḥyāʾ al-Maʿārif al-Nuʿmāniyya, 1936); al-Shaybānī, *Kitāb al-Āthār*, ed. Khālid ʿAwwād (Damascus: Dār al-Nawādir, 2008). On the authenticity of al-Shaybānī's works, see Sadeghi, "Authenticity of Two Ḥanafī Legal Texts."

[17] Al-Shaybānī, *Muwaṭṭaʾ al-Imām Mālik*, ed. ʿAbd al-Wahhāb ʿAbd al-Laṭīf (Cairo: al-Majlis al-Aʿlā li-l-Shuʾūn al-Islāmiyya, 1962). The editor as well as many subsequent scholars have considered this work to represent al-Shaybānī's recension of Mālik's *Muwaṭṭaʾ*; however, the divergence between it and the other extant recensions is significant enough to indicate, as Jonathan Brockopp and Yasin Dutton have concluded, that it is a quasi-independent work by al-Shaybānī, in which he draws on his studies with Mālik. See Dutton's review of *Early Mālikī Law: Ibn ʿAbd al-Ḥakam and His Major Compendium of Islamic Jurisprudence*, by Jonathan Brockopp, *Journal of Islamic Studies*, 13 (2002): 42–49, at 44.

Medinans claimed to base their judgments, namely, Medinan Companions such as ʿUmar b. al-Khaṭṭāb and his son ʿAbd Allāh b. ʿUmar.[18]

Al-Shāfiʿī's *Ikhtilāf ʿAlī wa-Ibn Masʿūd* turns this strategy against al-Shaybānī himself. The entire work – 130 pages in the most recent edition[19] – follows a simple and consistent format. Al-Shāfiʿī seeks to discredit the Ḥanafīs' claim to represent the Kufan tradition by systematically juxtaposing the opinions of Abū Ḥanīfa, al-Shaybānī, and Abū Yūsuf with the opinions of prominent Kufan Companions in order to expose the discrepancies between the two. For example, on the question of the legal status of an *umm walad*, a slave woman who has given birth to her master's child, al-Shāfiʿī points out that while ʿAlī believed that such a woman would remain a slave after the master's death, the followers of Abū Ḥanīfa disagree with ʿAlī on this issue – as does al-Shāfiʿī himself – and follow the contrary opinion of ʿUmar b. al-Khaṭṭāb instead. Al-Shāfiʿī criticizes the Ḥanafīs' divergence from ʿAlī's precedent: given that they provide no countervailing evidence to refute the report from ʿAlī, he argues, "if they consider it authentic then they are bound by it."[20] This criticism is repeated on a number of different occasions,[21] and it demonstrates that al-Shāfiʿī perceived a prima facie obligation on the part of the Ḥanafīs to adhere to the Kufan Companions' opinions.

It is easy to understand how reports about the Companions of the Prophet were localized in this manner: the Companions settled and lived in towns throughout the Islamic empire, and their unique characteristics and experiences combined with local cultures and practices to form distinctive regional traditions. But prophetic Hadith were different. The details of the Prophet's life in Mecca and Medina had a significance in defining Islam and Muslim life that was in theory universal. This universality formed the basis of Mālik's belief in the normativity of Medinan practice, modeled on the example set by the Prophet, even beyond the boundaries of the city; and it was also acknowledged by the Ḥanafīs, who formulated justifications for the normativity of prophetic Hadith that al-Shāfiʿī would later adopt verbatim in his work on legal theory.[22]

[18] For examples, see al-Shaybānī's *Ḥujja*, 1:24–33, and al-Shaybānī's *Muwaṭṭaʾ*, 1:79.

[19] *Umm*, 8:391–521.

[20] *Umm*, 8:440.

[21] See also, e.g., *Umm*, 8:451 and 463.

[22] Al-Shāfiʿī quotes al-Shaybānī on two occasions as calling the prophetic example "an indicator toward the meaning that God has intended [in the Quran]" (*dalīlan ʿalā mā arāda Allāh*); *Umm*, 7:319 and 8:41. That al-Shāfiʿī's unnamed opponent in this exchange is in fact al-Shaybānī is confirmed by Ibn al-Humām in *Sharḥ Fatḥ al-qadīr*, 7 vols.

Nonetheless, al-Shāfiʿī's debates with the Iraqi Ḥanafīs, as documented in the *Umm*, reveal that the claim of the universal normativity of Hadith, wielded by al-Shāfiʿī as the primary weapon in his debates with the Ḥanafīs, represented a serious challenge to Ḥanafī doctrine.

An illustrative example of this challenge can be found in an important section of the *Umm* where al-Shāfiʿī spends a full sixty-eight pages recounting a debate on the seemingly minor question of whether a solitary witness statement accompanied by an oath suffices as evidence in certain types of court cases.[23] The Ḥanafīs claim that a Quranic verse that prescribes two male witnesses or two females and one male for recording a debt (2:282) contradicts a prophetic Hadith according to which one witness statement supported by an oath constitutes decisive evidence in court. The Ḥanafīs therefore reject the Hadith and the practice that it permits. Al-Shāfiʿī's response consists of listing similar cases in which the Ḥanafīs do permit Hadith reports to modify apparently unequivocal Quranic injunctions. One such case is that of the Quranic verses 4:22–24, which prohibit certain types of marriage but declare everything beyond those to be permissible. However, both al-Shāfiʿī and his Ḥanafī opponent in the debate consider it prohibited for a man to marry a woman as well as her aunt, even though such a scenario is not explicitly mentioned in the Quranic verses, and both justify their positions by reference to a prophetic Hadith.[24] Al-Shāfiʿī thus accuses the Ḥanafīs of inconsistency. The Ḥanafī scholar replies that the two cases are marked by a significant difference: in the latter case, the Hadith report is supported by the fact that people agree upon it, which renders it normative. Al-Shāfiʿī retorts that this consensus simply represents the consensus on following a Hadith with a sound chain of transmission, since God has obliged humankind to follow His Prophet – an obligation, al-Shāfiʿī pointedly remarks, that the Ḥanafīs seem to have the confidence to ignore.

This debate shows that for al-Shāfiʿī the authenticity of a Hadith report, as vouchsafed by a sound chain of transmission, was sufficient to establish its normative force.[25] This was the case even for so-called single-transmitter reports (*akhbār al-āḥād*), that is, Hadith reports whose

(Damascus: Dār al-Fikr, n.d.), 5:357. For al-Shāfiʿī's adoption of this argument, compare the quotation with *Risāla*, in *Umm*, 1:43 (para. 308).

[23] *Umm*, 8:15–83. Al-Shāfiʿī even prefaces the report by saying that he has expended considerable efforts in order to condense his discussions on the subject.

[24] *Umm*, 8:48.

[25] This is evident in al-Shāfiʿī's famous statement "If the Hadith is correct, it is my *madhhab*"; see my "First Shāfiʿī," 320.

chains of transmission from the Prophet rested at some point on the strength of a single transmitter or at most a few transmitters.[26] In principle, then, al-Shāfiʿī considered all authentic Hadith formally equal. By adopting this view of Hadith, al-Shāfiʿī was moving away from the perception, characteristic of the regional legal schools, of Hadith as embedded in local practice and in the direction of the position held by the traditionalists or "Hadith folk" (*ahl al-ḥadīth/aṣḥāb al-ḥadīth*),[27] Hadith-oriented scholars whose emphasis on the primacy and sufficiency of Hadith as the basis of law led them to view speculative legal reasoning as a deeply suspect, even impious, imposition on revelation.[28]

Al-Shāfiʿī's metamorphosis from a loyal disciple of Mālik to an independent scholar with a traditionalist view of Hadith most likely began in Iraq. It was probably there that he met the most important traditionalist scholar of his time, Aḥmad b. Ḥanbal (d. 241/855), initiating a fruitful intellectual exchange: al-Shāfiʿī learned about the developing methods of Hadith criticism from Aḥmad and in turn taught Aḥmad legal hermeneutics.[29] The shift in al-Shāfiʿī's opinions can be observed within the text of the Iraqi debates in al-Shāfiʿī's *Umm*. For example, in debates that most probably form part of the older material in the *Umm*, al-Shāfiʿī stresses the religious authority of Medina,[30] uses Medinan practice as a legal argument,[31] and argues that although a particular Hadith report has no continuous chain of transmission, "I have seen that some of the people of knowledge in our region know it and follow it, and therefore I, too,

[26] Such uncorroborated or weakly corroborated reports were juxtaposed with concurrent reports (*akhbār mutawātira*), which, for Muslim scholars, could give rise to certain as opposed to merely probable knowledge. See Zysow, "Economy of Certainty," 11.

[27] "Hadith folk" is one of the terms used for the *ahl al-ḥadīth* by Christopher Melchert; see Melchert, "The Piety of the Hadith Folk," *International Journal of Middle East Studies* 34 (2002): 425–39. I prefer George Makdisi's term "traditionalists"; see Makdisi, "Ashʿarī and the Ashʿarites in Islamic Religious History I," *Studia Islamica*, no. 17 (1962): 37–80.

[28] Note that the term "traditionalist" (*ahl al-ḥadīth*) is not synonymous with "Hadith scholar" (*muḥaddith*, occasionally translated as "traditionist"). The former denotes a certain attitude toward Hadith, the latter scholarly expertise in their study.

[29] On their meetings and Aḥmad's praise of al-Shāfiʿī's work on legal theory, see Ibn Abī Ḥātim, *Ādāb al-Shāfiʿī*, 44, 55–63. Aḥmad's son ʿAbd Allāh quotes al-Shāfiʿī from his father's handwritten notes in Aḥmad b. Ḥanbal, *al-ʿIlal wa-maʿrifat al-rijāl*, ed. Waṣī Allāh ʿAbbās, 4 vols. (Riyadh: Dār al-Khānī, 1988), 2:383 and 3:422–24. Al-Shāfiʿī's expression of confidence in Aḥmad's Hadith expertise is quoted in Ibn Abī Yaʿlā al-Farrāʾ, *Ṭabaqāt al-ḥanābila*, ed. ʿAbd al-Raḥmān al-ʿUthaymīn, 3 vols. (Riyadh: al-Amāna al-ʿĀmma li-l-Iḥtifāl bi-Murūr Miʾat ʿĀm ʿalā Taʾsīs al-Mamlaka, 1999), 1:13.

[30] *Umm*, 7:158 and 160.

[31] *Umm*, 7:358.

follow it."[32] Such simple acceptance of the authority of the Medinan tradition is alien to al-Shāfiʿī's later thought, as exemplified by his arguments in the case involving legal evidence quoted previously: in that debate he gives no credit to local traditions[33] and considers a Hadith report's sound chain of transmission to render it prima facie unassailable.

By contrast, the Ḥanafī position on Hadith that emerges from the preceding exchange bears a surprising similarity to Mālik's view of Hadith discussed in Chapter 1: for al-Shāfiʿī's Ḥanafī opponent, as for Mālik, the normativity of a Hadith report is not automatic but rather hinges on its acceptance by the community.[34] This distinction is already evident in Abū Yūsuf's refutation of the Syrian jurist al-Awzāʿī (d. 157/774), quoted by al-Shāfiʿī, where Abū Yūsuf notes that the number of available Hadith reports has increased greatly and argues that "those reports are to be excluded that are unknown or not known to the jurists, as well as those that agree with neither the Quran nor the Sunna. And beware of irregular Hadith (*shādhdh*), and keep to those Hadith to which the community adheres and which the jurists know."[35] The Ḥanafī approach thus prioritized Hadith that had taken root in communal life or scholarly usage, while branding others "irregular"[36] and consequently not normative. This indicates that the Ḥanafīs saw Hadith not as discrete blocks of data but rather as integrally connected to communal religious life and identity. Accordingly, the recognized practice of local Companions could support a weak Hadith or even replace a sound one as evidence for a legal ruling. An example is provided by one of the debates between al-Shāfiʿī and al-Shaybānī in the *Umm*, where al-Shāfiʿī cites a sound Hadith in support of his own position and then points out that a Hadith report used by the Ḥanafīs as a proof text for their opposing position lacks a continuous chain of transmission and is consequently critically weakened.[37] Al-Shaybānī's response consists of citing two Kufan Companion traditions

[32] *Umm*, 7:368.

[33] In fact al-Shāfiʿī considers his opponent's argument, "that is what our fellow [Ḥanafīs] say," a sign of intellectual bankruptcy; see *Umm*, 7:41.

[34] As for Mālik, "community" for the Ḥanafīs did not mean the masses but rather referred to the carriers of religious tradition – primarily the scholars.

[35] Abū Yūsuf in *Siyar al-Awzāʿī*, reproduced with comments in al-Shāfiʿī's *Umm*, 9:188–89.

[36] An irregular Hadith later came to be defined as a unique report that contradicts other, more reliable reports (reliability being determined by the strength of the chain of transmission); see Brown, *Canonization of al-Bukhārī and Muslim*, 249. However, as seen in Chap. 8 of this volume, for Ḥanafīs at this time the term held other meanings.

[37] *Umm*, 7:322.

that also support his position, one going back to ʿAlī and the other to Ibn Masʿūd.[38]

The Ḥanafī view of Hadith – as well as its precariousness – can be better understood if we consider the state of Hadith in the late second/eighth century. In contrast to just a century later, when Hadith reports had been assembled, evaluated, classified, and made available in well-organized collections and concordances, at this time the great movement of systematic Hadith collection was still under way. This movement had begun with the generation of scholars who died in the first quarter of the second Islamic century (before ca. 750 CE),[39] and it had grown into a loose network of countless itinerant Hadith scholars who traveled to centers of learning throughout the Islamic world in search of localized Hadith reports, gathering, recording, and disseminating them along the way. This process led to the wide circulation of thousands of Hadith that had previously been known only in particular locales. The spread of Hadith was further accelerated by the migration of senior Hadith collectors to major cities; the illustrious Hadith scholar Ibn Shihāb al-Zuhrī (d. 124/742), for example, moved from Medina to the Umayyad capital of Damascus, taking with him an unprecedented wealth of Hadith reports.[40] For the Iraqis, too, Medina was a major source of newly gathered Hadith. Several Medinan Hadith scholars, including ʿAbd al-ʿAzīz b. al-Mājishūn (see Chapter 1), traveled to Baghdad in the early Abbasid period (the 130s and 140s/750s and 760s) at the request of the caliph al-Manṣūr and taught Hadith to Abū Yūsuf and other Ḥanafīs.[41] Al-Shaybānī also went to Medina himself to study with Mālik for three years and returned to Baghdad with Hadith that he had learned from Mālik.[42]

The effect of the influx of "new," hitherto unknown prophetic Hadith on local legal traditions, including that of Iraq, was profoundly unsettling. As seen in the previous chapter, the dialectical method of *raʾy* perfected by the Ḥanafīs in Iraq had created a proliferating, internally consistent body of legal rulings that were based on a limited number of generally accepted first principles, including some widely known Hadith. Such a body of rulings could not accommodate anomalous Hadith reports and was thus

[38] *Umm*, 7:323–24.

[39] As has been convincingly argued by Harald Motzki; see, for example, his "Whither Ḥadīth Studies?" in *Analysing Muslim Traditions*, 50–52.

[40] Michael Lecker, "Biographical Notes on Ibn Shihāb al-Zuhrī," *Journal of Semitic Studies* 41 (1996): 21–63.

[41] Ibn Taymiyya, *Ṣiḥḥat uṣūl ahl al-Madīna*, 20:170.

[42] Ibn Abī Ḥātim, *al-Jarḥ wa-l-taʿdīl*, 1:4.

severely undermined by the appearance, in ever greater numbers, of new Hadith that had been vetted and declared authentic by scholars specializing in the evaluation of Hadith, but that frequently contradicted established Ḥanafī positions.

The Ḥanafī response to this threat, then, was to declare the community a gatekeeper of normativity: Hadith that were known and accepted in local tradition enjoyed priority over Hadith that were not. The extant writings of Abū Ḥanīfa's students show that although in some cases they did revise their legal positions to conform to conflicting Hadith,[43] in many instances they asserted the primacy of the local legal tradition and their systematizations of the law over isolated Hadith reports and simply let the contradictions stand, leaving it to later generations of Ḥanafīs to construct justifications for these positions.[44] The Iraqi legal tradition and the discourse of Hadith thus developed on parallel tracks in Ḥanafī thought, without being integrated into a methodologically coherent overall approach. Al-Shaybānī, for example, held popular lessons on Hadith as well as giving lessons on law that contradicted the content of the Hadith that he transmitted.[45]

The Ḥanafīs' seemingly cavalier attitude toward Hadith scandalized al-Shāfiʿī. He quotes – with disapproval – a Ḥanafī jurist (probably al-Shaybānī) calmly acknowledging the incompatibility of his opinion with a particular Hadith: "The Hadith is authentic, but the jurists ignore it."[46] For al-Shāfiʿī, such eclecticism – accepting the authenticity of Hadith but selectively rejecting their implications – was unacceptable. In his attacks on this feature of Ḥanafī law we can see the ruthless consistency that came to constitute a central feature of al-Shāfiʿī's hermeneutic approach. While the Ḥanafīs had sought to systematize the edifice of the law by subjecting its individual rulings to the test of *raʾy*, al-Shāfiʿī went deeper by striving to systematize the methodological basis of the law as a whole.

In spite of the centrality of questions related to Hadith and their role in law, al-Shāfiʿī's debates with the Ḥanafīs were not exclusively about

[43] Compare, for example, Abū Ḥanīfa's position with that of his students in al-Sarakhsī, *al-Mabsūṭ*, 1:34–35 and 188.

[44] For examples of such justifications, see Abū Jaʿfar al-Ṭaḥāwī, *Sharḥ maʿānī al-āthār*, 4:17–22, and ʿAlāʾ al-Dīn Abū Bakr b. Masʿūd al-Kāsānī, *Badāʾiʿ al-ṣanāʾiʿ fī tartīb al-sharāʾiʿ*, ed. Aḥmad ʿAbd al-Mawjūd and ʿAlī Muʿawwaḍ, 10 vols. (Beirut: Dār al-Kutub al-ʿIlmiyya, 1997), 8:436.

[45] Ibn Abī Ḥātim, *al-Jarḥ wa-l-taʿdīl*, 1:4.

[46] *Umm*, 10:276.

Hadith. In fact, al-Shāfiʿī took great pleasure in challenging the Ḥanafīs in their own area of strength, complex legal reasoning. To take an example, all jurists agree on the impermissibility of a man's marrying both a woman and her mother. According to al-Shāfiʿī's account, the Ḥanafīs argued that extramarital intercourse between a man and his wife's mother would dissolve his marriage with the daughter. Al-Shāfiʿī responded: "How can an illegal act invalidate something that is legal?" His Ḥanafī opponent replied meekly that Abū Ḥanīfa had drawn an analogy with talk unrelated to worship during prayer. Al-Shāfiʿī retorted that such talk invalidates the prayer in question, but in order for the analogy to hold it would also have to invalidate subsequent prayers. He concluded: "Had anyone else than your master drawn this analogy, what would you have said to him? Wouldn't you have said, 'You have no business talking about law'?"[47]

The formative influence of al-Shāfiʿī's debates with al-Shaybānī on the development of his legal-theoretical thought is evident in the multiple roles that these debates play in his writings. An illustrative example is afforded by the discussion, mentioned earlier, of the validity of a witness statement and an oath as evidence in a court case. In a section on positive law in the *Umm*, al-Shāfiʿī quotes extensively from his notes on a debate with "*baʿḍ al-nās*," that is, with al-Shaybānī, in order both to support his position on this specific issue and to develop a critique of al-Shaybānī's selective use of Hadith.[48] The same debate, in a much more abridged form, also provided material for al-Shāfiʿī's old, Iraqi *Risāla*, where al-Shāfiʿī draws on his exchange with al-Shaybānī (who is there named explicitly) to make the legal-theoretical argument that the Sunna serves as an indication of the meaning of the Quran.[49] Finally, in the new, Egyptian *Risāla*, the abstract principle at the heart of the debate is again mentioned, but most of the substantial legal discussions have been removed and al-Shaybānī's identity has been erased.[50] Al-Shāfiʿī's oral debate with al-Shaybānī on a particular point of positive law thus found its way, via repeated written reworking and analysis, into al-Shāfiʿī's mature, abstracted legal theory.

Al-Shāfiʿī's double-pronged attack on Ḥanafism via both Hadith and reasoning demonstrates that he was not simply a convert to traditionalism who was intent on discrediting legal reasoning. Rather, his argumentative

47 *Umm*, 8:71. For another similar instance, see *Umm*, 7:419.
48 *Umm*, 8:15–83.
49 Badr al-Dīn al-Zarkashī, *al-Baḥr al-muḥīṭ*, ed. ʿAbd al-Qādir ʿAbd Allāh al-ʿĀnī, ʿUmar Sulaymān al-Ashqar, et al., 6 vols. (Kuwait: Wizārat al-Awqāf wa-l-Shuʾūn al-Islāmiyya, 1992), 4:121.
50 *Risāla*, in *Umm*, 1:43–47 (paras. 308–35).

strategy in the debates with the Ḥanafīs reveals an ambitious goal of synthesis. For al-Shāfiʿī, both Hadith and analogy were valid and necessary materials for the jurist: each had its distinctive role that complemented, rather than undermined, that of the other.

IBN ʿULAYYA'S THEORY OF CONSENSUS

While the communitarian doctrines of Mālik and the Ḥanafīs accommodated Hadith in lawmaking, albeit selectively and – for al-Shāfiʿī – inconsistently, al-Shāfiʿī also found himself defending the normativity of Hadith against an all-out attack from the perspective of rationalist theology. According to al-Shāfiʿī's own description, his treatise "The Sum of Knowledge" (*Jimāʿ al-ʿilm*),[51] included in the *Umm*,[52] reproduces his debates with two groups of theologians who deny the validity of single-transmitter Hadith (*akhbār al-āḥād*). The names of these scholars are not mentioned anywhere in the work.[53] However, the Egyptian legal historian Muḥammad al-Khuḍarī (d. 1927) has argued that al-Shāfiʿī's opponents were from the theological milieu of Basra,[54] and with almost another century of published material at our disposal, the combined analysis of biographical sources, quotations in works of theology, and the *Jimāʿ al-ʿilm* itself enables us to identify at least one of the opponents with a high degree of probability as the Basran jurist and theologian Ibrāhīm b. ʿUlayya (d. 218/834).[55] Al-Khaṭīb al-Baghdādī's history of Baghdad contains an anecdote told by al-Ḥārith b. Surayj (d. 236/850 or 851), a student of al-Shāfiʿī, in which al-Ḥārith describes entering a house in Baghdad and finding it full of well-known scholars, among them Aḥmad b. Ḥanbal, observing a debate between al-Shāfiʿī and Ibn ʿUlayya. Al-Ḥārith asks al-Shāfiʿī incredulously:

"You have the best scholars with you, and yet you have given your attention to this [heretical] innovator to debate with him?" Al-Shāfiʿī said to me with

[51] Aisha Y. Musa translated the title as "The Amalgamation of Knowledge" in her translation of the work in *Ḥadīth as Scripture: Discussions on the Authority of Prophetic Traditions in Islam* (New York: Palgrave Macmillan, 2008), 113–56.

[52] *Umm*, 9:5–55. The treatise seems to end on p. 42, but as is so often the case in the *Umm*, the subchapter and chapter divisions are not clear.

[53] Given the opponents' rejection of Hadith, Joseph Schacht speculated that they were members of one of the "ancient" schools of law; see Schacht, *Origins*, 40. In fact, as I argue here, the view represented by the opponents was radically new.

[54] Muḥammad al-Khuḍarī, *Tārīkh al-tashrīʿ al-islāmī* (Cairo: Dār al-Istiqāma, 1967), 153–56.

[55] On Ibn ʿUlayya, see van Ess, *Theologie und Gesellschaft*, 2:418–22.

a smile: "My debating him in their presence is more beneficial for them than my talking to them [directly]." They said: "That is true!" Al-Shāfiʿī then turned to [Ibn ʿUlayya] and said to him: "Do you not claim that the [ideal] proof is consensus (*ijmāʿ*)?" He said: "Yes." Al-Shāfiʿī said: "Then tell me about sound single-transmitter Hadith: is it on the basis of consensus that you reject them, or on the basis of something other than consensus?" Ibrāhīm was unable to respond and the people were delighted.[56]

The anecdote's identification of Ibn ʿUlayya as a proponent of consensus is repeated in a statement attributed to Aḥmad b. Ḥanbal: "Whoever claims consensus is a liar; this is the claim of Bishr [al-Marīsī, d. 218/833] and Ibn ʿUlayya, who intend to cancel out the traditions of the Prophet."[57] Another report likewise depicts al-Shāfiʿī and Ibn ʿUlayya engaging in a debate, this time in the ʿAmr mosque in Fustat (old Cairo): each sat in a corner of the mosque teaching a circle of students, who ran back and forth between them ferrying refutations and counterrefutations.[58]

Ibrāhīm b. ʿUlayya was the son of the famous Hadith scholar Ismāʿīl b. ʿUlayya (d. 193/809), with whom al-Shāfiʿī had studied Hadith in Medina.[59] Ibn ʿUlayya *fils* became the disciple of the Basran theologian ʿAbd al-Raḥmān Kaysān al-Aṣamm (d. around 200/816)[60] and eventually settled in Egypt, where his ideas remained prominent throughout the third/ninth century. Al-Aṣamm and Ibn ʿUlayya can be described as rationalists because of their relentless and systematic pursuit of certainty, which drove them to dismiss large parts of the prophetic tradition. While they have been considered to belong to the dominant theological movement in early Islam, Muʿtazilism, they represent a marginal orientation within the movement that neither displays a clear connection with any of the principal streams of Muʿtazilī thought nor forms part of a lasting school among the Muʿtazilīs.[61]

56 Al-Khaṭīb al-Baghdādī, *Tārīkh Madīnat al-Salām*, 6:512.

57 Ibn Taymiyya, *Iqāmat al-dalīl ʿalā ibṭāl al-taḥlīl*, in *al-Fatāwā al-kubrā*, ed. Muḥammad ʿAṭā and Muṣṭafā ʿAṭā, 6 vols., 6:5–320 (Beirut: Dār al-Kutub al-ʿIlmiyya, 1987), at 6:286. The account reproduced by Aḥmad's son ʿAbd Allāh reads: "Whoever claims consensus is a liar, for people may have disagreed; this is the claim of Bishr al-Marīsī and al-Aṣamm [Ibn ʿUlayya's teacher]." See Aḥmad b. Ḥanbal, *Masāʾil al-Imām Aḥmad b. Ḥanbal: Riwāyat ibnihi ʿAbd Allāh b. Aḥmad*, ed. Zuhayr al-Shāwīsh (Beirut: al-Maktab al-Islāmī, 1981), 439.

58 Al-Khaṭīb al-Baghdādī, *Tārīkh Madīnat al-Salām*, 6:512.

59 Al-Shāfiʿī transmits several Hadith from Ibn ʿUlayya *père* in the *Umm*; see, for example, *Umm*, 6:454.

60 Van Ess, "al-Aṣamm," in *EI2*, 12:88–90.

61 Van Ess, *Theologie und Gesellschaft*, 2:397.

Ibn ʿUlayya's works appear to have been lost, and references to his positions in other works are meager, but they suffice to establish the remarkable correspondence between his often idiosyncratic ideas and those put forward by al-Shāfiʿī's second opponent in the "Sum of Knowledge": a demand for certainty in the law, intolerance of differences in legal reasoning, and the elevation of consensus to the position of the ideal proof in matters of religion.[62] This, together with the anecdotes that show al-Shāfiʿī debating with Ibn ʿUlayya on precisely these topics, strongly suggests that al-Shāfiʿī's interlocutor in the second and most significant part of *Jimāʿ al-ʿilm* is Ibrāhīm b. ʿUlayya.[63] This hypothesis is further supported by Ibn Taymiyya's (d.728/1328) tantalizingly brief reference to a debate between al-Shāfiʿī and Ibn ʿUlayya as the cause of the first tract on legal theory (what that is he does not say).[64] In addition, the jurist Dāwūd al-Ẓāhirī (d. 270/884), who studied with al-Shāfiʿī, mentions that Ibn ʿUlayya penned a refutation of al-Shāfiʿī, which Dāwūd considered a sufficiently serious challenge to require a counterrefutation.[65] A reconstruction of Ibn ʿUlayya's legal theory and of al-Shāfiʿī's critique of it sheds light on the formation of al-Shāfiʿī's own ideas about Hadith, consensus, and their respective roles in the process of lawmaking.

The first section of the *Jimāʿ al-ʿilm* recounts a debate with a different opponent, but it nevertheless sets the subject of the tract as a whole, namely, the theologians' search for certainty in the law. Al-Shāfiʿī's unnamed opponent in this section may have been the theologian Bishr al-Marīsī, who is known to have met and debated with al-Shāfiʿī and to have rejected the normativity of single-transmitter Hadith.[66] In al-Shāfiʿī's text, this opponent holds up the Quran as the ideal of certainty in transmission and clarity of expression. In the presence of this rock of certainty, the opponent considers al-Shāfiʿī's imposition of analytical categories on the text outright impious. By finding certain Quranic expressions to be of general import and others to be specific, and by interpreting imperative statements as sometimes imposing obligation and at other times embodying simply prudent direction, al-Shāfiʿī is, from this perspective,

[62] See van Ess's discussions of both Ibn ʿUlayya and his teacher al-Aṣamm in *Theologie und Gesellschaft*, 2:414–22.

[63] *Umm*, 9:19–42.

[64] Ibn Taymiyya, *al-Istiqāma*, ed. Muḥammad Rashshād Sālim, 2 vols. (Medina: Jāmiʿat Muḥammad b. Saʿūd, 1983), 1:337. I am grateful to Aron Zysow for this reference.

[65] Al-Khaṭīb al-Baghdādī, *Tārīkh Madīnat al-Salām*, 6:513–14.

[66] Van Ess, *Theologie und Gesellschaft*, 3:178. See also "The Ḥanafīs" and "Other Scholars" in Chap. 8 of this volume.

willfully and arbitrarily distorting the divine message. This is especially the case since most of these interventions are carried out on the strength of single-transmitter Hadith, which, the opponent remarks, even Hadith scholars acknowledge to be subject to their transmitters' forgetfulness and errors.[67] The anonymous theologian is thus adopting the ideal of certainty represented by the Quran and criticizing al-Shāfiʿī for diluting this certainty by allowing reports that are by their nature uncertain to influence the interpretation of the Quran, thereby allowing uncertainty to infect the entire edifice of the law.

Al-Shāfiʿī counters these idealistic concerns with a very practical argument, probably drawn from his experience serving as a judge in Yemen: one must use the best evidence one has available. He mentions confessions, the testimony of two witnesses, and various forms of oath, noting that these types of evidence become progressively less reliable.[68] However, they are nonetheless explicitly endorsed by scripture, which demonstrates that certainty is not a prerequisite for religiously sanctioned judicial decisions. In fact, al-Shāfiʿī points out, condemning a man to death on the basis of two witness testimonies amounts to repealing what is certain – a man's right to life – by means of evidence that is only probable. Furthermore, he argues, the Quran itself implicitly calls for and thereby approves of its elaboration by the prophetic tradition when it imposes general obligations, such as prayer and charity, without providing sufficient detail as to how they are to be fulfilled. The fact that al-Shāfiʿī and his contemporaries were already separated from the prophetic Sunna by four or five generations meant that the latter could be recaptured only through the formalized reports that, in most cases, relied on single transmitters within their chains of transmission.[69]

The first part of the work thus lays out the theological critique of single-transmitter Hadith in law as too uncertain, and al-Shāfiʿī's response to this critique: scripture calls for prophetic elaboration, and using evidence that falls short of certainty is explicitly justified for the judiciary and can be analogized to the use of Hadith in law. The second part of the work, which reproduces al-Shāfiʿī's debates with Ibrāhīm b. ʿUlayya, lays out the theologian's alternative legal theory, which claims to eradicate

[67] *Umm*, 9:6. Musa, *Ḥadīth as Scripture*, 115.
[68] *Umm*, 9:6. This point is made even more clearly in a parallel statement in the *Risāla*, in *Umm*, 1:276 (para. 1821).
[69] *Umm*, 9:8. Musa, in *Ḥadīth as Scripture*, 116, omits this section, as her translation is based on an edition that is in turn based on an incomplete manuscript; see the editor's notes in the *Umm*, 9:7–8.

uncertainty in the law. It also contains al-Shāfiʿī's refutation of this theory. In the transcript, Ibn ʿUlayya describes his theory of interpretation as follows, punctuated by al-Shāfiʿī's comments:

> **[Ibn ʿUlayya said:]** Knowledge derives from different directions. Among them is what a multitude has transmitted from a multitude, which I therefore attribute to God and His Messenger; for example, the outlines of the religious obligations.
>
> **[Al-Shāfiʿī] said:** This is the aforementioned [kind of] knowledge, regarding which no one disagrees with you.
>
> **[Ibn ʿUlayya continued:]** Among them is scripture that permits interpretation, leading to disagreement about it. When there is disagreement about it, it [must be interpreted] according to its apparent and general meaning, never according to a nonapparent meaning, even if one is possible, except by the agreement of jurists[70] upon it. If they disagree, the apparent meaning is adopted. And among them is that on which the Muslims agree and about which they relate the agreement of previous generations, with no disagreement. Even if they do not base it on the Book or the prophetic tradition, I consider it equal to an agreed-upon tradition. This is because their agreement cannot stem from legal reasoning (*raʾy*), given that had reasoning been involved, differences would have emerged.
>
> **[Al-Shāfiʿī] said:** Describe to me what comes after it.
>
> **He said:** And among [the kinds of knowledge] is individually held information, and no proof is established through it, unless its transmission was of the kind that precludes error. Finally, the last one is analogy. One thing is not analogized with another unless subject, source, and endpoint (*mubtadaʾuhu wa-maṣdaruhu wa-maṣrifuhu*)[71] are the same from beginning to end, so that [the new case] possesses the same underlying qualities as the original case. Disagreement is not possible in any of the paths toward knowledge that I have described. Things remain in their original [legal] state until the general public decides to alter their state. And consensus is proof that supersedes anything, because it excludes the possibility of error.[72]

The legal theory outlined in this section reflects the theologians' concern with certainty, as outlined in the first section of *Jimāʿ al-ʿilm*. This preoccupation has given rise to a theory of interpretation that excludes the possibility of differences of opinion. If scripture permits a nonobvious

[70] In Ibn ʿUlayya's usage as occasionally in al-Shāfiʿī's, *nās* (literally "people") refers to jurists. For Ibn ʿUlayya, see *Umm*, 9:22; for al-Shāfiʿī, see *Umm*, 2:40.

[71] Beyond the general gist that the new case and the original case must be closely similar, it is not clear to me to what specifically these conditions refer. Musa translates the three conditions as "its subject, its source, and requirements"; *Ḥadīth as Scripture*, 129.

[72] *Umm*, 9:21. The translation is mine and diverges in important respects from Musa's in *Ḥadīth as Scripture*, 128–29.

interpretation, there is the danger of disagreement; therefore, it can only be interpreted in this way if everyone agrees on the interpretation. When such unanimity is absent, only the superficially apparent meaning (*ẓāhir*) can be assumed. In this view, consensus represents a truthful and certain representation of prophetic tradition as transmitted from generation to generation, because had it originated in individual legal opinions, no consensus would have arisen. Difference of opinion is thus seen as a sure sign of the fallible human element in lawmaking, while consensus and certainty are qualities of truth and revelation. The only Hadith that are accepted are those whose transmission is as certain as that of the Quran – thus excluding the vast majority of Hadith because of their single chains of transmission. Analogical reasoning is limited to cases of essential sameness, not simply resemblance, because the latter would inevitably lead to differences of opinion. Ibn ʿUlayya concludes by mentioning the general principle from which his rule for interpreting scripture is derived: everything is assumed to remain in its original state until it is transformed by decisive evidence. This is a rationalist principle that is not based on scripture, but rather establishes rules for interacting with scripture. In the realm of human deeds, this principle translates to the assumption that all actions are permissible until proven otherwise. It also gives rise to hermeneutic rules: the "original state" of interpretation is reliance on the most obvious meaning of a statement, unless decisive indicators justify a different interpretation.

The main thrust of al-Shāfiʿī's arguments against Ibn ʿUlayya's theory consists of criticizing the latter's notion of consensus and demonstrating how inconsistent and communally destructive Ibn ʿUlayya's search for certainty in consensus is. Unsurprisingly, al-Shāfiʿī's critique of Ibn ʿUlayya in the *Jimāʿ* is much more sophisticated than that mentioned in the report about their debate in Baghdad. The essence of the critique is nonetheless the same in both, though developed in greater detail in the former.[73]

Al-Shāfiʿī begins his critique of Ibn ʿUlayya by probing the question of who participates in the consensus and how its existence can be ascertained. Ibn ʿUlayya defines binding consensus as the agreement of those who have been deemed knowledgeable by their respective local communities.[74] When pressed by al-Shāfiʿī, he admits that this does not

[73] Al-Ḥārith b. Surayj, the narrator of the debate in Baghdad, was clearly more interested in the anecdotal value of his story than in the details of the debate, which is likely to have been much more extensive than the two-sentence exchange that he transmitted.

[74] *Umm*, 9:23.

include every scholar, but he refuses to specify the extent of the necessary majority.[75] Al-Shāfiʿī points out that, first, people differ regarding who is a scholar.[76] Second, in order to verify that a consensus reaches beyond a particular community, information regarding the opinions of scholars located in different countries has to circulate in what amount to single-transmitter reports. Therefore, establishing consensus would implicitly require the acceptance of such single-transmitter reports, which Ibn ʿUlayya categorically rejects. Third, al-Shāfiʿī demonstrates, drawing on the impressive historical and geographical breadth of his knowledge of legal positions, that even within particular localities scholars disagree and positions change over time. Given this, he queries, how likely is the emergence of a universal consensus across space and time?[77] Fourth, al-Shāfiʿī notes that Ibn ʿUlayya's definition of consensus is based on the assumption that dissenting scholars make known their disagreement, but evidence indicates that this is not a valid assumption.[78] Finally, al-Shāfiʿī shows that the very scholars whom his opponent considers the participants in a binding consensus in fact accepted single-transmitter reports as well as disagreed with each other. He thus concludes that there is an implicit consensus that contradicts Ibn ʿUlayya's theory of consensus.[79]

At the heart of the disagreement between al-Shāfiʿī and Ibn ʿUlayya lies the issue of Hadith, as Aḥmad recognized. For Ibn ʿUlayya, the claim to consensus solves the epistemological challenge posed by the less-than-certain status of Hadith reports. Consensus allows the jurist to fill in the vast areas of the law that are not covered by the Quran with rulings that enjoy a guarantee of epistemological certainty. For al-Shāfiʿī, on the other hand, consensus is a much more limited juristic tool: it cannot replace Hadith, but it can express a residual normative memory of the community.[80] Like Hadith, this memory is prone to the epistemological difficulties of transmission; therefore, rather than dogmatically asserting censensus on any given issue, al-Shāfiʿī often simply stated, "I know of no difference of opinion regarding it" (*lā aʿlamu fīhi khilāf*).[81]

75 *Umm*, 9:24.
76 *Umm*, 9:28; Musa, *Ḥadīth as Scripture*, 138.
77 *Umm*, 9:25–28.
78 *Umm*, 9:31–32.
79 *Umm*, 9:31.
80 For a discussion of al-Shāfiʿī's views on consensus, see Joseph E. Lowry, *Early Islamic Legal Theory: The Risāla of Muḥammad ibn Idrīs al-Shāfiʿī* (Leiden: Brill, 2007), chap. 7.
81 See, for example, *Umm*, 2:378, 4:289, and 6:18, and Ibn Taymiyya's discussion in his *Majmūʿat al-fatāwā*, ed. ʿĀmir al-Jazzār and Anwar al-Bāz, 20 vols. (Mansura: Dār al-Wafāʾ, 1997), 9:147.

Al-Shāfiʿī thus criticized Ibn ʿUlayya's excessive reliance on consensus and rejection of single-transmitter Hadith as a misguided imposition on a legal discourse that is necessarily divided on both the specifics of the law and the authority of those who interpret it. Furthermore, al-Shāfiʿī saw the theory not only as unrealistic, but also as a dangerous attempt to import the sectarian nature of theological discussions into law. While many aspects of the debate remain implicit in the text, it is clear that Ibn ʿUlayya sought to exclude many theologians with whom he disagreed from the community of scholars whose consensus he claimed to be normative. This agenda led al-Shāfiʿī to fear that Ibn ʿUlayya's approach would reproduce the factionalism of theology in the realm of law. Elsewhere in the *Umm*, al-Shāfiʿī sketches a legal system that contains a multiplicity of jurists who may disagree with each other but do not declare each other religiously deviant or heretical for these differences.[82] Given that, for al-Shāfiʿī, most parts of the law fall within the realm of probability, a jurist can accommodate the possibility that he is wrong and his opponent is right.[83] By contrast, given its insistence on black-and-white categories of certainty, Ibn ʿUlayya's model contains the seeds for the emergence of a separate legal consensus within each theological faction; each would justify its particular legal system as based on certainty and therefore objectively true, thus creating mutually exclusive and incommensurable doctrines of law. It was this danger that prompted al-Shāfiʿī to accuse his opponent of sowing division in the name of establishing consensus and certainty.[84] His fear of communal divisions born of mutual anathemization led him to be deeply wary of theology. When a student asked him about a point of theology, al-Shāfiʿī replied, "Ask me about something regarding which if I were to err, you would tell me 'You have erred,' rather than about something on which if I were to err, you would say 'You have fallen into disbelief!'"[85]

[82] See, for example, *Umm*, 8:130.

[83] This principle was expressed in a famous statement on interschool relations: "Our way is right but could conceivably be wrong; the way of our opponents is wrong but could conceivably be right" ("Madhhabunā ṣawāb yaḥtamilu al-khaṭaʾ, wa-madhhab mukhālifīnā khaṭaʾ yaḥtamilu al-ṣawāb"). While the statement is often attributed to al-Shāfiʿī himself, the earliest source that I have found attributes it to the Ḥanafī jurist Abū al-Barakāt al-Nasafī (d. 710/1310); see Zayn al-Dīn b. Nujaym (d. 970/1563), *al-Ashbāh wa-l-naẓāʾir*, ed. Muḥammad Muṭīʿ al-Ḥāfiẓ (Damascus: Dār al-Fikr, 2005), 452.

[84] *Umm*, 9:28; Musa, *Ḥadīth as Scripture*, 134.

[85] Shams al-Dīn Abū ʿAbd Allāh al-Dhahabī, *Siyar aʿlām al-nubalāʾ*, ed. Shuʿayb al-Arnāʾūṭ and Muḥammad Nuʿaym al-ʿArqasūsī, 25 vols. (Beirut: Muʾassasat al-Risāla, 1401–9/1981–88), 10:28.

Al-Shāfiʿī's struggle with the theologians' approach to religion sheds light on the long-term process by which law rather than theology came to constitute the central arena of Sunni Muslim thought. Divine revelation had ceased, but the eschaton had yet to dawn. In the interim, revelation remained accessible as an artifact of oral texts that had to be interpreted by fallible human beings – a situation that inevitably created a religious landscape of irreconcilable diversity. Theological discourse had at first proven the most intellectually innovative approach, but its twin pillars of extrarevelatory reason and a demand for certainty had entrenched religious divisions instead of providing a way to accommodate diversity under a common umbrella. The Byzantine approach of enforcing a singular orthodoxy by means of ruthless state power was attempted by the Abbasid caliphs not long after al-Shāfiʿī's death, but the failure of the infamous Quranic Inquisition (discussed in detail in Chapter 5) signaled the ascendancy of law over theology among the Sunnis. By justifying itself as an interpretive effort based on the textual remains of revelation, Islamic law gained the status of an authoritative discourse. In contrast to theology, where differences of opinion represented an insurmountable theoretical conundrum, law was able to accommodate and legitimize difference as the natural outcome of the process of interpretation. This was made possible by al-Shāfiʿī's novel conceptualization of revelation as language, a step that is analyzed in Chapter 3.

AL-SHĀFIʿĪ'S CRITIQUE OF MĀLIK

On his journeys to Medina and Baghdad, al-Shāfiʿī thus encountered circles of scholars who tried to formulate Islamic law in ways that would anchor it in the face of several interlocking threats. Local practice was by its nature fluid, but it relied on a sense of continuity that was threatened by the conceptually aggressive nature of legal reasoning (*ra'y*), especially as developed in and exported from Iraq. At the same time, the systematization of Hadith collection and transmission provided a powerful measure by which to criticize local legal teachings. In his debates with the Ḥanafīs and the theologians, al-Shāfiʿī argued strongly for a systematic and consistent use of single-transmitter Hadith in law. In the Ḥanafī debates, he still paid lip service to the Medinan legal tradition,[86] but in the debate with Ibn ʿUlayya he already declared local traditions to be unstable and equivocal.[87] It was in his third debate, directed against the

[86] See, for example, *Umm*, 8:66, 84, and 90.

[87] *Umm*, 9:25–26.

teachings of his former teacher Mālik, that al-Shāfiʿī would finally abandon the concept of a local legal tradition entirely.

After moving in (or around) 198/814 to Egypt, where he would spend the last five or six years of his life, al-Shāfiʿī's mounting criticisms of communitarian legal approaches matured into a fundamental critique of Mālik's theory of the law and its central feature, Medinan practice (*ʿamal*). The critique found expression in one of the great polemical works of Islamic legal literature, the *Ikhtilāf Mālik* ("Disagreement with Mālik"). This work, included in the *Umm*,[88] is presented in the form of a debate between al-Shāfiʿī and one of his Egyptian Mālikī students, who attempts to defend Mālik's teaching against al-Shāfiʿī's attacks.[89] It represents the most thoroughly methodological and, for the history of Islamic law, most significant contribution to the debate regarding the authenticity of Medinan practice and the true normative basis of Islamic law. In this work, al-Shāfiʿī synthesized his myriad departures from Mālik's precedent into a systematic attack on tradition-bound jurisprudence.

The essence of al-Shāfiʿī's argument against Mālik is eloquently summarized in a passage that ostensibly deals with an obscure case of criminal law. The question at hand was whether a runaway slave was to be considered a free man or a slave in terms of his legal liability for theft. As a free man, he would be subject to the amputation of his hand, whereas as a slave he would receive a lesser punishment. Al-Shāfiʿī's argument focuses on highlighting the multiple inconsistencies of the Mālikī position by contrasting it with a specific historical case. ʿAbd Allāh b. ʿUmar, the Medinan Companion and jurist, had demanded that the hand of his escaped slave be amputated; Saʿīd b. al-ʿĀṣ al-Umawī al-Qurashī (d. 59/679),[90] the governor, had refused to follow the judgment of Ibn ʿUmar and to order the punishment; and Ibn ʿUmar had subsequently carried it out of his own accord. As al-Shāfiʿī points out, the example shows not only that jurists and governors – both carriers of the normative *ʿamal* in the Mālikī framework – disagreed on individual issues, but also that these sources in fact contradict the Mālikī position that claims to be based on

[88] *Umm*, 8:513–778.

[89] Al-Shāfiʿī's interlocutor in *Ikhtilāf Mālik* is either al-Rabīʿ b. Sulaymān or, according to Abū Bakr al-Ṣayrafī (d. 330/941), Abū Yaʿqūb al-Buwayṭī; see Ibn al-Ṣalāḥ al-Shahrazūrī, *Ṭabaqāt al-fuqahāʾ al-shāfiʿiyya*, ed. Muḥī al-Dīn ʿAlī Najīb, 2 vols. (Beirut: Dār al-Bashāʾir al-Islāmiyya, 1992), 2:683. Within the text the interlocutor appears to be al-Rabīʿ, but this may be the effect of al-Rabīʿ transmitting al-Buwayṭī's first-person report of the debate.

[90] Appointed governor of Medina by Muʿāwiya, died in office; see Khayr al-Dīn al-Ziriklī, *al-Aʿlām*, 8 vols. (Beirut: Dār al-ʿIlm li-l-Malāyīn, 1980), 3:96.

them: though Mālik believed, along with Ibn ʿUmar, that an escaped slave should forfeit his hand for theft, he also held that a slave owner was not permitted to carry out a punishment not sanctioned by the authorities.[91] Addressing his Mālikī interlocutor in *Ikhtilāf Mālik*, al-Shāfiʿī queries:

Where is *ʿamal* here? If it is the practice of the governor, then Saʿīd was not of the opinion that the hand of the runaway slave who stole should be amputated, while you believe that it should be amputated. Or if *ʿamal* is established by Ibn ʿUmar's opinion, then [know that] Ibn ʿUmar amputated his hand, while you are of the opinion that one is not allowed to do so [if the authorities disagree]. So I cannot comprehend what you mean when you say "*ʿamal*," nor do you seem to know it yourself according to what you have told me, nor could I find clarification with any one of you about what *ʿamal* or consensus (*ijmāʿ*) are. I am forced to conclude, then, that you simply call your own opinions "*ʿamal*" and "consensus."[92]

What al-Shāfiʿī points out in this passage is that the anonymous "*ʿamal* of Medina" cannot in fact produce a single coherent result: it contains multiple contradictory voices but does not offer any systematic method for adjudicating among them.[93] Although Mālik did, as seen in the previous chapter, recognize complex gradations within the body of material upon which *ʿamal* was based, these gradations did not translate into a reproducible methodology of rule derivation. The reasons why certain sources – prophetic reports, scholars' opinions, and so on – were accepted as normative while others were not could not be deduced from an examination of the sources themselves, but only by reference to their reception, that is, whether or not they were followed by the community. This opacity rendered Mālik's *ʿamal* a "black box." One could not trace the reasoning that led to a particular ruling; one could only follow it blindly.

For al-Shāfiʿī, such following was an instance of what he called *taqlīd*, conformism or "blind following." A definition of the term *taqlīd* common among later Shāfiʿīs is "the acceptance of a position without evidence" (*qabūl qawl bi-lā ḥujja*),[94] and al-Shāfiʿī's usage of the term demonstrates

[91] Saḥnūn, *al-Mudawwana al-kubrā*, 16 vols. in 6 (Cairo: Maṭbaʿat al-Saʿāda, 1322/1905 or 1906; repr., Beirut: Dār Ṣādir, n.d.), 6:182 (Fī iqāmat al-ḥadd ʿalā al-ābiq), 6:257 (Fī al-sayyid yuqīmu ʿalā ʿabīdihi al-ḥudūd).

[92] *Umm*, 8:738–39.

[93] Al-Shāfiʿī had already argued in Baghdad that the concept of local practice had no substantial content beyond the subjective preferences of those invoking it; see *Umm*, 10:232.

[94] Possibly the earliest example of this definition is found in Abū Bakr al-Khaffāf's (d. around 330/941) *al-Aqsām wa-l-khiṣāl* (Dublin: Chester Beatty, MS Arabic 5115 [43 fols., copied 660/1262]; mistakenly attributed to Abū al-ʿAbbās b. Surayj in the catalog), fol. 5a. On later debates regarding the definition of *taqlīd* in the Shāfiʿī school, see al-Zarkashī, *al-Baḥr al-muḥīṭ*, 6:270–74.

that this is also how he understood it.[95] The most likely source for the term in al-Shāfiʿī's thought is represented by the legal and theological circles of Iraq, where it was already used in the latter half of the second/eighth century in discussions relating to the derivation of religious knowledge. The term is found in the work of al-Shaybānī as well as in that of Bishr al-Marīsī.[96] Al-Shāfiʿī was familiar with these theorizations of *taqlīd*, and it seems plausible to conclude that he adopted the term and the associated methodological rigor, which linked the strength of a legal argument to its basis in the sources, from his Iraqi companions. However, in the usage of al-Shāfiʿī, unlike that of al-Shaybānī or Bishr, the concept took on a central role within an explicit and comprehensive overall theory of the law.[97] As a consequence, al-Shāfiʿī's conception of *taqlīd* was to exert a uniquely powerful influence both within and beyond the school that he founded.

The crucial characteristic of al-Shāfiʿī's definition of *taqlīd* is the absence of a transparent connection between a legal ruling and the normative evidence on which it is based. This is the feature that al-Shāfiʿī highlighted in the "black box" of Mālik's *ʿamal*. While Mālikī legal reasoning in the earlier slave example does include pieces of historical information – namely, the opinions of Ibn ʿUmar and Saʿīd b. al-ʿĀṣ – the synthetic Medinan practice cannot be justified with reference to either of these pieces of information in any systematic way; in other words, they are not used as evidence. This is because, for Mālik, Medinan practice is the manifestation of the normative content of historical reports that by themselves are indeterminate. Medinan *ʿamal* constitutes evidence, while historical reports do not.

Al-Shāfiʿī, however, no longer shared Mālik's confidence in the unerring wisdom of the "hidden hand" of tradition. In the time that had passed since his studies with Mālik, he had come to see Medinan practice as an aggregate position devoid of any intelligible logic, artificially created by jurists who picked and chose among existing positions and practices and selectively declared some of them normative. The evolution

95 In the *Umm*, 8:346, al-Shāfiʿī asks rhetorically, "If you follow (*wa-in kunta tuqallid*) ʿUmar b. al-Khaṭṭāb alone on issues regarding which you have no evidence beyond following him (*lā ḥujja laka fī shayʾ illā taqlīduh*), then how could you disagree with him when he is supported by the Quran, analogy (*qiyās*), common sense (*maʿqūl*), and other Companions of the Prophet?"

96 For details, see my "Rethinking *Taqlīd*," 4–5.

97 This is not to deny the possibility that al-Shaybānī or Bishr may have developed such a theory, but no comprehensive legal theory attributed to either of them appears to have survived.

of al-Shāfiʿī's relationship with Mālik's thought can be seen clearly in al-Shāfiʿī's treatment of the exchange between Mālik's teacher Rabīʿa and Saʿīd b. al-Musayyab, recounted in Mālik's *Muwaṭṭa'* (and discussed in Chapter 1), regarding the blood-money payable to a woman in compensation for severed fingers. Ibn al-Musayyab had justified his seemingly arbitrary ruling on the matter by claiming that it represented the tradition (*sunna*). In his defense of Mālik against al-Shaybānī's criticism, al-Shāfiʿī had justified Mālik's agreement with Ibn al-Musayyab by arguing that although their position "contradicted analogy and common sense," Ibn al-Musayyab's statement indicated that it stemmed from the practice of the Prophet and was thus unquestionably normative. However, this passage in the *Umm* is followed by a later addition, in which al-Shāfiʿī notes, "I used to hold this opinion with this justification, but I stopped doing so, and may God grant me what is best; because I found some of them [i.e., the Medinans] claiming [it as] tradition (Sunna), but then I did not find their claimed tradition to reach back to the Prophet. Therefore, I [now] prefer analogy in this case."[98]

The addendum reveals al-Shāfiʿī's later disenchantment with Medinan tradition: rather than representing an organic connection to the prophetic age, it now seemed to him to contain a mixture of heterogeneous elements that were nevertheless justified with the blanket label of "tradition." Such a methodology, al-Shāfiʿī had grown to believe, would eventually sever the Muslim community's connection to divine revelation by superimposing the collective judgments of fallible scholars upon the guidance provided by God and His infallible Prophet. In this sense, al-Shāfiʿī considered Mālik's theory to differ only in degree from the doctrine of Ibn ʿUlayya. In *Ikhtilāf Mālik*, al-Shāfiʿī rebukes his Mālikī opponent by likening the latter's approach to that of Ibn ʿUlayya: "This is the method of those who abolish prophetic reports in their entirety, saying 'We adhere to consensus.'"[99] In al-Shāfiʿī's view, then, the "living tradition" model based on communal practice not only provided an inconsistent and unreliable channel to the age of revelation, but ultimately smothered it in the name of local or partial agreements between scholars in the present.

With this debate, al-Shāfiʿī left behind both his own past as a disciple of Mālik and the hitherto dominant conception of Islamic law as rooted in local legal traditions. He had encountered a coherent countermodel to the latter in the teaching of Ibn ʿUlayya, but had found its central

[98] *Umm*, 9:105.
[99] *Umm*, 8:750.

principle of consensus to be unworkable. Instead, al-Shāfiʿī developed his own approach out of his critique of Mālik, drawing on the various intellectual exchanges that had helped to form his ideas and uniting them in a systematic methodology based on a single unifying idea: that of God's unmediated communication with humanity in divine revelation. This idea, and the legal theory that al-Shāfiʿī constructed around it, laid the basis for the canonization of the Quran and Hadith as sources of the law and the consequent transformation of the discourse of Islamic law.

Chapter 3

From Local Community to Universal Canon

Al-Shāfiʿī's solution to the problems that he identified in the methods of the Ḥanafīs, Ibn ʿUlayya, and Mālik consisted of a radically new legal hermeneutic, at the core of which lay the canonization of Quran and Hadith as the distinctively authoritative sources of religiolegal norms. Al-Shāfiʿī's theory incorporated a conceptual repertoire of interpretive strategies: in his legal-theoretical writings, al-Shāfiʿī developed and elaborated on a range of specific hermeneutic techniques, especially abrogation (*naskh*) and particularization (*takhṣīṣ*) for reconciling seemingly contradictory scriptural statements and analogical reasoning (*qiyās*) for extending existing rules to new cases.[1] But he subjected these tools to a hierarchy that clearly prioritized the Quran and the prophetic Sunna, including single-transmitter Hadith reports, while excluding the indeterminate category of local practice. In *Ikhtilāf Mālik*, al-Shāfiʿī lays out this hierarchy thus:

> Law consists of numerous layers (*al-ʿilm ṭabaqāt shattā*).[2] The first is the Quran and the Sunna, provided that the Sunna is accurately transmitted. The second is consensus with regard to issues on which the Quran and the Sunna are silent. The third is what some Companions of the Prophet have said if we know of no other Companions who contradict them. The fourth is the opinions that were disputed among the Companions. The fifth is analogy on one of the previous layers. When the Quran and the Sunna are present [i.e., applicable], no other [layer] is consulted; and law (*al-ʿilm*) is derived from the highest [available layer].[3]

[1] For detailed analysis of these techniques and of al-Shāfiʿī's overall legal theory, see Lowry, *Early Islamic Legal Theory*, and Mohyddin Yahia, *Šāfiʿī et les deux sources de la loi islamique* (Turnhout, Belgium: Brepols, 2009).

[2] Al-Shāfiʿī and his students frequently used the word *ʿilm*, "knowledge," to mean law (*fiqh*); see, for example, Ibn Abī Ḥātim, *Ādāb al-Shāfiʿī*, 231.

[3] *Umm*, 8:764. Al-Shāfiʿī's work also contains other, slightly different versions of this hierarchy, but the absolute primacy of the Quran and Sunna remains constant. See, for example, *Risāla*, in *Umm*, 1:275 (paras. 1810–11).

The revolutionary feature of al-Shāfiʿī's theory was its isolation of the sacred past as a clearly defined and uniquely normative category. In al-Shāfiʿī's formulation, this past was enshrined in and accessible through verifiable reports consisting of the Quran and prophetic Hadith, of which other sources such as consensus (*ijmāʿ*) and the opinions of the Companions were derivations. The circumscribed sacred past thus provided an unchanging and authoritative measuring stick – a *canon* – by means of which the jurist could evaluate and categorize new cases.[4] Although al-Shāfiʿī's position regarding what, precisely, fell within the boundaries of this canon appears to have undergone some change,[5] his canonization project applied first and foremost to the sacred sources as a distinct category, rather than to any specific set of texts within this category.[6] Within such a framework, following divine guidance meant adhering to positions that were connected in an intelligible and reproducible way to the canonized sources and through them to the age of revelation.

This transparency was in stark contrast to the opaque conformism (*taqlīd*) that al-Shāfiʿī had decried in Mālikism.[7] By erecting a clear barrier between the normativity of the sources and communal practice, al-Shāfiʿī hoped to salvage the authentic memory of the prophetic age and delegitimize the later accretions to the law that had been sanctioned by appeal to *ʿamal* or consensus. In the process, he reworked Islamic normativity from an organic tradition into a legal "science" characterized by a transparent and systematic interpretive methodology.[8] The significance of al-Shāfiʿī's innovation is expressed in the reported statement of al-Shāfiʿī's Iraqi student al-Karābīsī (d. 248/862): "We did not know what the Quran and the Sunna were until we heard al-Shāfiʿī."[9] This does not mean that al-Karābīsī encountered these sources for the first time through al-Shāfiʿī. Rather, al-Shāfiʿī's canonization of the sacred texts as part of his novel

[4] J. Assmann, *Das kulturelle Gedächtnis*, 103–29.

[5] See Éric Chaumont, "Le 'dire d'un Compagnon unique' (*qawl al-wāḥid min l-ṣaḥāba*) entre la *sunna* et l'*iǧmāʿ* dans les *uṣūl al-fiqh* šāfiʿites classiques," *Studia Islamica*, no. 93 (2001): 59–76. See also my "First Shāfiʿī," 317–18.

[6] Wheeler, *Applying the Canon in Islam*, 59.

[7] There were two areas in which al-Shāfiʿī's own practice could be seen as falling under his definition of *taqlīd*, namely, in the acceptance of the expertise of Hadith scholars and in the ascertainment of paternity by traditional physiognomists; however, these exceptions can be argued to fit into al-Shāfiʿī's overall conception of the law. See my "Rethinking *Taqlīd*."

[8] As D. W. Hamlyn points out, "the word 'science' is ... simply the traditional translation of the term 'episteme' as Aristotle uses it, and that, as he so often says, is *knowing the reason why*"; "Aristotle on Dialectic," *Philosophy* 65 (1990): 465–76, at 475 (emphasis mine).

[9] Ibn Abī Ḥātim, *Ādāb al-Shāfiʿī*, 57.

legal hermeneutic endowed them with a new authority and meaning that transformed the way in which they were perceived.

THE LINGUISTIC TURN

It must have been a weighty step for al-Shāfiʿī to abandon the living tradition of Mālik in favor of a novel scientific venture. Gone was the existential certainty of being part of an organic stream of normative tradition flowing continuously from the prophetic time to the present. The essentially communal activity of mimesis gave way to the individual task of hermeneutics. The gap between the sources and their interpreter that opened up as a result of this move deprived the jurist of the pragmatic context[10] that communal practice within Mālik's framework had provided for Quranic scripture and for individual reports from the Prophet and other authorities. With communal practice no longer providing an authoritative basis for the interpretation of sacred texts, the jurist had to look elsewhere for guidance in deciphering the prohibitions and commandments contained in revelation. Among Imāmī Shiʿis, this guidance was provided by the imam, whose interpretation of the sources was considered infallible and thus definitive. For proto-Sunnis such as al-Shāfiʿī, however, there was no uniquely authoritative interpreter.[11] The explanatory context that could illuminate the correct meaning of the revealed sources had to be discovered within the sources themselves.

The challenges of departing from the zone of communally established normativity were already encountered by the Ḥanafīs in Iraq because of the inherently centripetal tendencies of *raʾy* as a discursive practice. Even though the Iraqi jurists continued to justify themselves as the heirs of ʿAlī b. Abī Ṭālib and Ibn Masʿūd, the internal logic of *raʾy* developed its own momentum that alienated the Iraqis' doctrine from the "living tradition" of the Companions. Instead, Ḥanafī doctrine grew like a web, suspended on and spreading out from the fixed points of agreed-upon propositions through the graded series of *raʾy* questions. To the Iraqis, to understand a source meant exploring its implications within the web constituted by the implications of all other accepted propositions. Early Ḥanafī doctrine thus resembled a structuralist "system of differences," as defined by Ferdinand de Saussure, in which the meanings of signs come about through their relationship with and relative distance from other signs,

[10] See Chapter 1, n. 87.
[11] On al-Shāfiʿī's theological positions, see al-Bayhaqī, *Manāqib al-Shāfiʿī*, 1:385–98.

rather than through a connection to an outside referent.[12] *Ra'y* questions, then, created a structuralist semantic context for an accepted source or opinion by placing it in the context of other cases with varying degrees of similarity and difference.

From al-Shāfiʿī's perspective, Ḥanafī structuralism was unacceptable, because it operated on a strong presumption of consistency in the law, which generally did not admit the existence of individual exceptions to general rules. This meant that the analogical extensions of generally accepted reports necessarily trumped any anomalous rules that were grounded in single-transmitter Hadith. In order to uphold the primacy of the sacred texts, including single-transmitter reports, al-Shāfiʿī thus had to develop an alternative theory of revelation. He found the basis for such a theory in the nature of the Arabic language itself. In his *Risāla* – his primary treatise on legal theory – al-Shāfiʿī lays out his understanding of the linguistic nature of the Quran as follows:

> God addressed His book to the Arabs in their language according to what they know of its features. And among those features of it with which they are familiar is the multiplicity of ways in which meaning is imparted (*ittisāʿ lisānihā*). It is part of [the Quran's] nature (*fiṭratahu*)[13] that in each part of it, it speaks in a manner that is explicitly unrestricted (*ʿāmman ẓāhiran*), with a meaning that is intended to be explicitly unrestricted;[14] ... or in a manner that is explicitly unrestricted, with a meaning that is unrestricted but that contains some restriction, which is indicated by an element within that which is expressed; or in a manner that is explicitly unrestricted, but with a meaning that is specific (*khāṣṣ*); or in a manner that appears explicit, but in its context is understood to mean something other than its apparent meaning.[15] Information about all of this is present either in the beginning, the middle, or the end of the utterance. An utterance of [the Arabs] may proceed so that the beginning of the pronouncement explicates (*yubayyin*) the end, or so that the end explicates the beginning, or they communicate something by

[12] Ferdinand de Saussure, *Saussure's Third Course of Lectures on General Linguistics (1910–1911): From the Notebooks of Emile Constantin*, ed. Eisuke Komatsu, trans. Roy Harris (Oxford: Pergamon, 1993), chap. 6.

[13] My translation here agrees with that of Joseph Lowry, who renders this phrase as "the nature of God's language"; it disagrees with those of Majid Khadduri ("[God's] divine disposition") and Sherman Jackson (the "primordial nature" of the Arabs). See al-Shāfiʿī, *The Epistle on Legal Theory*, trans. Joseph E. Lowry (New York: New York University Press, 2013), 73; al-Shāfiʿī, *Al-Shāfiʿī's Risāla: Treatise on the Foundations of Islamic Jurisprudence*, trans. Majid Khadduri (Cambridge: Islamic Texts Society, 1987), 94; and Sherman A. Jackson, "Fiction and Formalism: Toward a Functional Analysis of *Uṣūl al-Fiqh*," in *Studies in Islamic Legal Theory*, ed. Bernard G. Weiss, 177–201 (Leiden: Brill, 2002), 190.

[14] On al-Shāfiʿī's use of *ʿāmm* and *ẓāhir*, see Lowry, *Early Islamic Legal Theory*, 86.

[15] Khadduri conflates these four categories into one; *Al-Shāfiʿī's Risāla*, 95.

conveying a message without a clear utterance, the way that a gesture conveys [a message] (*tuʿarrifuhu bi-l-maʿnā dūna al-īḍāḥ bi-l-lafẓ kamā tuʿarrifu al-ishāra*). This is the highest form of speech among them, due to the exclusive knowledge of their scholars regarding it that excludes those who are ignorant of it. One thing is referred to by many different names, and one word is used to express many different meanings.[16]

This passage demonstrates al-Shāfiʿī's view of the role of language in revelation. The audience of the Quran does not encounter revelation as pure meaning, but rather as speech (*kalām*) directed at it. This speech displays the same structure as ordinary Arabic, and its intuitive understanding thus requires competence in the expressions and idioms of the Arabic language.[17] Without such competence, aspects of the revealed message that utilize particular features of Arabic – such as the capacity, mentioned by al-Shāfiʿī, of indicating something specific through an expression that on the surface appears general in its purview – would remain incomprehensible. The central term through which al-Shāfiʿī describes the characteristic capacity of language to convey information is "clarity" (*bayān*). The Quran refers to itself frequently as "clear" and "clarifying" (*mubīn*, from the same root as *bayān*),[18] and it also postulates an innate human capacity to speak clearly.[19]

The clarity of revelation, however, does not preclude difficulties in comprehension. One set of obstacles is faced by those whose native tongue is not Arabic. This is because revelation is in the first instance directed "at those who are addressed by it among those in whose language the Quran was revealed. For them [its expressions] are equally direct,[20] even if some are more emphatic than others, while they differ in the perception of those who are ignorant of the Arabic language."[21] The reason

[16] *Risāla*, in *Umm*, 1:22 (paras. 173–77).

[17] Already Sībawayh (d. ca. 180/796), the author of the first work on Arabic grammar, stated that "God's servants were addressed in their own way of speaking and the Quran came to them in their own language"; quoted in Michael Carter, "Foreign Vocabulary," in *The Blackwell Companion to the Qurʾān*, ed. Andrew Rippin, 120–39 (Malden, MA: Blackwell, 2006), 121.

[18] See, for example, Quran 11:6 and 15:1. Other wording is also used; for example, Quran 16:89 describes the Quran as "a clarification for everything" (*tibyānan li-kulli shayʾ*). For description of the prophetic message in general as clear/clarifying, see, for example, Quran 16:35 and 16:82. This characteristic of the Quran is used by al-Shāfiʿī's opponent in the first part of *Jimāʿ al-ʿilm* to argue for the superfluousness of Hadith; *Umm*, 9:6.

[19] Quran 55:1–4: "The Merciful taught the Quran, created man, [and] taught him clear speech (*al-bayān*)."

[20] For the most likely meaning of *istiwāʾ* as directness, see Edward W. Lane, *Arabic-English Lexicon*, 2 vols. (Cambridge: Islamic Texts Society, 1984), 1:1477.

[21] *Risāla*, in *Umm*, 1:7 (para. 54).

why God's expressions are economical to the point of causing confusion for non–Arabic speakers lies in the basic nature of communication: "The clarity of these verses does not differ for the Arabs, since the more succinct expression suffices for them, making the longer one superfluous; all that the hearer wants is to understand what the speaker has to say, so the shortest expression that conveys the meaning is enough for him."[22] A second source of confusion lies in the fact that the inherent clarity of revelation as language does not imply the absence of ambiguity. Al-Shāfiʿī acknowledged that the language of revelation often contained an element of ambiguity that was not due to a deficiency in revelation but was simply part and parcel of language.[23] Acceptance of this fact did not, however, make him into a relativist: he believed that clear language could convey meaning and that the better one's familiarity with the features of a language, the more accurately one could decipher this meaning.

The striking feature of al-Shāfiʿī's description of the way in which Arabic conveys meaning is his distinction between sentence meaning and utterance meaning.[24] This distinction is obvious in al-Shāfiʿī's remark that the Arabs "communicate by conveying a message without a clear utterance, the way that a gesture conveys [a message]." In other words, the Arabs convey utterance meanings that go beyond the formal content, or sentence meaning, of the words that they utter. It is those gestures of language, which transcend the actual phrases in which they are transmitted, that according to al-Shāfiʿī represent the highest form of expression in Arabic, but they also present a challenge to the interpreter of Arabic speech, since their meaning cannot be captured through the purely semantic analysis of an utterance.

This challenge is illustrated in the example of the famous prophetic Hadith according to which the Prophet said, "If you have no shame, do whatever you want" (*idhā lā tastaḥī fa-'ṣnaʿ mā shi't*). Muslim scholars were aware that the sentence meaning of this statement – ordering

[22] *Risāla*, in *Umm*, 1:27 (para. 206). Al-Shāfiʿī here anticipates Grice's maxim of quantity: "Make your contribution as informative as is required for the current purposes of the exchange, and do not make your contribution more informative than is required." See Paul Grice, "Logic and Conversation," in *Pragmatics: A Reader*, ed. Steven Davis, 305–15 (New York: Oxford University Press, 1991), 308.

[23] See my review of *The Formation of Islamic Hermeneutics: How Sunni Legal Theorists Imagined a Revealed Law*, by David Vishanoff, *Journal of the American Oriental Society* (forthcoming).

[24] In modern linguistics and philosophy of language, this distinction was introduced by Paul Grice; see, for example, his "Utterer's Meaning, Sentence-Meaning, and Word-Meaning," in *Pragmatics: A Reader*, 65–76.

those who have no shame to do whatever they wished – did not reflect the actual message, or utterance meaning, that the Prophet intended to convey. A variety of interpretations of the latter were proposed. Some scholars claimed that the underlying utterance meaning was "You may do anything, as long you do not have to be ashamed of it"; others held that the statement conveys a threat to those who have lost their sense of shame regarding the consequences of their actions: "Just wait and see what will happen to you." A third explanation described the gap between sentence meaning and utterance meaning in this instance as follows: "The wisdom behind the expression that uses the imperative instead of the indicative mood is that it indicates that it is shame that prevents the human being from doing evil, so whoever loses it will be compelled by his lower nature to do every kind of evil."[25] The discussions surrounding this prophetic report were therefore concerned with what the Prophet intended to communicate with his statement, rather than the meaning of the statement in isolation.

Given al-Shāfiʿī's stress on the divergence between sentence meaning and utterance meaning, it is clear that he viewed a merely semantic approach to the sacred sources as insufficient for understanding the true message of divine revelation. Instead, the scholar must engage in an interpretive analysis that focuses on the underlying message communicated through the sources. Within modern linguistics, such interpretation is the occupation of *pragmatics*,[26] a field whose domain is "speakers' communicative intentions, the uses of language that require such intentions, and the strategies that hearers employ to determine what these intentions and acts are, so that they can understand what the speaker intends to communicate."[27] God could be conceptualized as a "speaker," given that al-Shāfiʿī, like other legal theorists after him, conceived of revelation as a continuously unfolding speech act addressed to the believer – a model that was facilitated by memorization, which turned a text into a "virtual oral event."[28]

[25] All three explanations are reported by Ibn Ḥajar al-ʿAsqalānī in *Fatḥ al-bārī*, 13:694; the final quotation is attributed to Ḥamd b. Muḥammad al-Khaṭṭābī (d. 388/998).

[26] On pragmatics in medieval Muslim thought, see Mohamed Mohamed Yunis Ali's excellent discussion in *Medieval Islamic Pragmatics: Sunni Legal Theorists' Models of Textual Communication* (Richmond: Curzon, 2000).

[27] Steven Davis, introduction to *Pragmatics: A Reader*, 11.

[28] Michael Carter, "Pragmatics and Contractual Language in Early Arabic Grammar and Legal Theory," in *Approaches to Arabic Linguistics: Presented to Kees Versteegh on the Occasion of His Sixtieth Birthday*, ed. Everhard Ditters and Harald Motzki, 25–44 (Leiden: Brill, 2007), 36.

Revelation therefore presents itself as a relationship between a divine speaker who intends to express himself and a listener who wants to understand what the speaker has to say. Mālik – representing the dominant trend in his time – believed that the listener ought to approach revelation within the context formed by the cumulative understandings of preceding generations. Al-Shāfiʿī, on the other hand, had come to see this organically grown context as something akin to a game of telephone, in which the last listener in the chain tries to decipher the garbled message that has accrued over time. Given that, for al-Shāfiʿī, revelation possessed the quality of *bayān*, that is, the inherent capacity to express its communicative intentions, such an approach was both dangerous and unnecessary. If the quality of *bayān* existed, and if it was a feature of revelation as language rather than any supernatural characteristic, then there was no need for interpretive contexts such as Medinan practice that were external to revelation itself.[29] In his *Risāla*, al-Shāfiʿī thus set out to develop a hermeneutic theory that made visible the various modes through which revelation expressed the divine speaker's communicative intentions. Al-Shāfiʿī achieved this by showing how the two genres of revelation – Quran and Hadith – interacted, how revelation functioned diachronically (abrogation), and how utterance meanings could be understood in cases where they diverged from sentence meanings (e.g., via the general/specific distinction).

A large part of the argumentative strategy in al-Shāfiʿī's legal discussions consists of his persuasive attempts to show that instances of apparent contradiction within revelation actually represent higher forms of coherence. A good example is afforded by the case mentioned in Chapter 1 involving the sale and subsequent return of a cow. According to a single-transmitter Hadith, the Prophet had ordered a man who had bought a cow with full udders, milked it, and then returned it because of an unrelated fault in the animal to pay a specified amount of dates to the seller as compensation for the milk. The Ḥanafīs considered this report to conflict with the well-known Hadith that states, "With liability comes [the entitlement to] profit." They argued that since the buyer was liable for the cow while it was in his possession, he was entitled to the milk extracted during that time. The Ḥanafīs consequently disregarded the first, single-transmitter, Hadith by appealing to the second, universally known, Hadith. Al-Shāfiʿī,

[29] The intimate link between hermeneutics and theories of language is explored by Paul Hardy in "Epistemology and Divine Discourse," in *The Cambridge Companion to Classical Islamic Theology*, ed. Timothy J. Winter, 288–307 (Cambridge: Cambridge University Press, 2008).

by contrast, was deeply opposed to dismissing any sound Hadith, and he pointed out that the two Hadith reports were in fact not contradictory: the liability-profit principle, he argued, refers to profit accrued during ownership, but in this case the milk in the udders was produced while the cow was still in the possession of the seller, and thus the dates payable by the buyer represent compensation for the reduced value of the cow at the time of the return.[30] In his quest to defend his view of the law as both coherent and grounded in the sacred foundations of revelation, al-Shāfiʿī was thus proposing a synthesis of the approaches of *raʾy* and Hadith.[31]

THEORIES OF LANGUAGE

As seen earlier, for Mālik Medinan practice functioned as a pragmatic context that ensured that the protonormative material derived from the Quran and from reports about the Prophet as well as prominent later Muslims was translated into an authentic normative tradition. Such a model entails a view of revelatory language as chronically underdetermined and therefore in constant need of contextualization through an aggregate history of reception. In al-Shāfiʿī's view, however, the postulation that revelation was underdetermined ignored the fact that the Quran itself calls revelation "clear" and "clarifying." Al-Shāfiʿī's belief in the inherent clarity of revealed language did not make him into a literalist who adopts the apparent implications of verses or reports in isolation. To the contrary, he advocated a contextualist approach that interpreted individual sentences in the context of revelation as a whole. Al-Shāfiʿī did not perceive revelation as an amorphous, undifferentiated corpus, but rather identified three layers of information within it, layers whose interaction resulted in the overall clarity of the revealed message.

The first of these layers consists of God's speech, the Quran. In some instances the Quran itself achieves absolutely clear expression (*ghāyat al-bayān*), in which case the hearer is in no need of further clarifying information.[32] In other instances, the Quran mentions obligations in a general fashion, necessitating clarification of the details. At this point the

[30] *Umm*, 10:274.

[31] Such an epistemology combines both foundationalist and coherentist approaches, in the same way that solving a crossword puzzle involves answering questions as well as making sure that the answers fit together. In the modern study of epistemology, this approach has been developed by Susan Haack; see her article "A Foundherentist Theory of Empirical Justification," in *Epistemology: Contemporary Readings*, ed. Michael Huemer, 417–30 (London: Routledge, 2002).

[32] *Risāla*, in *Umm*, 1:12 (para. 98).

second level, the prophetic tradition, intervenes, since "God's Messenger clarified (*bayyana*) on God's behalf" how, by whom, and under what circumstances these obligations must be discharged.[33] For al-Shāfiʿī, the clarification offered by the prophetic tradition was intimately tied to human responsibility. He argued that if revelation were incapable of expressing itself clearly, God would have no valid claim against people on the Day of Judgment. Therefore, al-Shāfiʿī concludes, God "placed them under obligation[34] by indicating to them, through the traditions of His Messenger, the meanings of what God intended by the obligations [imposed] in His Book."[35] As mentioned in Chapter 2, al-Shāfiʿī most probably adopted the justification of prophetic tradition as evidence of divine intention from the Ḥanafīs in Iraq.[36] His account of his debate with the Ḥanafīs suggests that the idea was originally put forward by the Ḥanafīs in the context of a debate with the Khārijīs, who did not permit Hadith to interfere with the meaning of a Quranic verse.[37] Al-Shāfiʿī thus seems to have adopted already developed ideas as components of his new system.

Al-Shāfiʿī identifies a second dimension in the layer of prophetic traditions, arguing that Hadith also establish obligations that are not mentioned in the Quran beyond the general injunction to follow the Prophet. The reason why the Sunna can act as an independent source of normative commandments lies in the fact that for al-Shāfiʿī it does not clarify God's *word*, but rather God's *intention*. This is a crucial difference that distinguishes al-Shāfiʿī from literalists such as the Ẓāhirīs. If revelation is an instance of Arabic speech, and if (correct) speech consists of the clarification of the speaker's intentions, then inferences about the speaker's intentions, even beyond what is actually covered in revelation, should be possible. The early Ẓāhirīs, in contrast, accepted only the direct import of revelation as sacred text, without the assumption of divine communicative intentions underlying this text.[38]

[33] *Risāla*, in *Umm*, 1:12 (para. 99).

[34] "Aqāma ʿalayhim ḥujjatahu." Lowry translates this phrase as "He established His proof for them" in *The Epistle on Legal Theory*, 118, but the preposition *ʿalā* implies the use of evidence *against* another party; cf. Quran 4:165, "Rusulan mubashshirīna wa-mundhirīna li-allā yakūna li-l-nās ʿalā Allāh ḥujjatun baʿd al-rusul" ("Messengers bearing good news and warnings, so that humankind should have no argument against God after the messengers").

[35] *Risāla*, in *Umm*, 1:43 (para. 308).

[36] See *Umm*, 7:319, 8:41.

[37] This is indicated by *Umm*, 7:319, combined with the identification of the Ḥanafīs' opponents as Khārijīs in *Umm*, 8:41.

[38] They consequently rejected analogical reasoning, which assumes a graspable logic underpinning the law such that the extension of known rules to novel cases is possible. See

The Quran and the Sunna form the two principal layers of revelation; the first consists of direct divine speech and the second of the wisdom (*ḥikma*) embodied in the example of God's Prophet as clarification for God's speech. The third and final layer of information that bears upon the interpretation of revelation is provided by the occasions (*asbāb*) that caused the Prophet to act or to speak, and that therefore represent the context within which the prophetic tradition manifested itself. Knowledge of this context is important, since "a man might relate a saying from [the Prophet] having caught the answer but not the question, which could have indicated to him the true nature (*ḥaqīqa*) of the answer through knowledge of the occasion (*sabab*) from which the answer sprang."[39] It is the context provided by the occasion that allows the jurist to extract normative Sunna from the textual form of a Hadith report. If a report lacks information regarding the occasion, this report is deficient for al-Shāfiʿī.[40]

It is significant that in contrast to Mālik's concept of Medinan practice, which understands revelation through its reception by the Muslim community throughout the ages, al-Shāfiʿī interprets Hadith reports not through their *reception*, but rather through their *occasion*. The latter approach cuts out the subjective element of reception by ordinary human beings, since in al-Shāfiʿī's scheme the social context constitutes merely the setting for the speech or practice of the infallible Prophet, not its interpreter. While al-Shāfiʿī considered the occasions that gave rise to Hadith, he does not appear to have taken into account occasions for Quranic verses – what later became known as *asbāb al-nuzūl* – in his legal theory.[41] The Sunna is the only context through which to understand the Quran, and the Sunna in turn can be properly understood only within the context formed by the occasions of individual reports. Consequently, each of the two sources of the law possesses its own auxiliary information that clarifies it.

Revelation is thus a complete and self-sufficient statement, which, like other statements in the Arabic language, contains instances of

Zysow, "Economy of Certainty," 294–23, and David Vishanoff, *The Formation of Islamic Hermeneutics: How Sunni Legal Theorists Imagined a Revealed Law* (New Haven, CT: American Oriental Society, 2011), chap. 3.

39 *Risāla*, in *Umm*, 1:93 (para. 577).

40 Accordingly, al-Shāfiʿī's discussion of Hadith that lack mention of the occasion is found in the *Risāla*'s chapter on deficient reports (Bāb ʿilal al-aḥādīth): *Risāla*, in *Umm*, 1:93 (paras. 576–77).

41 Hans-Thomas Tillschneider, "Typen historisch-exegetischer Überlieferung: Formen, Funktionen und Genese des *Asbāb al-Nuzūl* Materials" (PhD diss., University of Freiburg, Germany, 2009), 258–60.

self-clarification; as al-Shāfiʿī expressed it in the passage quoted earlier, "the beginning of the pronouncement explicates the end, or ... the end explicates the beginning." Accordingly, the interpreter must move back and forth between parts of the speech of revelation to gain a complete understanding of it within its context. Normativity is, in this sense, diffused throughout the corpus of sacred sources; correct answers to legal dilemmas cannot be obtained through the analysis of isolated parts or the external context of a "living tradition," but rather must be sought in a holistic consideration of revelation in its entirety.

In the first draft of the *Risāla*, which al-Shāfiʿī wrote in Iraq, the opinions of the Companions of the Prophet appear to have had normative weight of their own.[42] In his mature legal theory, however, Companion opinions are considered only in the absence of prophetic reports as indicators toward the likely content of the revealed message. The sidelining of reports about the Prophet's Companions is consistent with the logic of al-Shāfiʿī's theory of revelation. Within the corpus of the Quran and Hadith, seeming contradictions could be eliminated through the interpretive techniques of abrogation and particularization that were mentioned earlier. Such techniques could not, however, be applied to the opinions of prophetic Companions, since they were separate, noninspired individuals. Al-Shāfiʿī continued to quote the opinions of Companions and of later scholars in the *Umm* in support of his positions, not because he thought them normative, but rather in order to convince his audience, as he explains himself:

> Regarding what I have written of [postprophetic] reports after mentioning the Quran, prophetic tradition (Sunna), and consensus, this is not because any of it would strengthen the tradition of the Prophet or, were [such reports] to contradict it or not be preserved, weaken it. Nay: it is [prophetic tradition] through which God removes the possibility of excuse [for failing to fulfill obligations].[43] However, I hope for divine reward in guiding those who hear what I have written; so what I have written contains things that open their hearts to its acceptance, for if their heedlessness were to dissipate from them they would be like me in contenting themselves with the book of God and secondarily with the tradition of His Prophet.[44]

The answers that the interpreter finds through a study of revelation are approximations of an independently existing truth. That al-Shāfiʿī believed in the existence of objectively true answers to normative

[42] Al-Bayhaqī, *Manāqib al-Shāfiʿī*, 1:442–43.
[43] Literally, "through which God makes excuses impossible."
[44] *Umm*, 4:187.

questions – a position that Joseph Lowry describes as "metaphysical realism"[45] – can be seen most clearly in al-Shāfiʿī's immensely influential metaphor of the direction of prayer (*qibla*). This recurs time and again in his writings and likens the objective basis of the revealed message to the physical presence of the holy shrine of the Kaʿba in Mecca, toward which all Muslims turn in their daily prayers.[46] The truth of certain propositions is clear to literally any Muslim, just as the correct direction of prayer is clear to anyone who stands within sight of the Kaʿba. However, as soon as direct vision is insufficient, it becomes necessary for the jurist to infer the correct direction by using indicators, such as geography, the stars, or the angle of the sun.

Transferring the implications of the metaphor to the realm of law, it is clear that beyond a small core of legal issues that, like the direction of the Kaʿba when one stands next to it, are intuitively certain, the answers that the jurist can reach for the vast majority of legal questions can be only approximations characterized by varying degrees of probability.[47] Al-Shāfiʿī saw the reasons for this uncertainty to lie not only in the problems of authenticating prophetic reports (and, as in the case of the *qibla*, of obtaining sufficient factual information), but also in the inherent limitations of language. Since, as seen earlier, al-Shāfiʿī distinguished between sentence meaning and utterance meaning, the full understanding of a textual source necessarily involved complex processes of inference that sought to grasp God's intentions beyond the formal content of the revealed message. Revelation could not be simply decoded as with a key, which could have yielded certain knowledge. Rather, accessing it required the interpretation of signs analogous to the physical indicators of the *qibla* outside Mecca and consequently could produce only probable conclusions.[48]

Believing that every question has a single correct answer corresponding to God's communicative intention, but that as a result of the limitations of language this answer may be inaccessible to human understanding, gives rise to an apparent paradox: God imposes on humanity an obligation to

[45] Lowry, *Early Islamic Legal Theory*, 246.

[46] This recurring metaphor is explained most clearly in al-Shāfiʿī's *Jimāʿ al-ʿilm*, in *Umm*, 9:15–17.

[47] Aron Zysow has analyzed the divide between legal theories that conceive of Islamic law as a realm of probability (formalism) and those that demand certainty (materialism) in "Economy of Certainty."

[48] On the difference between the code model and the inference model, see Dan Sperber and Deirdre Wilson, *Relevance: Communication and Cognition* (Cambridge, MA: Harvard University Press, 1986), chap. 1.

obey Him but then communicates His commandments in language that contains the possibility of ambiguity. Al-Shāfiʿī solves this dilemma by arguing that humans are required only to exert themselves in deciphering the indicators of revelation; they are not obliged to arrive at the correct result.[49] This position, widely accepted by Muslim legal scholars and also held by Mālik,[50] is expressed in the common maxim "Every qualified jurist hits the mark" (*kullu mujtahid muṣīb*)[51] – that is, every jurist possessing the qualifications for *ijtihād* (independent legal reasoning) who strives to identify the correct answer to a question discharges his obligation in the matter, whether or not the answer that he reaches is in fact the correct one.

However, although both al-Shāfiʿī and Mālik appear to have subscribed to this maxim, Mālik, unlike al-Shāfiʿī, did not base his position on metaphysical realism. This difference explains a crucial feature in the disagreement between Mālik and his students. The criticisms leveled against Mālik's theory of Medinan practice by al-Shaybānī and al-Shāfiʿī were rooted in a realist perspective. For example, al-Shaybānī attacked the reliability of *ʿamal* as an indicator of true normativity by pointing out that retaliation (*qiṣāṣ*) for severed fingers – defended by Mālik as part of *ʿamal* – was not practiced in Medina until it was introduced by the judge ʿAbd al-ʿAzīz b. al-Muṭṭalib[52] in the early Abbasid period (mid-second/eighth century). Al-Shaybānī's critique was based on the assumption that the correct normative answer was as real and unchanging as the Kaʿba in Mecca: either retaliation was due for severed fingers or it was not, and this normative fact would be valid for all times. Mālik's frank affirmation that the practice of Medina had changed represented for al-Shaybānī an admission of its deficiency.

Mālik, on the other hand, appears not to have posited an objective reality underpinning the correct answers provided by Medinan practice; rather, the correctness of the answers was a product of the discursive practice that constituted *ʿamal*. The disagreement between Mālik and his critics was not merely a symptom of a clash between sophisticated and primitive modes of legal reasoning but rather reflects fundamentally

[49] *Risāla*, in *Umm*, 1:227 (para. 1381); see also *Jimāʿ al-ʿilm*, in *Umm*, 9:15–17.

[50] See, for example, Ibn al-Qaṣṣār's (d. 397/1006 or 1007) *Muqaddima fī al-uṣūl*, ed. Muḥammad b. al-Ḥusayn al-Sulaymānī (Beirut: Dār al-Gharb al-Islāmī, 1996), 113–14.

[51] Josef van Ess, *The Flowering of Muslim Theology*, trans. Jane Marie Todd (Cambridge, MA: Harvard University Press, 2006), 174.

[52] Judge of Medina during the reign of the second Abbasid caliph, Abū Jaʿfar al-Manṣūr (r. 136–58/754–75); d. unknown. See Muḥammad b. Saʿd, *al-Ṭabaqāt al-kubrā* [partial

different conceptions of the nature of revelation: for al-Shāfiʿī and al-Shaybānī, the language of revelation was self-sufficient, whereas for Mālik it was chronically underdetermined. In the example of severed fingers that was raised by al-Shaybānī, the Quranic verse 5:45, which stipulates the forfeit of an eye for an eye,[53] makes no explicit mention of the appropriate penalty in the case of severed fingers. Under Mālik's view of language, therefore, whether or not fingers fall within the purview of retaliation as outlined in this verse cannot be gleaned from the text itself, but rather is determined by the actions and decisions that constitute normative practice, including the judgment of ʿAbd al-ʿAzīz b. al-Muṭṭalib and its subsequent endorsement by Medinan scholars. In Mālik's theory, Medinan authorities and scholars held the right to determine the precise meaning of revelation. There is no indication that they believed that the Quranic text, though outwardly silent on fingers, in reality referred to a clearly demarcated set of injuries that are subject to retaliation. Rather, it was up to the Medinan scholars to set the boundaries of this definite but underdefined category.

Al-Shāfiʿī's view, which did presuppose a fully determined truth underpinning even apparently underdetermined language, already found its theoretical justification in Greek philosophy; this stance has been termed the "magic language theory" by Samuel Wheeler.[54] If one accepts the premise of magic language that words and phrases correspond to specific and defined meanings, the task of the scholar is simply one of discovery – of gathering evidence to discover in which direction from one's present position the Kaʿba lies, or what injuries are included in the predetermined set to which the Quranic verse refers. Since al-Shāfiʿī's theory makes judgments contingent on evidence, most judgments can amount only to probable interpretations. For Mālik, on the other hand, the scholar actively determines, not merely discovers, the specific meaning implied by revelatory language.[55] The "path of the believers" is not a road map that

ed.], ed. Ziyād Muḥammad Manṣūr (Medina: Maktabat al-ʿUlūm wa-l-Ḥikam, 1987), 460–61.

[53] Quran 5:45: "We ordained therein for them: 'Life for life, eye for eye, nose for nose, ear for ear, tooth for tooth, and wounds equal for equal.'"

[54] Samuel C. Wheeler III, *Deconstruction as Analytic Philosophy* (Stanford, CA: Stanford University Press, 2000), 3.

[55] The theory of language at the heart of Mālik's model of Medinan practice displays parallels to the rabbinic use of language in the Talmud; see Samuel Wheeler, "Rabbinic Philosophy of Language," in *Deconstruction as Analytic Philosophy*. I do not mean to argue that Mālik's theory is derived from Judaic law, nor that al-Shāfiʿī's conception of "magic language" was necessarily inspired by Greek philosophy; however, these

reproduces an independently existing normative landscape in the mind of God, as it is for al-Shāfiʿī. Rather, it is the product of the actual practice of those who witnessed and were transformed by revelation and whose legacy is perpetuated and safeguarded through continuous reenactment by successive generations of their descendants. Therefore, the judgments of Medinan authorities, once they have been accepted as part of *ʿamal*, actually constitute truth and not merely approximations of it – but it is a different kind of truth, one not grounded in an objective reality and thus open to the possibility of change over time, as illustrated by the example of the penalty for severed fingers.

COMMUNITARIANISM VERSUS INDIVIDUALISM

The disagreement between Mālik and al-Shāfiʿī regarding the nature of revelatory language was closely connected to their differing views on the relationship between revelation and the Muslim community. For Mālik, the normative meaning of revelation could unfold only in the practice of the Medinan community; revelation and community were thus inseparable. For al-Shāfiʿī, God spoke through revelation to the individual Muslim, and it was the responsibility of the individual (insofar as he or she possessed the requisite juristic qualifications)[56] to understand the normative implications of this message by applying the insights of legal theory to the canon of sacred sources, unfettered by the interpretations of the rest of the community. While Mālik's hermeneutic perspective was thoroughly communitarian, al-Shāfiʿī's theory of the nature and interpretation of divine law embodied a radical individualism that represented a fundamental challenge to the communitarian status quo.

Mālik's deeply held trust in the communal wisdom and essential rightness of the Muslim community of Medina is evident in his letter to al-Layth b. Saʿd, in which Mālik justifies the Medinan normative tradition as both certain knowledge of revelation in action and the outcome of cumulative wisdom on issues not clearly dealt with in revelation. He argues that if scholars and authorities in Medina

> did not possess [certain] knowledge, they would inquire [among themselves] about it and would adopt the strongest position that they found according to their judgment (*ijtihādihim*) and their closeness to the prophetic age (*ḥadāthat*

similarities could serve as bridges into broader discussions in modern scholarship, which has thus far largely ignored theories of language embodied in Islamic law.

[56] *Risāla*, in *Umm*, 1:164–65 (paras. 961–65).

'ahdihim). If someone disagreed with them, or voiced a different opinion that was stronger than theirs and preferable to it, they would abandon their [old] opinion and act according to the other opinion. Those who succeeded them followed the same approach.[57]

This is the "hidden hand" that Mālik envisaged at work guiding the community toward truth, a cumulative effect that emerges out of the fallible efforts of individuals. The resulting tradition – at home in the sacred space of the Prophet's city – represented the fusion of community and revelation.

Al-Shāfiʿī, on the other hand, had fewer such communitarian roots and lost any that he may have had over the course of his peripatetic life. From such a cosmopolitan vantage point, the fusion of revelation to a particular community would appear problematic. This was the feature that al-Shāfiʿī highlighted in his critiques both of Mālik and of Ibn ʿUlayya, pointing out that the communitarianism of the former amounted to a less extreme but also less coherent form of the theological absolutism of the latter. On one occasion in *Ikhtilāf Mālik*, al-Shāfiʿī despairs when his Mālikī opponent dismisses a Hadith that al-Shāfiʿī has mentioned with the explanation that "it is simply not acted upon"; he exclaims in reply, "If your abandonment of reports of the Prophet of God is due to the weak argument that you have described, then how can one blame those theologians (*ahl al-kalām*) who abandon some Hadith and justify their abandonment of them with [arguments] that are better and stronger than your weak arguments?"[58]

It appears, then, that al-Shāfiʿī had come to see community as overshadowing and – taken to its logical conclusion – strangling revelation in the Medinan normative tradition. By extracting revelation from the grip of communal tradition and interrogating it by means of a repertoire of systematic interpretive techniques wielded by the individual interpreter, al-Shāfiʿī sought to save revelation from domination by the community. Instead of Mālikī communitarianism, al-Shāfiʿī proposed a starkly individualist model of interpretation. In his metaphor of the direction of prayer (*qibla*), there are only the interpreter of signs – the *mujtahid* – and the signs that he is interpreting. The landscape of the law is divided into the immediate vicinity of the Kaʿba in Mecca on the one side and an endless, uninhabited desert on the other. Al-Shāfiʿī remains silent regarding what the interpreter should do if he were to find himself in a Muslim city that already has an established prayer direction.

[57] Abū Ghudda, *Namādhij*, 31.
[58] *Umm*, 10:171.

Such an individualistic model has profound implications for the foundations of the Muslim community, the *umma*. The unitary, shared *qibla* is a perennial symbol of the communal unity of the Muslims, so much so that theologians often refer to the *umma* as a whole – beyond sectarian differences – as the "people of the *qibla*."[59] To deny the validity of the communal *qibla* and impose on each individual the personal obligation to determine the correct direction for him- or herself, even if the result contradicts that reached by other Muslims, amounts to turning the performance and experience of the crucial ritual of prayer into a purely individualistic enterprise and thus questioning the very basis of the communal aspect of religion. The idea that even the *qibla* of established mosques should be viewed as provisional and subject to repeated recalculation implies a profound distrust in the generations of Muslims after the Companions, and by extension in the lived connection of Muslim communities back in time. Al-Shāfiʿī's theory of the law thus represented a potentially dramatic challenge to the still-dominant normative order of the second Hijri century, which was based on the primacy of community and communal interpretation.

This conclusion partly agrees with but more significantly differs from the theory proposed by Patricia Crone and Martin Hinds regarding the balance of power between political leaders and religious scholars in the determination of Islamic law. As mentioned in the Introduction, Crone and Hinds have argued that the second/eighth century witnessed a shift from a caliphal to a prophetic normative tradition. This movement involved the projection of norms back to the prophetic age and an end to the possibility of evolution within the tradition, thereby disenfranchising politicians in favor of scholars as the guardians of Islam.[60] By contrast, my findings here suggest that the primary shift was from a strong communal legal tradition, in which prophetic Hadith were embedded, to a scientific hermeneutic system that isolated Hadith from the communal context and subjected them to "neutral" hermeneutic principles. In terms of religiopolitics, this transformation dethroned the makers of the ancient normative traditions – caliphs, governors, and judges, as well as scholars – and gave rise to a new class of jurists who derived their authority from their role as the expert interpreters of sacred texts.

Al-Shāfiʿī did not, of course, entirely dismiss the role of the community in the process of lawmaking. Although he drew an unequivocal distinction

[59] Van Ess, *Flowering of Muslim Theology*, 40–42.
[60] Crone and Hinds, *God's Caliph*, 58–96.

between the sources of the law, enshrined in a fixed category of canonical texts, and the community that sought to interpret these sources, he granted a position to communal consensus (*ijmāʿ*) as the repository of religious knowledge.[61] While Mālik, as seen in the previous chapter, still employed the Quranic threat to those who contravened the "way of the believers" as a justification for the living tradition of Medina, al-Shāfiʿī interpreted this verse as a proof text for consensus. *Ijmāʿ* in the usage of al-Shāfiʿī had no generative power, but rather served as a residual category of communal memory relating to the interpretation of the sacred sources.

If the central thrust of al-Shāfiʿī's doctrine indeed consisted of the dual aims of canonizing (and thus safeguarding) the sacred sources and essentially disenfranchising the Muslim community in the determination of Islamic normativity, one cannot but ask: Why did al-Shāfiʿī's ideas catch on? Why, instead of becoming a mere curiosum of history like the consensus-based doctrine of Ibn ʿUlayya, did Shāfiʿism both give rise to one of the enduring schools of Islamic law and also exert a profound influence on the legal theory of the other schools? At least part of the answer to these questions lies in the turbulent social and cultural history of the young Abbasid empire in general and its Egyptian province in particular.

[61] Lowry, *Early Islamic Legal Theory*, chap. 7.

PART II

COMMUNITY IN CRISIS

Chapter 4

Status, Power, and Social Upheaval

In order to understand why al-Shāfiʿī's radical theory of the law attracted a following, it is necessary to appreciate the historical context within which it was formulated and received. The success of al-Shāfiʿī's ideas cannot be explained wholly as the result of social forces. However, the fundamental shifts under way in Muslim societies in the late second/eighth century created a receptive environment for a legal approach that distanced itself from the hitherto hegemonic understanding of normativity as grounded in communal practice. These shifts are well illustrated in the history of Egypt, the place where al-Shāfiʿī formulated the definitive statement of his legal theory and where his teaching flourished after his death. But they also characterized the Muslim realm more broadly, which explains why al-Shāfiʿī's project of canonization, though initially launched in the specific context of Egypt, found a receptive audience across the empire. Fortunately, detailed and early sources on Egypt in this period have survived, and they allow the construction of a reasonably coherent account of the province's sociopolitical history.

In this chapter I examine the social and political situation of Egypt at this time, highlight the major trends that were beginning to transform Egyptian society, and demonstrate how these developments laid the basis for the adoption of al-Shāfiʿī's doctrine and for its growth into a prominent and politically patronized school (the subject of the following chapter). In particular, I focus on the declining social and political fortunes of the established Arab aristocracy, the growing presence of non-Arab Muslims in both politics and religious scholarship, and the impact of an increasingly powerful and ambitiously centralizing Abbasid state apparatus.

Together, these trends progressively eroded the basis of the Egyptian elite's vision of a secure and autonomous communal tradition connecting the individual in the present back in time to the original Muslim community and the moment of revelation. The communal dislocations affecting second-/eighth-century Egypt (as well as the Muslim world more generally) therefore prepared the ground for al-Shāfiʿī's abandonment of communal practice and his proposed canonization of the sacred sources that invested normativity in texts alone.

The primary source for the sociopolitical history of Egypt in this period is the work of the historian Muḥammad b. Yūsuf al-Kindī (d. 350/961). Al-Kindī's *Kitāb al-Wulāt* (Book of Governors) and *Kitāb al-Quḍāt* (Book of Judges)[1] offer a detailed account of the political and judicial governance of Egypt during the first three centuries of its Islamic history. As the scion of a respected old family with a long history in Egypt, al-Kindī also had access to and preserved significant amounts of material from older Egyptian historians, whose own work is no longer extant. Al-Kindī's writings paint a vivid picture of the kind of society that al-Shāfiʿī encountered when he arrived in Egypt around the year 198/814.[2] This society was dominated by an aristocratic class of Arab notables (*wujūh*) who traced their roots back to the Muslim conquest of Egypt in the Hijri year 18 or 19 (639 or 640 CE). The conquest replaced the old Byzantine elite, which had governed Egypt as vassals of Constantinople, with a new ruling class composed of Southern Arabian (Yemeni) Arabs led by the prophetic Companion ʿAmr b. al-ʿĀṣ (d. 43/664). The old elite had created a Hellenic enclave in Alexandria, from which Constantinople could be reached easily by ship, while ruling over a landed Coptic population whom they considered both culturally inferior and religiously deviant. The Arabs, in contrast, built their garrison town, Fustat, roughly 150 miles to the south on the east bank of the Nile, directly on the caravan route to the Hejaz.

Egypt's value as a province lay in its agricultural output, which became the second largest source of revenue for the caliphate after the fertile

[1] Published together (in Arabic) as *The Governors and Judges of Egypt, or Kitāb el ʿumarāʾ (el wulāh) wa Kitāb el quḍāh of el Kindī*, ed. Rhuvon Guest (Leiden: E. J. Brill, 1912).

[2] Al-Kindī, *Governors and Judges*, 154. There is some disagreement regarding this date, with Ibn Yūnus, in *Tārīkh Ibn Yūnus al-Ṣadafī*, comp. ʿAbd al-Fattāḥ Fatḥī ʿAbd al-Fattāḥ, 2 vols. (Beirut: Dār al-Kutub al-ʿIlmiyya, 2000), 2:191, giving the year as 199/814 or 815. A possible explanation is furnished by Jonathan Brockopp's thesis that al-Shāfiʿī temporarily left Egypt during the civil war; see Brockopp, *Early Mālikī Law: Ibn ʿAbd al-Ḥakam and His Major Compendium of Jurisprudence* (Leiden: Brill, 2000), 27–28, 42.

lands of southern Iraq.[3] After the conquest, ownership of all agricultural lands formally passed to the Muslim community as a whole; the peasants who continued to work the land were required to pay a land tax, *kharāj*, on agricultural produce to the governor.[4] The Arab conquerors themselves were prohibited by the caliph ʿUmar from settling among the indigenous population and from engaging in agriculture. In return for their services during the invasion, they were granted a pension (*ʿaṭāʾ*) that was paid to them and their descendants, with the sole condition that they serve in the local militia (*jund*). The *dīwān*, or register of the recipients of this pension, was fixed after the first decades of the Hijra.[5] As a result, a distinct aristocratic class of urban Arabs emerged, with a strong self-consciousness.

Over the first two centuries of Egypt's Islamic history, this aristocratic class ensured the loyalty of Egypt to the Rāshidūn, Umayyad, and Abbasid caliphs. Thanks to its tribal homogeneity, the Arab aristocracy did not suffer the dramatic communal discord that plagued Syria: for a long time the Egyptian elite consisted overwhelmingly of Southern (Yemeni) Arabs. Northern (Qaysī) Arabs settled in Egypt only a century after the conquest, when the caliph Hishām (r. 105–25/724–43) broke with ʿUmar's decree and permitted his chief tax collector ʿUbayd Allāh b. al-Habḥāb, a Qaysī, to settle some of his fellow tribesmen in the eastern Nile delta (Ḥawf) region, away from the capital, Fustat.[6] However, thanks to their distance from Fustat, the cultural impact of the Qaysī Arabs on the established Arab elite was initially negligible.

The relationship between the caliph and the province remained for the most part stable. Apart from exceptional circumstances, the caliph appointed both the governor and the chief judge, and each then selected his own personnel. Governors were overwhelmingly non-Egyptian Arabs, sometimes members of the caliphal family. Their tenures often lasted for less than a year; this possibly reflected a deliberate strategy on the caliph's part to ensure that the appointees would not have the opportunity to

[3] Hugh Kennedy, "Central Government and Provincial Elites in the Early ʿAbbasid Caliphate," *Bulletin of the School of Oriental and African Studies* 44 (1981): 26–38, at 33.

[4] Hossein Modarressi, *Kharāj in Islamic Law* (London: Anchor Press, 1983); Kōsei Morimoto, *The Fiscal Administration of Egypt in the Early Islamic Period* (Kyoto: Dohosha, 1981).

[5] Hugh Kennedy, "Egypt as a Province in the Islamic Caliphate, 641–868," in *The Cambridge History of Egypt*, vol. 1, *Islamic Egypt, 640–1517*, ed. Carl Petry, 62–85 (Cambridge: Cambridge University Press, 1998), 65.

[6] Al-Kindī, *Governors and Judges*, 75–76.

build local bases of power. As a result of the transitory nature of this arrangement, governors relied heavily on local officials to enable them to govern effectively. The most prominent of such officials was the police chief, *ṣāḥib al-shurṭa*, whose role was effectively that of a deputy governor.[7] The *ṣāḥib al-shurṭa* was the executive agent of the governor: he was responsible for public order, and he led the militia in quelling rebellions. In contrast to the governors, the *ṣāḥib al-shurṭa* was in most cases a native of Egypt and a member of the indigenous aristocracy and often served under several governors.[8] While the primary ruler of the province was thus appointed from the outside, the day-to-day running of the province must have been predominantly determined by the local elite, whose families held important administrative positions throughout the first two centuries of Islamic rule.

The chief judge of Egypt was generally also appointed directly by the caliph. Unlike governors, however, judges not uncommonly held office for a decade or more, enabling them to shape Egyptian society more consistently than was possible for transient governors.[9] In addition, the caliph often appointed as judges either Egyptians or jurists who were already resident in Egypt before their appointment, who thus enjoyed greater familiarity with the local situation and normative practice. Those judges who were appointed from the outside often relied on local experts, whom they employed in the role of secretary (*kātib*) or witness examiner (*ṣāḥib al-masāʾil*). Such local input was important in preventing faux pas that could expose judges to the derision of the local population or, more seriously, undermine the integrity of and respect for legal institutions that were crucial to society.

The self-understanding and normative values of the Arab aristocracy in late second-/early ninth-century Egypt were conservative. Families that were influential in public life traced their lineages to prominent personalities among the conquerors, many of whom were Companions of the Prophet, thus providing the Egyptian Arabs with a direct connection to the Prophet.[10] This sense of continuity, together with the perceived distinctness and cohesion of the notable class, was reflected in the Arabs' view of the relationship between their communal normative values and

[7] Hugh Kennedy, "Miṣr," in *EI2*, 7:146.

[8] On the prominence of successive members of, for example, the al-Khawlānī and ʿAssāma families as *aṣḥāb al-shurṭa*, see Kennedy, "Central Government," 36.

[9] Hallaq discusses the role of judges in the articulation of early Islamic law in general in *Origins and Evolution*, 57–101.

[10] See, for example, Kennedy, "Egypt as a Province," 64–65.

the original Muslim community as the repository of the sacred law. A clear articulation of this view is provided by the following passage from a letter written by the Egyptian jurist al-Layth b. Saʿd to Mālik b. Anas in Medina:

> Indeed, many of the "first and foremost" (*al-sābiqūn al-awwalūn*)[11] left [their homeland] in order to strive in the path of God in pursuit of His good pleasure. They founded their garrison towns and the people gathered around them. They openly displayed the Book of God and the example of His Prophet, and they never concealed anything that they knew. So in every garrison town there was a group that acted in accordance with (*yaʿmalūna bi*) the Book of God and the example of His Prophet, and they would not conceal from them anything that they knew.... They strove to arrive at sound opinions (*yajtahidūna raʾyahum*) regarding anything that the Quran or the Sunna did not explain. Abū Bakr, ʿUmar, and ʿUthmān,[12] whom the Muslims had chosen for themselves [as leaders], corrected them [in these efforts] and were neither neglectful nor careless with regard to them. They would write [to the Companions] even about small matters to maintain the religion and to warn against disagreement with the Book of God and the example of His Messenger. They never failed to inform them about issues that had been explained in the Quran, or acted upon by the Prophet, or regarding which they had consulted with each other. So if an issue arises upon which the Companions of the Messenger of God in Egypt, Syria, or Iraq acted during the lifetime of Abū Bakr, ʿUmar, and ʿUthmān, without the latter ordering them to act otherwise, we do not consider it permissible for the inhabitants of the Muslims' garrison towns to come up with something new today that was not done by their predecessors among the Companions of the Messenger of God and their Successors; because most of the scholars have passed away, and those who remain do not resemble those of old.[13]

Al-Layth thus justified local normative traditions, such as the one that had grown in Egypt, as fully legitimate representations of the sacred law, since they were rooted in the teachings of the Companions who had settled in the garrison towns, in their knowledge of the religion and their legal reasoning. Their direct contact with the "rightly guided caliphs" meant that any differences of opinion had remained within acceptable limits. The same was true for the immediate Successors (*tābiʿūn*) of these Companions, as illustrated by a case involving debt servitude that arose in an Egyptian court during the reign of the Umayyad caliph ʿUmar b. ʿAbd al-ʿAzīz, a member of the Successor generation. The Egyptian judge sought the caliph's guidance on the issue, and the caliph's response

[11] Quran 9:100; for al-Layth, this phrase refers to the Companions of the Prophet.

[12] The first three Rāshidūn, or "rightly guided," caliphs, all of whom were Companions of the Prophet.

[13] Abū Ghudda, *Namādhij*, 35.

became part of the Egyptian legal tradition.[14] As seen in the first chapter, al-Layth concluded by postulating a break between the earlier Muslim generations and his contemporaries and arguing that the latter should not be permitted to disagree with the former. Al-Layth's theory of the sacred law, based on the authority of the local normative tradition, was structurally similar to the teaching of Mālik, with the exception that Mālik posited the absolute superiority of Medina, while al-Layth argued for the legitimacy of multiple normative traditions rooted in the teachings of the Companions.

Because of this fundamental similarity in outlook, and the fact that both the Arabs of Medina and those of Egypt belonged to Yemeni tribes, several Egyptian scholars of al-Layth's generation had traveled to Medina to study with Mālik; the most prominent such figures were Ibn Wahb (d. 197/812), Ibn al-Qāsim (d. 191/806), Ashhab (d. 204/820), ʿAbd Allāh b. ʿAbd al-Ḥakam (d. 214/829), and Aṣbagh b. al-Faraj (d. 225/840), who, however, arrived in Medina only to find that Mālik had died shortly before. The material that they took back to Egypt – copies of Mālik's *Muwaṭṭaʾ* as well as other lecture notes from their lessons with Mālik – was then used to turn Mālik's teaching into a textual tradition disconnected from the actual locality of Medina. After Mālik's death in 179/795, the primary center for the study and development of his thought shifted to Egypt, where his students formed an indigenous group of prominent jurists who dedicated themselves to the preservation, elaboration, and perpetuation of the Islamic normative tradition as defended by Mālik. However, their efforts, influenced by the polycentric perspective described by al-Layth, gave rise to a distinctly Egyptian form of Mālikism, in which the communal tradition of the Egyptian Arabs played an important normative role.

THE CHANGING ECONOMY OF STATUS

The original Arab conquerors had established their settlement as a tiny ruling minority among Coptic Christians. The Coptic community had, beyond its clergy, no educated or scholarly class of its own, since it had already been a subaltern majority under Byzantine rule. The identity of the Egyptian Arabs as a cultural and intellectual elite was therefore much

[14] Al-Kindī, *Governors and Judges*, 336–37. See also Harald Motzki, "The Prophet and the Debtors: A *Ḥadīth* Analysis under Scrutiny," in *Analysing Muslim Traditions*, 125–208, at 195–200.

more secure than that of the Iraqi Arabs, since in Iraq indigenous Persian aristocracy and high culture continued to represent a rival source of identity and status.

The Arabs' elite identity was nevertheless potentially open to challenge, given that non-Arabs could convert to Islam and thereby appropriate one of the central markers of elite status. However, since religion, though important, was only one element of a communal identity that also encompassed ethnic and tribal affiliations, simple conversion did not bestow on non-Arabs the social status required to interact on an equal basis with Arabs in Egypt. The substantial barriers that hindered Copts' social mobility and the resulting problems are illustrated by the Ḥaras affair, which shook Egypt in the late 180s/early 800s. The people of Ḥaras, a village in eastern Egypt,[15] appear to have been Coptic converts to Islam who were subjected to provocation and humiliation by prominent Arab Egyptians, particularly members of the Khawlān and Kinda clans;[16] the exact nature of this harassment is unclear. The people of Ḥaras then consulted Zakariyyā b. Yaḥyā (d. 242/856 or 857),[17] a native of Ḥaras, who, as the secretary (*kātib*) of Egypt's chief judge ʿAbd al-Raḥmān al-ʿUmarī (in office 185–94/801–10), was presumably the most prominent member of the community. Zakariyyā advised them to acquire a false Arab identity by having themselves registered with the judge as members of the Arab clan of Ḥawtaka. Through the payment of bribes to officials and the securing of false witnesses, the people of Ḥaras succeeded in achieving official recognition as Arabs and were registered in the *dīwān* as recipients of the pension.

The reaction of the local Arab elite to this blatant fraud was intense. In al-Kindī's histories of the governors and judges of Egypt, the Ḥaras affair receives more extensive treatment than any other single event in the first three centuries of Islamic rule in Egypt, including the conquest itself.[18] That this was not simply a personal preoccupation of al-Kindī is demonstrated by the voluble amount of poetry that was composed to lament the injustice of the genealogical forgery; to air accusations against

[15] Ḥaras is described as a village by Yāqūt al-Ḥamawī, who, however, notes that al-Dāraquṭnī thought it to represent an urban quarter within Fustat; see Yāqūt al-Ḥamawī, *Muʿjam al-buldān*, 5 vols. (Beirut: Dār Iḥyāʾ al-turāth al-ʿArabī, 1979), 2:240.

[16] Al-Kindī, *Governors and Judges*, 397.

[17] Shams al-Dīn al-Dhahabī, *al-Kāshif fī maʿrifat man lahu riwāya fī al-kutub al-sitta*, ed. Muḥammad ʿAwwāma and Aḥmad Muḥammad Nimr al-Khaṭīb, 2 vols. (Jedda: Dār al-Qibla, 1992), 1:406.

[18] Al-Kindī discusses the affair in his entries on the judges al-ʿUmarī and Hishām al-Bakrī; *Governors and Judges*, 397–414.

the judge, al-ʿUmarī, who permitted it; and to praise the new judge who eventually reversed the registration. A passage in a poem written around this time by Yaḥyā al-Khawlānī (d. unknown) indicates the enormity of the perceived transgression:

> And what a strange thing it was that a group
> Of Copts among us suddenly became Arabs
> Saying, "Our fathers are Ḥawtak," though their fathers
> Were heathen Copts with unclear genealogies
> They brought oaths from the delta, claiming
> That they were from them – what folly! – and they succeeded
> Truly, may the Merciful curse the one who accepts
> Them ... as long as the sun sets in the west.[19]

Given that the people of Ḥaras had converted to Islam, the term "Copts" was used as a designator of social differentiation.[20] The practical significance of this differentiation is suggested by the comment of the poet Muʿallā al-Ṭāʾī, who lived in the late second/early ninth century, to the judge al-ʿUmarī, who was instrumental in the genealogical forgery: "If indeed you consider them Arabs, then give them your daughters in marriage!"[21] An Arab, it seems, would not have permitted his daughter to marry an Egyptian of Coptic descent, even if he were Muslim.

The scope of the Ḥaras scandal prompted the Egyptian aristocracy to send a delegation to Baghdad to the caliph al-Amīn (r. 193–98/809–13), who in turn advised the new judge of Egypt, Hishām al-Bakrī (in office 194–96/810–11), to reopen the case. After summoning several witnesses, al-Bakrī overturned his predecessor's decision, prompting the following triumphant statement from the poet Yaḥyā al-Khawlānī: "The Copts have returned to their origins and a manifest injustice had been reversed."[22]

The basis of the social division laid open by the Ḥaras affair was not ethnicity properly speaking, but rather status in a society where status emerged from a complex combination of origins, affiliations, and personal merit.[23] Although Arabness remained an inviolate category, the institution

[19] Al-Kindī, *Governors and Judges*, 399.

[20] Maged Mikhail notes that writings from this period often use the term *qibṭ* (Copt) to mean "Egyptian" as opposed to "Arab"; see Maged S. A. Mikhail, "Egypt from Late Antiquity to Early Islam: Copts, Melkites, and Muslims Shaping a New Society" (PhD diss., University of California at Los Angeles, 2004), 195.

[21] Al-Kindī, *Governors and Judges*, 401.

[22] Al-Kindī, *Governors and Judges*, 415.

[23] For a general discussion on the interaction of background (*nasab*) and merit (*ḥasab*) in determining status, see Roy P. Mottahedeh, *Loyalty and Leadership in an Early Islamic Society*, 2nd ed. (London: I. B. Tauris, 2001), 98–104.

of clientage (*walā'*), practiced across the Muslim world, increasingly provided a way for non-Arabs to participate in the status that was enjoyed by members of the elite.[24] A good example of the functioning of this system is the judge's secretary, Zakariyyā, who had achieved a successful career in the judiciary despite his Coptic origins. Most sources refer to him as Zakariyyā al-Quḍā'ī,[25] the Quḍā'a being a large Arab tribe of which the Ḥawtaka were a clan. It is likely that Zakariyyā gained this appellation through clientage: he or one of his ancestors either was the manumitted slave of a member of this tribe or had entered into a contractual relationship with a member. Such a relationship transferred inheritance rights and legal liability onto the patron (*mawlā*), as well as providing the client (also known as *mawlā*) with an adopted Arab genealogy. As indicated by Yaḥyā al-Khawlānī's poem, the absence of a genealogy was often highlighted as the distinguishing mark between Arabs and non-Arabs.[26]

Clientage as practiced by Muslim Arabs thus served to integrate non-Arabs as individuals into Arab tribal society, with its web of social and legal relations, and promoted their cultural assimilation. Accordingly, when the second Hijri century witnessed the emergence of literary genres in the Islamic sciences, scholars of client background played a key role in the development of this written discourse in Egypt and beyond.[27] More generally, clientage permitted non-Arab Muslims to enter into Arab society and to attain high scholarly, cultural, and political rank. The first two centuries of Muslim rule in Egypt saw clients as governors, *aṣḥāb al-shurṭa*, and judges, and al-Kindī composed an entire (now lost) work to extol the achievements of the clients (*mawālī*) in Egypt.[28]

[24] On the position of clients under the Umayyads and the Abbasids, see 'Abd al-'Azīz al-Dūrī, *al-Judhūr al-tārīkhiyya li-l-shu'ūbiyya* (Beirut: Dār al-Ṭalī'a, 1962).

[25] Al-Dhahabī, *Kāshif*, 1:406.

[26] Patricia Crone, "Walā'," in *EI2*, 6:874.

[27] Harald Motzki cautions against overestimating the role of non-Arab clients in Islamic scholarship in "The Role of Non-Arab Converts in the Development of Early Islamic Law," *Islamic Law and Society* 6 (1999): 293–317. However, Christopher Melchert points out that the sources used by Motzki are likely to understate the importance of clients; see "The Early History of Islamic Law," in *Method and Theory in the Study of Islamic Origins*, ed. Herbert Berg, 293–324 (Leiden: Brill, 2003), 302–3, n. 35. John Nawas has argued that by the mid-third/ninth century, non-Arabs constituted more than half of all jurists in the Muslim world; "The Emergence of *Fiqh* as a Distinct Discipline and the Ethnic Identity of the *Fuqahā'* in Early and Classical Islam," in *Studies in Arabic and Islam: Proceedings of the 19th Congress, Halle 1998*, ed. S. Leder, H. Kilpatrick, B. Martel-Thoumian, and H. Schönig, 491–99 (Sterling, VA: Peeters, 2002), 496.

[28] Rhuvon Guest, introduction to al-Kindī, *Governors and Judges*, 10; Abū al-Ḥasan al-Dāraquṭnī, *al-Mu'talif wa-l-mukhtalif*, ed. Muwaffaq b. 'Abd Allāh b. 'Abd al-Qādir, 5 vols. (Beirut: Dār al-Gharb al-Islāmī, 1986), 2:76.

The system of clientage operated on an individual level, based on personal relationships between non-Arab clients and their Arab patrons, and thus differs from what the people of Ḥaras sought to accomplish in two ways. A client's status, though linked to that of his patron, remained a distinct category, without entitlement to the state pension; and the system of clientage absorbed only individuals and their descendants, rather than entire communities, into the framework of Arab society. The complex nature of the relationship between clientage and status is exemplified by the case of Aṣbagh b. al-Faraj. Aṣbagh was a leading Mālikī scholar in Egypt, who claimed to be the descendant of a client of the Umayyads. Al-Kindī's evaluation of this claim illustrates the fine gradations of a class-conscious society. Aṣbagh's ancestor, determined al-Kindī, was not a client of the Umayyad dynasty, but rather a slave donated by the Umayyads for service in a mosque.[29] Aṣbagh was therefore a mere impostor: this seemingly slight difference meant that he had no specific Arab patron and therefore no genuine clientage.

Nonetheless, the increasing success and prominence of the *mawālī* in Egyptian society appear to have created anxieties among the Arabs of Egypt, who recognized the trend of relative decline in the prestige and exclusivity of the Arab elite as more non-Arabs took positions of leadership in politics and intellectual life. Saʿīd b. ʿUfayr (d. 226/841), poet, historian, and member of the Egyptian Arab aristocracy, reported the following highly tendentious statement attributed to the Prophet: "If you see the Arabs scorn the Quraysh, and the clients scorn the Arabs, and the non-Muslim subjects of the land (*musālamat al-arḍ*) scorn the clients, then the signs of the last hour have reached you."[30] The gradual erosion of the social hierarchy, and the concerns that it provoked among the Arabs, are further indicated by numerous anecdotes from this period that demonstrate the declining social cachet of mere membership in the Arab elite when juxtaposed with other factors conferring individual status. Such factors included not only ethnicity and clientage, both of which can be subsumed under the Arabic term *nasab* (genealogy), but also the accomplishments and qualifications of an individual as well as his patron, if the individual was a client. For example, when the judge Isḥāq b. al-Furāt (in office 184–85/800–801) demanded of the abovementioned Saʿīd b. ʿUfayr

[29] Quoted in Taqī al-Dīn al-Maqrīzī, *al-Muqaffā al-kabīr*, ed. Muḥammad al-Yaʿlāwī, 8 vols. (Beirut: Dār al-Gharb al-Islāmī, 1990), 2:214; the source is probably al-Kindī's lost *Kitāb al-Mawālī*.

[30] Al-Dāraquṭnī, *al-Mu'talif wa-l-mukhtalif*, 2:81.

that the latter hand over the property of an orphan to him for supervision, Ibn ʿUfayr initially refused, alluding to the fact that Isḥāq was a mere client. Isḥāq replied: "Do you know Muʿāwiya b. Ḥudayj,[31] lord of everyone between al-Faramā [in Egypt] and Andalusia?" When Ibn ʿUfayr answered in the affirmative, Isḥāq continued: "He is my patron – so who are you?" To this, Ibn ʿUfayr apparently had no response.[32] Judge Isḥāq's persuasive argument was thus that the merit (*ḥasab*) of his patron outshone the lineage of Ibn ʿUfayr.

The possibility of a career based on merit that could overcome the limitations of client status existed already among the Umayyads. The caliph ʿUmar b. ʿAbd al-ʿAzīz (r. 99–101/717–20) appointed three Egyptians to issue legal opinions (*fatāwā*); one of these appointees was an Arab, while two were clients. When the Arabs of Egypt protested about this preference for clients, the caliph is said to have retorted, "It is not my fault that the clients are reaching prominence through their own efforts (*tasmū bi-anfusihā*) and that you are not."[33] The two client appointees, ʿUbayd Allāh b. Abī Jaʿfar (d. 132/749 or 750) and Yazīd b. Abī Ḥabīb (d. 128/745 or 746), reached positions of such importance that they were the first Egyptians to give the oath of allegiance (*bayʿa*) to a new caliph.[34]

The changing nature of the economy of status is also indicated by another anecdote involving Ibn ʿUfayr. In a heated debate before the Abbasid general ʿAbd Allāh b. Ṭāhir in 212/827 regarding the possible appointment of Aṣbagh b. al-Faraj as chief judge, Ibn ʿUfayr appears to have considered the simple fact of Aṣbagh's client status insufficient grounds to object to the appointment. Instead, he attempted to use an alternative argument to discredit Aṣbagh, asking rhetorically, "What is the use of mentioning the sons of dyers and tailors in connection with a position for which God Almighty has not made them suitable?" To this, Aṣbagh retorted, "The general has ordered the jurists and scholars to

[31] Muʿāwiya b. Ḥudayj (d. 52/672) was a Companion of the Prophet and a military commander in North Africa; his son and grandson were also powerful men in the region under the Umayyads. See al-Ziriklī, *Aʿlām*, 7:260, 3:338, and 4:95.

[32] Quoted from al-Kindī's lost *Kitāb al-Mawālī* by Ibn Ḥajar al-ʿAsqalānī in *Rafʿ al-iṣr ʿan quḍāt Miṣr*, ed. Ḥāmid ʿAbd al-Majīd, Muḥammad al-Mahdī Abū Sinna, and Muḥammad Ismāʿīl al-Sāwī, 2 vols. (Cairo: Maṭbaʿat al-Amīriyya, 1957–61), 1:115. I read Isḥāq's statement as "he is my patron" (*huwa mawlāyā*), given that Isḥāq is known to have been a client of Muʿāwiya b Ḥudayj.

[33] Reported by Ibn Yūnus; quoted by al-Maqrīzī in *al-Khiṭaṭ*, 2:332.

[34] While ʿUbayd Allāh's background is unknown, Yazīd's father had been brought to Egypt as a slave from the Dongola region of Sudan. See Motzki, "Prophet and Debtors," 198–99.

attend [this meeting], not the poets and soothsayers," referring to the fact that he, Aṣbagh, was a recognized authority in law, whereas Ibn ʿUfayr was a poet and a local historian.[35] While Ibn ʿUfayr appealed to the allegedly lowly occupations of Aṣbagh's forefathers to support his objection to his appointment, Aṣbagh countered by pointing out that in the here and now he was a distinguished jurist, unlike Ibn ʿUfayr, who was not qualified to speak on the topic. Neither genealogy nor class background could therefore predetermine Aṣbagh's status and social aspirations.[36]

A final example of the erosion of simple correlations between ethnicity and status is the governor Ibn Mamdūd (in office 162–64/779–80), who was not only a former slave but also of Turkic heritage. Al-Kindī's discussion of the governor is nonetheless positive, highlighting the fact that Ibn Mamdūd's mother was the aunt of the (non-Muslim) king of Tabaristan and that Ibn Mamdūd's governorship was characterized by unprecedented law and order.[37] Thus both class deriving from an illustrious non-Arab genealogy as well as professional merit played a role in the perception and negotiation of status.

This short exposition has sought to demonstrate the complexity of the construction of status among Egyptians in the second/eighth and third/ninth centuries and to indicate the gradual but – at least in the perception of the old elite – dramatic social transformations that were under way as the result of the increasing presence and prominence of non-Arabs in Egyptian society. While established Egyptian Arabs still possessed a firm bedrock of status through their genealogy that was so closely tied to the history of Islamic Egypt and through the financial distinction afforded by the state pension, non-Arabs from Egypt as well as elsewhere were able to construct status capital via alternative avenues, even reaching positions that permitted them to challenge directly the dominance of members of the Arab aristocracy. One possible such avenue, as mentioned earlier, was excellence in Islamic legal scholarship.

The declining eminence of the Arab elite in Egyptian society was accompanied by the dilution of tribal loyalties among the Arabs due to

[35] Al-Kindī, *Governors and Judges*, 434. Ibn ʿUfayr had studied with Mālik and transmitted his *Muwaṭṭaʾ* but achieved no recognition in the field of law; see al-Dhahabī, *Siyar aʿlām al-nubalāʾ*, 10:583–86.

[36] The exchange appears, however, to have deterred Ibn Ṭāhir, who appointed ʿĪsā b. al-Munkadir instead of Aṣbagh to the judgeship.

[37] Al-Kindī, *Governors and Judges*, 122–23. Al-Kindī reports that public order under Ibn Mamdūd was so exemplary that the he forbade the Egyptians to lock their doors, promising to provide personal compensation for anything that was stolen.

the emergence of competing economic interests. This trend was the result of growing numbers of Arabs contravening the original orders of the caliph ʿUmar by settling in the Egyptian countryside and taking up agriculture. This process had begun in the mid-second/eighth century, when the caliph Hishām, as mentioned earlier, had permitted Qaysī Arabs from Syria to move to the Nile delta as a means of suppressing occasional tax revolts by indigenous Egyptian peasants. Subsequently, Arabs of both Qaysī and Yemeni descent engaged in farming in the delta.[38] After a generation had passed, however, the economic interests of the settled Arabs had become fused with the interests of those whom they were meant to police. This shift led to new tax revolts that this time saw Coptic Christians and Muslim Arabs of various tribes allied against the elite Arab militia.[39] Thus the neat order of Arab Muslims loyal to the empire extracting taxes from non-Muslim and non-Arab peasants began to break down.

THE CENTRALIZING STATE

The second principal source of social upheaval in Egypt at the time of al-Shāfiʿī's arrival sprang from the increasingly aggressive centralizing agenda pursued by both Umayyad and Abbasid caliphs throughout the second Hijri century (718–815 CE). Their far-reaching efforts at centralization within the empire had a direct impact on the autonomy of the local Arab Muslim community in the Egyptian province by progressively disenfranchising the indigenous elite in the management of communal affairs and the daily life of the polity. Many central social functions that had hitherto been the domain of the Arab families became enshrined in legal institutions administered by centrally appointed agents of the state, further contributing to the Arabs' sense that the foundations of their social order and way of life were under threat.

An important example of such a transfer of responsibility is the change in the administration of religious endowments (*aḥbās* or *awqāf*) that was effected by the Umayyad-appointed judge Tawba b. Namir (in office 115–20/733–38) in 118/736.[40] Religious endowments generally consisted of institutions dedicated to providing a public benefit – such as mosques, bathhouses, and soup kitchens – that were donated or bequeathed to the community by individual Muslims. Such endowments, traditionally

[38] Mikhail, "Egypt from Late Antiquity to Early Islam," 195–205.
[39] Mikhail, "Egypt from Late Antiquity to Early Islam," 202.
[40] Al-Kindī, *Governors and Judges*, 342.

supervised privately by the heirs of the original donor or the executors of his or her will, appear to have played an important part in Egyptian life of the second Hijri century. Tawba's decree, justified as a measure to prevent irregularities in the administration of endowments that could diminish their value, placed all endowments in Egypt under the supervision of the chief judge. As a result of the decision, an enormous *dīwān* was set up to facilitate the centralized management of the endowments – though it is not clear whether the term simply refers to a special register kept by the judge or whether he actually established an administrative division dedicated to this task.

Less than two decades later, during the second tenure of judge Khayr b. Nuʿaym (133–35/751–53), the supervision of the property of orphans was likewise removed from the private sphere and added to the responsibilities of the judge, necessitating rigorous bookkeeping regarding the usage of these funds.[41] A predecessor of Khayr's, Ibn Ḥudayj (in office for six months in 86/705), had already compiled a central list of orphans' property,[42] but the management of these assets had remained a tribe-internal matter until the 130s/750s, when the caliph initiated the reform.[43] As in the case of the endowments, this measure moved control over substantial assets from private hands (the orphans' guardians within the framework of families and tribes) to the office of the judge. Increased centralization went hand in hand with increased record keeping. For example, the judge Mufaḍḍal b. Faḍāla (first term in office 168–69/785–86) significantly increased the volume of official files (*sijillāt*) by adding to them copies of wills, debts, and endowment documents,[44] thereby permitting more reliable adjudication in cases of dispute, but also facilitating more intrusive supervision of private transactions by state agents.

These policies encroached on local autonomy and self-regulation and caused mistrust among the population, expressed in rumors and suspicions regarding the conduct of government officials. In the late 170s/790s a rumor spread throughout Fustat that the disliked judge Ibn Masrūq (in office 177–84/793–800), a foreigner from Iraq, was planning to transfer

[41] Al-Kindī, *Governors and Judges*, 355.
[42] Al-Kindī, *Governors and Judges*, 325.
[43] Al-Kindī claims that the centralization of orphans' property management was carried out on the orders of the caliph al-Manṣūr, but al-Manṣūr acceeded to the throne in 136/754, while al-Kindī records the centralization as having taken place between 133/750 and 135/752.
[44] Al-Kindī, *Governors and Judges*, 379.

the assets of both the endowments and all orphans of Egypt to the caliph Hārūn al-Rashīd in Baghdad.[45] In another incident in the 180s/800s, the Egyptian poet Yaḥyā al-Khawlānī accused the administration of judge ʿAbd al-Raḥmān al-ʿUmarī, likewise a foreigner, of misappropriating orphans' property.[46]

Communal autonomy was also being eroded by centralization in the judicial sphere, especially through the reform of the witness system. It seems that in the first Hijri century, Egyptian judges accepted the witness statement of any male Muslim as long as there were no obvious reasons to discount him as untrustworthy; in cases of doubt, a character reference was sought from the neighbor of the potential witness.[47] In the small and close-knit tribal community of Fustat in the first century of Muslim rule, such a procedure that rested on the reliability of individuals' reputations appears to have been workable.[48] At the beginning of the second Hijri century, however, judge Tawba b. Namir began to exclude automatically any Yemeni Arab's testimony against a Qaysī Arab, and vice versa.[49] This policy was introduced at a time when the ethnic homogeneity of the predominantly Southern Egyptian Arab community was becoming diluted by an influx of Northern Arabs. Fear that the notorious Qays/Yaman rivalry would spill from Syria into Egypt through the judiciary thus appears to have prompted the new critical attitude toward witness statements by Muslims. The default assumption of trustworthiness also proved unsustainable in situations when the judge was called upon to adjudicate cases among Christians. Given that the Muslim judge was an outsider to Christian communal life, he had no way of assessing the credibility of witnesses who appeared in front of him. To address this problem, judge Khayr b. Nuʿaym began to make inquiries regarding the reliability of potential non-Muslim witnesses among their coreligionists.[50]

Reflecting a declining sense of trust in Muslim society, judge Ghawth b. Sulaymān, who served three terms between 135 and 168 (752 and 784), extended to Muslim witnesses Khayr's policy of making the acceptance of testimony conditional upon prior discreet investigations of character, thereby dismissing the long-established prima facie assumption of

[45] Al-Kindī, *Governors and Judges*, 390.
[46] Al-Kindī, *Governors and Judges*, 396.
[47] Al-Kindī, *Governors and Judges*, 361.
[48] "Have you ever known a village reputation to be wrong?" asks Stephen Maturin rhetorically in Patrick O'Brian's novel *Master and Commander* (New York: W. W. Norton, 1990), 230.
[49] Al-Kindī, *Governors and Judges*, 346.
[50] Al-Kindī, *Governors and Judges*, 351.

Muslims' trustworthiness.[51] During the second term of judge Mufaḍḍal b. Faḍāla (174–77/790–93), the task of assessing witness credibility was assigned to the newly created position of the witness examiner (*ṣāḥib al-masāʾil*). This system of determining the probity of witnesses was formalized during the judgeship of al-ʿUmarī, who not only required potential witnesses to pass the vetting of the examiner but subsequently had all approved witnesses entered into an official register.[52] These individuals acquired a previously unknown position, that of a professional witness.

This innovation had a dramatic impact on the nature of the judicial process. Before Mufaḍḍal, a court case had involved only the judge, his secretary, and the parties involved in the case, who could in principle call upon any member of the Muslim community to give testimony regarding the facts of the case. Uprightness (*ʿadāla*) had been assumed to represent a natural characteristic of every Muslim, to be questioned only in cases of manifest immorality or deviance. The presumption of uprightness allowed the community to participate actively in the judicial process: the testimony of one, two, or four upright witnesses (their number depending on the nature of the case) automatically settled a claim. In such a system, the role of the judge was primarily that of a guarantor of correct procedure; it was the Muslim public, through the witnesses drawn from it, who decided the case. Under the new system that arose in the decade spanning the tenures of Mufaḍḍal and al-ʿUmarī, however, a key role in the process of adjudication was given to the certified professional witnesses, who now held a monopoly on the ascertainment of facts pertaining to a court case. The functioning of this new system is illustrated by the case of the Ibn ʿUmar mosque in Fustat during al-ʿUmarī's tenure. When the neighbors of the mosque complained that it was about to collapse and requested that the judge allow the establishment of an endowment to support the repairs, the judge would not rely on their testimony but rather dispatched his witnesses to survey the situation before permitting the new endowment.[53]

The unprecedented restriction of acceptable witnesses to a small, preselected group that, according to al-Kindī, consisted of a mere ten individuals under Mufaḍḍal thus meant that the administration of justice, once a communal affair, was now the prerogative of a few appointed officials. Although later judges increased the number of certified witnesses – to one

[51] Al-Kindī, *Governors and Judges*, 361.

[52] Al-Kindī, *Governors and Judges*, 394.

[53] Al-Kindī, *Governors and Judges*, 308–9.

hundred under al-ʿUmarī, then back to thirty under Lahīʿa b. ʿĪsā (second term in office 199–204/814–20) – their number remained negligible in relation to the population as a whole.[54]

The certification of witnesses and the consequent exclusion of the majority of the population from the judicial process were perceived as an outrage by Egyptian Arabs.[55] Not only did the rejection of the assumption of uprightness cast implicit doubt on the personal integrity of community members; the small group of individuals who did achieve recognition as acceptable witnesses were considered by many to be unscrupulous people who were taking advantage of their favor with the judge. This was especially the case under al-ʿUmarī, who imported many of the witnesses whom he approved from his native Medina while scorning indigenous Egyptians. A local poet, Isḥāq b. Muʿādh (d. unknown), composed the following verses addressed to Mufaḍḍal, who initiated the system:

> I shall beseech my Lord until dawn
> That He may return you to [what you were,] an emaciated dog:
> You established injustice in judging between us
> And declared a group of thieves to be upright!
> None among those who have come before us ever heard
> That the number of upright people was so low.[56]

Within the span of seventy years between the centralization of endowment records by Tawba b. Namir in 118/736 and the formalization of the witness register under al-ʿUmarī in 185/801, the judges of Egypt effectively revoked much of the legal autonomy and self-regulation of Egyptian Muslim society. By the end of this period, it was the judge who decided which projects counted as valid endowments[57] and how they were to be managed, and the establishment of legal facts had been removed from the domain of the public to become the prerogative of de facto agents of the judge. This centralization not only limited the autonomy of Egyptians in the regulation of daily life; it also rendered the social order far more vulnerable to the politics of judicial appointments influenced by legal and theological doctrines, as will be seen in the following chapter.

While it appears that Egyptians largely accepted the appointment of foreigners as governors, the office of judge was connected more closely to local identity. In late 154 or early 155 (771 or 772) a delegation of

[54] Al-Kindī, *Governors and Judges*, 396 and 422.
[55] Al-Kindī, *Governors and Judges*, 386.
[56] Al-Kindī, *Governors and Judges*, 386.
[57] See the endowment document reproduced by al-Kindī, *Governors and Judges*, 407–10.

Egyptian notables visited Baghdad to meet with the Abbasid caliph al-Manṣūr.[58] The judge of Egypt, Abū Khuzayma, had just died, and al-Manṣūr was in the process of selecting his successor. ʿAbd Allāh b. Ḥudayj (d. unknown), a member of the Egyptian delegation, implored the caliph to appoint an Egyptian: "O prince of the believers, do you want to bring us to infamy among the provinces by appointing over us someone foreign, [so that it will be said] that our land has no one fit to serve as judge?" Al-Manṣūr appears to have been convinced by this argument; he appointed the Egyptian jurist ʿAbd Allāh b. Lahīʿa (in office 155–64/771 or 772–780 or 781) to the judgeship in spite of what he called "the inferiority of his doctrine (*sūʾ madhhabih*)," which could be a reference either to Ibn Lahīʿa's alleged Shiʿism or to his legal opinions. The caliph was thus willing to overlook his own objections to the appointee in order to name a judge for the Egyptians from among themselves.

A decade later, the new caliph, al-Mahdī (r. 158–69/775–85), took a different course. He deposed Ibn Lahīʿa and appointed the first Ḥanafī jurist, the Iraqi Ismāʿīl b. al-Yasaʿ al-Kindī (in office 164–67/781–83), as judge of Egypt. It is possible that al-Mahdī deliberately selected a member of the Kinda tribe, given that the Kinda were also prominent among Egyptian Arabs and Ismāʿīl's tribal affiliation might therefore have aided his acceptance by the Egyptians. However, the legal innovations introduced by the Kufan quickly overshadowed his genealogy and his personal qualities, which the Egyptians did not hesitate to praise. The most dramatic of these innovations was the abolition of religious endowments, a measure that was in accordance with Ismāʿīl's Ḥanafī doctrine[59] but that contradicted that of the Egyptian Mālikīs. According to al-Kindī, the measure "weighed heavily on the Egyptians and led them to hate him."[60] Eventually, al-Layth b. Saʿd wrote a letter to al-Mahdī, complaining about

[58] The visit is reported in al-Kindī, *Governors and Judges*, 368–69.

[59] This action was based squarely on the opinion of Abū Ḥanīfa and the first opinion of Abū Yūsuf, which allowed permanent endowments to be established only for the benefit of mosques; see al-Sarakhsī, *Mabsūṭ*, 12:26.

[60] Al-Kindī, *Governors and Judges*, 371. The founding deed of a mosque endowment reproduced by al-Kindī indicates that according to the dominant teaching in Egypt the basic conditions for the establishment of an endowment were simply that it would yield benefit for the Muslims and would not harm anyone ("manfaʿa li-l-muslimīn … wa-anna dhālika laysa bi-ḍarar ʿalā aḥad"). While the dearth of sources prevents a clear picture of the institutions financed by endowments, the low requirements for justifying their establishment and the severity of the Egyptians' reported response to their abolition suggest that already at this time endowments played an important role in the provision of a range of public services.

the abolition of endowments. This letter seems to have at least contributed to the replacement of the judge.[61]

For the next decade, the caliphs al-Mahdī, al-Hādī (r. 169–70/785–86), and Hārūn al-Rashīd appointed Mālikīs as judges for Egypt; two of the appointees were native Egyptians and the third, a Medinan, had studied in Egypt.[62] Toward the end of his reign, however, Hārūn al-Rashīd selected another Iraqi Ḥanafī, the already mentioned Ibn Masrūq, for the post. A possible reason for this was the fact that Abū Yūsuf, the judge of Baghdad and one of the principal students of Abū Ḥanīfa, exercised increasing influence over caliphal appointments in the provinces under Hārūn.[63] Ibn Masrūq's tenure proved as alienating to the local population as that of his Ḥanafī predecessor Ismā'īl b. al-Yasa'. Al-Kindī describes his measures as harsh and insensitive to the locals; he traded insults with them and quickly lost their trust.[64] His allegiance to Ḥanafī doctrine played a part in these problems as it had in the case of Ismā'īl. For example, the Egyptian/Medinan Mālikī teaching did not permit non-Muslims[65] to enter mosques on the basis of purity rules.[66] Therefore, Egyptian judges would adjudicate cases involving Christians and Jews either just outside the mosque or in the judges' own homes.[67] As a follower of Abū Ḥanīfa, however, Ibn Masrūq saw no legal obstacle to admitting non-Muslims into the central mosque of Fustat to attend his court sessions.[68] While this shift did not affect tangible economic interests, as had Ismā'īl b. al-Yasa''s abolition of endowments, it nevertheless posed a symbolic challenge to Egyptian Muslim identity because of the centrality of the mosque

[61] Al-Kindī, *Governors and Judges*, 371–72.

[62] Ghawth b. Sulaymān (three terms in office; d. 168/785) and Mufaḍḍal b. Faḍāla were Egyptians; 'Abd al-Malik b. Muḥammad al-Ḥazmī (in office 170–74/786–90) was a Medinan who had studied with Ibn Wahb in Egypt. See Ibn Ḥajar, *Raf' al-iṣr*, 2:372.

[63] Ibn 'Abd al-Barr, *Intiqā'*, 331; al-Maqrīzī, *Khiṭaṭ*, 2:333.

[64] Al-Kindī, *Governors and Judges*, 388–91.

[65] Al-Kindī mentions only Christians; *Governors and Judges*, 294. This probably reflects the fact that Christians constituted the vast majority of non-Muslims in Egypt; in addition, the Jews possessed their own religious law and legal institutions that sought to discourage Jews from taking recourse in other legal systems, thus giving them little reason to enter the mosque. Nevertheless, as al-Kindī reports (*Governors and Judges*, 351), Jews did on occasion call upon Muslim courts.

[66] For the Mālikī position, see Saḥnūn, *Mudawwana*, 3:107 (Kitāb al-li'ān).

[67] Al-Kindī, *Governors and Judges*, 391.

[68] For the Ḥanafī position, see al-Sarakhsī, *Mabsūṭ*, 1:48. The difference stems from divergent interpretations of the Quranic description of the unbelievers as impure (9:28). While for Mālikīs this impurity is physical because non-Muslims do not adhere to Muslim purity laws, Ḥanafīs and Shāfi'īs interpret it to refer to incorrect belief and thus not to constitute an impediment to entrance into a mosque.

in Muslim life as the community's public space par excellence: the central mosque was where all male members of the community congregated every week, where Islam was taught and Islamic normativity put into practice through the decisions of the judge.[69] By inviting non-Muslims into the mosque, Ibn Masrūq breached the exclusivity of the primary communal and ritual space, contributing to the Arabs' sense that the ethnic and religious boundaries that had defined their status and guaranteed their prestige since the Islamic conquest of Egypt were being eroded. The centralizing Abbasid state's instrumental logic of effective administration, supported by Ḥanafī legal doctrine, thus conflicted with and pushed back these boundaries on multiple fronts: through the meritocratic inclusion of non-Arab clients in prominent positions, the gradual restriction of the Egyptians' legal autonomy, and the disregard of highly significant symbolic boundaries of Islamic identity.

It is no coincidence that the historian ʿAbd al-Raḥmān b. ʿAbd al-Ḥakam (d. 257/871) penned his history of the conquest of Egypt at precisely this time, when the once-proud society that the conquerors had founded stood on the brink of collapse. ʿAbd al-Raḥmān's history depicts the Arab conquerors as fearless but humble warriors, against whom the cowardly and internally divided leaders of Egypt, steeped in luxury, stood little chance. Describing the conquerors through the eyes of a Byzantine diplomat, he writes, "We saw them as people to whom death is more dear than life, and humbleness is more dear than nobility. None of them has a desire concerning the world, nor any greed. Rather, their seats are on the ground and their food is on their knees and their prince is one of them."[70] The bitter irony would not have escaped any contemporary reader: now it was the descendants of these noble Arabs whose power was fading as a result of internal divisions and a sedentary lifestyle that had alienated them from their ancestors' nomadic virtues.[71] ʿAbd al-Raḥmān's account was thus both a tribute to the glory of the Arab conquerors and an obituary for the social order that they had founded.

An important marker of distinction for the Arab aristocracy was the pension that they received in recognition of the role of their families in

[69] Baber Johansen, "The All-Embracing Town and Its Mosques: Al-Misr al-Jami," *Revue de l'Occident Musulman et de la Méditerranée* 12 (1981–82): 139–61.

[70] ʿAbd al-Raḥmān b. ʿAbd al-Ḥakam, *The History of the Conquest of Egypt, North Africa and Spain* (*Futūḥ Miṣr wa-akhbāruhā*), ed. Charles Torrey (New Haven, CT: Yale University Press, 1922); translation by Yasmin Hilloowala, "The History of the Conquest of Egypt" (PhD diss., University of Arizona, 1998), 46.

[71] I owe this insight to Jon Powell.

the conquest of Egypt and of their continuing service in the militia (*jund*), which held responsibility for maintaining internal peace in the province. It was thus a severe blow to the Arabs when, in the 180s/800s, the caliph dispatched a permanent contingent of Iraqi/Khurasanian troops to Egypt to secure order. The reason for this move lay in the ineffectiveness and unwillingness of the Egyptian Arab militia in quelling taxation-related revolts by Arab tribes in the delta.[72] The sidelining of the indigenous militia removed the principal justification for the payment of the pension, which was subsequently discontinued in 218/833, thus depriving the elite of both an important source of income and a major signifier of social status.

With the dismantling of local military capacity in favor of forces sent from the imperial center, the province became vulnerable to chaos with the outbreak of the Abbasid civil war between al-Amīn and al-Ma'mūn (r. 198–218/813–33) in 193/809. Taking advantage of the power vacuum in Egypt, a commander of the Abbasid troops in Egypt, al-Sarī b. al-Ḥakam (d. 205/820), seized control of Egypt from Fustat southward, while a man by the name of ʿAbd al-ʿAzīz al-Jarawī (d. 205/820) led an Arab tribal alliance to rule northern Egypt – a division that persisted even after the civil war in Iraq had come to an end. Egypt thus witnessed a decade of periodic warfare between the two factions that claimed the lives of many of the militarily and politically active sons of the old Arab aristocracy.[73] The aristocracy, though not eradicated, was decisively weakened by the loss of life, property, and stability that accompanied this period of upheaval. Its role in public life was curtailed further: though al-Sarī at first adopted the practice of appointing the *ṣāḥib al-shurṭa* from among the local aristocratic families, he later began to prefer members of his own family for this position.[74] For a while, the Arab elite continued to exert "soft power"[75] in Egyptian politics and society; on two occasions when Fustat was besieged during the period of unrest, the notables of the city (*ahl Miṣr*) and especially the learned and pious among them (*ahl al-masjid*) successfully petitioned al-Jarawī and his son to spare the city from attack.[76] But the Arab elite never recovered from the loss of

[72] Kennedy, "Egypt as Province," 80.
[73] Kennedy, "Egypt as Province," 81.
[74] Compare the first and second period of his reign; al-Kindī, *Governors and Judges*, 128 and 132.
[75] The term was coined by Joseph Nye to describe noncoercive power based on diplomacy and prestige; see Nye, *Bound to Lead: The Changing Nature of American Power* (New York: Basic Books, 1990).
[76] Al-Kindī, *Governors and Judges*, 170 and 173.

its political, military, and judicial power and autonomy. The extent to which the foundations of the old social system had been corroded will be demonstrated by the events that led to its final collapse, discussed in the next chapter.

AL-SHĀFIʿĪ IN EGYPT

It was at this juncture, with the Egyptian Arab community feeling increasingly threatened by non-Arab social mobility, aggressive Abbasid centralization, and the encroachment of Ḥanafī doctrines in the judicial realm, that al-Shāfiʿī arrived in Egypt. With his noble Qurashī lineage extending back to the Prophet's great-uncle al-Muṭṭalib, his impeccable scholarly credentials, and his illustrious reputation, al-Shāfiʿī made an immediate impression on the Egyptian scholarly scene and attracted many students. According to Zakariyyā al-Sājī (d. 307/919 or 920), al-Shāfiʿī's arrival in Egypt was hailed as the coming of "a jurist from the Quraysh," and many prominent Mālikīs rushed to visit him.[77] As seen in previous chapters, al-Shāfiʿī had studied not only in the Hejaz, where he had been a close student of Mālik, but also in Iraq, where he had read the works of the leading Ḥanafī scholar al-Shaybānī and engaged him in debate.[78] This experience must have held a particular attraction for the Mālikī Egyptians, since what we have of the Mālikī writings of this era suggests that their ability to defeat Ḥanafī arguments in debate must have been very limited.[79]

ʿAbd Allāh b. ʿAbd al-Ḥakam, the leader of the prominent client family of Banū ʿAbd al-Ḥakam and the main facilitator of al-Shāfiʿī's move to Egypt,[80] was aware of this Mālikī vulnerability vis-à-vis Ḥanafī teaching. He sent his son Muḥammad (d. 268/882) to study with al-Shāfiʿī in the hope that the latter's methodology would prove a potent tool in defense of Mālik. ʿAbd Allāh instructed his son to "keep the company of this man, because he knows many [different ways of deriving] legal proofs; for if you were to leave this country and say [as evidence in a

[77] Ibn ʿAbd al-Barr, *Intiqāʾ*, 77–78.

[78] Ibn Abī Ḥātim, *Ādāb al-Shāfiʿī*, 201–3.

[79] For a discussion of the Mālikī style of jurisprudence in this period, see Jonathan E. Brockopp, "Competing Theories of Authority in Early Mālikī Texts," in *Studies in Islamic Legal Theory*, ed. Bernard G. Weiss, 3–22 (Leiden: Brill, 2002), as well as his *Early Mālikī Law*.

[80] ʿAbd Allāh housed al-Shāfiʿī, supported him financially, acted as the implementer of his will, and even provided a plot for al-Shāfiʿī's grave. See Brockopp, *Early Mālikī Law*, 27–28, and al-Qāḍī ʿIyāḍ, *Tartīb al-madārik*, 3:195.

legal debate], 'Ibn al-Qāsim said [so],' you would be laughed at."[81] This statement contains two revealing elements: first, it reveals a provincialist lack of self-confidence, which generates a fear of being ridiculed; and second, it juxtaposes the character of the indigenous Egyptian teaching, which is justified by reference to authorities ("Ibn al-Qāsim said"), with al-Shāfiʿī's method, which consists of a skilled deployment of legal proofs. ʿAbd Allāh b. ʿAbd al-Ḥakam seems to have recognized the latter as a distinctive feature of al-Shāfiʿī's legal theory and to have been willing, even eager, to harness it to the advantage of Egyptian Mālikī teaching.

Al-Shāfiʿī appears to have been a popular lecturer. He is said to have drawn an audience of up to three hundred students and listeners at his gatherings, which were held at a specific arch in the central mosque of Fustat.[82] Al-Shāfiʿī's lectures were not only about law but also covered the Hadith sciences and poetry, thereby drawing a varied audience[83] that included many occasional listeners, such as the poet al-Ḥusayn b. ʿAbd al-Salām al-Jamal (d. 258/872),[84] the judicial secretary (*kātib*) Ibrāhīm b. Abī Ayyūb ʿĪsā al-Ṭaḥāwī (d. 259/872),[85] and the Mālikī scholar Yūsuf b. Yazīd al-Qarāṭīsī (d. 287/900),[86] who heard al-Shāfiʿī's lectures as a child. While most listeners were men, at least one woman – the sister of Ismāʿīl b. Yaḥyā al-Muzanī (d. 264/877), one of al-Shāfiʿī's principal students – is said to have attended al-Shāfiʿī's lessons.[87]

However, it was not long before al-Shāfiʿī's position as a defender of the embattled Mālikī doctrine began to be questioned by his primarily Mālikī students. The jurists who frequented al-Shāfiʿī's teaching circle, as well as the broader community of scholars, became aware that al-Shāfiʿī held many positions that did not agree with those of Mālik. This in itself was not particularly unusual: the current leader of the Mālikīs in Egypt, Ashhab, himself diverged from Mālik's positions on many – for some too

[81] Al-Qāḍī ʿIyāḍ, *Tartīb al-madārik*, 4:161. For a slightly different version of this quotation that mentions Ashhab instead of Ibn al-Qāsim, see Ibn Khallikān, *Wafayāt al-aʿyān wa-anbāʾ abnāʾ al-zamān*, ed. Iḥsān ʿAbbās, 8 vols. (Beirut: Dār Ṣādir, 1398/1978), 4:194. Ibn ʿAbd al-Barr, in *Intiqāʾ*, 113, also reports that Ibn ʿAbd al-Ḥakam encouraged his son to study with al-Shāfiʿī.

[82] Al-Dhahabī, *Siyar aʿlām al-nubalāʾ*, 12:60; Ibn ʿAsākir, *Tārīkh madīnat Dimashq*, ed. Muḥī al-Dīn al-ʿAmrawī, 70 vols. (Beirut: Dār al-Fikr, 1995–2001), 51:405.

[83] Abū Zakariyyā Muḥī al-Dīn al-Nawawī, *Tahdhīb al-asmāʾ wa-l-lughāt*, 4 vols. (Cairo: Idārat al-Ṭibāʿa al-Munīriyya, 1927), 1:61.

[84] Ibn Yūnus, *Tārīkh Ibn Yūnus al-Ṣadafī*, 1:130.

[85] Ibn Yūnus, *Tārīkh Ibn Yūnus al-Ṣadafī*, 1:26.

[86] Al-Dhahabī, *Siyar aʿlām al-nubalāʾ*, 10:85.

[87] Jalāl al-Dīn al-Suyūṭī, *Ḥusn al-muḥāḍara*, ed. Muḥammad Abū al-Faḍl Ibrāhīm, 2 vols. (Cairo: ʿĪsā al-Bābī al-Ḥalabī, 1967–68), 1:399.

many – points.[88] But in the heated and lively debates between al-Shāfiʿī and his students, al-Shāfiʿī developed much more than merely differing conclusions on individual points of law. As seen in Chapters 2 and 3, al-Shāfiʿī put forward a critique of Mālik's fundamental approach, especially the latter's reliance on the opaque concept of communal practice (*ʿamal*), and proposed a radically different alternative theory that was based on the canonization of the sacred sources of Quran and Hadith.

The reactions of Egyptian scholars to this realization varied. Some experienced a "conversion" from Mālikism (or, more rarely, Ḥanafism) to Shāfiʿism that resulted in the creation of a distinct Shāfiʿī scholarly identity.[89] The most prominent such scholars were al-Rabīʿ b. Sulaymān al-Murādī, a prayer caller (*muʾadhdhin*) who became the principal transmitter of al-Shāfiʿī's writings; Ismāʿīl b. Yaḥyā al-Muzanī, a former Ḥanafī and a distinguished jurist; Ḥarmala b. Yaḥyā (d. 243/858), a member of an influential family of local government officials;[90] and Abū Yaʿqūb al-Buwayṭī (d. 231/846), a Mālikī scholar who became one of al-Shāfiʿī's closest students and his first successor. Al-Buwayṭī described the origin of his attachment to al-Shāfiʿī as follows: "Al-Shāfiʿī came to Egypt and began to voice much criticism of Mālik. I [first] reproached him for it, [then] remained in a state of confusion. I prayed much and asked God in the hope that He might show me the truth. Then I saw in my dream that the truth was with al-Shāfiʿī."[91] This group of students acquired a reputation that was based on their identification with the doctrine of al-Shāfiʿī. They preserved and taught al-Shāfiʿī's works, wrote compendia of his teaching, and used these as well as al-Shāfiʿī's own writings to popularize his ideas. The development and diffusion of Shāfiʿī doctrine by al-Shāfiʿī's students are examined in detail in Chapters 6 and 7.

Another group of students remained largely faithful to Mālikī doctrine in terms of individual legal positions, but they were nonetheless deeply influenced by al-Shāfiʿī's legal methodology. The most important of these students was Muḥammad b. ʿAbd al-Ḥakam, whose account of al-Shāfiʿī's break with Mālik sets a very different emphasis from the report of al-Buwayṭī: "Al-Shāfiʿī continued to adhere to Mālik's opinions, disagreeing with him

[88] Abd-Allah, "Mālik's Concept of *ʿAmal*," 1:108.

[89] The earliest evidence of a distinct collective identity ascribed to al-Shāfiʿī's students is contained in a poem written by al-Ḥusayn b. ʿAbd al-Salām al-Jamal (d. 258/872) in the early 230s/mid-840s; the poem is quoted in Chap. 5 of this volume and further discussed in Chap. 7.

[90] Ibn Yūnus, *Tārīkh Ibn Yūnus al-Ṣadafī*, 1:112.

[91] Ibn al-Ṣalāḥ, *Ṭabaqāt al-fuqahāʾ al-shāfiʿiyya*, 2:682–83.

only to the extent that Mālik's other students did, until Fityān pressed him hard. This led him to compose [his work] against Mālik."[92] This narrative focuses on the reason for the break and explains it as the result of provocation by a zealous Mālikī adherent (Fityān b. Abī Samḥ, d. 232/846 or 847) rather than as the necessary outcome of profound differences between the doctrines of al-Shāfiʿī and Mālik. The persona of al-Shāfiʿī that appears in this and other reports from Muḥammad is that of a Mālikī dissenter, whom circumstances compelled to criticize Mālik publicly. Muḥammad also continued to acknowledge his intellectual debt to al-Shāfiʿī, claiming that "had it not been for al-Shāfiʿī, I would not have known legal theory. It was he who taught me legal analogy."[93] Furthermore, we know that Muḥammad continued to teach and transmit al-Shāfiʿī's works even while proclaiming his primary allegiance to Mālik, though he held such lessons only in his home and was criticized by his fellow Mālikīs for them.[94]

The third reaction to al-Shāfiʿī is exemplified by the majority of the senior Mālikī scholars of Egypt, particularly Fityān b. Abī Samḥ, Ashhab, and ʿĪsā b. al-Munkadir (d. after 215/830). In the course of an impassioned debate between Fityān and al-Shāfiʿī, the former appears to have uttered something (the content of the exclamation is not preserved) that could have been construed as an insult to the Prophet Muḥammad. When word of Fityān's statement reached al-Sarī b. al-Ḥakam, he sentenced Fityān to public whipping as punishment for the affront to the Prophet. This incident, involving as it did a prominent and respected member of the Egyptian elite, led to a violent public outburst against al-Shāfiʿī, who was subsequently attacked by a mob and thereafter confined to his house until his death – for how long is not known.[95] That the incident did not simply reflect a personal conflict between al-Shāfiʿī and Fityān is indicated by the fact that both Ashhab and ʿĪsā b. al-Munkadir are reported to have prayed in public for al-Shāfiʿī's death.[96] ʿĪsā is quoted as having said to al-Shāfiʿī, "O you nothing (*yā kadhā*), when you came to our country, we were united and our doctrine was one; but then you sowed division and spread evil, so may God separate your body and soul!"[97]

[92] Al-Qāḍī ʿIyāḍ, *Tartīb al-madārik*, 3:179. The work referred to is al-Shāfiʿī's *Ikhtilāf Mālik*, discussed in detail in Chaps. 2 and 3 of this volume.
[93] Al-Qāḍī ʿIyāḍ, *Tartīb al-madārik*, 3:180.
[94] Ibn ʿAsākir, *Tārīkh madīnat Dimashq*, 53:362.
[95] Al-Qāḍī ʿIyāḍ, *Tartīb al-madārik*, 3:279–80. It is not clear whether al-Shāfiʿī's confinement was the result of injuries sustained in the attack, or whether it was caused by voluntary or involuntary house arrest.
[96] For Ashhab, see al-Qāḍī ʿIyāḍ, *Tartīb al-madārik*, 3:270.
[97] Al-Kindī, *Governors and Judges*, 438.

In spite of the pronounced animosity of many of the most prominent Egyptian scholars for al-Shāfiʿī, his students nonetheless succeeded in establishing themselves in Egypt and in attracting a growing number of students, leading to the first "golden age" of Shāfiʿism a mere half-century after al-Shāfiʿī's death. The reasons for their success are rooted in the radical transformations of the second/eighth century. As seen previously, the closely linked Medinan and Egyptian normative systems that were based on communal practice relied on a vision of the community as inextricably connected to the revelatory past through an unbroken succession of scholars and other transmitters that spanned the distance to the prophetic age. While this worldview may still have appeared natural for Egyptian Muslims who came of age in the first half of the second Hijri century, the subsequent social upheaval and military conflict, the trauma that was caused by the disruption of social patterns and hierarchies, and the decisive undermining of the political and economic foundations of the Arab aristocracy's position represented grave challenges to a vision predicated on continuity. In the state of flux that characterized Egyptian society and politics at the end of the second Hijri century, a stable communal identity could hardly be preserved. Given the close connection between community and normativity in Egyptian religious thought, the very basis of the Egyptians' normative understanding was thus under threat. Against this background, al-Shāfiʿī's innovative theory, based on the canonization of the sacred sources, offered the possibility of deriving normative values directly from the sources without recourse to the increasingly fictitious notion of a continuous communal practice.

It is likely that the increasing prominence of clients was also a factor in facilitating adoption of al-Shāfiʿī's ideas in Egypt. Many, though not all, of al-Shāfiʿī's students were of client background, most notably al-Rabīʿ, Muḥammad b. ʿAbd al-Ḥakam, Ḥarmala, and Yūnus b. ʿAbd al-Aʿlā (d. 264/877 or 878). Although clients possessed an adopted Arab genealogy by virtue of their association with an established tribe, their status within the social hierarchy, as noted earlier, remained distinct. As a consequence, the clients' self-image was not as closely wedded to the Mālikī notion of a continuous normative communal tradition, and they would thus have been more open to the merits of al-Shāfiʿī's textualist approach, which, in effect, leveled the playing field between Arabs and non-Arabs. In al-Shāfiʿī's system, access to revelation did not require membership in a particular tradition but could be secured simply by consulting the authoritative sources, and the correct understanding of these sources was based first and foremost on mastery of the Arabic language – an asset that, unlike a genuinely Arab genealogy, could be acquired.[98]

The stringent rejectionism of al-Shāfiʿī maintained by the Mālikī old guard was extinguished with the deaths of its last proponents. The new generation of Egyptian scholars, whose lives had been profoundly shaped by the events of the past decades, viewed al-Shāfiʿī's theory from a different perspective, and they showed its influence in their work whether or not they became part of the school that grew around it after al-Shāfiʿī's death. Understanding the dynamics that led to the establishment of this school during the third/ninth century and its eventual replacement of Mālikism as the predominant intellectual discourse in Egypt requires an appreciation of the significant impact of political and social shifts on legal scholarship in the century that followed al-Shāfiʿī's death. This forms the subject of the following chapter.

[98] Here I differ with Joseph Lowry's claim that al-Shāfiʿī's argument for the primacy of the Arabic language seeks to justify the "divinely sanctioned ethno-linguistic superiority" of the Arabs (Lowry, *Early Islamic Legal Theory*, 294–96). Al-Shāfiʿī's argument, made in the context of a discussion on the language of revelation, is that (a) languages are mutually incomprehensible; (b) consequently, one language must be dominant in revelation; and (c) in the case of Islam, this language is the language of its Prophet, that is, Arabic (*Risāla*, in *Umm*, 1:19, paras. 152–54). In fact, immediately prior to this argument, al-Shāfiʿī stresses that non-Arabs can become linguistically Arab (*min ahl lisānihā*), as long as they learn the language directly from native speakers (*Risāla*, in *Umm*, 1:17–18, paras. 143 and 147).

Chapter 5

Scholarship between Persecution and Patronage

The preceding chapter showed that the social and political transformations affecting Egypt in the beginning of the third/ninth century produced receptive conditions for al-Shāfiʿī's innovative theorization of the law, which entailed the abandonment of the ideal of normative communal practice. It is tempting to speculate that had al-Shāfiʿī developed his theory a mere few decades earlier, it would have found little resonance in the rigidly stratified and culturally conservative Arab society of Fustat. The increasing social mobility and heterogeneity that served to undermine the foundations of this society's self-understanding created an opening for the novel conception of religious and legal legitimacy proposed by al-Shāfiʿī.

However, for this new theory to spread beyond al-Shāfiʿī and his immediate disciples, it had to find its way into the broader scholarly discourse of the time through teaching and textual transmission. As seen at the end of the previous chapter, al-Shāfiʿī had – in spite of his notable standing and his initial popularity among the Mālikīs – formidable enemies in Egypt, who correctly perceived the challenge that his theory posed to the old normative order. Shāfiʿism at the end of the second/eighth century was decidedly an underdog: a doctrine that had gained several committed adherents but that lacked the backing provided by an established locus of power. Unlike Mālikism, which was firmly entrenched among the indigenous ruling elite, or Ḥanafism, which enjoyed the vigorous support of the imperial administration, Shāfiʿī teaching was initially carried forward by individuals who often possessed considerable personal status but did not represent an independent social constituency. That al-Shāfiʿī's students were nonetheless able to propagate their master's thought and writings with such success, achieving their diffusion throughout the Islamic world within a single generation, can be explained only with reference to the shifting currents of political patronage for religious learning in third-/ninth-century Egypt.

This chapter identifies the major trends of persecution, tolerance, and endorsement that shaped the trajectory of early Shāfiʿī sholarship; analyzes their causes; and traces their impact on the lives and activities of al-Shāfiʿī's students. In particular, it focuses on two central events in the early history of Shāfiʿism: the Quranic Inquisition of the early third/mid-ninth century and the reign of the Tulunid dynasty in Egypt (254–92/868–905). Though the paucity of sources from this period renders the following account necessarily sketchy, combining information from historical chronicles and biographical dictionaries with the available data regarding the historical transmission of Shāfiʿī works permits the construction of a coherent narrative that connects the sociopolitical history of Egypt and the history of Shāfiʿī scholarship over the third/ninth century. This narrative shows that the social "rootlessness" of Shāfiʿism as a new and still-marginal intellectual doctrine was a crucial factor both in its long suppression during and after the Inquisition and in its subsequent rise to prominence under the Tulunids.

At al-Shāfiʿī's death in 204/820, deep divisions surfaced among his closest students.[1] The immediate issue was the question of who was to succeed al-Shāfiʿī – both physically, as the occupant of the particular space in the central mosque of Fustat where al-Shāfiʿī had convened his teaching circle, and intellectually and symbolically, as the primary teacher and interpreter of the master's ideas. The principal contenders for leadership of al-Shāfiʿī's circle were Abū Bakr al-Ḥumaydī (d. 219/834), Muḥammad b. ʿAbd al-Ḥakam, and Abū Yaʿqūb al-Buwayṭī. The Meccan al-Ḥumaydī, a proficient Hadith scholar, had become a disciple of al-Shāfiʿī already in Mecca[2] and could thus claim seniority among his Egyptian students. Muḥammad, as seen in the previous chapter, was a scion of the prominent Mālikī client family of Banū ʿAbd al-Ḥakam and the son of al-Shāfiʿī's principal sponsor in Egypt. Al-Buwayṭī was, like Muḥammad, a former Mālikī with close links to the indigenous elite, and, like al-Ḥumaydī, he could boast of

[1] Some reports suggest that the succession struggle had already begun while al-Shāfiʿī was on his deathbed; see Ibn ʿAsākir, *Tārīkh madīnat Dimashq*, 53:359.

[2] See, for example, Tāj al-Dīn al-Subkī, *Ṭabaqāt al-shāfiʿiyya al-kubrā*, ed. Maḥmūd Muḥammad al-Ṭanāḥī and ʿAbd al-Fattāḥ Muḥammad al-Ḥulw, 10 vols. (Cairo: ʿĪsā al-Bābī al-Ḥalabī, 1964–76; repr., Cairo: Dār Iḥyāʾ al-Kutub al-ʿArabiyya, 1413/1992 or 1993), 2:140.

a Qurashī Arab heritage[3] and tended to grant Hadith a central role in his legal reasoning.[4] It appears that al-Ḥumaydī made an initial bid for the leadership, but this was countered by Muḥammad, who is reported to have formed an alliance against him (*taʿaṣṣaba ʿalayh*),[5] possibly using his local stature to marginalize the foreigner al-Ḥumaydī. In response, al-Ḥumaydī threw his support behind al-Buwayṭī. Ibn Khuzayma (d. 311/923), the famous Hadith scholar who studied with al-Shāfiʿī's students al-Rabīʿ and al-Muzanī, transmitted this account of the succession struggle by Abū Jaʿfar al-Sukkarī (d. unknown), a friend of al-Rabīʿ:

> Muḥammad b. ʿAbd al-Ḥakam contested al-Buwayṭī regarding al-Shāfiʿī's place [of teaching in the mosque]. Al-Buwayṭī said, "I have more right to it than you," and Ibn ʿAbd al-Ḥakam said, "I have more right to his place than you." Al-Ḥumaydī, who was in Egypt at the time, intervened and claimed that al-Shāfiʿī had said, "No one has more right to my place than Yūsuf b. Yaḥyā al-Buwayṭī, and none of my companions is more knowledgeable than him." Muḥammad b. ʿAbd Allāh b. ʿAbd al-Ḥakam said, "You are lying." He replied, "No; you are lying, and your father is lying, and your mother is lying." Ibn ʿAbd al-Ḥakam became angry, and moved further and sat at the third arch [of the mosque], leaving an arch between the place of al-Shāfiʿī and his own place. Al-Buwayṭī then sat in al-Shāfiʿī's place.[6]

Al-Buwayṭī thus prevailed and took over the leadership of al-Shāfiʿī's teaching circle, which was subsequently described by al-Rabīʿ as the largest gathering in the central mosque.[7] Relatively little information is available on al-Buwayṭī's career during the next quarter-century. Though he continued to give lessons in the central mosque, there is no explicit evidence that he transmitted al-Shāfiʿī's writings to other scholars – with the exception of al-Rabīʿ, who acknowledged having received parts of al-Shāfiʿī's *Umm*, which he compiled, from al-Buwayṭī (see Chapter 6). Rather, al-Buwayṭī taught his own compendium (*Mukhtaṣar*) of al-Shāfiʿī's work. According to some reports, he had authored this text already before al-Shāfiʿī's death;[8]

3 For al-Buwayṭī's Arab ancestry, see Ibn Yūnus, *Tārīkh Ibn Yūnus al-Ṣadafī*, 1:524, and Abū ʿĪsā al-Tirmidhī, *al-Jāmiʿ al-ṣaḥīḥ* [*al-Sunan*], ed. Aḥmad Muḥammad Shākir, Muḥammad Fuʾād ʿAbd al-Bāqī, and Ibrāhīm ʿAṭwa ʿAwaḍ, 5 vols. (Cairo: Muṣṭafā al-Bābī al-Ḥalabī, 1937–62), 5:693.

4 See El Shamsy, "First Shāfiʿī," and Chap. 7 of this volume.

5 Al-Dhahabī, *Tadhkirat al-ḥuffāẓ*, ed. Zakariyyā ʿUmayrāt, 5 vols. (Beirut: Dār al-Kutub al-ʿIlmiyya, 1998), 2:3; al-Dhahabī, *Siyar aʿlām al-nubalāʾ*, 10:619.

6 Ibn ʿAsākir, *Tārīkh madīnat Dimashq*, 53:358; see also al-Dhahabī, *Siyar aʿlām al-nubalāʾ*, 12:60.

7 Ibn ʿAsākir, *Tārīkh madīnat Dimashq*, 53:359.

8 The Egyptian Mālikī judge Ibn Abī Maṭar (d. 339/950 or 951) claimed that al-Buwayṭī had composed his work already during al-Shāfiʿī's lifetime; see Ibn al-Ṣalāḥ, *Ṭabaqāt al-fuqahāʾ al-shāfiʿiyya*, 2:684.

it certainly appears to have been completed by 220/835, when he taught it during a visit to Baghdad.[9] We also know that al-Buwayṭī was a prominent figure in the Egyptian legal community, with the governor and ordinary people alike consulting him on matters of law.[10] However, the doctrine that he represented – Shāfiʿism – initially remained marginal in comparison with the two primary competitors on the intellectual stage of Egypt, Mālikism and Ḥanafism. The fierce rivalry between these two schools profoundly shaped the tumultuous century that followed al-Shāfiʿī's death.

MĀLIKISM VERSUS ḤANAFISM

For the first century of Abbasid rule, the judicial governance of Egypt had relied on a fine balance between the autonomy claims of the powerful local elite and the requirement of allegiance to the Abbasid state. As long as the Egyptian elite had retained the capacity to guarantee both the security and the loyalty of the province, this balance had safeguarded indigenous Mālikī legal practice against the encroachment of Ḥanafī policies promoted by centrally appointed Abbasid officials. However, the military, political, and economic decline of the Egyptian aristocracy over the course of the second/eighth century undermined the basis of the old accommodation between local and external legal institutions, creating a vacuum of legal legitimacy in Egypt.

The ensuing conflict between two sources of legal authority – recognition by the community, on the one hand; sanction by the state, on the other – is illustrated by the judicial instability that characterized the first decade of the third Hijri century, when Fustat and southern Egypt were under the control of the renegade Abbasid commander al-Sarī b. al-Ḥakam and subsequently his sons Abū al-Naṣr (r. 205–6/820–22) and ʿUbayd Allāh (r. 206–11/822–26). Exercising what was generally a caliphal prerogative, al-Sarī and his sons appointed the chief judge of Egypt directly during their reign. Al-Sarī's first appointee in 204/820 was the Mālikī Ibrāhīm b. Isḥāq al-Qārī (in office until 205/820), who was selected in consultation with local notables

[9] Al-Buwayṭī is reported to have visited Aḥmad b. Ḥanbal in prison. This would mean that he would have been in Baghdad between 218 and 220 (833 and 835); see Ibn al-Ṣalāḥ, *Ṭabaqāt al-fuqahāʾ al-shāfiʿiyya*, 2:684. Aḥmad's student Abū Bakr al-Athram describes a session in which al-Buwayṭī taught the compendium, and it is probable that the session took place during this visit to Baghdad; ibid., 2:681–82.

[10] Ibn ʿAsākir, *Tārīkh madīnat Dimashq*, 53:359; al-Kindī, *Governors and Judges*, 434–35.

(*ahl al-balad*).[11] However, six months into his tenure, al-Qārī refused to consider al-Sarī's intercession for a defendant, prompting al-Sarī to remove him from office.[12]

Al-Sarī replaced al-Qārī with Ibrāhīm b. al-Jarrāḥ (in office 205–11/820–26), whose background was very different. Ibn al-Jarrāḥ was a Ḥanafī rather than a Mālikī; originally from Merv in Central Asia, he had studied in Iraq and was a strong believer in the createdness of the Quran. This controversial doctrine, which had obscure origins in rationalist theology, postulated that the Quran had been created by God along with all other elements of His creation.[13] The doctrine appears to have become a religiocultural litmus test in the last decades of the second/eighth century, when the rationalist reconceptionalization of Islam proposed by the theologians provoked vehement opposition among sections of the scholarly class. Subsequently, rationalist theological ideas, of which the createdness doctrine was emblematic, became deeply divisive. Given the marginality of rationalism in Egypt at the time, the doctrine was regarded with deep hostility in mainstream Muslim discourse;[14] indeed, proponents of related theological propositions had previously been excluded from serving as court witnesses on account of their perceived deviance.[15]

It is noteworthy that Ibn al-Jarrāḥ appears to have made a deliberate effort to acknowledge the legitimacy of Mālikī positions in his legal reasoning. According to his secretary, his method of recording a legal ruling (*sijill*) consisted of writing a list enumerating the positions of Abū Ḥanīfa, Ibn Abī Laylā, Abū Yūsuf, and Mālik on the issue, and then making a mark after the position that he personally supported.[16] Ibn al-Jarrāḥ thus included, at least nominally, Mālik's opinions on an equal basis alongside those of the three Ḥanafī authorities. (Al-Shāfiʿī's opinions were clearly not influential enough to be considered.) Nonetheless, the Egyptians' reaction to the new judge was hostile. When Ibn al-Jarrāḥ had his prayer mat placed in the central mosque of Fustat, the locals threw it out onto the

[11] Wakīʿ, *Akhbār al-quḍāt*, 3:239; Ibn Ḥajar, *Rafʿ al-iṣr*, 1:21–22.

[12] Al-Kindī, *Governors and Judges*, 427.

[13] Opponents of this doctrine did not generally argue that the Quran was eternal instead; rather, they insisted on refraining from speculation regarding the nature of the Quran. For more on this controversy, see Wilferd Madelung, "The Origins of the Controversy Concerning the Creation of the Koran," in *Orientalia Hispanica*, vol. 1, ed. J. M. Barral, 504–25 (Leiden: E. J. Brill, 1974).

[14] Note Ḥarmala's shocked reaction to Ibn al-Jarrāḥ's creed and the stigma it created for those associated with Ibn al-Jarrāḥ; al-Kindī, *Governors and Judges*, 429.

[15] Al-Kindī, *Governors and Judges*, 422.

[16] Al-Kindī, *Governors and Judges*, 432.

street. Subsequently, Ibn al-Jarrāḥ never returned to the central mosque and held his court sessions in his home.[17]

Al-Sarī thus faced a dilemma of legitimacy. His first appointee was chosen by consulting local notables, thus endowing the selected judge with a strong sense of independence from al-Sarī, which was incompatible with the latter's desire to exert influence in the judicial realm. With his second appointment he avoided the input of the local community by selecting an outsider who adhered to a foreign doctrine. This, however, caused the appointee to be rejected by the indigenous population.

The same challenge confronted the Abbasid general ʿAbd Allāh b. Ṭāhir, who finally brought Egypt back under direct imperial control in 211/826. He dismissed Ibn al-Jarrāḥ and, as al-Sarī had initially done, invited the Egyptian notables to advise him on the appointment of the next judge. One of these notables was Abū Yaʿqūb al-Buwayṭī, who resolved what appears to have been a gridlocked debate by presenting Ibn Ṭāhir with a short list of six candidates for the position.[18] That al-Buwayṭī was present at the gathering, and that Ibn Ṭāhir accepted his suggestion, indicate his status in Egypt at this time.

What is even more interesting, however, is what al-Buwayṭī's choice of jurists to recommend reveals both about the balance between the Mālikīs and the Ḥanafīs and about the complex interconnections among the rival legal schools. Three of the jurists on al-Buwayṭī's list were Mālikīs, indicating the sustained stature of Mālikī teaching in Egypt in spite of the declining fortunes of its adherents. These three were ʿAbd Allāh b. ʿAbd al-Ḥakam, the friend of al-Shāfiʿī and father of Muḥammad b. ʿAbd al-Ḥakam; Saʿīd b. Hāshim b. Ṣāliḥ al-Fayyūmī (d. 214/829 or 830), a client of the clan of Makhzūm;[19] and ʿĪsā b. al-Munkadir, who had accused al-Shāfiʿī of sowing dissent among the Egyptians.[20] Remarkably, however, the remaining three candidates appear to have been Ḥanafīs. They included a man by the name of Jaʿfar b. Hārūn al-Kūfī (d. unknown), whose Kufan appellation indicates that he was an Iraqi and consequently most probably a Ḥanafī, and two unnamed sons of Maʿbad b. Shaddād (d. unknown). One of these must have been ʿAlī b. Maʿbad b. Shaddād (d. 218/833), a Ḥanafī scholar who had been a student of al-Shaybānī at the court of Ḥārūn al-Rashīd, transmitted al-Shaybānī's *al-Jāmiʿ al-kabīr*

[17] Al-Kindī, *Governors and Judges*, 428.
[18] Al-Kindī, *Governors and Judges*, 434–35.
[19] Al-Dhahabī, *Tārīkh al-islām wa-wafayāt al-mashāhīr wa-l-aʿlām*, ed. ʿUmar ʿAbd al-Salām Tadmurī, 52 vols. (Beirut: Dār al-Kitāb al-ʿArabī, 1987), 15:175.
[20] Al-Kindī, *Governors and Judges*, 438.

and *al-Jāmiʿ al-ṣaghīr*, and later studied with al-Shāfiʿī in Egypt.[21] Nothing is known about Maʿbad b. Shaddād's other son, but he is likely to have been a Ḥanafī like his brother.

Al-Buwayṭī's inclusion of three Ḥanafīs on his short list seems surprising. However, part of an explanation is suggested by the fact that ʿAlī b. Maʿbad, the only one of the three about whom I have found detailed information, was a Hadith scholar (*muḥaddith*). He had studied not only with al-Shāfiʿī but also with al-Shāfiʿī's teacher Ibn ʿUyayna as well as with al-Layth b. Saʿd and the Mālikī Ibn Wahb, and he is known to have taught Abū Ḥātim al-Rāzī (d. 277/890), Abū ʿUbayd al-Qāsim b. Sallām (d. probably 224/838 or 839), Isḥāq al-Kawsaj (d. 251/865 or 866), and Yaḥyā b. Maʿīn (d. 233/847).[22] ʿAlī was thus intimately integrated into a network of prominent *muḥaddithūn* with close links to al-Shāfiʿī and Mālik. This strongly suggests that in spite of his Ḥanafī legal affiliation, he did not subscribe to rationalist theological tenets such as the createdness of the Quran that made many Ḥanafīs so suspect to Egyptian Mālikīs. Al-Buwayṭī's list thus indicates that the divisions between the legal schools at this time, though real and often acrimonious, were not absolute. Rather, they interacted with a complex web of multiple and overlapping identities that were defined not only by legal affiliation but also by theological stance and disciplinary orientation (particularly commitment to Hadith). The apparent acceptance of the theologically and methodologically Hadith-oriented Ḥanafī ʿAlī b. Maʿbad contrasts vividly with the opprobrium heaped on Abū ʿAbd al-Raḥmān al-Shāfiʿī (d. after 230/845). The latter, though a prominent student of al-Shāfiʿī in Baghdad, came to be considered deviant and an embarrassment to his fellow Shāfiʿīs because of his adherence to Muʿtazilī doctrines and his active participation in the Inquisition.[23]

Ibn Ṭāhir selected ʿĪsā b. al-Munkadir for the judgeship, and the latter in turn appointed ʿAbd Allāh b. ʿAbd al-Ḥakam his witness examiner (*ṣāḥib al-masāʾil*). It could be assumed that this appointment of a Mālikī judge implied a restrengthening of the old Arab aristocratic order. This, however, was not the case. The evidence available to us regarding Ibn al-Munkadir's two-year term in office suggests that he maintained order not primarily through an established court system but rather

[21] Ibn Abī al-Wafāʾ, *Jawāhir al-muḍiyya*, 2:614–16; al-Kindī, *Governors and Judges*, 442–43; al-Dhahabī, *Siyar aʿlām al-nubalāʾ*, 10:631–32.

[22] Al-Dhahabī, *Siyar aʿlām al-nubalāʾ*, 10:631.

[23] Ibn ʿAsākir, *Tārīkh madīnat Dimashq*, 51:358, quoting Abū Dāwūd al-Sijistānī (d. 275/889). On Abū ʿAbd al-Raḥmān, see van Ess, *Theologie und Gesellschaft*, 3:292–95.

via an informal group dedicated to enforcing public morality (*ṭāʾifa … yaʾmurūna bi-l-maʿrūf wa-yanhawna ʿan al-munkar*).[24] Ibn al-Munkadir's vigilantist approach was likely a pietistic reaction to the lawlessness of the civil war period, and it was marked by an egalitarian streak that contrasted sharply with the rigid social divisions maintained by the old elite. Weavers, peddlers, and other individuals of low social standing were admitted to serve as court witnesses under Ibn al-Munkadir and Ibn ʿAbd al-Ḥakam, sparking an angry tirade from a member of the Egyptian Arab aristocracy directed at the latter: "O son of ʿAbd al-Ḥakam, this was a closed matter, and you ripped it open and brought in as witnesses those who do not deserve it." To which ʿAbd Allāh answered, "This matter is part of religion, and I am only doing my duty."[25]

It is understandable that the central Abbasid administration did not look favorably on Ibn al-Munkadir's and Ibn ʿAbd al-Ḥakam's autonomous strategy. When in 214/829 the caliph al-Maʾmūn named his brother Abū Isḥāq (who later became the caliph al-Muʿtaṣim, r. 218–27/833–42) the governor of Egypt, Ibn al-Munkadir attempted to assert his group's independence by calling for Abū Isḥāq's dismissal. The request landed both him and Ibn ʿAbd al-Ḥakam in prison.[26] Subsequently, the pendulum swung once more in the direction of Ḥanafism: for the next three years, the interim judge of Egypt was a Ḥanafī by the name of Muḥammad b. ʿAbbād b. Muknif (d. unknown).[27] In the meantime, al-Maʾmūn attempted to fill the post permanently by appointing ʿAlī b. Maʿbad b. Shaddād, but the latter declined to accept the appointment. This indicates that the Abbasids continued to face the dilemma that had already plagued al-Sarī b. ʿAbd al-Ḥakam: naming a judge who was sufficiently qualified and locally accepted, but also willing to serve as a loyal agent of the state.

The deadlock was temporarily resolved by the appointment of Hārūn b. ʿAbd Allāh al-Zuhrī (in office 217–26/832–40), who originated from Medina and adhered to Mālik's teaching. Hārūn appears to have enjoyed local popularity (possibly due to his Mālikī affiliation) and might consequently have been able to reestablish judicial continuity in Egypt,

[24] Al-Kindī, *Governors and Judges*, 440. For a parallel phenomenon during the Abbasid civil war in Baghdad, see Ira M. Lapidus, "The Separation of State and Religion in the Development of Early Islamic Society," *International Journal of Middle East Studies* 6 (1975): 363–85, at 372–74.

[25] Al-Kindī, *Governors and Judges*, 436.

[26] Al-Kindī, *Governors and Judges*, 440–41. For an alternative interpretation of this episode, see Brockopp, *Early Mālikī Law*, 45–46.

[27] Al-Kindī, *Governors and Judges*, 441.

had it not been for al-Ma'mūn's last great project, which he initiated four months before his death in Rajab 218/August 833: the Quranic Inquisition (*miḥnat al-Qur'ān*).

THE QURANIC INQUISITION

The *miḥna*, which began in 218/833 and lasted until 234/849, was one of the defining episodes in the development of Sunni scholarship and self-consciousness. The theological doctrine whose public acceptance the Inquisition sought to enforce – namely, the createdness of the Quran – was itself of little consequence: beliefs regarding the nature of the Quran as either created or otherwise had no effect on how it was read and interpreted. Rather, the central struggle at the heart of the Inquisition took place between Sunni scholars and the Abbasid ruling apparatus regarding the question of who had the authority to decide such points of creed. While the causes, events, and consequences of the Inquisition as it unfolded in Iraq have been the subject of several studies,[28] the significant impact that it had on the intellectual history of Egypt has thus far been largely ignored.[29] The beginning of the Inquisition in Egypt can be located in a letter, preserved by al-Kindī, that the caliph al-Ma'mūn's brother and successor, Abū Isḥāq, sent to the governor of Egypt, Kaydur Naṣr b. ʿAbd Allāh (in office 217–19/832–34), on the caliph's behalf in Jumādā II 218 (June or July 833). In the letter, Abū Isḥāq informed the governor that he had written to the judges of the realm and instructed them to "test those who attend court to bear witness, and to accept only those who profess to the createdness of the Quran and who are trustworthy."[30] He ordered the governor to apply the same test to the judge himself and to relieve the latter of his office if he refused to endorse the proposition that the Quran was created. Furthermore, Abū Isḥāq commanded the governor to "forbid anyone who is consulted in matters of law among the *ahl al-ḥadīth* to teach or to issue legal opinions as long as he has not ascribed to this article of faith," adding that he had written

[28] See, for example, Walter M. Patton, *Aḥmed ibn Ḥanbal and the Miḥna: A Biography of the Imâm Including an Account of the Moḥammedan Inquisition Called the Miḥna, 218–234 A. H.* (Leiden: E. J. Brill, 1897); van Ess, *Theologie und Gesellschaft*, 3:446–508; and John Nawas, "A Reexamination of Three Current Explanations for al-Ma'mun's Introduction of the *Miḥna*," *International Journal of Middle East Studies* 26 (1994): 615–29.

[29] For a short account, see van Ess, *Theologie und Gesellschaft*, 3:477–79.

[30] Al-Kindī, *Governors and Judges*, 446.

to the judge and directed him, too, to enforce this rule.[31] A month after this letter was written, al-Maʾmūn died and Abū Isḥāq succeeded him as the caliph al-Muʿtaṣim.

At first glance, these orders appear severe: not only the judiciary, consisting of the judge and court witnesses, was to be subjected to the Inquisition, but also the broader realm of religious and legal scholarship. Consequently, jurists alongside court personnel were officially required to affirm their belief in the createdness doctrine. Most of them apparently did so, and those who did not are said to have fled, which may mean that they left the country or simply that they kept a low profile, ceased teaching, or went into hiding.[32] However, for most of the eight years that constituted al-Muʿtaṣim's reign as caliph and Hārūn b. ʿAbd Allāh's as judge of Egypt, the implementation of the Inquisition in Egypt remained relatively lenient. The historian Ibn Qudayd (d. 312/925) described this period as "easy," reporting that "people were not punished, whether they agreed or disagreed with [the createdness doctrine]."[33] There are no accounts from this period of penalties meted out for failing to affirm the doctrine. This laxness was probably due to a lack of political will on the part of al-Muʿtaṣim, as well as to Hārūn's reluctance to persecute Egyptian scholars – most of whom were, after all, fellow Mālikīs. While Hārūn's long term in office indicates that he must have given a public affirmation of the createdness doctrine, later Sunni authors did not consider him to have genuinely held this position.[34]

During the last months of al-Muʿtaṣim's life, however, the Inquisition in Egypt took a dramatic turn. In 225 or 226/839–41, an imperial decree ordered Hārūn to transport recalcitrant jurists to Iraq for questioning.[35] When Hārūn made clear his unwillingness to carry out this command, Ibn Abī Duwād, the imperial grand judge (in office probably 218–37/833–851 or 852), delegated the task to Muḥammad b. Abī al-Layth al-Aṣamm (d. 251/865 or 866), who shortly thereafter replaced Hārūn as judge of Egypt.

Ibn Abī al-Layth was a Ḥanafī jurist from Khwarazm in Central Asia and had worked as a copyist (*warrāq*) before going to Egypt in 205/820 or 821.[36] Put in control of implementing the Inquisition in the province,

[31] Al-Kindī, *Governors and Judges*, 447–48.
[32] Al-Kindī, *Governors and Judges*, 447 and 453.
[33] Al-Kindī, *Governors and Judges*, 451.
[34] Al-Kindī, *Governors and Judges*, 443–49.
[35] Al-Kindī, *Governors and Judges*, 447.
[36] Al-Kindī, *Governors and Judges*, 449.

Ibn Abī al-Layth set upon his task with ferocious zeal. According to al-Kindī, "it was as if a fire had been lit":

He left no jurist, traditionist (*muḥaddith*), caller to prayer (*mu'adhdhin*), or teacher (*mu'allim*) untested. Subsequently many people fled and the prisons were filled with those who had failed the Inquisition. Ibn Abī al-Layth ordered that the sentence, "There is no deity but God, Lord of the [created] Quran," be inscribed on the mosques, and it was written on the mosques of Fustat. And he prevented Mālikī and Shāfiʿī jurists from sitting in the mosque and even from approaching it.[37]

The first part of this account demonstrates the dramatic intensification of the Inquisition under Ibn Abī al-Layth's reign: religious leaders and scholars were systematically questioned, and harsh penalties were imposed on those who refused to profess allegiance to the createdness doctrine, which was furthermore etched into mosque walls as a visible reminder. However, the focus of the report then shifts from the theological realm to the suppression of Shāfiʿī and Mālikī legal teaching in mosques. It is true that the majority of Shāfiʿīs and Mālikīs rejected the createdness doctrine, and that these primarily legally defined groups thus also held distinct theological positions. But additional evidence reveals that Ibn Abī al-Layth's campaign had a legal dimension that was independent of the theological goal of the Inquisition, though carried out under its guise. A poem written at the time by al-Ḥusayn b. ʿAbd al-Salām al-Jamal (d. 258/872)[38] to honor Ibn Abī al-Layth paints a vivid picture of the latter's motivations. Addressing Ibn Abī al-Layth, the poet says,

You defended the rightly guided teaching of Abū Ḥanīfa,
Muḥammad [al-Shaybānī], the renowned Yūsufī,[39]
Ibn Abī Laylā, and the positions of their peer
Zufar, the master of analogy....[40]
And you smashed the teaching of al-Shāfiʿī and his followers (*wa-ṣaḥbih*),
And halted the spread of Ibn ʿUlayya's doctrine.
....
And the Mālikīs, having enjoyed widespread renown –
You extinguished their fame so that they are no longer remembered.
....
All of them now proclaim the createdness of the Quran.
You pilloried[41] them by means of a previously little-known doctrine,

[37] Al-Kindī, *Governors and Judges*, 451.
[38] Ibn Yūnus, *Tārīkh Ibn Yūnus al-Ṣadafī*, 1:130.
[39] I.e., Abū Yūsuf.
[40] All were prominent Ḥanafī scholars.
[41] Reading "shahhartahum" instead of "shahartahum."

And you were not content with mere utterances
But persisted until the mosques no longer denied its createdness.[42]

Al-Jamal's fame was primarily based on the composition of praise poetry for dignitaries such as the caliph al-Ma'mūn and ʿAbd Allāh b. Ṭāhir, and this poem is clearly intended as a similar work. It is thus remarkable that in addressing Ibn Abī al-Layth's achievements al-Jamal focuses on his defense of Ḥanafism and his persecution of other legal doctrines before mentioning the implementation of the theological position ostensibly at the heart of the purge. Furthermore, the reference to Ibn ʿUlayya is surprising, given that Ibn ʿUlayya is said to have been a proponent of the createdness of the Quran.

These features are explained by the element of legal partisanship that was integral to Ibn Abī al-Layth's enforcement of the Inquisition. Ibn ʿUlayya, for example, was a jurist as well as a theologian, and he had authored a book dedicated to refuting Abū Ḥanīfa.[43] The main thrust of al-Jamal's poem is to celebrate Ibn Abī al-Layth's role in promoting the legal doctrine of Ḥanafism and in suppressing its rivals.[44] Even though the poem likely reflects the motivations of its author before those of its subject, it is probable that a prominent poet would have made sure to praise a notable personality for achievements of which the latter was particularly proud. Ibn Abī al-Layth thus appears to have used his position at the helm of the Inquisition as an opportunity to refashion radically the legal landscape of Egypt, "smashing" the Shāfiʿīs and "extinguishing" Mālikism.

Given the status of Mālikism as the dominant doctrine associated with the indigenous elite, Ibn Abī al-Layth singled out Mālikī scholars for public humiliation. Muḥammad b. ʿAbd al-Ḥakam and Fityān b. Abī Samḥ were stripped to their underwear and whipped in the central mosque.[45] Ibn Abī al-Layth also banned both Mālikīs and Shāfiʿīs from teaching in the central mosque, which at this time represented the primary venue for

[42] Al-Kindī, *Governors and Judges*, 452–53.

[43] Al-Shaykh al-Mufīd, *al-Masāʾil al-ṣāghāniyya*, vol. 3 of *Muṣannafāt Abī ʿAbd Allāh Muḥammad b. Muḥammad b. al-Nuʿmān b. al-Muʿallim al-ʿUkbarī al-Baghdādī*, 14 vols. (Qum: al-Muʾtamar al-ʿĀlamī li-Alfiyyat al-Shaykh al-Mufīd, 1993), 67–68. I am grateful to Aron Zysow for pointing out that al-Mufīd mentions this work.

[44] This feature of al-Jamal's poem was also noted by ʿAbd al-Raḥmān al-Muʿallimī (d. 1965 or 1966) in *al-Tankīl bi-mā fī taʾnīb al-Kawtharī min al-abāṭīl*, 2nd ed., ed. Muḥammad Nāṣir al-Albānī and ʿAbd al-Razzāq Ḥamza, 2 vols. (Riyadh: Maktabat al-Maʿārif, 1406/1985 or 1986), 1:261.

[45] Muḥammad b. Aḥmad Abū al-ʿArab al-Tamīmī, *al-Miḥan*, ed. ʿUmar b. Sulaymān al-ʿUqaylī (Riyadh: Dār al-ʿUlūm, 1983), 449 and 469.

promulgating and popularizing legal teaching. The campaign against the Mālikīs culminated in 237/851, when Ibn Abī al-Layth accused the Banū ʿAbd al-Ḥakam of misappropriating government property. The family was ordered to pay a colossal fine of 1,404,000 dinars, and Muḥammad's eldest brother, ʿAbd al-Ḥakam b. ʿAbd Allāh b. ʿAbd al-Ḥakam, died under torture that was used to extract information about the family fortune. Other members of the family were imprisoned and their houses were razed to the ground.[46] Though Muḥammad survived the Inquisition and remained one of the most distinguished Egyptian scholars until his death in 268/882, the dominance of the Mālikī elite in Egypt had been broken forever. Subsequently, the focal point of Mālikī scholarly activity shifted westward to Qayrawān, where Mālikism became the dominant doctrine under the semi-independent Aghlabid dynasty.[47]

The Shāfiʿīs also felt the force of Ibn Abī al-Layth's zeal. As already mentioned, Shāfiʿīs alongside Mālikīs were banned from conducting their lessons in the central mosque. Ibn Abī al-Layth accused Yūnus b. ʿAbd al-Aʿlā, a student of al-Shāfiʿī, of misappropriating an orphan's property; Yūnus was found guilty and was imprisoned until 235/850.[48] Hārūn b. Saʿīd al-Aylī (d. 253/867)[49] was another Shāfiʿī to suffer: Ibn Abī al-Layth's assistant dragged him through the mosque and the streets of Fustat, while Hārūn was forced to proclaim, "The Quran is created."[50]

But the main Shāfiʿī victim of the Inquisition was Abū Yaʿqūb al-Buwayṭī. Al-Buwayṭī had stubbornly refused to obey the command to declare public adherence to the createdness doctrine. Al-Dhahabī reports that he was first taken before the governor, who was most likely ʿAlī b. Yaḥyā al-Armanī (in office 226–28/841–43 and 234–35/849–50).[51] Al-Armanī was well disposed toward al-Buwayṭī and encouraged him to utter the required words in order to evade further persecution. Al-Buwayṭī, however, was determined to take a stand, arguing that his capitulation, even if a sham, would lead many others astray: "A hundred thousand would follow me without recognizing [the insincerity of my statement]."[52] Some reports preserved by the Shāfiʿī tradition suggest that al-Buwayṭī's downfall may have been hastened by a conspiracy involving al-Muzanī, Ḥarmala, and one of al-Shāfiʿī's sons; the conspiracy would

46 Al-Kindī, *Governors and Judges*, 464–65.
47 Joseph Schacht, "Aghlabids," in *EI2*, 1:247.
48 Al-Kindī, *Governors and Judges*, 454–55.
49 Ibn ʿAbd al-Barr, *Intiqāʾ*, 176.
50 Al-Kindī, *Governors and Judges*, 451–52.
51 Al-Kindī, *Governors and Judges*, 195–98.
52 Al-Dhahabī, *Siyar aʿlām al-nubalāʾ*, 12:60–61.

probably have consisted of drawing the attention of the authorities to al-Buwayṭī.[53] As a result of his refusal to comply, al-Buwayṭī was arrested and dispatched to Baghdad for interrogation, probably no later than 228/842 or 843.[54] Al-Rabīʿ described the scene of al-Buwayṭī's transfer to Baghdad as follows: "I saw him riding a donkey, an iron collar around his neck, his legs shackled, and between the shackles and the collar an iron chain with a stone weighing 40 *raṭl*.[55] He was shouting, 'God has created creation by [saying] "be"; if that [speech] were created, creation would be created by means of creation.'"[56]

Al-Buwayṭī, along with a number of other Egyptian scholars, was imprisoned in Iraq. At some point during his imprisonment, al-Buwayṭī wrote a letter to al-Rabīʿ, advising him to "have patience with strangers and perfect your character toward the members of your teaching circle, for I have heard al-Shāfiʿī recite repeatedly the line [of poetry], 'I humble myself before them, so that they might honor me, for no soul shall be honored that has not been humbled.'"[57] A possible interpretation of this message is that al-Buwayṭī was thereby appointing al-Rabīʿ as his successor. Al-Buwayṭī died imprisoned in Baghdad in 231/846. The Inquisition formally ended in 234/849, when the caliph al-Mutawakkil (r. 232–47/847–61) prohibited further arguments about the nature of the Quran.[58] However, Ibn Abī al-Layth remained in office until 237/851 and continued his persecution of rival scholars until the end of his tenure.

[53] Al-Subkī, *Ṭabaqāt al-shāfiʿiyya al-kubrā*, 2:164. The unnamed son of al-Shāfiʿī was probably either Abū ʿUthmān (d. after 240/854) or Abū al-Ḥasan (d. 231/846); see al-Subkī, *Ṭabaqāt*, 2:71–73. Al-Subkī interprets al-Buwayṭī's ambiguity on this point as a sign of respect for his teacher al-Shāfiʿī. On the other hand, Josef van Ess believes "Ibn al-Shāfiʿī" to refer to Abū ʿAbd al-Raḥmān al-Shāfiʿī, al-Shāfiʿī's Muʿtazilī student from Baghdad; see van Ess, *Theologie und Gesellschaft*, 3:477, n. 35.

[54] Al-Buwayṭī is reported to have been sent to Baghdad together with Nuʿaym b. Ḥammād, who died in prison in 228/842 or 843. See Ibn Saʿd, *al-Ṭabaqāt al-kubrā* [partial ed.], ed. ʿAlī Muḥammad ʿUmar, 11 vols. (Cairo: Maktabat al-Khānjī, 2001), 9:527, and al-Ziriklī, *Aʿlām*, 8:40. On Nuʿaym, see van Ess, *Theologie und Gesellschaft*, 2:723–26; note that van Ess argues that al-Buwayṭī and Nuʿaym were transported separately.

[55] One *raṭl* approximates to one pound.

[56] Al-Dhahabī, *Siyar aʿlām al-nubalāʾ*, 12:61. This argument became an important proof for the noncreatedness of the Quran in the repertoire of the traditionalists. See Abū al-Qāsim Ismāʿīl b. Muḥammad al-Taymī al-Iṣbahānī, *al-Ḥujja fī bayān al-maḥajja*, 2nd ed., ed. Muḥammad al-Madkhalī, 2 vols. (Riyadh: Dār al-Rāya, 1999), 1:243, and Abū al-Qāsim al-Lālakāʾī, *Sharḥ uṣūl iʿtiqād ahl al-sunna wa-l-jamāʿa*, ed. Aḥmad b. Saʿd al-Ghāmidī, 4 vols. (Riyadh: Dār Ṭayyiba, 1402/1981 or 1982), 2:217–18.

[57] Abū al-ʿAbbās al-Aṣamm, *Musnad al-Imām Muḥammad b. Idrīs al-Shāfiʿī*, ed. Rifʿat Fawzī ʿAbd al-Muṭṭalib, 3 vols. (Beirut: Dār al-Bashāʾir al-Islāmiyya, 2005), 2:2000.

[58] Al-Kindī, *Governors and Judges*, 197.

Even though the ruthlessness of Ḥanafization in the judicial realm waned after the Inquisition, Ḥanafī encroachment in public life became increasingly aggressive, leading to a further erosion of traditional structures and legal practices. This trend was due to the ascendancy of a new breed of Abbasid officials as governors of Egypt: military men of primarily Turkic and Armenian origin, often recent converts to Islam. The rapid rise to power of this class in Egypt as well as elsewhere within the Islamic empire reflected the changing ethnic and cultural composition of the Abbasid state apparatus. In 221/836, the caliph al-Muʿtaṣim had moved the imperial capital to Samarra, about eighty miles to the north of Baghdad, where he relied increasingly on his praetorian guard of foreign-born slave soldiers to fill military and administrative posts. Under al-Muʿtaṣim's successors, especially after the death of the caliph al-Mutawakkil in 247/861, these officials became the de facto power holders in the Abbasid empire, ruling both the capital as commanders and the provinces as governors.

The new Turkic and Armenian rulers generally had little experience with or interest in the scholarly discourse of law. Nonetheless, they had absorbed basic Ḥanafī teaching as part of their training in Iraq and, once in Egypt, seem to have had no scruples in applying this teaching with utter disregard for local practice. A prominent example is the case of a police chief by the name of Azjūr "the Turk," appointed in 253/867, who forbade the imam of the central mosque of Fustat to recite the *basmala*[59] aloud, as well as forbidding the caller to prayer to perform *tathwīb*.[60] These ritual practices, adhered to by both Mālikīs and Shāfiʿīs, had formed part of the performance of communal prayer in Egypt ever since the Muslim conquest; but they were not sanctioned by Ḥanafī teaching and were thus banned by Azjūr. To add insult to injury, the change was implemented in a particularly insensitive fashion by an agent of Azjūr brandishing a whip in the mosque to ensure compliance.[61] Simultaneously, the new administration made little pretense of participating in the cultural practices of the community. ʿAnbasa b. Isḥāq al-Ḍabbī (in office 238–42/852–56), the last Arab governor of Egypt, had still led the congregation of Fustat in communal prayers as all his predecessors had, but with his Turkic successors this centuries-old custom came to an end.[62]

[59] The phrase "in the name of God, most gracious, most merciful" (*bi-'sm Allāh al-raḥmān al-raḥīm*), which is found in the beginning of every chapter of the Quran save one.

[60] The *tathwīb* consists of adding the line "prayer is better than sleep" (*al-ṣalāt khayrun min al-nawm*) to the call for the morning prayer.

[61] Al-Kindī, *Governors and Judges*, 210.

[62] Al-Kindī, *Governors and Judges*, 202.

THE AFTERMATH

By at least the 220s/830s, a substantial body of Shāfiʿī literature must have been in existence: al-Rabīʿ was teaching al-Shāfiʿī's corpus that he had compiled into the *Umm* either before or after al-Shāfiʿī's death, and al-Buwayṭī had written and published his compendium (*Mukhtaṣar*) of al-Shāfiʿī's work. Nevertheless, for the three decades between the death of al-Shāfiʿī in 204/820 and the end of the Inquisition in 234/849, there are relatively few datable instances of al-Shāfiʿī's students' transmitting either al-Shāfiʿī's works or their own:

- The text of the chapter on pilgrimage (*kitāb al-ḥajj*) in al-Shāfiʿī's *Umm* specifies that an unnamed scholar completed his study of that part of the work with al-Rabīʿ in the year 207/822 or 823.[63]
- The Iraqi scholar Abū ʿUbayd al-Qāsim b. Sallām is reported to have studied al-Shāfiʿī's books with al-Rabīʿ during a visit to Egypt, probably between 210 and 213 (825 and 829).[64]
- Ibn Abī Ḥātim al-Rāzī (d. 327/938) reproduces a lengthy report by the Hadith scholar Abū Zurʿa al-Rāzī (d. 264/878), according to which Abū Zurʿa studied al-Shāfiʿī's works with al-Rabīʿ during his stay in Egypt at some point between 227/841 and 232/846. Abū Zurʿa also mentions a friend who studied both with al-Rabīʿ and with another of al-Shāfiʿī's students, Ḥarmala.[65]
- Ibn Qutayba quotes the compendium of al-Buwayṭī in his book *Gharīb al-ḥadīth* and notes that he received a copy of the book via correspondence from al-Rabīʿ;[66] it is likely that this correspondence took place between 228/842 and 236/850.[67]

The dearth of evidence of Shāfiʿī scholarly activity continues for a further decade after the end of the Inquisition. I have found no confirmed

63 *Umm*, 10:5.

64 Al-Bayhaqī, *Manāqib al-Shāfiʿī*, 2:251, quoting a lost book by Zakariyyā al-Sājī, who was a student of al-Rabīʿ and al-Muzanī. Regarding the dating of Abū ʿUbayd's visit, see Hans Gottschalk, "Abū ʿUbayd al-Qāsim b. Sallām: Studie zur Geschichte der arabischen Biographie," *Der Islam* 23 (1936): 245–89, at 272.

65 Ibn Abī Ḥātim, *al-Jarḥ wa-l-taʿdīl*, 1:344–45; see also Chap. 6.

66 Ibn Qutayba, *Gharīb al-ḥadīth*, ed. ʿAbd Allāh al-Jubūrī, 3 vols. (Baghdad: Maṭbaʿat al-ʿĀnī, 1397/1997), 1:200.

67 Given that Ibn Qutayba received the compendium via al-Rabīʿ rather than directly from al-Buwayṭī, it seems plausible that the transmission took place after al-Buwayṭī's imprisonment in Baghdad around 228/842. On the other hand, Gérard Lecomte has argued that Ibn Qutayba's *Gharīb al-ḥadīth* was composed no later than 236/850; see Joseph E. Lowry, "Ibn Qutayba: The Earliest Witness to al-Shāfiʿī and His Legal Doctrines," in *ʿAbbasid Studies*, ed. James E. Montgomery, 303–19 (Leuven: Peeters, 2004), 305.

instances of textual transmission in the 240s (late 850s or early 860s), though it is likely that one such instance did take place during that time: Isḥāq b. Mūsā al-Yaḥmadī (d. 300/912 or 913) studied al-Shāfiʿī's books with Ḥarmala, who died in 243/858.[68] Given that al-Yaḥmadī survived his teacher by half a century, it is probable that their encounter happened only shortly before Ḥarmala's death.

In part the lack of evidence regarding textual transmission in this period is no doubt due to the nature of the *isnād* system that governed the transmission of Hadith reports and that, as will be seen in Chapter 6, was also adopted for the transmission of al-Shāfiʿī's writings. Short chains of transmission involving a minimal number of transmitters were (and still are) considered more prestigious, because they minimize the distance between the original source of a text and its current transmitter. The longer the intervals between transmitters, the shorter the *isnād*; so later transmissions naturally came to be preferred to earlier ones. As transmissions with the smallest number of links were prioritized, those with longer *isnād*s became marginalized and were gradually lost, thus eradicating evidence of early instances of transmission.

However, the bias generated by the preference for short chains of transmission does not constitute the full explanation: three practical factors contributed to the apparent lull in Shāfiʿī scholarship immediately after the Inquisition. The first of these was the continuing ban on Shāfiʿīs holding their lessons in the central mosque – a policy that was initiated by Ibn Abī al-Layth but was perpetuated after his removal from office by the next judge of Egypt, the Mālikī al-Ḥārith b. Miskīn (in office 237–245/851–859). Al-Ḥārith took revenge on Ibn Abī al-Layth and his associates for their persecution of Mālikīs during the Inquisition. He had Ibn Abī al-Layth tortured to gain information about funds that he had allegedly embezzled;[69] he rejected the testimony of two court witnesses simply on the basis that they had been deemed acceptable by his predecessor; and he confiscated property that had been bequeathed to a man connected to Ibn Abī al-Layth because of that connection.[70] Al-Ḥārith also adopted in reversed form Ibn Abī al-Layth's policy of suppressing rival legal schools: under al-Ḥārith, it was now the Shāfiʿīs and the Ḥanafīs who were barred

[68] Ḥamza b. Yūsuf al-Sahmī, *Tārīkh Jurjān*, ed. Muḥammad ʿAbd al-Muʿīd Khān (Beirut: ʿĀlam al-Kutub, 1981), 518.

[69] Al-Kindī, *Governors and Judges*, 468–69. Al-Ḥārith eventually resigned from the judgeship after the caliph overturned a decision that al-Ḥārith had issued on the basis of Mālikī doctrine; the caliph prioritized the Ḥanafī position on the question.

[70] Al-Kindī, *Governors and Judges*, 474.

from teaching in the central mosque. The Shāfiʿīs were thus denied access to this important arena for disseminating legal doctrines for nearly two decades, until the end of al-Ḥārith's tenure in 245/859.

A second factor in the post-Inquisition quietude of the Shāfiʿīs was the apparent disgrace of one of the leading Shāfiʿī scholars in Egypt, Ismāʿīl b. Yaḥyā al-Muzanī. Al-Muzanī had been a Ḥanafī before becoming a student of al-Shāfiʿī, and sources suggest an association between him and Ibn Abī al-Layth. Al-Kindī remarks that while Ibn Abī al-Layth had forbidden scholars to wear traditional tall caps (*al-qalānis al-ṭiwāl*) in his presence, al-Muzanī did not return to this fashion after Ibn Abī al-Layth's removal; this indicates indirectly that al-Muzanī had attended Ibn Abī al-Layth's gatherings.[71] The grave allegation that al-Muzanī had conspired against al-Buwayṭī to effect the latter's arrest has already been mentioned; further, there seem to have been suspicions that he in fact genuinely believed in the createdness of the Quran (or at least in the createdness of its utterance). Abū Yaʿlā al-Khalīlī (d. 446/1054) intimates that Abū Zurʿa al-Rāzī, who studied with al-Rabīʿ in Egypt, shunned al-Muzanī as a teacher specifically because of the rumors regarding the latter's theological stance.[72] These aspersions deeply tarnished al-Muzanī's reputation for at least a decade and a half afterward. Ibn ʿAbd al-Barr (d. 463/1071) reports that his teaching circle in Fustat dwindled to no more than a handful of students.[73]

Finally, a third reason why al-Shāfiʿī's written corpus – contained in the *Umm* – does not seem to have enjoyed wide circulation in the first half of the third Hijri century was most likely the daunting length and density of the work, which in the most recent edition runs to eleven volumes,[74] and in which the discussion of any given subject is often scattered across several parts of the work. Already al-Buwayṭī appears to have considered the length of al-Shāfiʿī's writings to represent an impediment to their popularization: he told al-Shāfiʿī, "You are excessively wordy (*tataghannī*) in composing your works, and consequently people ignore you and your books."[75] The *Umm*, rambling and disorganized, was clearly not suitable to serve as a teaching text. It is therefore not surprising that it did not

[71] Al-Kindī, *Governors and Judges*, 460–61.

[72] Al-Khalīlī argues that al-Muzanī's position was that the utterance (*lafẓ*) of the Quran was created; see Abū Yaʿlā al-Qazwīnī al-Khalīlī, *Kitāb al-Irshād fī maʿrifat ʿulamāʾ al-ḥadīth*, ed. Muḥammad Saʿīd b. ʿUmar Idrīs, 3 vols. (Riyadh: Maktabat al-Rushd, 1989), 1:431. On the other hand, Ibn ʿAbd al-Barr, in *Intiqāʾ*, 170, claims that al-Muzanī believed in the createdness of the Quran itself.

[73] Ibn ʿAbd al-Barr, *Intiqāʾ*, 170.

[74] Rifʿat Fawzī ʿAbd al-Muṭṭalib's edition for Dār al-Wafāʾ, published in 2001.

[75] Ibn ʿAsākir, *Tārīkh madīnat Dimashq*, 51:364–65.

attract large numbers of students at a time when Egypt's scholarly circles as well as the cosmopolitan community of traveling scholars still consisted overwhelmingly of Mālikīs and Ḥanafīs, as well as Hadith scholars who lacked a strong interest in law. There was little incentive for such scholars to dedicate the time necessary to study a voluminous legal text written by a scholar with whom they disagreed. It was thus the compendia written by al-Shāfiʿī's students al-Buwayṭī and al-Muzanī that played a central role in introducing al-Shāfiʿī's ideas to a broad audience during the early decades after al-Shāfiʿī's death and thus prompting an increasing number of scholars to commit to studying al-Shāfiʿī's original, much more extensive work with his students later on.

The growing interest in al-Shāfiʿī's works from the 250s/860s onward heralded the turning of the tide for Shāfiʿī scholarship. In contrast to the scarce evidence of Shāfiʿī teaching and transmission up to the 240s/850s, the two and a half decades between 246/860 and 270/884 represent a "golden age" of scholarly activity on the part of al-Shāfiʿī's students. Al-Muzanī's reputation appears to have recovered by this time: he attracted students such as the great traditionist Ibn Abī Ḥātim al-Rāzī, who had traveled to Egypt to study,[76] and he authored a still extant mainstream Sunni creed that displays no traces of the theological deviance alleged by some earlier sources.[77] It is possible that this work formed part of an effort by al-Muzanī to rehabilitate himself among Sunni scholars.

Particularly active in this period was al-Rabīʿ, who did not – in contrast to his peers al-Buwayṭī and al-Muzanī – write and teach his own works but rather specialized in transmitting the writings of al-Shāfiʿī, as well as teaching the compendium of al-Buwayṭī. With the exception of a small collection of Hadith,[78] all of al-Shāfiʿī's written work that is extant today (namely, the *Umm*, including the *Risāla*) was transmitted from him by al-Rabīʿ. Already in the early third/ninth century, al-Rabīʿ was recognized as the primary teacher of al-Shāfiʿī's books; Yaḥyā b. Maʿīn reported that al-Rabīʿ was considered by his contemporaries to be the best person with whom to study the *Umm*.[79] Al-Rabīʿ's student Abū Ismāʿīl al-Tirmidhī (d. 280/893) is said to have compiled a list of those

[76] Al-Dhahabī, *Siyar aʿlām al-nubalāʾ*, 12:493.

[77] See van Ess, *Theologie und Gesellschaft*, 2:727. Al-Muzanī's creed is reproduced in Ibn Qayyim al-Jawziyya, *Ijtimāʿ al-juyūsh*, ed. Bashīr Muḥammad ʿUyūn (Damascus: Maktabat Dār al-Īmān, 2000), 121, and published separately as *Sharḥ al-sunna*, ed. Jamāl ʿAzzūn (Riyadh: Dār al-Minhāj, 2009).

[78] Al-Shāfiʿī, *al-Sunan al-maʾthūra* [al-Ṭaḥāwī's transmission through al-Muzanī], ed. ʿAbd al-Muʿṭī Qalʿajī (Beirut: Dār al-Maʿrifa, 1986).

[79] Al-Nawawī, *Tahdhīb al-asmāʾ wa-l-lughāt*, 1:60.

who transmitted al-Shāfiʿī's books from al-Rabīʿ that contained two hundred names.[80] Though that list is no longer extant, we know of dozens of scholars who studied al-Shāfiʿī's works with al-Rabīʿ and/or al-Muzanī's compendium with al-Muzanī in the 250s and 260s, up to al-Muzanī's death in 264/877 and al-Rabīʿ's in 270/884.[81] These scholars include the Andalusian Mālikī Ibn al-Kharrāz, who studied al-Shāfiʿī's *Risāla* as well as al-Muzanī's compendium in Egypt in the early 250s/mid-860s;[82] the Ḥanafī jurist and traditionist Abū Jaʿfar al-Ṭaḥāwī (d. 321/933), who was al-Muzanī's nephew and studied Shāfiʿī works probably in the 250s or early 260s (late 860s to mid-870s);[83] the famous historian and exegete Muḥammad b. Jarīr al-Ṭabarī (d. 310/923), who studied the *Umm* with al-Rabīʿ in either 253/867 or 256/870;[84] and the great traditionist of Nishapur Abū al-ʿAbbās al-Aṣamm (d. 346/957), who completed his study of the *Umm* with al-Rabīʿ in 266/880.[85] The next chapter examines the process of transmission of al-Shāfiʿīs writings in more detail.

THE RISE OF THE SHĀFIʿĪS

The "golden age" of Shāfiʿism in the second half of the third/ninth century was inaugurated by the repeal of the long ban on Shāfiʿīs teaching in the central mosque. The ban was rescinded by the new judge who succeeded the Mālikī al-Ḥārith: Bakkār b. Qutayba (in office 246–70/860–84), a Ḥanafī jurist from Basra who had studied law with ʿĪsā b. Abān (d. 220/835) and Hadith with Abū Dāwūd al-Tayālisī (d. 203/819).[86] Unlike many of his Ḥanafī predecessors, Bakkār became an accepted member of Egyptian scholarly society and enjoyed good relations with members of other schools, particularly Shāfiʿī-leaning Hadith scholars. This is demonstrated by the fact that such prominent Shāfiʿī *muḥaddithūn* as Ibn Khuzayma, Abū ʿAwāna al-Isfarāyīnī (d. 316/928 or 929), and Abū al-ʿAbbās al-Aṣamm transmitted Hadith from him.[87]

[80] Ibn ʿAbd al-Barr, *Intiqāʾ*, 177.
[81] For details, see my "Al-Shāfiʿī's Written Corpus."
[82] ʿAbd Allāh b. Muḥammad b. al-Faraḍī, *Tārīkh al-ʿulamāʾ wa-l-ruwāt li-l-ʿilm bi-l-Andalus*, ed. ʿIzzat al-ʿAṭṭār al-Ḥusaynī, 2 vols. (Cairo: Maktabat al-Khānjī, 1954), 2:182–83.
[83] Al-Ṭaḥāwī, *Sharḥ mushkil al-āthār*, ed. Shuʿayb al-Arnaʾūṭ, 16 vols. (Beirut: Muʾassasat al-Risāla, 1994), 7:228. The year of birth given for al-Ṭaḥāwī ranges from 229/844 to 239/853. Given that he died in 321/933, the latter date is more likely; that date would make any meaningful legal training before the late 250s/early 870s improbable.
[84] C. E. Bosworth, "al-Ṭabarī," in *EI2*, 10:11–15.
[85] Al-Aṣamm, *Musnad al-Shāfiʿī*, 2:2000.
[86] Ibn Ḥajar, *Rafʿ al-iṣr*, 1:140.
[87] Al-Dhahabī, *Siyar aʿlām al-nubalāʾ*, 12:599.

Like Muḥammad b. ʿAbd al-Ḥakam, Bakkār authored a refutation of al-Shāfiʿī's doctrine where it disagreed with that of his imam (in Bakkār's case, Abū Ḥanīfa).[88] However, as with Muḥammad, Bakkār's differences with the Shāfiʿīs in substantive law did not preclude a shared legal discourse and deep personal bonds of respect. Bakkār clearly knew of al-Shāfiʿī and his students before moving to Egypt: his teacher ʿĪsā b. Abān had written a refutation of al-Shāfiʿī's ideas regarding the usage of Hadith.[89] Several reports attest to Bakkār's favorable opinion of the Shāfiʿīs, particularly of al-Muzanī. One such report depicts Bakkār presiding in court in Egypt and asking a potential witness for his name; when the latter replied that he was Ismāʿīl b. Yaḥyā al-Muzanī, Bakkār asked, "The student of al-Shāfiʿī?" Upon receiving an affirmative answer, he immediately declared al-Muzanī a trustworthy witness.[90] On another occasion, a companion of Bakkār's, following the latter's request, challenged al-Muzanī to a debate by asking how the total Shāfiʿī ban on small amounts of intoxicating drinks (*nabīdh*) could be sustained, given that there were Hadith that forbade and others that permitted them. Al-Muzanī replied that one of the two groups of Hadith must have abrogated the other, and given the common agreement that intoxicating drinks were allowed before Islam, the Hadith reports that permit intoxicating drinks must predate and have been abrogated by Hadith that ban them. Hearing al-Muzanī's reply, Bakkār is said to have exclaimed, "Exalted is God; if argumentation (*kalām*) could ever be more subtle than poetry, this would be it."[91]

Bakkār was also closely familiar with Shāfiʿī doctrine. This is evident from his judgment in a case where the sale of a piece of land was contested by the owner of an adjacent property, who claimed that he had the right of preemption (*shufʿa*) in the sale. The plaintiff could provide no witnesses to support his claim, and the defendant – the seller – was willing to swear an oath to deny the claimed right to preemption, which would have decided the case in his favor. Bakkār, however, knew that the defendant was a Shāfiʿī and that according to Shāfiʿī doctrine the right of preemption does not apply to adjacent but otherwise distinct property;

[88] Ibn Ḥajar, *Rafʿ al-iṣr*, 1:151, quoting a now-lost book by the historian Ibn Zūlāq (d. 386/996).

[89] See Murteza Bedir, "An Early Response to al-Shāfiʿī: ʿĪsā b. Abān on the Prophetic Report (*khabar*)," *Islamic Law and Society* 9 (2002): 285–311, as well as Chap. 8.

[90] Ibn Ḥajar, *Rafʿ al-iṣr*, 1:145.

[91] Ibn Ḥajar, *Rafʿ al-iṣr*, 1:150, quoting Ibn Zūlāq; Ibn Ḥajar adds that Bakkār abstained from *nabīdh*, possibly having being convinced by al-Muzanī's reasoning.

hence the defendant's willingness to give the oath. Bakkār thus fine-tuned the required oath to specify that the plaintiff had no right of preemption according to those who believe in this right for adjacent property – that is, non-Shāfi'īs. The seller could not in good faith give this oath and was thus forced to grant preemption. When the seller informed al-Muzanī of this incident, al-Muzanī praised Bakkār's sharp legal mind.[92]

Bakkār's decision to rescind the ban on Shāfi'īs teaching in the central mosque represented a significant point in the development of Shāfi'ism in Egypt, because it enabled al-Shāfi'ī's surviving students to reach out once again to a broader audience through the public platform of the mosque. But a second factor was at least equally important in raising the profile of Shāfi'ī scholarship and teaching in Egypt as well as farther afield. This was the shift in patterns of patronage and political support for legal scholarship in Egypt that was initiated by the appointment of another Turkic military leader, Aḥmad b. Ṭūlūn (r. 254–70/868–84), as the governor of Egypt. Ibn Ṭūlūn was the son of a Turkish military slave at the court of al-Ma'mūn. He grew up as a Muslim, receiving both military and religious training. When his stepfather, the Turkish general Bākbāk, was appointed governor of Egypt in 254/868, he sent Ibn Ṭūlūn to Egypt to rule on his behalf. Ibn Ṭūlūn soon embarked on the pursuit of financial, political, and military independence from the Abbasid state. Five years after his arrival, a revolt by the governor of Jordan and Palestine, 'Īsā b. al-Shaykh (d. 269/882), and 'Īsā's confiscation of a tax payment from Egypt enabled Aḥmad b. Ṭūlūn to obtain the caliph's permission to raise his own army of Turkic and Sudanese soldiers against 'Īsā.[93] Thus, for the first time since the dissolution of the Egyptian militia in the beginning of the third/ninth century, the governor of Egypt controlled an army independently of the caliph, and in contrast to the old militia system, Ibn Ṭūlūn's army owed its loyalty to the governor alone.

The military power embodied in the army, together with the internal weakness of and external challenges to the Abbasid caliphate, allowed Ibn Ṭūlūn to make Egypt into a de facto independent state. The caliph

[92] Ibn Ḥajar, *Raf' al-iṣr*, 1:153–54. For the two positions, compare al-Muzanī, *Mukhtaṣar kitāb al-Umm li-l-Shāfi'ī*, ed. Khalīl Shīḥā (Beirut: Dār al-Ma'rifa, 2004), 168 (Mukhtaṣar al-shuf'a min al-Jāmi'), with al-Ṭaḥāwī, *Mukhtasar al-Ṭaḥāwī*, 120–24. Subsequent references to al-Muzanī's *Mukhtaṣar* are to this edition, except where specified. To facilitate locating references in alternative editions of this work, I include chapter titles in all subsequent citations.

[93] Al-Kindī, *Governors and Judges*, 214–15. A more extensive source is Abū al-Ḥusayn al-Razī's (d. 347/958) account, quoted in Ibn 'Asākir, *Tārīkh madīnat Dimashq*, 47:311–12.

al-Muʿtamid (r. 256–79/870–92) was weak and had no power base of his own, while his brother and regent to the throne, al-Muwaffaq (d. 278/891), who commanded the Abbasid troops and the loyalty of the Turkish generals, was occupied with the tasks of keeping the Safarids at bay and retaking southern Iraq from the Zanj rebels.[94] Aḥmad b. Ṭūlūn could thus maintain nominal loyalty to the politically insignificant caliph while opposing his brother, defeating the army that the latter had dispatched to depose him in 263/877, and even extending his reach into Syria with a military expedition in 264/878.

Given the close alliance of the Ḥanafī establishment with the imperial administration, it is not surprising that a gap began to emerge between Ibn Ṭūlūn and the Ḥanafīs. In 269/882, Ibn Ṭūlūn invited al-Muʿtamid to relocate to Egypt to escape al-Muwaffaq's sphere of influence. However, al-Muʿtamid was intercepted by an agent of al-Muwaffaq and confined to virtual house arrest.[95] In response, Ibn Ṭūlūn ordered the judges, jurists, and notables of his realm to gather in Damascus in order to declare al-Muwaffaq's regency to the throne annulled because of rebellion and disobedience, and to announce that *jihād* against al-Muwaffaq had therefore become obligatory. Most of those assembled signed the document; only three refused, most prominently the Ḥanafī judge Bakkār b. Qutayba. Back in Egypt, Ibn Ṭūlūn ordered Bakkār to appoint a deputy (Muḥammad b. Shādhān al-Jawharī, whose death date is unknown) and then had Bakkār arrested. Bakkār continued to teach Hadith during his imprisonment and attended court sessions but would then have to return to his cell.[96]

The Tulunids appear to have adopted a policy of gradual divestment from Ḥanafism. However, Ibn Ṭūlūn and his successors, probably aware of the symbolism and power of legitimization (and delegitimization) possessed by the legal-religious scholarly discourse, demonstrated great respect for correct form in their dealings with judicial officials. After Bakkār's refusal to renounce al-Muwaffaq, Ibn Ṭūlūn did not remove him from office – a caliphal prerogative and thus not formally within the governor's powers – but simply detained Bakkār and transferred most of the judge's day-to-day responsibilities to his deputy. After the deaths of Bakkār and Ibn Ṭūlūn in 270/884, the judgeship remained vacant for three years; then Ibn Ṭūlūn's son and successor, Khumārawayh (d. 282/896), appointed another Ḥanafī, Muḥammad b.

[94] Hugh Kennedy, "al-Muwaffaḳ," in *EI2*, 7:801.
[95] Al-Kindī, *Governors and Judges*, 226.
[96] Ibn Ḥajar, *Rafʿ al-iṣr*, 1:152 and 154.

ʿAbda b. Ḥarb al-ʿAbbādānī (d. 313/926 or 927), as an appeals court (*maẓālim*) judge – a lower appointment that was within his rights as the governor of Egypt. (Ibn Ḥarb named al-Muzanī's nephew, al-Ṭaḥāwī, his secretary.)[97] However, after a 280/893 agreement with the caliph al-Muʿtaḍid (r. 279–89/892–902) that transferred control over judicial appointments to the Tulunids in exchange for an annual tribute,[98] the first full judge appointed by the Tulunids was a Shāfiʿī: Muḥammad b. ʿUthmān Abū Zurʿa (in office 284–92/897–905; d. 302/914 or 915), a wealthy Damascene jurist from a family of Jewish converts to Islam.[99] Abū Zurʿa was initially named the judge of Damascus by Khumārawayh around 277/891[100] and was subsequently made chief judge of the entire Tulunid realm of Egypt and Syria in 284/897 by Khumārawayh's son Hārūn (r. 283–92/896–904). Abū Zurʿa used his office as judge as well as his personal wealth to promote Shāfiʿism.[101] Al-Dhahabī reports that he offered a reward of a hundred dinars to anyone who successfully memorized al-Muzanī's compendium.[102]

Already before this appointment, Shāfiʿism was elevated to an unprecedented position of official support and recognition by Ibn Ṭūlūn and his descendants. When Ibn Ṭūlūn's famous mosque in al-Qaṭāʾiʿ was completed in 266/879, Bakkār b. Qutayba, in his capacity as the chief judge, led the first Friday prayer in the mosque, but it was the Shāfiʿī al-Rabīʿ who afterward recited a text that he had composed on the virtues of building mosques. Ibn Ṭūlūn listened to the recitation and then sent his servant to reward al-Rabīʿ with a thousand dinars.[103] The fact that al-Rabīʿ was invited to play such an important ceremonial role in the inauguration of Ibn Ṭūlūn's greatest architectural monument demonstrates the status that he had achieved. Ibn Ṭūlūn not only honored al-Rabīʿ in public; he also invited al-Rabīʿ into his own household and encouraged members of his family to study al-Shāfiʿī's books with him. Ibn Ṭūlūn's son ʿAdnān (d. 325/936 or 937) is reported to have said:

> God showed His generosity by extending the life of al-Rabīʿ until the world had studied with him. We studied with him when we were still adolescents.... The

[97] See Ibn Ḥajar's *Rafʿ al-iṣr*, as quoted in the appendix to al-Kindī, *Governors and Judges*, 516; this section is not included in the incomplete published edition of *Rafʿ al-iṣr*.

[98] Al-Kindī, *Governors and Judges*, 240.

[99] Gerhard Conrad, *Die quḍāt Dimašq und der madhab al-Auzāʿī: Materialien zur syrischen Rechtsgeschichte* (Beirut and Stuttgart: F. Steiner, 1994), 270–74.

[100] Conrad, *Quḍāt Dimašq*, 274.

[101] Ibn Yūnus, *Tārīkh Ibn Yūnus al-Ṣadafī*, 2:217.

[102] Al-Dhahabī, *Siyar aʿlām al-nubalāʾ*, 14:233.

[103] Al-Maqrīzī, *Khiṭaṭ*, 2:265–66.

Mālikīs had been dominant in Egypt, but then God cast love for al-Shāfiʿī and his disciples into my father's heart. Disagreements and clashes broke out between the Shāfiʿīs and the Mālikīs in Egypt and my father always sided with the Shāfiʿīs.... He was generous toward al-Rabīʿ and supported him financially and ordered him to continue to visit us, and he prodded us to listen to al-Shāfiʿīs works. So we studied al-Shāfiʿī's books with al-Rabīʿ.[104]

ʿAdnān later taught what he had learned from al-Rabīʿ in Baghdad.[105] A manumitted slave by the name of Luʾluʾ al-Rūmī, who was part of Ibn Ṭūlūn's household, also studied with al-Rabīʿ and subsequently taught Shāfiʿī law in Baghdad.[106] Another Shāfiʿī scholar emerged from the family of a high-ranking Tulunid official. Abū al-Ṭayyib Aḥmad b. Akhī Ṭakhshī (d. 299/911)[107] was most probably the nephew of Ṭakhshī b. Baylabard (Balbard; d. unknown), who served the Tulunids both as a general and as a police chief.[108] Abū al-Ṭayyib is one of the known transmitters of al-Muzanī's compendium.[109]

Beyond ʿAdnān's comment about God "casting love for al-Shāfiʿī" into Aḥmad b. Ṭūlūn's heart, the reasons for the Tulunids' shift of support from the Ḥanafī to the Shāfiʿī school are nowhere explicitly discussed. However, it seems likely that the identity of Ḥanafism as the imperial doctrine of the Abbasids made it unsuitable for the independence project of the Tulunids, as demonstrated by the unwillingness of the Abbasid-appointed Bakkār to interfere in caliphal politics. On the other hand, Mālikism with its close links to the old Egyptian Arab elite must also have appeared unattractive. Against its two rivals, Shāfiʿism thus offered several advantages. It was allied with neither the imperial center nor the old Egyptian social order. And its textualism, which divorced law from particular local settings and located the fount of normativity in a disembodied corpus of canonical texts, fitted the needs of the essentially rootless Turkic newcomers. These sought not only political independence but also an independent basis of Islamic legitimacy, which was ideally provided by Shāfiʿī doctrine.

104 Ibn ʿAsākir, *Tārīkh madīnat Dimashq*, 40:54–55.

105 Ibn ʿAsākir, *Tārīkh madīnat Dimashq*, 40:54.

106 Al-Khaṭīb al-Baghdādī, *Tārīkh Madīnat al-Salām*, 14:545. This seems to be a different Luʾluʾ from the Tulunid general; see al-Kindī, *Governors and Judges*, 224.

107 ʿAbd al-Karīm b. Muḥammad al-Samʿānī, *al-Ansāb*, ed. ʿAbd Allāh al-Bārūdī, 5 vols. (Beirut: Dār al-Janān, 1988), 1:435.

108 Al-Kindī, *Governors and Judges*, 215–17.

109 See Hibat Allāh al-Akfānī (d. 524/1129), *Tasmiyat man rawā ʿan al-Muzanī al-Mukhtaṣar al-ṣaghīr min ʿilm al-Shāfiʿī* (Damascus: al-Ẓāhiriyya, MS Majmūʿ 94, fol. 85b [1 fol., copied 701/1301]).

The "golden age" of state-backed Shāfiʿism did not last very long. In 292/905, the Tulunid dynasty was overthrown by an Abbasid army from Baghdad, and many of the dynasty's Shāfiʿī appointees, including Abū Zurʿa, lost their positions in the judiciary. But the brief period of prominence led to a blossoming of Shāfiʿī thought and scholarship that had enduring consequences. Scores of jurists, from both Egypt and elsewhere, studied with al-Shāfiʿī's students, copied his works, and transmitted them to others. By the time Shāfiʿism lost the official support provided by the Tulunids, it was firmly established among Egyptian intelligentsia, and traveling scholars had spread Shāfiʿī doctrines from Egypt to all corners of the Muslim world. Historical sources tell us, for example, the names of the scholars who were the first to introduce al-Shāfiʿī's thought to the following locations:

- Bukhara in Central Asia: Abū Sahl al-Bāhilī (d. 250/864), who had studied with al-Buwayṭī[110]
- Astarabad: Isḥāq b. Mūsā al-Yaḥmadī (d. 300/912 or 913), a student of al-Shāfiʿī's disciple Ḥarmala[111]
- Granada in Muslim Spain: Abū Zakariyyā b. al-Kharrāz (d. 295/907), who transmitted both al-Muzanī's compendium and al-Shāfiʿī's *Risāla* in the early 250s/mid-860s[112]
- Merv in Khurasan: ʿAbadān ʿAbd Allāh b. Muḥammad b. ʿĪsā al-Marwazī (b. 220/835, d. 294/906), who taught al-Shāfiʿī's work as well as al-Muzanī's compendium[113]
- Shiraz: Nūḥ b. Mirdās Abū Muslim al-Sulamī (d. 295/907 or 908), who had studied al-Shāfiʿī's books with Yūnus b. ʿAbd al-Aʿlā and al-Rabīʿ in Egypt[114]
- Isfarayin in Khurasan: Abū ʿAwāna al-Isfarāyīnī (d. 316/928 or 929), who had studied with al-Rabīʿ and al-Muzanī[115]

Within a century of al-Shāfiʿī's death, then, his ideas had spread throughout the Islamic world, carried in al-Shāfiʿī's own writings as well as in the works of his students and disseminated by scholars who had

[110] ʿAlī b. Hibat Allāh b. Mākūlā, *al-Ikmāl fī rafʿ al-irtiyāb ʿan al-muʾtalif wa-l-mukhtalif min al-asmāʾ wa-l-kunā wa-l-ansāb*, 7 vols. (Hyderabad: Dāʾirat al-Maʿārif al-ʿUthmāniyya, 1962–), 7:271.
[111] Al-Sahmī, *Tārīkh Jurjān*, 518.
[112] Ibn al-Faraḍī, *Tārīkh ʿulamāʾ al-Andalus*, 2:182–83.
[113] Al-Subkī, *Ṭabaqāt al-shāfiʿiyya al-kubrā*, 2:297.
[114] Al-Subkī, *Ṭabaqāt al-shāfiʿiyya al-kubrā*, 2:346.
[115] Al-Dhahabī, *Tadhkirat al-ḥuffāẓ*, 3:3.

studied in Egypt during the "golden age" of Shāfiʿī scholarly activity in the 250s and 260s.

Shifting patterns of political persecution and patronage over the course of the third/ninth century thus had a profound effect on the fates of Shāfiʿī scholars and scholarship: the stifling of Shāfiʿī teaching during the Inquisition and its aftermath gave way to the resurgence of Shāfiʿism under the supportive conditions of the Tulunid reign. However, the narrative in this chapter also highlights the ultimately limited power of a medieval government to eradicate an already established legal doctrine. A sustained campaign of persecution by the powerful Ḥanafī school against its rival was made possible only by the relative weakness of the target – the terminally undermined Mālikī elite – and the identification of the target with a theological proposition that was defined as sufficiently heterodox to merit radical measures of suppression. (A similar harnessing of theology for interschool rivalry was later seen in the conflict between Shāfiʿīs and Ḥanafīs in fifth-/eleventh-century Nishapur.)[116] Finally, in spite of the severity of the harassment endured by the Mālikīs during the *miḥna*, Mālikism retained a permanent foothold in Egypt even after the rapid rise of Shāfiʿism under the Tulunids reduced it to the position of a minority doctrine. But it never regained its dominance. In both the short and the long term, Shāfiʿism was clearly the principal "winner" in the turmoil of the third/ninth century: the brief Shāfiʿī "golden age" described in this chapter was followed by others under the Ayyubids and the Mamluks, and Shāfiʿism remained the predominant legal school in Egypt into the modern period.

However, the kind of "school" that Shāfiʿism represented differs in a fundamental way from the Mālikism that preceded it. This chapter has been concerned with the scholars who made up the schools – their careers, teaching activities, and political and personal fates. I have thus far had little to say about the form and content of the teaching that they transmitted to their students, or about the ways in which they perceived their relationship with that teaching and with one another and how these were perceived by others around them. It is these features that define a legal school in the particular sense that became constitutive of classical Islamic law, and it is to a close examination of them that I now turn.

[116] See, for example, Heinz Halm, "Der Wesir al-Kundurī und die Fitna von Nīšāpūr," *Die Welt des Orients* 6 (1971): 205–33.

PART III

FOUNDATIONS OF A NEW COMMUNITY

Chapter 6

Authorship, Transmission, and Intertextuality

The establishment of a uniquely authoritative textual canon, divorced from the pragmatic context of communal tradition, created a need for interpretation. Hitherto, the scholar had been an organic part of the normative tradition, both shaping and embodying it. Al-Shāfiʿī recast the scholar as a systematic interpreter of the canonized sources, opening up a gulf between the two. This analytical distance would henceforth be bridged by the careful and methodical application of hermeneutic tools.

Canonization and the resulting hermeneutic discourse relied on the existence of a written culture that could support the determination of a textual canon and the development and elaboration of systematic techniques for its analysis. Part I of this book has shown that al-Shāfiʿī's theorization of canonization was both prompted and made possible by the birth of a culture of deliberately composed books, as exemplified by Mālik's *Muwaṭṭa'*. However, Mālik's precanonization work differs in a crucial respect from the writings of al-Shāfiʿī and the latter's successors. Although the *Muwaṭṭa'* represents Mālik's individual effort to articulate a definitive statement of Medinan practice, Mālik himself is not really the author of the doctrine presented in its pages; his role is that of a faithful, though critical, compiler. The *Muwaṭṭa'* embodies the written codification of an authoritative tradition, but it is not yet the written expression of a distinct authorial voice in the way that al-Shāfiʿī's writings would be.

This difference is rooted in the transformation of the task of the scholar as theorized by al-Shāfiʿī. In his new capacity as an autonomous interpreter of canonized scripture, the scholar could only speak for himself; his writings reflect his personal conclusions regarding legal dilemmas, not the authoritative positions of a collective tradition. Within such a framework, accuracy and precision gain a paramount importance: once the scholar has lost his mantle as the guardian of tradition, his claim to authority is now based solely on his expert handling of the textual sources.

The significance of accuracy is compounded by the shift in the perception of time that accompanies canonization. The lived normative tradition of Medina was sustained by constant repetition, giving rise to a cyclical sense of time. The use of writing for note taking does not disrupt this "ritual coherence," as Jan Assmann termed it: the cycle of notes based on oral lectures that are, in turn, based on previous notes and previous lectures erases the individual originators of statements and thereby creates a perception of permanent presentness. By contrast, the isolation of the sacred past in the fixed textual form of the canon ("textual coherence") generates the perception of relative time – history – as the chronological distance that separates the scholar from the canonized text and the moment of divine revelation that it encapsulates. Time thus becomes linear and in most cases is accompanied by a progressive degeneration, given that the growing distance from the sacred past is perceived as the source of inevitable corruption.[1] Meticulous attention to accuracy represents an attempt to counter this inevitable entropy.

Already before al-Shāfiʿī, scholars of Hadith had developed protocols of transmission that strove to protect the integrity of the transmitted material against the ravages of time. They insisted that each transmitted report include the name of its originator and all subsequent transmitters, and they formulated rules for ensuring accuracy in the process of scholar-to-scholar transmission. They did not, however, author books to interpret these reports. The fusion of this concern with accuracy with the concept of original authorship is the groundbreaking characteristic that marks the work of al-Shāfiʿī and his students. This chapter investigates the types and techniques of writing, transmission, and quotation employed by al-Shāfiʿī and his followers in order to demonstrate that the latter sought explicitly to adhere to the protocols of Hadith transmission in their engagement with textual material. However, they applied these standards not only to the canonized scriptures but also to other, interpretive texts, including al-Shāfiʿī's own corpus, thus enabling the identification and preservation of the precise authorship of these texts. This extension of rigorous criteria of authenticity and accuracy from the narrow field of Hadith study to religious scholarship more broadly was a

[1] J. Assmann, *Das kulturelle Gedächtnis*, 87–97.

function of canonization, and it laid the basis for the new kind of critical scholarship that subsequently came to characterize Islamic law.

I begin this chapter with a brief overview of al-Shāfiʿī's literary production to reveal five distinct types of writing that constitute his corpus of works, the *Umm*. (I have defended elsewhere the authenticity of the *Umm* as genuinely written by al-Shāfiʿī.)[2] The stylistic composition of the *Umm*, though heterogeneous, demonstrates the novel nature of the work: its voice, unlike that in Mālik's *Muwaṭṭaʾ*, is that of a singular author seeking to persuade the reader with an original argument. Turning then to an examination of the transmission of the *Umm*, we find al-Shāfiʿī and his students emulating the formal traditionist protocols of transmission and openly acknowledging where they fell short of this standard. They exhibited a critical attitude toward the texts and their potential weaknesses, an attitude that was also shared by their contemporaries, as evidence from other sources indicates. These scholars thus inaugurated a culture of writing in legal scholarship that recognized the interpreter as the author of his opinions and subsequently insisted on the correct reproduction and attribution of such opinions.

AL-SHĀFIʿĪ'S WRITING

As seen in Chapter 1, the culture of learning into which al-Shāfiʿī was socialized in his youth was a primarily aural one; he described sitting with scholars in the mosque, listening to and memorizing their lessons on Hadith and law, and subsequently writing down the material covered.[3] The writing materials that the young al-Shāfiʿī had at his disposal included animal bones as well as hides and palm bark,[4] materials that are said to have been in use already during the life of Muḥammad to record the text of the Quran.[5] The notes written on such rudimentary materials must have been fragmentary, unable to record lengthy passages of writing but suited for short texts, such as Hadith and individual points of law (*masāʾil*).

Al-Shāfiʿī's first known literary activities beyond such note taking are mentioned in connection with his studies with al-Shaybānī in Baghdad. He had acquired al-Shaybānī's books both by writing them out in his own hand (a quantity he described as "a whole camel load")[6] and by spending

[2] El Shamsy, "Al-Shāfiʿī's Written Corpus."
[3] Ibn Abī Ḥātim al-Rāzī, *Ādāb al-Shāfiʿī*, 24.
[4] Al-Bayhaqī, *Manāqib al-Shāfiʿī*, 1:93.
[5] See, for example, Abū ʿAmr al-Dānī, *Muqniʿ*, 46.
[6] Ibn Abī Ḥātim, *Ādāb al-Shāfiʿī*, 27–28.

sixty dinars – a formidable sum – on the purchase of al-Shaybānī's books from a bookseller.[7] Ibn Abī Ḥātim reports that al-Shāfiʿī wrote on the margins of these bought books, adding a Hadith to each of al-Shaybānī's points of law, probably in order to support or refute the point.[8]

Either still in Iraq or upon his return to Mecca,[9] al-Shāfiʿī began to produce his own writings on law. This early corpus is generally known as *al-Mabsūṭ* or *al-Ḥujja*,[10] and it is likely to have contained al-Shāfiʿī's counterrefutation of al-Shaybānī's attack on Mālik (*al-Radd ʿalā Muḥammad b. al-Ḥasan*);[11] commented-upon versions of Abū Yūsuf's work on the disagreement between Abū Ḥanīfa and Ibn Abī Laylā (*Ikhtilāf al-ʿIrāqiyyayn*)[12] as well as of Abū Yūsuf's refutation of al-Awzāʿī's work on the law of warfare (*Siyar al-Awzāʿī*);[13] and possibly al-Shāfiʿī's refutation of the Iraqi legal tradition (*Ikhtilāf ʿAlī wa-Ibn Masʿūd*).[14] (All of these were later subsumed into al-Shāfiʿī's magnum opus, the *Umm*.) What these writings have in common is that they engage with the Iraqi legal thought of al-Shāfiʿī's time but do so in a way that is undeveloped relative to al-Shāfiʿī's later work.[15] These texts take the form of commentaries or commentary-like works that consist primarily of substantial quotations of earlier texts, adding evidence and snippets of al-Shāfiʿī's own writing. In these works al-Shāfiʿī seems not yet to have found his own voice fully, and he limits himself to partial criticism and correction.

[7] Ibn Abī Ḥātim, *Ādāb al-Shāfiʿī*, 34.

[8] Ibn Abī Ḥātim, *Ādāb al-Shāfiʿī*, 34.

[9] Shams al-Dīn al-Munāwī, *Farāʾid al-fawāʾid*, ed. Abū ʿAbd Allāh Ismāʿīl (Beirut: Dār al-Kutub al-ʿIlmiyya, 1995), 56.

[10] See Muḥammad b. Isḥāq b. al-Nadīm, *Kitāb al-Fihrist*, ed. Ayman Fuʾād Sayyid, 2 pts. with 2 vols. each (London: Al-Furqan Islamic Heritage Foundation, 2009), pt. 1, 2:39–41, and Ibn Ḥajar al-ʿAsqalānī, *Tawālī al-taʾnīs bi-maʿālī Ibn Idrīs*, ed. ʿAbd Allāh al-Kandarī (Beirut: Dār Ibn Ḥazm, 2008), 180, quoting al-Bayhaqī. (Earlier editions of this book carry the title *Tawālī al-taʾsīs*.) Ibn al-Nadīm notes that the structure of the *Mabsūṭ* as transmitted by al-Shāfiʿī's Iraqi student Abū ʿAlī al-Ḥasan b. Muḥammad al-Zaʿfarānī (d. 260/874) corresponds to the structure of al-Rabīʿ's transmission of this work, lending further support to the thesis that it (or substantial parts of it) later became part of the *Umm*.

[11] *Umm*, 9:85–169.

[12] *Umm*, 8:217–390. For Abū Yūsuf's original work, see Abū Yūsuf, *Ikhtilāf Abī Ḥanīfa wa-Ibn Abī Laylā*, ed. Abū al-Wafāʾ al-Afghānī (Hyderabad: Lajnat Iḥyāʾ al-Maʿārif al-Nuʿmāniyya, 1938 or 1939).

[13] *Umm*, 9:171–277.

[14] *Umm*, 8:391–512.

[15] Schacht, in *Origins*, appendix I, also hypothesizes that these works represent some of al-Shāfiʿī's earliest writings.

This rudimentary type of writing, which I will refer to as commentary notes, represents the first of five distinct forms of writing that can be identified in the *Umm*. The second type is epistolary writing, sustained prose that makes a larger point by means of complex argumentation. The aim of this kind of writing is to convince the reader of an overall position. The most important example of this type is al-Shāfiʿī's famous *Risāla*.[16] The original version of this work is reported to have been an actual epistle written to ʿAbd al-Raḥmān b. Mahdī (d.198/814) in Basra,[17] but the extant version was composed about a quarter-century later in Egypt, when al-Shāfiʿī revised the work in accordance with his changed opinions regarding legal theory.[18]

The third recognizable type of writing in al-Shāfiʿī's works is segmented writing, which consists of a succession of seemingly self-sufficient discussions on individual points of law (*masāʾil*), grouped according to the area of the law with which they deal. The discussion of a new point of law is sometimes introduced by "al-Shāfiʿī said" (*qāla al-Shāfiʿī*) or simply "he said" (*qāla*), in order to signify a break between consecutive points. Al-Shāfiʿī's segmented writing addresses the myriad detailed and often hypothetical questions generated by Iraqi jurists but mostly dispenses with the *raʾy* question format that characterizes al-Shaybānī's texts. Instead, al-Shāfiʿī foregrounds scriptural evidence and uses the explicit techniques of interpretation and reconciliation developed in his legal-theoretical works to answer legal questions. Occasionally these *masāʾil* feature hypothetical objections ("in qīla ... qult ..."; "if it were said ... I would reply ..."), which al-Shāfiʿī uses to bolster and further develop his argument.[19]

The fourth type of writing consists of written records of actual debates in which al-Shāfiʿī had participated. In contrast to the hypothetical questions that sometimes structure al-Shāfiʿī's *masāʾil*, these texts feature sustained back-and-forth exchanges of arguments with an opponent who is usually not named but can nonetheless often be identified: al-Rabīʿ notes that when al-Shāfiʿī quotes "one/some of the jurists" (*baʿḍ al-nās*) in the *Umm*, he means specifically Ḥanafīs, while the expressions "one/some of our fellows" (*baʿḍ aṣḥābinā*) and "one/some of our compatriots" (*baʿḍ*

[16] It is very likely that the *Risāla* was from the beginning transmitted as part of the *Umm*; see the editor's introduction in the *Umm*, 1:24.

[17] Al-Bayhaqī, *Manāqib al-Shāfiʿī*, 1:230–33; see also 1:442 for a quotation from the old *Risāla*, which appears to have been still available to al-Bayhaqī.

[18] See Aḥmad Shākir's introduction to his edition of the *Risāla*, 11.

[19] See, for example, *Umm*, 2:138.

ahl baladinā) refer to Mālikīs.[20] Such debate records are found throughout the *Umm*, though they are concentrated in the last four volumes. Some constitute an entire book (such as *Ikhtilāf Mālik*) or a subsection (such as a debate regarding the status of an incomplete act of worship).[21] The substantial material on al-Shāfiʿī's Iraqi debates, discussed in Chapter 2, is largely in this form.[22] That the placement of such records within the body of the *Umm* is not arbitrary is indicated by the fact that al-Shāfiʿī often prefaces them with the comment that although he possesses even more material on the subject at hand from his debates, he has reproduced in the text only as much as is required for the purpose of the chapter.[23] It thus seems that al-Shāfiʿī selectively integrated notes from his debates into the text of the *Umm*.

The fifth type of writing consists of templates of legal documents for specific practical purposes. In the *Umm*, al-Shāfiʿī provides model documents for a poll tax (*jizya*) contract between a Muslim authority and a non-Muslim community under its rule,[24] for the annulment of a marriage, the manumission of a slave, and the rental of a house.[25] The *Umm* also contains the deed for an endowment established by al-Shāfiʿī, dated Safar 203/August 818,[26] as well as al-Shāfiʿī's will, dated Shaʿbān 203/ February 819.[27] While al-Shāfiʿī dictated the former document to his students for use as a template, the latter was added to the *Umm* later by al-Rabīʿ.

Among these five types of prose – commentary notes, epistolary writing, segmented writing, debate records, and legal documents – segmented writing is the dominant style. It is dominant in the sense that it represents the majority of al-Shāfiʿī's written work, but also in the sense that other types of writing often tend to drift into segmented form. The *masʾala*

20 *Umm*, 7:417. Al-Shāfiʿī's student al-Ḥumaydī also referred to Abū Ḥanīfa as *baʿḍ al-nās* when lecturing at the Kaʿba in Mecca in order to avoid mentioning his name in such a hallowed place; see Abū Ḥātim al-Bustī, *al-Majrūḥīn*, ed. Maḥmūd Ibrāhīm Zāyid, 3 vols. (Aleppo: Dār al-Waʿī, 1976), 2:330. Al-Bukhārī, in his *Saḥīḥ*, appears to use the same designation, *baʿḍ al-nās*, to refer to Abū Ḥanīfa; see, for example, Ibn Ḥajar al-ʿAsqalānī, *Fatḥ al-bārī*, 3:364. Later Ḥanafīs have rejected this link; see ʿAbd al-Ghanī Maydānī, *Kashf al-iltibās ʿammā awradahu al-Imām al-Bukhārī ʿalā baʿḍ al-nās*, ed. ʿAbd al-Fattāḥ Abū Ghudda (Aleppo: Maktab al-Maṭbūʿāt al-Islāmiyya, 1993). I am grateful to Garrett Davidson for the reference to Maydānī's work.

21 For the latter, see *Umm*, 2:648–65.

22 This material represents roughly two of the eleven volumes of the *Umm*.

23 See, for example, *Umm*, 8:81–82.

24 *Umm*, 5:471–75.

25 *Umm*, 7:474–80.

26 *Umm*, 7:455–58.

27 *Umm*, 5:262–66. For both documents, see Friedrich Kern, "Zwei Urkunden vom Imām Šāfiʿī," *Mitteilungen des Seminars für Orientalische Sprachen* 7 (1904): 53–68.

was the basic unit of oral dialectical engagements characterized by the use of the *ra'y* questions discussed in Chapter 1. Consequently, records of debates by their very nature resemble the literary form of segmented writing. Al-Shāfiʿī's epistolary writing also appears on many occasions to circumvent the need for a clear structure of argument by taking the form of a debate with a seemingly hypothetical interlocutor.[28] This permits al-Shāfiʿī to cover a number of related issues without having to define their exact interconnections, by simply presenting them as questions asked. Such exchanges generally cause al-Shāfiʿī's text to shift from epistolary to segmented style.[29]

What unites all of these types of writing in the *Umm* is the fact that al-Shāfiʿī employs them in a deliberate and sophisticated way to make coherent original arguments. As noted previously, he does not, for example, simply reproduce "raw" debate transcripts in the text but rather draws on them creatively to support and illustrate his larger points. Although the arrangement of the component works within the *Umm* is, to a large extent, attributable to al-Shāfiʿī's successors, and although it is very probable that this corpus does not contain the entirety of al-Shāfiʿī's written production,[30] each of the individual works in the *Umm* represents a coherent text authored by al-Shāfiʿī and reflecting his views, not those of an amorphous school.

Within the various types of writing, al-Shāfiʿī employs a range of literary techniques, including abridgment (*ikhtiṣār*), quotation of other works, and cross-referencing of his own work as well as replication of passages in it. Introducing the record of one particular debate, he specifies

[28] Lowry, *Early Islamic Legal Theory*, 375–82.

[29] This classification, and particularly the dominance of the segmented writing type, can serve as a useful map to al-Shāfiʿī's large corpus and its internal structure, as a starting point for future studies into al-Shāfiʿī's Arabic style, and as a note of caution to those who seek to apply analytical tools developed for other types of writing (especially biblical narratives) to analyze Islamic legal texts. The latter approach was used notably by Norman Calder in his *Studies in Early Muslim Jurisprudence*; I discuss the weaknesses of Calder's methodology in "Al-Shāfiʿī's Written Corpus."

[30] Other students of al-Shāfiʿī besides al-Rabīʿ, including al-Muzanī, Ḥarmala, and al-Zaʿfarānī, are also known to have compiled their own collections of al-Shāfiʿī's writings, under various titles. For al-Muzanī's *Mabsūṭ*, see Ibn Ḥajar, *Tawālī al-ta'nīs*, 170; al-Muzanī himself refers to *al-Jāmiʿ* in the *Mukhtaṣar*, e.g., at 168 (Mukhtaṣar al-shufʿa min al-Jāmiʿ). For Ḥarmala's *Umm*, see al-Bayhaqī, *Manāqib al-Shāfiʿī*, 2:347; and for al-Zaʿfarānī's *Mabsūṭ*, see Ibn al-Nadīm, *Fihrist*, pt. 1, 2:42. While these are likely to have overlapped substantially with al-Rabīʿ's recension of the *Umm*, we also know of individual sections that appear to have been included in only some of these collections; see, for example, al-Muzanī's reference to al-Shāfiʿī's "al-Imlā' ʿalā masā'il Mālik" in the *Mukhtaṣar*, 115 (Bayʿ al-laḥm bi-l-laḥm).

that the text "is an abridgment of it, and what I have written contains an indication of what I did not write."[31] Similarly, another chapter on his Iraqi debates is prefaced by the statement that "the script (*kitāb*) of this is long; this is the abridgment of what they said and what I said."[32] Al-Shāfiʿī reproduces extensive and accurate quotations from the works of other scholars, attributing in each instance the quoted material to its originator. For example, he quotes hundreds of Hadith[33] from Mālik's *Muwaṭṭa'* as well as at least two dozen passages of Mālik's prose, which match the surviving recensions of the *Muwaṭṭa'*,[34] and he includes numerous lengthy quotations from al-Shaybānī's refutation of Mālik (*al-Ḥujja ʿalā ahl al-Madīna*) in his counterrefutation, *al-Radd ʿalā Muḥammad b. al-Ḥasan*.[35] Al-Shāfiʿī also provides numerous cross-references within the text of the *Umm* itself, directing the reader to other, named sections and chapters that bear upon his current topic.[36] Finally, al-Shāfiʿī occasionally includes the same passage of text in several of his works. For example, a central element of al-Shāfiʿī's refutation of juridical preference (*istiḥsān*), namely, a set of conditions that he outlines for the proper application of analogy, is repeated in substantially the same form both in his treatise on the subject, *Ibṭāl al-istiḥsān*, and in the *Risāla*.[37]

TRANSMISSION OF AL-SHĀFIʿĪ'S WORKS

A close examination of the writings of al-Shāfiʿī and of his students reveals that the transmission of al-Shāfiʿī's written corpus to the next generation of scholars took place through four different methods, all of which

31 *Umm*, 8:81–82.

32 *Umm*, 8:196.

33 Rifʿat Fawzī ʿAbd al-Muṭṭalib has diligently traced these in the notes to his edition of the *Umm*. Compare, for example, Mālik's *Muwaṭṭa'*, 1:96, with *Umm*, 8:522; *Muwaṭṭa'*, 2:727, with *Umm*, 8:531; *Muwaṭṭa'*, 1:136, with *Umm*, 8:537; *Muwaṭṭa'*, 1:75, with *Umm*, 8:541–42; and *Muwaṭṭa'*, 1:206, with *Umm*, 8:548.

34 Compare, for example, Mālik's *Muwaṭṭa'*, ed. ʿAbd al-Bāqī, 2:859, and *Muwaṭṭa'*, ed. al-Aʿẓamī, 5:1259, with *Umm*, 8:776; *Muwaṭṭa'* (ʿAbd al-Bāqī), 1:184, and *Muwaṭṭa'* (al-Aʿẓamī), 2:256, with *Umm*, 2:217–18; and *Muwaṭṭa'* (ʿAbd al-Bāqī), 2:656, and *Muwaṭṭa'* (al-Aʿẓamī), 4:950, with *Umm*, 4:23. In spite of slight discrepancies, probably attributable to copying mistakes by al-Shāfiʿī himself as well as by later copyists, these citations clearly originate in the *Muwaṭṭa'*.

35 Compare, for example, al-Shaybānī's *Ḥujja*, 4:404–7, with *Umm*, 9:162–63; *Ḥujja*, 4:413–17, with *Umm*, 9:167–68; and *Ḥujja*, 4:285–94, with *Umm*, 9:105–6.

36 Dozens of such cross-references can be found in the *Umm*. See, for example, *Umm*, 7:487 (referring to 7:633), 5:297, 5:683, 6:720, and 8:309.

37 Compare the *Risāla*, in *Umm*, 1:237 (paras. 1472–73), with *Ibṭāl al-istiḥsān*, in *Umm*, 9:76.

originate in the repertoire of Hadith transmission. The first of these was *samāʿ* ("hearing"), or viva voce transmission, in which students listened to al-Shāfiʿī reading out a section of his writing that they had generally copied for themselves prior to the lecture. The students would compare al-Shāfiʿī's recitation with the text of their own copies and correct any mistakes in the latter. Al-Rabīʿ indicates the use of this method in the text of the *Umm* by phrases such as *samiʿtu al-Shāfiʿī yaqūl*, "I heard al-Shāfiʿī say."[38] A variant of this method is dictation from written notes (*imlāʾ*), in which students wrote down al-Shāfiʿī's work as he read it to them rather than copying it in advance of the lesson. There are at least eleven instances in the *Umm* in which al-Rabīʿ states that he received a particular chapter through dictation.[39]

The second type of transmission, *qirāʾa* ("reading"), was based on the practice of students copying the work of al-Shāfiʿī and then reading it back to him to allow him to point out any errors in the copy. Al-Muzanī claims to have learned many prophetic Hadith from al-Shāfiʿī through *qirāʾa*.[40] Al-Rabīʿ is reported to have missed al-Shāfiʿī's lesson on a three-page section of his book on sales but implored al-Shāfiʿī to permit him nonetheless to transmit the text, to which al-Shāfiʿī is said to have replied, "Read it to me, as it was read to me [in your absence]."[41] In a variation of this practice, a student of al-Shāfiʿī, Ibrāhīm b. Haram al-ʿĀmirī (d. unknown),[42] copied a section of al-Shāfiʿī's work, and al-Buwayṭī then used this copy to read the work to al-Shāfiʿī for verification. Afterward other students would write their own copies on the basis of Ibn Haram's copy.[43] According to Ibn Abī Ḥātim, al-Rabīʿ made use of such copies in compiling the *Umm* because he also served as al-Shāfiʿī's personal assistant (*ghulām*) and consequently often found himself forced to miss al-Shāfiʿī's lectures because of more practical obligations.[44]

The third method by which al-Shāfiʿī's work was transmitted to his students consisted of simple copying of written text that had been neither heard from (*samāʿ*) nor read to (*qirāʾa*) al-Shāfiʿī for authentication. In Hadith circles, such transmission was known as *wijāda*, literally

[38] See, for example, *Umm*, 2:38 and 7:516.

[39] *Umm*, 4:463, 4:479, 4:489, 5:125, 5:256, 5:258, 7:250, 7:449, 7:474, 7:485, and 7:557. These passages constitute roughly fifty pages in the text of the *Umm*.

[40] Al-Shāfiʿī, *al-Sunan al-maʾthūra*, 173 and 174.

[41] Badr al-Dīn al-Zarkashī, *al-Nukat ʿalā Muqaddimat Ibn al-Ṣalāḥ*, ed. Zayn al-ʿĀbidīn b. Muḥammad Bilā Farīj, 4 vols. (Riyadh: Maktabat Aḍwāʾ al-Salaf, 1998), 3:503.

[42] Ibn ʿAbd al-Barr, *Intiqāʾ*, 176.

[43] Ibn Abī Ḥātim, *Ādāb al-Shāfiʿī*, 71.

[44] Ibn Abī Ḥātim, *Ādāb al-Shāfiʿī*, 71.

"discovery" (of a written text),[45] and on at least one occasion, al-Rabīʿ uses the exact phrase associated with this method, *wajadtu bi-khaṭṭih* ("I found in his [own] handwriting"), for a text that he acquired from al-Shāfiʿī in this way.[46] Sometimes students copied texts written by al-Shāfiʿī himself; on other occasions the source was a copy of al-Shāfiʿī's work written by an unnamed copyist, who was probably the abovementioned Ibn Haram. Al-Rabīʿ admits openly in connection with one section of the *Umm* that "we wrote this book from al-Shāfiʿī's text, written in his own hand; we did not hear it from him."[47] On another occasion, al-Rabīʿ expresses doubt regarding the accuracy of the text, saying, "I fear that this is a mistake by the copyist, since it was neither read to al-Shāfiʿī nor heard from him."[48] Likewise, al-Muzanī introduces two texts of al-Shāfiʿī on which he draws in his compendium by noting, "al-Shāfiʿī wrote this in his own hand but I do not know that it was heard from him [by anyone]."[49] By contrast, al-Rabīʿ introduces al-Shāfiʿī's endowment deed in the *Umm* by specifying that the original document both was written in al-Shāfiʿī's own hand and had been read aloud in his presence,[50] and it thus enjoys a kind of "double guarantee."

In the fourth method of transmission students took notes on al-Shāfiʿī's lectures on individual points of law (*masāʾil*). For example, al-Muzanī begins several of the chapters in his compendium with the information that al-Shāfiʿī's positions as given in the text originate in "separate points of law that I have gathered from his oral presentation" (*masāʾil shattā jamaʿtuhā minhu lafẓan*).[51] The same kind of lecture notes most likely form the basis of some of al-Rabīʿ's interjections in the text of the *Umm*, for example, on occasions when he gives an opinion of al-Shāfiʿī and then mentions an alternative, prefaced by "and he has another opinion …" (*wa-lahu qawl ākhar* …).[52] Al-Shāfiʿī's student Ḥarmala is

[45] Ibn al-Ṣalāḥ al-Shahrazūrī, *An Introduction to the Science of the Ḥadīth (Kitāb Maʿrifat anwāʿ ʿilm al-ḥadīth)*, trans. Eerik Dickinson (Reading: Garnet, 2006), 125–27.

[46] *Umm*, 7:455. Ibn al-Ṣalāḥ notes that the Shāfiʿīs, in contrast to most Mālikīs, endorsed the acceptability of acting upon material transmitted through *wijāda*; *Introduction*, 127.

[47] *Umm*, 5:187.

[48] *Umm*, 5:230.

[49] Al-Muzanī, *Mukhtaṣar*, 185 (Kitāb iḥyāʾ al-mawāt), 194 (Iltiqāṭ al-manbūdh).

[50] *Umm*, 7:455.

[51] Al-Muzanī, *Mukhtaṣar*, 175 (Bāb al-musāqā); see also 182 (Kitāb al-muzāraʿa wa-kirāʾ al-arḍ), 194 (Iltiqāṭ al-manbūdh), 259 (Bāb al-ṭalāq qabl al-nikāḥ), 390 (Bāb mukhtaṣar al-aymān wa-l-nudhūr), 405 (al-Shahādāt fī al-buyūʿ), and 421 (Bāb mukhtaṣar min jāmiʿ al-daʿwa wa-l-bayyināt).

[52] See, for example, *Umm*, 2:104, 5:60, and 8:181.

reported to have claimed that he had a sack full of assorted notes from al-Shāfiʿī's lectures.[53] A collection of such notes transmitted through several of al-Shāfiʿī's students is also found in Ibn Abī Ḥātim al-Rāzī's *Ādāb al-Shāfiʿī*.[54]

These methods of transmission were also employed by the next generation of Shāfiʿī scholars, who studied al-Shāfiʿī's works with al-Rabīʿ as well as al-Shāfiʿī's other students. By this time a new product had become widely available, one that enabled the rapid dissemination of writings across the Muslim world: paper. Much cheaper than parchment and well suited to preserving long arguments in the manageable form of the codex (in contrast to the scrolls characteristic of papyrus works), paper furnished the material basis for the knowledge explosion experienced by the Muslim world in the third/ninth and fourth/tenth centuries.[55]

An illuminating description of how the process of studying and copying al-Shāfiʿī's works played out in actual practice is afforded by the following anecdotes by the Hadith scholar Abū Zurʿa al-Rāzī, as quoted in the work of his student Ibn Abī Ḥātim:

> I left Rayy for the second time in 227 [841 or 842 CE] and returned in early 232 [846 CE].... I stayed in Egypt for fifteen months. In the beginning of my sojourn in Egypt I resolved to make my stay a short one, but when I saw the abundance of knowledge there and the abundance of benefit, I decided to settle [for longer]. I had not intended to hear al-Shāfiʿī's books, but when I decided to settle, I headed for the most knowledgeable man with regard to al-Shāfiʿī's works in Egypt and I agreed to pay him eighty dirhams to copy all of them, and I provided him with the paper.... I bought one hundred sheets of paper for ten dirhams,[56] and on these al-Shāfiʿī's books were written.[57]

[53] Al-Bayhaqī, *Manāqib al-Shāfiʿī*, 1:255.

[54] Ibn Abī Ḥātim, *Ādāb al-Shāfiʿī*, 280–309.

[55] According to one estimate quoted by Jonathan Bloom, six hundred thousand manuscript books written in the Muslim world between 700 and 1500 CE remain extant today; significantly more works were produced in this period but have been lost. See Bloom, *Paper before Print: The History and Impact of Paper in the Islamic World* (New Haven, CT: Yale University Press, 2001), 93.

[56] The total cost was thus ninety dirhams, i.e., no more than nine dinars, or less than one-seventh of the amount paid by al-Shāfiʿī for al-Shaybānī's books four decades earlier. For the theoretical exchange rate, see *Umm*, 9:85–86; for historical fluctuations, see G. C. Miles, "Dirham," in *EI2*, 3:319.

[57] Ibn Abī Ḥātim, *al-Jarḥ wa-l-taʿdīl*, 1:340. Note that the length of the copied works cannot be established from this report, given that the size of sheets as well as the way in which they were cut and/or folded varied significantly; see Adam Gacek, *Arabic Manuscripts: A Vademecum for Readers* (Leiden: Brill, 2009), 104–5. The extant manuscripts of the *Umm* contain between 850 and 2,000 folios (see editor's introduction to the *Umm*, 1:30–33). One report quotes al-Rabīʿ as saying that the *Umm* consisted of 2,000 pages (*waraqa*); see Ibn Ḥajar al-ʿAsqalānī, *Tawālī al-taʾnīs*, 194.

That al-Rabīʿ was not the only one of al-Shāfiʿī's students to transmit the master's corpus is evident from Abū Zurʿa's anecdote regarding an unnamed friend who complained that he had not yet finished studying all of al-Shāfiʿī's works with his teacher Ḥarmala: "I asked him: 'Would you agree if al-Rabīʿ were to read to you [the rest]?' He said yes. When I met al-Rabīʿ I told him this story and asked him whether he could come and recite to him what he was still missing, so he came at night and read to him."[58] Finally, Abū Zurʿa was asked whether it was true that he had heard the whole corpus of al-Shāfiʿī from al-Rabīʿ in forty days, and he answered: "No, my son, I studied with him when I was free from other obligations. I was attending his classes in the central mosque and sometimes I was late, or did not go at all, and he [waited for me and] would not go home. So he said: 'If you cannot come, leave a note on the column so that I can go home.'"[59]

These accounts offer an insight into how an aspiring student would have gone about studying al-Shāfiʿī's work in third-/ninth-century Egypt. (The process sketched here is strikingly similar to the method of instruction in Mālik's circle in Medina, as encountered in Chapter 1, indicating a continued emphasis on aural transmission; I return to this point later.) First one needed a copy of al-Shāfiʿī's works. It seems that one first chose a teacher, then had that teacher's copy of al-Shāfiʿī's writings copied for oneself. Professional copyists could provide this service, and some seem to have specialized in the copying of al-Shāfiʿī's work; the particular copyist (*warrāq*) mentioned by Abū Zurʿa was probably Abū al-Ḥusayn al-Iṣbahānī (d. 262/876), a student of al-Shāfiʿī and the *warrāq* of al-Rabīʿ.[60] After acquiring a copy of al-Shāfiʿī's corpus according to the recension of one of his students, the novice would then attend the lectures of this teacher to hear the complete work read out by the teacher – that is, transmission by *samāʿ*. In the process, the student could correct any copyist mistakes in the written text and hear the teacher explain and elucidate on al-Shāfiʿī's prose. The student might also add the teacher's explanations to his own copy of the text as marginal notes. A student was not, however, bound to one particular teacher, as indicated by the example of Abū Zurʿā's friend, who began his studies with Ḥarmala but completed them with al-Rabīʿ. In addition, Abū Zurʿa's report suggests

58 Ibn Abī Ḥātim, *al-Jarḥ wa-l-taʿdīl*, 1:344–45.
59 Ibn Abī Ḥātim, *al-Jarḥ wa-l-taʿdīl*, 1:345.
60 Al-Maqrīzī, *Muqaffā*, 6:126–27. For the phenomenon of the *warrāq* as a personal copyist/bookseller, see Johannes Pedersen, *The Arabic Book*, ed. Robert Hillenbrand, trans. Geoffrey French (Princeton, NJ: Princeton University Press, 1984), 45.

that a student could have studied (that is, heard in lectures) al-Shāfiʿī's entire corpus in about forty days, if he had the financial means to dedicate his time to studying free of other obligations.

While Abū Zurʿa still heard al-Rabīʿ in his fifties reading out al-Shāfiʿī's work himself, ʿAdnān, the son of the governor Aḥmad b. Ṭūlūn, encountered al-Rabīʿ several decades later: "He [al-Rabīʿ] came to us, and his son read out [the works] to him while we listened."[61] In his eighties or early nineties, al-Rabīʿ no longer recited al-Shāfiʿī's corpus himself for students. Rather, in a variant of *qirāʾa*, he had the material that he had gathered decades earlier read out by his son, vouching for its authenticity by his presence.

STANDARDS OF TRANSMISSION

The evidence presented here regarding the early transmission of al-Shāfiʿī's work shows that both al-Shāfiʿī and his students consciously sought to follow the rigorous protocols that scholars of Hadith had developed for the transmission of Hadith reports and were careful to note any potential shortcomings in the transmitted text.[62] Al-Shāfiʿī, for example, doubts his notes on one occasion in the *Umm*, when he reproduces a Hadith whose chain of transmission contains one link fewer than in the version of the chain transmitted by other scholars. He comments: "I do not know … whether or not it was left out of my text when I transferred it from [my] original [notes]. The original [notes] from the day when I wrote this [Hadith] are not with me."[63] In another instance, al-Shāfiʿī quotes a Hadith that he had heard from Sufyān b. ʿUyayna but then raises a problem: "That is how I have heard it from him all my life, but then I found in my notebook [the same Hadith with a crucial addition]; so this is either a mistake in my notes, or a mistake on Sufyān's part."[64] Al-Shāfiʿī contrasts the two versions of the Hadith using alternative chains of transmission and argues that the shorter version is the correct one, concluding that "I have heard from more than one person who studied with Sufyān in the old days that he did not use to make this addition … and some were amazed when I told them that I found [it] in my notes … and said that this might be his mistake or an oversight that I preserved from him."[65]

[61] Ibn ʿAsākir, *Tārīkh madīnat Dimashq*, 40:54.

[62] Mohyddin Yahia has arrived at very similar conclusions regarding the transmission of al-Shāfiʿī's work; see his *Šāfiʿī et les deux sources*, chap. 3.

[63] *Umm*, 10:205. For a similar admission, see the *Risāla*, in *Umm*, 1:198–99 (para. 1184).

[64] *Umm*, 9:307.

[65] *Umm*, 9:307.

In yet another discussion, al-Shāfiʿī relates a report from Mālik's *Muwaṭṭa'* in which the prophetic Companion Ṭalḥa b. ʿUbayd Allāh urges someone to "wait until my treasurer comes back." Al-Shāfiʿī adds: "I read [this passage] correctly to Mālik, there is no doubt about that; but much time has passed since then and I no longer remember exactly, so I am unsure whether the word was 'treasurer' (masculine) or 'treasurer' (feminine). Others transmit this from him as 'treasurer' (masculine)."[66] He then goes on to narrate the same report from Ṭalḥa via a different chain of transmission, featuring the word "treasurer" in its masculine form. The fact that al-Shāfiʿī stubbornly insists on admitting his uncertainty regarding the precise wording of the transmission from Mālik and refuses to extrapolate, even though he possesses unambiguous corroborating evidence, demonstrates a meticulous attention to accuracy.

Al-Shāfiʿī thus used writing critically, comparing his written notes with information that he had memorized and with alternative written and aurally transmitted sources and openly acknowledging weaknesses in his sources or his memory. He also explicitly addressed the problem of correct transmission in the context of recording debates in which he had participated:

> Some people disagreed with me on this point, so I debated with some of them, and they put forward some of the arguments that I mentioned in the discussion on this point of law. I paraphrased [their position], and they answered me with what I have summarized here; however, I am not sure whether I might have clarified my own position when writing it down beyond what I actually uttered when I was speaking. I do not like to report anything other than what I actually said, even when I am only paraphrasing what I said.[67]

Another section he prefaces with the following disclaimer: "God willing, I will relate what Muḥammad b. al-Ḥasan and others who follow his way said to me in debate. I may not distinguish between his words and those of the others, but most of it is his words."[68] These reflections on the pitfalls of reporting a debate indicate a critical awareness of the challenge of accuracy in turning the spoken words of an interpersonal encounter into written text. Al-Shāfiʿī specifically mentions the tendency on the part of the reporting party to lump together the arguments of several opponents, as well as the temptation to clarify, enlarge, and sharpen his arguments retroactively and thereby to skew the record.

[66] *Umm*, 4:53–54. Al-Shāfiʿī's observation that other students of Mālik relate the word in the masculine form matches the extant transmissions of the *Muwaṭṭa'*; see *Muwaṭṭa'*, ed. ʿAbd al-Bāqī, 2:636–37, and *Muwaṭṭa'*, ed. al-Aʿẓamī, 4:920–21.

[67] *Umm*, 2:648.

[68] *Umm*, 9:106.

Al-Rabīʿ also demonstrated a prima facie commitment to the exacting standards established for the transmission of Hadith in his treatment of al-Shāfiʿī's writings. His comments in the *Umm* show great precision in specifying both the method of transmission used for particular passages and any departures from the proper protocol of transmission. According to al-Khaṭīb al-Baghdādī (d. 463/1071), al-Rabīʿ was instructed by al-Shāfiʿī to use the phrase *akhbaranā* ("he told us") to mark passages received through *qirāʾa* and its near-synonym *ḥaddathanā* to indicate *samāʿ*,[69] a distinction that later became part of standard Hadith terminology.[70] A survey of al-Rabīʿ's usage of these terms in the *Umm* suggests that they are generally, though not uniformly, employed in this manner.[71] On the other hand, al-Rabīʿ admits openly where he, for example, has copied a text from al-Shāfiʿī's documents without having studied it with him, is aware of a missing section within the text, suspects a copyist error, or has reproduced a passage from memory.[72] These notes thus show al-Rabīʿ as a careful transmitter, who readily acknowledged shortcomings and gaps in the material. The following is a sampling of examples from the *Umm* that indicate al-Rabīʿ's critical attitude toward the text:

- In the *Umm*'s chapter on alms, al-Rabīʿ notes, about a page into the text, that "I heard the whole chapter, but I did not present/collate (*lam uʿāriḍ*) it from here until the end."[73] Depending on the meaning of the ambiguous verb *ʿāraḍa*, two interpretations are possible. The first is that although al-Rabīʿ heard the entire chapter recited in al-Shāfiʿī's presence through *qirāʾa*, the last section was not read by al-Rabīʿ himself but rather by another student. Alternatively, the chapter may have been transmitted through *samāʿ*, and al-Rabīʿ may have had the opportunity to collate (i.e., compare) his copy of the text with an authoritative version only for the first part of the chapter.[74]

[69] Al-Khaṭīb al-Baghdādī, *al-Kifāya fī ʿilm al-riwāya*, ed. Abū ʿAbd Allāh al-Sawraqī and Ibrāhīm Ḥamdī al-Madanī (Medina: al-Maktaba al-ʿIlmiyya, 1980), 303.

[70] Ibn al-Ṣalāḥ, *Introduction*, 98–101.

[71] See, for example, *Umm*, 5:256, 5:258, 7:250, 7:449, and 7:557, where al-Rabīʿ employs the specific phrase *ḥaddathanā al-Shāfiʿī imlāʾan*. However, there are also a few instances where al-Rabīʿ uses *akhbaranā* to introduce a passage received through dictation; see *Umm*, 4:479, 4:489, and 5:125. These may be copyist errors, but they may also indicate that al-Rabīʿ's usage of this terminology was not consistent.

[72] For the latter, see *Umm*, 6:21.

[73] *Umm*, 3:158.

[74] "Lam uʿāriḍ" could, in the terminology of textual transmission, refer either to presentation (*ʿarḍ*) in the course of *qirāʾa* or to the collation of different manuscripts of a text (*muʿāraḍa*); see Ibn al-Ṣalāḥ, *Introduction*, 100, and al-Zarkashī, *Nukat*, 3:582. The

- In another chapter al-Rabīʿ says, "I missed this part of the book, but I heard it *viva voce* (*samiʿtu*) from al-Buwayṭī, and I know that it is al-Shāfiʿī's words (*aʿrifuhu min kalām al-Shāfiʿī*)";[75] three pages later he notes, "my *viva voce* reception (*samāʿī*) from al-Buwayṭī ends here."[76] Al-Rabīʿ thus acknowledges that his formal chain of transmission (*isnād*) for this material runs through al-Buwayṭī. It is noteworthy that the four Hadith that al-Rabīʿ quotes from al-Shāfiʿī within this section all include al-Buwayṭī in their chains of transmission; this contrasts with Hadith quoted before and after this section, whose *isnāds* go straight from al-Shāfiʿī to al-Rabīʿ.[77]
- At one point, al-Rabīʿ admits that he did not hear a particular chapter directly from al-Shāfiʿī, but asserts – without specifying the reason – that he is nevertheless sure of its authenticity.[78]
- In a passage in the *Umm*'s book on admission (*iqrār*), al-Shāfiʿī mentions that he has given the evidence for a particular position in his "book on duress" (*kitāb al-ikrāh*). A student of al-Rabīʿ adds the following note: "al-Rabīʿ was asked about the book on duress, and he said 'I don't know it.'"[79]
- On the subject of wills, the text poses a legal problem, but then breaks off in midsentence. Al-Rabīʿ comments that "this is as much as there is in al-Shāfiʿī's book (*kitāb al-Shāfiʿī*) on this point of law; the answer is missing."[80]
- In a discussion on the alms payable on livestock, al-Rabīʿ adds a note of caution: "I suspect that instead of 'two-year-old calf' (*musinna*) it should say 'one-year-old calf' (*tabīʿ*); this is a copyist mistake, since the end of the sentence indicates that [al-Shāfiʿī] means a one-year-old calf."[81]

Some evidence in the *Umm* as well as in other sources suggests that al-Rabīʿ drew to some extent on the notes of his peer al-Buwayṭī in compiling the *Umm*. As seen earlier, al-Rabīʿ admits as much at one point in the *Umm*, stating that he received a particular text via al-Buwayṭī.[82]

former possibility is supported by the phrase "akhbaranā" that introduces the chapter; the latter use of the term is, however, more common.

75 *Umm*, 2:252.
76 *Umm*, 2:255.
77 Abū al-ʿAbbās al-Aṣamm also notes this difference in his *Musnad al-Shāfiʿī*, 1:268–72.
78 *Umm*, 2:639.
79 *Umm*, 4:498.
80 *Umm*, 5:208.
81 *Umm*, 3:28.
82 *Umm*, 2:252.

Elsewhere, the text includes a note that may represent a marginal comment made by al-Buwayṭī on his notes of the *Umm*.[83] More substantial borrowing by al-Rabīʿ was alleged by his contemporary Yūsuf b. Yazīd al-Qarāṭīsī (d. 287/900);[84] the same allegation was repeated a century later by Abū Ṭālib al-Makkī (d. 386/996)[85] and has most recently been aired by Zakī Mubārak (d. 1952).[86] The precise extent of al-Rabīʿ's reliance on al-Buwayṭī's notes is probably impossible to ascertain, but such borrowing was not limited to al-Rabīʿ: al-Muzanī is also said to have made use of al-Rabīʿ's notes for material that he had missed from al-Shāfiʿī.[87]

Basing one's transmission on someone else's notes would have been considered unacceptable in the context of Hadith transmission; indeed, precisely this transgression is reported to have led to the disgrace of Muḥammad b. ʿAbda b. Ḥarb al-ʿAbbādānī, the Ḥanafī judge mentioned in Chapter 5.[88] However, it seems that although al-Shāfiʿī's students clearly modeled their transmission practices on Hadith standards, in practice their adherence to those standards with respect to the formal aspects (though not substantive content) of transmission was not as rigid. This is understandable given that the material being transmitted lacked the grave religious significance of Hadith reports, and its source – al-Shāfiʿī – lay within the students' own lifetimes, in contrast to the era of the Prophet, from which this generation of scholars was separated by more than two centuries.

The concern of al-Shāfiʿī and his students for correct transmission was noted by Ḥusayn Wālī in his 1933 study of the nature and textual history of the *Umm*.[89] Furthermore, evidence indicates that this concern was shared by other third-/ninth-century Egyptian scholars and was applied to the works of the emerging Shāfiʿī school by contemporary observers. The first example is furnished by the abovementioned Yūsuf b. Yazīd al-Qarāṭīsī, an Egyptian Mālikī scholar and a transmitter of ʿAbd Allāh

[83] *Umm*, 4:327.

[84] Ibn Ḥajar al-ʿAsqalānī, *Tahdhīb al-Tahdhīb*, 3:246.

[85] Abū Ṭālib al-Makkī, *Qūt al-qulūb*, ed. ʿAbd al-Munʿim al-Ḥifnī, 3 vols. (Cairo: Dār al-Rashād, 1991), 458.

[86] Zakī Mubārak, *Iṣlāḥ ashnaʿ khaṭaʾ fī tārīkh al-tashrīʿ al-islāmī* (Cairo: al-Maktaba al-Tijāriyya al-Kubrā, 1352/1934). See also Melchert's discussion of Mubārak's work in "The Meaning of *Qāla 'l-Shāfiʿī* in Ninth Century Sources," in *ʿAbbasid Studies*, ed. James E. Montgomery, 277–301 (Leuven: Peeters, 2004), 298–301.

[87] This claim was made by al-Khalīlī in *Kitāb al-Irshād*, 1:429: "al-Muzanī maʿa jalālatihi istaʿāna fī mā fātahu ʿan al-Shāfiʿī bi-kitāb al-Rabīʿ."

[88] Al-Kindī, *Governors and Judges*, 515 (appendix).

[89] Ḥusayn Wālī, "Kitāb al-Umm wa-mā yuḥīṭu bih," *Majallat nūr al-islām* 4 (1352/1933 and 1934): 656–88.

b. ʿAbd al-Ḥakam's compendium.[90] Al-Qarāṭīsī is reported to have seen al-Shāfiʿī as a child but not to have become his student. He was both thoroughly acquainted with al-Shāfiʿī's work and involved in the Mālikī efforts to refute al-Shāfiʿī's criticism of Mālik; one of al-Qarāṭīsī's students, Yūsuf b. Yaḥyā al-Azdī al-Maghāmī (d. 288/901),[91] wrote a refutation of al-Shāfiʿī. His son Idrīs b. Yūsuf al-Qarāṭīsī (d. unknown), on the other hand, was a devoted Shāfiʿī.[92] Al-Qarāṭīsī is reported to have cast doubt on the directness of al-Rabīʿ's transmission of al-Shāfiʿī's works by claiming that "the material that al-Rabīʿ b. Sulaymān received aurally from al-Shāfiʿī was not reliable, and he took most of the books from the family of al-Buwayṭī after al-Buwayṭī's death."[93] The truth or otherwise of this claim, mentioned earlier, is here irrelevant. What is significant is that al-Qarāṭīsī, a member of a rival school and a contemporary of al-Rabīʿ, was informed enough about the textual history of al-Shāfiʿī's corpus to make such a claim and that he used this particular claim to denigrate al-Rabīʿ as a transmitter of al-Shāfiʿī's work. This demonstrates that there was a critical public of scholars outside the immediate Shāfiʿī circle who were willing to question the precise transmission of al-Shāfiʿī's works. The fact that al-Qarāṭīsī's challenge to the Shāfiʿīs consisted of the rather limited charge that al-Rabīʿ's transmission was based not on his own notes but on those of al-Buwayṭī indicates the absence of concerns regarding the bigger issue of the content of the transmitted works. Had al-Qarāṭīsī had any reason to suspect that al-Rabīʿ either alone or in concert with other Shāfiʿī scholars was actively manipulating the text, he would hardly have focused his criticism on such a minor detail.

That third-/ninth-century scholars had an interest in ascertaining the real source of written material is demonstrated by the apparent outrage of al-Shāfiʿī's Iraqi student al-Karābīsī upon discovering what he believed to be a case of blatant plagiarism of al-Shāfiʿī's work by Abū ʿUbayd al-Qāsim b. Sallām. Al-Karābīsī read Abū ʿUbayd's works and claims to have noted that the author "uses al-Shāfiʿī's arguments and copies his wording (*yaḥkī lafẓahu*) but does not name him." This anonymous

[90] On al-Qarāṭīsī's biography, see Ibn al-Qaṭṭān al-Fāsī, *Bayān al-wahm wa-l-īhām al-wāqiʿayn fī kitāb al-Aḥkām*, ed. al-Ḥusayn Saʿīd, 6 vols. (Riyadh: Dār Ṭayyiba, 1997), 5:554; on his transmission of the *Mukhtaṣar*, see al-Qāḍī ʿIyāḍ, *Tartīb al-madārik*, 3:365.

[91] Al-Dhahabī, *Siyar aʿlām al-nubalāʾ*, 13:337.

[92] Abū ʿAbd Allāh al-Ṣaymarī, *Akhbār Abī Ḥanīfa wa-aṣḥābih*, ed. Abū al-Wafāʾ al-Afghānī (Hyderabad: Lajnat Iḥyāʾ al-Maʿārif al-Nuʿmāniyya, 1974; repr., Beirut: ʿĀlam al-Kutub, 1985), 128.

[93] Ibn Ḥajar al-ʿAsqalānī, *Tahdhīb al-Tahdhīb*, 3:246.

borrowing angered al-Karābīsī, and when he later met Abū ʿUbayd, he confronted him: "What is wrong with you, O Abū ʿUbayd, that you say in your works, 'Muḥammad b. al-Ḥasan said,' and 'So-and-so said,' but you do not mention al-Shāfiʿī, even though you plagiarized (*saraqta*) his reasoning from his books?"[94] There is also specific evidence to indicate that third-/ninth-century scholars studying the work of al-Shāfiʿī expected the material that they received to be fully authentic. When the Ḥanafī judge of Egypt, Bakkār b. Qutayba, set out to write a refutation of al-Shāfiʿī's critique of Abū Ḥanīfa, he dispatched two court witnesses to al-Muzanī to have him testify formally that the opinions included in his compendium were indeed those held by al-Shāfiʿī.[95] And an unnamed student of al-Rabīʿ is reported to have insisted that al-Rabīʿ vouch for the content of his lecture explicitly by uttering the formula "This is how it was read to me and how al-Shāfiʿī transmitted it to us," signifying authentic verbatim transmission.[96]

The preoccupation of third-/ninth-century scholars with ascertaining the aural transmission history of al-Shāfiʿī's works indicates the existence of what might be described as a developmental time lag in the evolution of Islamic law. Previous chapters have argued that this period witnessed a shift from a primarily oral mode of legal discourse, supported by mnemonic written texts, to one based primarily on purposefully composed books. However, the evidence presented in this chapter demonstrates that the transmission of these works continued to be governed by the principles of an oral culture with its emphasis on direct aural transmission. As an example, Ibn Khuzayma, who studied with al-Shāfiʿī's students, dismissed the learning of his fellow Shāfiʿī Ibn Surayj with the rhetorical question "Has he taken his knowledge from any but borrowed books?"[97] – in contrast to Ibn Khuzayma himself, who was connected to al-Shāfiʿī by means of a sound chain of transmission. For Ibn Khuzayma, the organic connection of an unbroken chain of transmission was still a *conditio sine qua non* for a claim to real knowledge of a scholar's work; a book was not yet considered an exclusively written artifact. With time this attitude changed with regard to legal works. This shift was probably assisted both by the burgeoning of legal literature, which made the expectation of an impeccable transmission history for each work unrealistic, and by the

[94] Ibn Ḥajar al-ʿAsqalānī, *Tahdhīb al-Tahdhīb*, 2:361.
[95] Al-Kindī, *Governors and Judges*, 511–12 (appendix).
[96] Al-Khaṭīb al-Baghdādī, *Kifāya*, 281.
[97] Ibn ʿAsākir, *Tārīkh madīnat Dimashq*, 54:247.

emergence of "standard" recensions of particularly influential texts. In the ninth/fifteenth century, Ibn Ḥajar al-ʿAsqalānī (d. 852/1449) observed that no part of al-Shāfiʿī's corpus with the exception of the *Risāla* and the *Ikhtilāf al-ḥadīth* still possessed an unbroken chain of transmission.[98]

Al-Shāfiʿī's legacy was not perpetuated only through the vehicle of his own writing: his powerful authorial voice and systematic approach to law prompted some of his students to compose books that were in close dialogue with his work. In contrast to the intertextual form that we have encountered thus far – namely, the refutation – the works of al-Shāfiʿī's students formed a symbiotic relationship with al-Shāfiʿī's oeuvre, building on his methodology and opinions and extending them to new cases. The emergence of such a relationship between texts, explored in the next chapter, is a sign of the formation of a new kind of community to replace the regional normative traditions of old.

[98] Ibn Ḥajar al-ʿAsqalānī, *al-Imtāʿ bi-l-arbaʿīn al-mutabāyina al-samāʿ*, ed. Abū ʿAbd Allāh Muḥammad Ismāʿīl (Beirut: Dār al-Kutub al-ʿIlmiyya, 1997), 103. Ṣalāḥ al-Dīn Khalīl b. Kaykaldī al-ʿAlāʾī (d. 761/1359) provides a continuous *isnād* for the *Risāla* until his time in *Ithārat al-fawāʾid al-majmūʿa fī al-ishāra ilā al-farāʾid al-masmūʿa*, ed. Marzūq b. Hayyās Āl Marzūq al-Zahrānī, 2 vols. (Medina: Maktabat al-ʿUlūm wa-l-Ḥikam; Damascus: Dār al-ʿUlūm wa-l-Ḥikam, 2004), 1:112–13.

Chapter 7

A Community of Interpretation

The previous chapter explored al-Shāfiʿī's written works and the transmission of these works by al-Shāfiʿī's immediate students, highlighting the attention to accuracy and correct attribution that characterized the process of transmission. But al-Shāfiʿī's students also composed their own writings based on the master's work. Two of these compendia are extant: those of Abū Yaʿqūb al-Buwayṭī (d. 231/846) and Ismāʿīl b. Yaḥyā al-Muzanī (d. 264/877). An examination of these works reveals that they neither simply reproduce al-Shāfiʿī's ideas nor develop their own sui generis interpretations of the sacred canon. Instead, they organize, digest, complement, and critique al-Shāfiʿī's arguments and evidence. This critical engagement creates a hierarchy of authority between the first tier of interpretive writing – that of al-Shāfiʿī – and the secondary literature produced by his students. This does not mean that the students in effect canonized their master's work: al-Shāfiʿī's corpus remained distinct from the sacred canon, its authority contingent on and derivative of the authority of the texts that it interpreted. Rather, through their creative engagement with al-Shāfiʿī's writings, the students synthesized his thought into an impersonal doctrine – a Shāfiʿī paradigm – around which grew a new, communal institution: the school of law (*madhhab fiqhī*) as a community of interpretation.

Throughout the classical period, the four orthodox legal schools (Mālikī, Ḥanafī, Shāfiʿī, and Ḥanbalī) dominated the theory and practice of Sunni Islamic law, structuring and constraining the individual interpretive work of their members and thus circumscribing the parameters of the Islamic normative discourse. The hegemonic authority of these institutions is perhaps the central feature of Islamic law in its classical manifestation, and it is directly rooted in the canonization project of al-Shāfiʿī. Although the local legal traditions of Medina, Iraq, and so on, that predated al-Shāfiʿī can also be called schools of law, these differed in a fundamental way from the classical *madhhab*. The former were founded on communal tradition, whereas the latter was defined by a particular interpretive stance vis-à-vis the newly canonized sources. This chapter demonstrates how al-Shāfiʿī's students, through their textual and analytical engagement with the work of their teacher, laid the basis for the classical model of the legal school as a paradigmatic institution.

To date, most studies on the Islamic legal schools have been guided by three principal theories regarding the origins and nature of the schools of law. The first of these was formulated by Joseph Schacht, who proposed a two-phase trajectory of evolution that was largely drawn from the classical Muslim narrative of Islamic legal history.[1] According to Schacht, the earliest, "ancient," legal schools, which were based on and justified in terms of local normative traditions, were in the late second/eighth and early third/ninth centuries transformed into "personal" schools, defined by adherence to the school founder, an eponymous imam. This shift was made possible by the emergence of legal theory, which enabled legal opinions to be derived directly and systematically from textual sources, rather than from local traditions.

The second theory, put forward by George Makdisi and most forcefully developed by Christopher Melchert, takes as its starting point Schacht's periodization but identifies and focuses on a third, "classical," phase, in which the schools functioned as de facto guilds of law. The constitutive elements of the *madhhab*-as-guild-school were social structures of initiation, reproduction, and leadership.[2] Given that these ingredients were not yet evident in the third/ninth century, Melchert dates the birth of the schools proper to the fourth/tenth century. A corollary of his argument is the conclusion that the role of the so-called founder-imams in the establishment of the schools is in fact fictitious and should be dismissed: "no more should textbook-writers tell us that the eponyms founded their schools."[3]

1 Schacht, *Origins*, as well as *Introduction to Islamic Law*, chaps. 6, 9, and 10. See also Noel J. Coulson, *A History of Islamic Law* (Edinburgh: Edinburgh University Press, 1964), chaps. 6–8.

2 George Makdisi, *The Rise of Colleges: Institutions of Learning in Islam and the West* (Edinburgh: Edinburgh University Press, 1981), and Melchert, *Formation of the Sunni Schools*. See also Knut Vikør, *Between God and the Sultan: A History of Islamic Law* (Oxford: Oxford University Press, 2005), chap. 6.

3 Melchert, *Formation of the Sunni Schools*, xxv.

Most recently, Wael Hallaq has proposed an alternative historical trajectory, rejecting Schacht's notion of regional schools and arguing that the personal schools (which he relocates to the second/eighth century) were followed in the late third/ninth century by a distinctly "doctrinal" developmental stage.[4] According to Hallaq, the doctrinal schools, only nominally based on the work of their eponyms, were primarily characterized by a complex system of authority. This included substantive as well as theoretical rules and was fueled by the principle of *taqlīd*, or legal conformism.[5]

Each of the three models places primary emphasis on a particular dimension of the legal schools: Schacht focuses on law and legal theory, Makdisi and Melchert on social structures, and Hallaq on authority and doctrinal change within the schools. However, a comprehensive account of the *madhhab* and its emergence must incorporate all of these perspectives in order to do justice to this complex historical phenomenon. In this chapter, I survey the available internal evidence regarding third-/ninth-century scholars' perception of the putative Shāfiʿī school and offer an analytical account of the legal works and thought of the students of al-Shāfiʿī. I argue that we can indeed observe a phenomenon that merits the appellation *madhhab*, encompassing a distinct group identity, a common literature, and a shared intellectual discourse.

AL-SHĀFIʿĪ'S FOLLOWERS

Already in the early third-/ninth-century literature we find references to "al-Shāfiʿī's followers" (*aṣḥāb al-Shāfiʿī*), indicating that the disciples of al-Shāfiʿī formed a distinct, identifiable cluster defined not in terms of their geographical affiliation (as the "Meccans" or the "Iraqis," for example) or of their theoretical orientation (as *aṣḥāb al-ḥadīth* or *aṣḥāb al-raʾy*) but rather in terms of their attachment to al-Shāfiʿī as an individual. The earliest example is found in al-Jamal's poem in praise of judge Ibn Abī al-Layth, quoted in Chapter 5, which makes explicit reference to "al-Shāfiʿī and his followers (*wa-ṣaḥbih*)."[6] Given the unpopularity of the Inquisition and of Ibn Abī al-Layth, there could have been no reason

[4] Hallaq, "From Regional to Personal Schools"; *Origins and Evolution*, 150–77; *Authority, Continuity and Change* (Cambridge: Cambridge University Press, 2001).

[5] Beyond these theories, Nurit Tsafrir's and Nimrod Hurvitz's studies of early Ḥanafism and Ḥanbalism, respectively, avoid theoretical models of the *madhhab* in favor of microhistorical analyses of scholarly circles, their social interactions and values. See Nurit Tsafrir, *The History of an Islamic School of Law: The Early Spread of Hanafism* (Cambridge, MA: Islamic Legal Studies Program at Harvard Law School, 2004), and Nimrod Hurvitz, *The Formation of Ḥanbalism: Piety into Power* (London: RoutledgeCurzon, 2002).

[6] Quoted in al-Kindī, *Governors and Judges*, 452.

for al-Jamal to compose the poem after Ibn Abī al-Layth's removal from office, which means that it must have been written before 237/850.

The term "al-Shāfiʿī's followers" (*aṣḥāb al-Shāfiʿī*) was also used by three contemporaries of al-Shāfiʿī's students, who compiled lists of al-Shāfiʿī's principal disciples. These lists are given in the following table; the numbers indicate the original ordering, but two of the three lists have been rearranged to facilitate comparison. The added letters in parentheses refer to the locality with which each student is primarily associated in the biographical literature: E = Egypt, B = Baghdad, M = Mecca.

Aḥmad b. Shuʿayb al-Nasāʾī (d. 303/915)[7]	**Abū Dāwūd al-Sijistānī (d. 275/889)**[8]	**Dāwūd al-Ẓāhirī (d. 270/884)**[9]
1. al-Muzanī (E)	9. al-Muzanī (E)	13. al-Muzanī (E)
2. Abū Thawr (B)[10]	5. Abū Thawr (B)	5. Abū Thawr (B)
3. al-Buwayṭī (E)	3. al-Buwayṭī (E)	7. al-Buwayṭī (E)
4. Ibn Abī al-Jārūd (M)[11]	6. Ibn Abī al-Jārūd (M)	10. Ibn Abī al-Jārūd (M)
5. al-Ḥumaydī (M)	1. al-Ḥumaydī (M)	3. al-Ḥumaydī (M)
	2. Aḥmad b. Ḥanbal (B)	1. Aḥmad b. Ḥanbal (B)
	4. al-Rabīʿ (E)	9. al-Rabīʿ (E)
	7. al-Zaʿfarānī (B)[12]	6. al-Zaʿfarānī (B)
	8. al-Karābīsī (B)[13]	8. Ḥarmala (E)
	10. Ḥarmala (E)	2. Sulaymān b. Dāwūd (B)[14]
	11. Abū ʿAbd al-Raḥmān (B)	4. al-Ḥusayn al-Qallās (B)[15]
		11. al-Ḥārith b. Surayj (B)[16]
		12. Aḥmad al-Khallāl (B)[17]

[7] Abū ʿAbd al-Raḥmān Aḥmad b. Shuʿayb al-Nasāʾī, *Tasmiyat fuqahāʾ al-amṣār min aṣḥāb rasūl Allāh wa-man baʿdahum*, ed. Muḥammad Ibrāhīm Zāyid (Aleppo: Dār al-Waʿī, 1950), 127–28.

[8] Reproduced in Ibn ʿAsākir, *Tārīkh madīnat Dimashq*, 51:358, as well as in al-Maqrīzī, *Muqaffā*, 5:377.

[9] Reproduced in Ibn ʿAsākir, *Tārīkh madīnat Dimashq*, 51:358.

[10] Ibrāhīm b. Khālid al-Kalbī (d. 240/854).

[11] Abū al-Walīd Mūsā b. Abī al-Jārūd (d. unknown).

[12] Abū ʿAlī al-Ḥasan b. Muḥammad al-Zaʿfarānī (d. 259/873).

[13] Abū ʿAlī al-Karābīsī (d. 248/862).

[14] Sulaymān b. Dāwūd al-Hāshimī (d. 219 or 220/834 or 835); see al-Subkī, *Ṭabaqāt al-shāfiʿiyya al-kubrā*, 2:139.

[15] The text reads "al-Fallās"; my emendation is based on al-Subkī, *al-Ṭabaqāt al-shāfiʿiyya al-kubrā*, 1:127. Al-Qallās's death date is unknown.

[16] Al-Ḥārith b. Surayj (d. 236/850 or 851) was known as "the carrier" (*al-naqqāl*), because he was said to have delivered the first, "Iraqi" version of al-Shāfiʿī's *Risāla* to ʿAbd al-Raḥmān b. Mahdī (d. 298/824); see al-Dhahabī, *Siyar aʿlām al-nubalāʾ*, 10:44. Al-Ḥārith is not to be confused with Abū al-ʿAbbās b. Surayj (d. 306/918), who belonged to the next generation of Shāfiʿī scholars.

[17] Aḥmad b. Khālid al-Khallāl (d. 246 or 247/860–62).

These lists were clearly not aimed at providing an exhaustive index of all scholars who studied with al-Shāfiʿī; Abū al-Ḥasan al-Dāraquṭnī (d. 385/995) compiled such a comprehensive directory a century later, and it included more than a hundred names.[18] Nor do they simply list members of al-Shāfiʿī's study circle in any particular location, as the geographical diffusion of the scholars included in the lists demonstrates. Rather, it seems to me that the lists seek to identify the principal carriers of al-Shāfiʿī's intellectual legacy, as determined by the compiler. They could thus be seen as antecedents of the school-specific biographical dictionaries (*ṭabaqāt*) that began to appear a century later and that Melchert considered a mark of the classical schools of law.[19] Like the later *ṭabaqāt* works, the lists differ in their selection of scholars. Nonetheless, there is considerable overlap among the three.

It is noteworthy that all three lists omit Muḥammad b. ʿAbd al-Ḥakam, in spite of his prominence among al-Shāfiʿī's Egyptian students and his important role in the dissemination of al-Shāfiʿī's ideas. The likely reason for this is that, as seen in previous chapters, Muḥammad distanced himself from al-Shāfiʿī after the latter's death by authoring a refutation of his work from a Mālikī perspective, and he retained a clear and public affiliation to the Mālikī school to the end of his life. It thus seems reasonable to exclude him from a listing of al-Shāfiʿī's primary intellectual heirs. Against this background, it may appear odd that two of the three lists include Aḥmad b. Ḥanbal, the illustrious Hadith scholar (*muḥaddith*) after whom the fourth Sunni legal school is named. However, we know that Aḥmad studied jurisprudence with al-Shāfiʿī in Mecca before the latter's departure for Egypt,[20] and the abundance of statements attributed to Aḥmad regarding al-Shāfiʿī (discussed in Chapter 8) suggests that the encounter made a strong impression on him. Subsequently, important contemporary scholars such as Muḥammad b. Jarīr al-Ṭabarī (d. 310/923)[21] and Ibn Khuzayma (d. 311/923) argued that, whatever his merits in the field of Hadith, Aḥmad's highest achievement as a jurist was to be "nothing but one of the disciples (*ghulām min ghilmān*) of

[18] Ibn ʿAsākir, *Tārīkh madīnat Dimashq*, 51:358. This work was titled "Dhikr man rawā ʿan al-Shāfiʿī"; see al-Dāraquṭnī, *Mawsūʿat aqwāl Abī al-Ḥasan al-Dāraquṭnī*, ed. Muḥammad al-Muslimī, ʿIṣām Maḥmūd, Ayman al-Zāmilī, et al., 2 vols. (Beirut: ʿĀlam al-Kutub, 2001), 1:19. Ibn Ḥajar al-ʿAsqalānī includes a list of 164 transmitters from al-Shāfiʿī in his *Tawālī al-taʾnīs*, 182–93.

[19] Melchert, *Formation of the Sunni Schools*, 87.

[20] See, for example, Éric Chaumont, "al-Shāfiʿī," in *EI2*, 9:181–85.

[21] See the editor's introduction to al-Ṭabarī, *Ikhtilāf al-fuqahāʾ*, ed. Friedrich Kern (Beirut: Dār al-Kutub al-ʿIlmiyya, 1990), 10.

al-Shāfiʿī."[22] Indeed, Aḥmad is also included in the most extensive biographical dictionary of the Shāfiʿī school, that of Tāj al-Dīn al-Subkī (d. 771/1370), which was written in the eighth/fourteenth century.[23]

It appears, then, that there existed in the third/ninth century an identifiable group of scholars characterized as al-Shāfiʿī's followers or associates. However, such external identification does not yet tell us what the nature of this association with al-Shāfiʿī was. A more significant question, then, concerns the substantive features of this group: to what extent, if at all, were these scholars united by a distinctly Shāfiʿī scholarly discourse?

A useful starting point for answering this question is provided by the following brief description of al-Shāfiʿī's followers written by Ibn Yūnus al-Ṣadafī (d. 347/958 or 959), the fourth-/tenth-century historian of Egypt and the grandson of al-Shāfiʿī's student Yūnus b. ʿAbd al-Aʿlā:

> Mālik's school (*madhhab Mālik*) remained common in Egypt until Muḥammad b. Idrīs al-Shāfiʿī arrived in Egypt with [the new governor] ʿAbd Allāh b. al-ʿAbbās ... in the year 198 [814 CE]. A group of notables from the people of Egypt joined him (*ṣaḥibahu*), such as Ibn ʿAbd al-Ḥakam, al-Rabīʿ b. Sulaymān, Abū Ibrāhīm Ismāʿīl b. Yaḥyā al-Muzanī, and Abū Yaʿqūb Yūsuf b. Yaḥyā al-Buwayṭī. They wrote down what al-Shāfiʿī composed and adopted his positions (*ʿamilū bi-mā dhahaba ilayh*); and his school (*madhhab*) continues to grow stronger in Egypt and its fame is spreading.[24]

This description shows that Ibn Yūnus conceptualized and juxtaposed the adherents of Mālik and al-Shāfiʿī as "schools" (*madhāhib*, sing. *madhhab*). Although the term *madhhab* can also carry other meanings, such as referring to a legal opinion sanctioned by a particular scholar's approach,[25] Ibn Yūnus's focus on textual and doctrinal student-teacher relations in his description supports reading *madhhab* in its primary sense as legal school in this context. Ibn Yūnus characterized the relationship of al-Shāfiʿī's close students with al-Shāfiʿī in two ways: as a textual continuity that was based on studying and copying al-Shāfiʿī's works, and as adherence to al-Shāfiʿī's legal positions. These two factors laid the foundations for the fundamental elements of a school of law: a secondary literature, which presented the opinions of the school founder while

[22] Al-Dhahabī, *Siyar aʿlām al-nubalāʾ*, 10:59. Though these claims have some merit, the substantial body of Aḥmad's legal opinions preserved in the *masāʾil* works of his students demonstrates that he was also a jurist in his own right. See also Christopher Melchert, *Ahmad ibn Hanbal* (Oxford: Oneworld, 2006).

[23] Al-Subkī, *Ṭabaqāt al-shāfiʿiyya al-kubrā*, 2:27.

[24] Quoted in al-Maqrīzī, *Khiṭaṭ*, 2:334.

[25] See Hallaq, *Origins and Evolution*, 150–53.

elucidating and extending his original insights, and a school doctrine – Shāfiʿism – that, though rooted in the legacy of al-Shāfiʿī, transcended his writings and historical personality. These characteristics, discussed in detail in the next section, justify the conclusion that the Shāfiʿī school, as it emerged in the generations that followed al-Shāfiʿī, formed the model for the *madhhab* as an interpretive community that subsequently came to characterize the entire discourse of Islamic law.

THE EMERGENCE OF A SHĀFIʿĪ PARADIGM

Al-Shāfiʿī's students, particularly al-Rabīʿ, taught al-Shāfiʿī's works for more than sixty years after al-Shāfiʿī's death. The preservation and continued transmission of al-Shāfiʿī's writings were important factors in popularizing his ideas, but they were neither sufficient nor necessary preconditions for the formation of a school. Abū ʿUbayd al-Qāsim b. Sallām, for example, wrote several books that his students continued to transmit without, however, forming a recognizable school.[26] On the other hand, Abū Ḥanīfa's students preserved a substantial body of notes from their teacher, but they did not transmit a single coherent work written by him. As a result, Abū Ḥanīfa's ideas can be accessed only through the writings of his students, depriving him of the distinct authorial voice inherent in a fully published book and rendering the precise attribution of foundational Ḥanafī texts and opinions ambiguous. This ambiguity is reflected in the common recognition of al-Shaybānī and Abū Yūsuf, the principal students of the eponymous imam, as cofounders of the school. While the preservation of al-Shāfiʿī's own writings was thus essential for the establishment of his – as distinct from his students' – intellectual contribution as the basis of the nascent school, it was not a requirement for the founding of a school per se.[27]

The defining textual manifestation of a school is a secondary literature, consisting of texts written by the students or followers of a scholar with the aim of abridging, popularizing, extending, and defending the works and ideas of the founder(s).[28] It is the development of a secondary

[26] Görke, *Das Kitāb al-Amwāl*, chap. 3.

[27] Shāh Walī Allāh al-Dihlawī (d. 1176/1762) praised the Shāfiʿī school for its unique attention to maintaining the distinction between the opinions of the founder and those of his students; see his *al-Inṣāf*, 85. I am grateful to SherAli Tareen for drawing my attention to this reference.

[28] It seems that already Ibn al-Nadīm (d. 380/990) viewed legal schools primarily as constellations of texts; see Devin Stewart, "The Structure of the *Fihrist*: Ibn al-Nadim as Historian of Islamic Legal and Theological Schools," *International Journal of Middle*

Shāfiʿī literature that specifically characterizes the generation of al-Shāfiʿī's students in Egypt and constitutes the reason why this study focuses on them, largely ignoring al-Shāfiʿī's Meccan and Baghdadi students. Among al-Shāfiʿī's Egyptian students, at least three are known to have authored a compendium (*mukhtaṣar*) of al-Shāfiʿī's works. While the compendium of Ḥarmala appears to have been lost (though Shāfiʿīs in the fifth/eleventh century still seem to have known the work),[29] the compendia of al-Muzanī and al-Buwayṭī remain extant. A study of the format and contents of these two secondary texts permits an illuminating insight into the formation of the second key characteristic of a legal school: a school doctrine, based on but not limited to the work of al-Shāfiʿī himself.

The compendia of al-Buwayṭī and al-Muzanī each comprise a single volume. The former runs to about 100,000 and the latter about 160,000 words, constituting roughly 10 percent and 16 percent, respectively, of the total length of al-Shāfiʿī's *Umm* as we have it today. Both works consist overwhelmingly of material that originates directly in al-Shāfiʿī's work but has been abridged and paraphrased. Al-Buwayṭī's compendium digests al-Shāfiʿī's writing to a much lesser degree than does al-Muzanī's book: the chapter divisions of the original are kept, and each chapter is abridged separately. Al-Muzanī condenses and reorganizes al-Shāfiʿī's material in chapters of his own design, but he prefaces most chapters by naming the part of al-Shāfiʿī's work on which that chapter draws. In both compendia, material from the *Umm* is introduced by the phrase *qāla al-Shāfiʿī*, "al-Shāfiʿī said." This serves as a marker of paraphrased transmission that contrasts with the verbs *ḥaddathanā*, *anbaʾanā*, and *akhbaranā*, which are used only rarely in the compendia to denote verbatim quotation in cases where the authors cite Hadith on al-Shāfiʿī's authority.[30]

East Studies 39 (2007): 369–87, at 374. Christopher Melchert also posits transmission of the founder's writings and development of a secondary literature as hallmarks of a legal school, but his reliance on Calder's questionable redating of foundational texts and his exclusive focus on commentaries as secondary texts lead Melchert to postpone the emergence of the legal schools to the fourth/tenth century. See his *Formation of the Sunni Schools*, 60.

[29] The editor of Ibn al-Mundhir's *al-Awsaṭ* notes that Abū al-Ṭayyib al-Ṭabarī (d. 450/1058), al-Maḥāmilī (d. 415/1024), Ibn al-Ṣabbāgh (d. 477/1084), and al-Rūyānī (d. 501/1107) all refer to Ḥarmala's *Mukhtaṣar*; see *al-Awsaṭ fī al-sunan wa-l-ijmāʿ wa-l-ikhtilāf* [partial ed.], ed. Ṣaghīr Aḥmad Muḥammad Ḥanīf, 11 vols. (Riyadh: Dār Ṭayyiba, 1985–99), 1:130, n. 80.

[30] For this phenomenon in al-Buwayṭī's compendium, see my "First Shāfiʿī," 314; contrast with al-Rabīʿ's use of these phrases as discussed in Chap. 6. On *qāla al-Shāfiʿī*, see Melchert, "Meaning of *Qāla 'l-Shāfiʿī*."

Another indicator of the paraphrased nature of the text attributed to al-Shāfiʿī is the complete absence of references to mode of transmission (e.g., *samāʿ*, *qirāʾa*, *imlāʾ*); by contrast, such references are conspicuous in the *Umm*, which – as seen in Chapter 6 – claims to embody al-Shāfiʿī's exact words as written down by his students. Al-Muzanī's introduction to his work makes this project of abridged paraphrasing explicit: he explains that his work is based on the "legal learning (*ʿilm*) of Muḥammad b. Idrīs al-Shāfiʿī ... and the import of his doctrine (*maʿnā qawlih*)."[31] Comparing the compendia with the text of al-Shāfiʿī's *Umm* (as I have elsewhere)[32] demonstrates that in spite of the necessary condensation, rephrasing, and omission of material involved in the production of an abridgment, the original text and arguments remain in most cases easily recognizable. In addition to material attributed to al-Shāfiʿī, both compendia contain comments by their authors that elucidate al-Shāfiʿī's arguments. One manuscript of al-Buwayṭī's compendium further includes brief comments by al-Rabīʿ, Abū Ḥātim al-Rāzī, and Abū Thawr. These features of the two compendia – the explicit paraphrasing, the close correlation with the text of the *Umm*, and the fact that it is al-Shāfiʿī's statements, rather than those of the authors, that are given center stage – demonstrate the secondary nature of the two works: they are original writings by al-Shāfiʿī's disciples that nonetheless claim to speak in the name of al-Shāfiʿī and to represent his ideas faithfully.

The significance of the emergence of such secondary works cannot be overemphasized. For the nascent Shāfiʿī school, they mark the birth of what Thomas Kuhn has termed "normal science," which he defined as "research firmly based upon one or more past scientific achievements, achievements that some particular scientific community acknowledges for a time as supplying the foundation for its further practice."[33] In al-Buwayṭī's and al-Muzanī's compendia, al-Shāfiʿī's work, and particularly his novel legal theory, represents that foundational achievement. Al-Shāfiʿī's arguments furnish a set of accepted assumptions, defined methods for expanding these assumptions, and further questions to be

[31] Ismāʿīl b. Yaḥyā al-Muzanī, *Mukhtaṣar al-Muzanī* (Beirut: Dār al-Kutub al-ʿIlmiyya, 1998), 1; translated by Joseph Lowry in "The Reception of al-Shāfiʿī's Concept of *Amr* and *Nahy* in the Thought of His Student al-Muzanī," in *Law and Education in Medieval Islam*, ed. Joseph E. Lowry, Devin J. Stewart, and Shawkat M. Toorawa, 128–49 (Cambridge: E. J. W. Gibb Memorial Trust, 2004), 131.

[32] See my "Al-Shāfiʿī's Written Corpus," 214–18.

[33] Thomas Kuhn, *The Structure of Scientific Revolutions*, 3rd ed. (Chicago: University of Chicago Press, 1996), 10. Kuhn focused on the natural sciences but suggested that his theory might also be true for other fields, including law.

explored, as well as a wealth of possible answers. These form the basis of a distinctly Shāfiʿī paradigm, upon which the students then build. It is this relationship between the work of al-Shāfiʿī and that of his students that allows us to speak of the Shāfiʿī school as a substantive institution already in the third/ninth century, and of al-Shāfiʿī as its genuine founder.

Kuhn's argument is that the lion's share of all scientific inquiry consists of the puzzle-solving work of normal science, which can proceed only against the background of an accepted paradigm. Furthermore, the acceptance and internalization of a scholar's paradigm by a group of students open the way for a higher and more mature form of scholarly inquiry. As Kuhn observed of physicists studying optics before the emergence of an accepted paradigm:

> Those men were scientists. Yet anyone examining a survey of physical optics before Newton may well conclude that, though the field's practitioners were scientists, the net result of their activity was something less than science. Being able to take no common body of belief for granted, each writer on physical optics felt forced to build his field anew from its foundations.[34]

A paradigm justifies certain problems as significant and specific tools and materials as appropriate to their investigation. It thereby establishes an exemplar, a "concrete problem-solution,"[35] that students internalize and then use to tackle the outstanding questions raised by the paradigm. By adopting such an exemplar, students become socialized into a particular profession and join a "community of scholars"[36] whose efforts, thanks to a shared paradigm, are compatible and can build on each other. The exemplar thus inaugurates a cumulative process of knowledge construction around the structure provided by the original paradigm.

In the legal realm, al-Shāfiʿī's style of legal argument established an exemplar for addressing a legal problem by identifying appropriate sources of evidence, methods for extracting their legal significance, and ways of reconciling any contradictions through mechanisms such as abrogation and especially particularization.[37] Al-Shāfiʿī's exemplar was not a finished methodological template that could simply be applied to novel cases as they arose. Rather, by accepting al-Shāfiʿī's paradigm, his followers inherited a broad but incomplete framework of questions, answers,

[34] Kuhn, *Structure of Scientific Revolutions*, 13.

[35] Kuhn, *Structure of Scientific Revolutions*, 187.

[36] Douglas E. Eckberg and Lester Hill, "The Paradigm Concept and Sociology: A Critical Review," *American Sociological Review* 44 (1979): 925–37, at 928.

[37] Al-Shāfiʿī's *Ikhtilāf al-ḥadīth* (vol. 10 of the *Umm*) is in essence a "how-to" manual for reconciling apparent contradictions between Hadith reports.

and the sources and methods that connected them. The followers' task, then, was to flesh out this framework by interpreting, evaluating, extending, and negotiating its components, a process that gives rise to a shared discourse.

The strongly communal nature of "normal science" is, of course, a far cry from the stark individualism inherent in al-Shāfiʿī's original conception of the hermeneutic process, as described in Chapter 3. By accepting al-Shāfiʿī's paradigm as the common foundation of their scholarly activities, al-Shāfiʿī's students in effect reintegrated into law the communal element that al-Shāfiʿī's theory of canonization had initially excised. However, the resulting "community of scholars" was very different from the community that had formed the vessel of Mālik's Medinan practice: while Mālik had envisioned a community of *tradition*, the school that grew around al-Shāfiʿī's paradigm was first and foremost a community of *interpretation*. This was defined by its members' shared commitment to a particular interpretive methodology and, more broadly, to the very idea of law as an interpretive rather than mimetic venture.

The beginning of a shared school discourse rooted in al-Shāfiʿī's paradigm is evident in the compendia of al-Buwayṭī and al-Muzanī. Both digest al-Shāfiʿī's positions, juxtapose them with each other and with the evidence, offer additional proofs and examples, analyze al-Shāfiʿī's reasoning, extend it to new cases, and on occasion disagree explicitly with the master. Later Shāfiʿīs called this activity *ijtihād fī al-madhhab* (school-internal, or "intra-madhhabic," reasoning),[38] and though neither al-Buwayṭī nor al-Muzanī uses the term, their treatment of al-Shāfiʿī's work in their compendia is structured by a set of distinct techniques of interpretation and extension that came to constitute the basis of the later school's analytical repertoire – that is, the methodological basis of Shāfiʿī school doctrine.[39]

The first technique employed by al-Shāfiʿī's students in their engagement with the master's work consists of the elucidation and reinforcement of al-Shāfiʿī's opinions by means of explanations and/or additional

[38] On *ijtihād fī al-madhhab*, see, for example, Bernard G. Weiss, *The Spirit of Islamic Law* (Athens: University of Georgia Press, 1998), 130–32. The term "intra-madhhabic" was coined by Eyyüp Said Kaya in "Continuity and Change in Islamic Law: The Concept of Madhhab and the Dimensions of Legal Disagreement in Hanafi Scholarship of the Tenth Century," in *The Islamic School of Law: Evolution, Devolution, and Progress*, ed. Peri Bearman, Rudolph Peters, and Frank Vogel, 26–40 (Cambridge, MA: Islamic Legal Studies Program, 2005), 39.

[39] This does not mean that all of the techniques described here were used by later generations of Shāfiʿīs; see my "Rethinking *Taqlīd*."

evidence; these are appended to al-Shāfiʿī's positions via markers such as *qāla al-Muzanī* or *qāla Abū Yaʿqūb* [*al-Buwayṭī*].[40] Al-Muzanī often employs the former approach (explanation), supplementing al-Shāfiʿī's prose with brief clarifications prefaced by "this means" (*yaʿnī*)[41] or "in my opinion the meaning of this is" (*wa-maʿnāhu ʿindī*).[42] The latter feature (additional evidence) is particularly prominent in al-Buwayṭī's compendium, where it accounts for the majority of al-Buwayṭī's writing within the text. On several occasions, al-Buwayṭī's comments bolster al-Shāfiʿī's arguments by, for example, citing a further relevant Hadith report[43] or adding an alternative transmission of a particular Hadith that offers stronger support for al-Shāfiʿī's opinion.[44]

The second technique that can be identified in the two compendia involves selecting among differing opinions attributed to al-Shāfiʿī regarding a particular issue. Such conflicting views were recorded on separate occasions in al-Shāfiʿī's writings, developed at different points during his career – in Iraq versus in Egypt – or given side by side without a decisive judgment in favor of any specific position. The comments added to al-Buwayṭī's compendium by al-Rabīʿ often clarify instances of such ambiguity through a brief statement identifying what al-Rabīʿ considered to be the correct opinion.[45] (Al-Rabīʿ also provided such clarifications in his comments within the *Umm*.)[46] This technique is also used by al-Muzanī to prioritize subordinate viewpoints within al-Shāfiʿī's corpus, a procedure later known as the establishment of preponderance (*tarjīḥ*).[47] On several occasions, al-Muzanī departs from the general assumption that a later opinion supersedes an earlier one by favoring an older opinion of al-Shāfiʿī. He defends his choice by arguing that the earlier position

[40] For a detailed discussion of al-Muzanī's use of all of these techniques, see Muḥammad Nabīl Ghanāyim, *al-Muzanī wa-atharuhu fī al-fiqh al-shāfiʿī* (Cairo: Dār al-Hidāya, 1998), 157–205.

[41] See, e.g., al-Muzanī, *Mukhtaṣar*, 400 (Bāb al-nudhūr) and 136 (Bāb al-rahn).

[42] See, e.g., al-Muzanī, *Mukhtaṣar*, 280 (Bāb mā yujziʾu min al-ʿuyūb fī al-riqāb al-wājiba).

[43] Abū Yaʿqūb al-Buwayṭī, *Mukhtaṣar al-Buwayṭī* (Istanbul: Süleymaniye, Murad Molla, MS 1189 [196 fols., copied 625/1228]), fol. 30b (Bāb fī al-ṣalāt): "Qāla Abū Yaʿqūb: wa-l-ḥujja ayḍan fī ḥadīth al-nabī ..." Unless otherwise specified, all subsequent references to al-Buwayṭī's *Mukhtaṣar* are to this manuscript.

[44] Al-Buwayṭī, *Mukhtaṣar*, fol. 14a (Bāb al-jahr bi-bism Allāh al-raḥmān al-raḥīm); here al-Buwayṭī adds another version of a particular Hadith, which includes Abū Hurayra's clarification of its legal significance.

[45] Al-Buwayṭī, *Mukhtaṣar*, 104b (Bāb al-rahn) and 165a (Bāb al-shahādāt).

[46] See, e.g., *Umm*, 3:133.

[47] On the origins of this term, see Ulrich Rebstock, "Vom Abwägen (*tarǧīḥ*): Stationen einer Begriffskarriere" (paper presented at the 30th Deutscher Orientalistentag, Freiburg im Breisgau, Germany, Sept. 25, 2007); available online at http://orient.ruf.uni-freiburg.de/dotpub/rebstock.pdf. Neither al-Rabīʿ nor al-Muzanī used the term *tarjīḥ*.

is closer to the available evidence or more consonant with al-Shāfiʿī's approach as a whole.[48]

The third type of technique became known as *takhrīj*: the extension of a known opinion of al-Shāfiʿī to a case not explicitly addressed by him.[49] For example, on the topic of *ḥawāla* (the payment of a debt through the transfer of a claim), al-Muzanī introduces a passage of his own writing in his compendium with the following explanation: "regarding these questions, I reasoned on the basis of the underlying meanings of al-Shāfiʿī's responses on *ḥawāla*" (*hādhihī masāʾil taḥarraytu fīhā maʿānī jawābāt al-Shāfiʿī fī al-ḥawāla*).[50] In another instance, he introduces a new ruling as "the analogical extension of [al-Shāfiʿī's] opinion" (*qiyās qawlih*).[51] By using the term *qiyās*, al-Muzanī draws an explicit parallel between analogical reasoning as a hermeneutic method of extending the sacred sources of the Quran and Sunna, on the one hand, and *takhrīj* on the basis of the corpus of al-Shāfiʿī's work, on the other. The founder's writings, in this framework, constitute a textual source to which hermeneutic techniques can be applied, analogously to the interpretation of the canonical sources.

The fourth technique used by al-Buwayṭī and al-Muzanī in their engagement with their teacher's work is particularly revealing. In several instances, both students openly amend al-Shāfiʿī's opinions but then attribute the changed opinion to al-Shāfiʿī, with the implicit or explicit justification that this is, in fact, what the latter would have said had he been fully consistent or aware of all the relevant evidence. An eloquent example is provided by an anecdote reported by Abū Bakr al-Athram (d. around 260/873), a companion of Aḥmad b. Ḥanbal, who attended al-Buwayṭī's lesson in Baghdad:

[Al-Buwayṭī] read to us that al-Shāfiʿī held the view that ablution in the absence of water (*tayammum*) consists of beating [the palms of the hands on earth] twice. I told him: "There is a reliable transmission by ʿAmmār b. Yāsir that *tayammum*

[48] See, for example, al-Muzanī, *Mukhtaṣar*, 138 (Bāb al-rahn), 20 (Bāb al-masḥ ʿalā al-khuffayn), 24 (Bāb ṣifat al-adhān), and 40 (Bāb ikhtilāf niyyat al-imām wa-l-maʾmūm wa-ghayr dhālika).

[49] The term *takhrīj* was used already a few decades after al-Muzanī's death by his fellow Shāfiʿīs; see, for example, Ibn al-Qāṣṣ (d. 335/946 or 947), *Adab al-qāḍī*, ed. Ḥusayn al-Jubūrī, 2 vols. (Taʾif: Maktabat al-Ṣiddīq, 1409/1989), 1:68. For a discussion of this technique, see Hallaq, *Authority, Continuity and Change*, 43–56, and Ahmad Atif Ahmad, *Structural Interrelations of Theory and Practice in Islamic Law: A Study of Six Works of Medieval Islamic Jurisprudence* (Leiden: Brill, 2006).

[50] Al-Muzanī, *Mukhtaṣar*, 148 (Bāb al-ḥawāla).

[51] Al-Muzanī, *Mukhtaṣar*, 339 (Bāb mā yusqiṭu al-qasāma min al-ikhtilāf wa-lā yusqiṭuhā).

consists of only one beating." So he erased "two beatings" from his notes and changed it to one on the basis of ʿAmmār's report. And then he said: "Al-Shāfiʿī said that if you find reliable reports from the Prophet [that contradict my opinion], abandon my opinion and hold to the prophetic tradition, as that is my [true] opinion."[52]

Al-Buwayṭī thus openly and confidently rewrote al-Shāfiʿī's opinion as presented in his compendium and justified the revision by citing al-Shāfiʿī's well-known command to consider any authentic Hadith to represent his genuine opinion (*in ṣaḥḥa al-ḥadīth fa-huwa madhhabī*).[53] The same "Hadith principle" was used explicitly by al-Shāfiʿī's (and al-Buwayṭī's) Meccan student Ibn Abī al-Jārūd (d. unknown), who explained his amendment of al-Shāfiʿī's opinion regarding the medical procedure of cupping by saying, "given the Hadith, 'the one who gives and the one who receives cupping have broken their fast,' I say that al-Shāfiʿī said (*fa-anā aqūlu qāla al-Shāfiʿī*) that the one who gives and the one who receives cupping have broken their fast."[54]

Al-Muzanī employed a different form of this technique: he isolated general rules from al-Shāfiʿī's writings and used them to overrule his individual opinions. An example is the legal maxim "every worshipper [acts] for himself (*kullu muṣallin li-nafsih*)," which al-Shāfiʿī used to encapsulate his view that even in collective prayers the validity of each individual prayer is independent of the validity of the prayers of the other worshippers and the imam. [55] Al-Muzanī, in his compendium, applies this maxim to the case of a person who joins a collective prayer late and justifies his revision of al-Shāfiʿī's known position on the issue by arguing that the revised position "is more befitting [al-Shāfiʿī's] principle (*aqyas ʿalā aṣlih*), since he considers every worshipper to act for himself."[56] Al-Muzanī then uses the same maxim to overrule al-Shāfiʿī on a related question regarding the validity of participating in a collective prayer led by an imam who does not fulfill the requirements of that role, arguing, pace al-Shāfiʿī, that such prayers are nonetheless valid.[57]

[52] Ibn al-Ṣalāḥ, *Ṭabaqāt al-fuqahāʾ al-shāfiʿiyya*, 2:681–82. All of the manuscripts of al-Buwayṭī's compendium that I have examined contain the unchanged version of this passage.

[53] Al-Dhahabī, *Siyar aʿlām al-nubalāʾ*, 10:33–35; see also my "First Shāfiʿī," 317–21.

[54] Ibn al-Ṣalāḥ, *Adab al-muftī wa-l-mustaftī*, ed. Muwaffaq ʿAbd Allāh ʿAbd al-Qādir (Beirut: Maktabat al-ʿUlūm wa-l-Ḥikam, 1407/1986 or 1987), 119–20.

[55] *Umm*, 10:127.

[56] Al-Muzanī, *Mukhtaṣar*, 28 (Bāb ṣifat al-ṣalāt).

[57] Al-Muzanī, *Mukhtaṣar*, 40 (Bāb ikhtilāf niyyat al-imām wa-l-ma'mūm wa-ghayr dhālika).

Finally, in a number of instances, both al-Buwayṭī and al-Muzanī disagree outright with al-Shāfiʿī's positions. Al-Buwayṭī, in his compendium, cites al-Shāfiʿī's opinion that a man may acknowledge another as his consanguine brother but then argues against it, pointing out that this would entail an admission of paternity by the man on behalf of his father, which is not acceptable.[58] Similarly, al-Muzanī mentions that al-Shāfiʿī believed that someone who forgets the prohibition against the use of perfume during the annual pilgrimage is exempt from the requirement of expiation (*fidya*), based on an analogy on a Hadith according to which the Prophet did not order expiation in the case of a Bedouin who violated other formalities of the pilgrimage. Al-Muzanī, however, justifies his rejection of this conclusion by noting that a similar Hadith regarding the unintentional breaking of the fast during the month of Ramadan also makes no explicit mention of expiation, even though scholars agree that it – in the form of an additional day of fasting – is nonetheless obligatory in such a case.[59] In addition, a rare note preserved in the text of the *Umm* contains both al-Buwayṭī's disagreement with al-Shāfiʿī's opinion regarding the paternity of a child born to a slave woman who was used as security for a debt (*rahn*), as well as al-Rabīʿ's comment to the effect that he, too, concurs with al-Buwayṭī's dissent on the matter.[60]

The application of these five techniques by al-Buwayṭī and al-Muzanī demonstrates that, though the primary purpose of their works was to abridge their teacher's writings and to present his central arguments in a concise, clear format, their efforts were not limited to mere summarizing. Through their subtle engagement with al-Shāfiʿī's work – their evaluation of the master's arguments and evidence, their interpretation and extension of his paradigm, and their assertion of divergent opinions justified in terms of al-Shāfiʿī's own vocabulary – the students inaugurated a distinct school doctrine. This took al-Shāfiʿī's writings as its starting point (*qāla al-Shāfiʿī*), creating a genealogical relationship between the words of al-Shāfiʿī and those of his successors, but it was not circumscribed by al-Shāfiʿī's written corpus. Rather, the work of al-Shāfiʿī's students gave rise to an ongoing project of legal inquiry based on al-Shāfiʿī's

[58] Al-Buwayṭī, *Mukhtaṣar*, fol. 122a (Masʿala fī al-waṣiyya): "Qāla Abū Yaʿqūb: lā yajūzu dhālika ʿindī.... "

[59] Al-Muzanī, *Mukhtaṣar*, 98 (Bāb fī mā yamtaniʿu ʿalā al-muḥrim min al-lubs).

[60] *Umm*, 4:327. This passage casts doubt on Kevin Jaques's hypothesis that later Shāfiʿī scholarship sought to suppress evidence of disagreements between al-Rabīʿ and al-Shāfiʿī. See Jaques, "The Other Rabīʿ: Biographical Traditions and the Development of Early Shāfiʿī Authority," *Islamic Law and Society* 14 (2007): 143–79.

paradigm but sparking heated debates on issues such as the precise status of the founder's opinions and the appropriate limits of disagreement. Shāfiʿī doctrine was continuously reformulated and negotiated by successive generations of Shāfiʿī scholars, beginning with the generation of al-Shāfiʿī's immediate students.

The "community of interpretation" that grew around al-Shāfiʿī's teaching in the third/ninth century thus represents a radical break from the old model of legal schools justified in terms of locality-based normative traditions. The nascent Shāfiʿī school was, in Schacht's sense, *personal*,[61] in that it was squarely rooted in the work of a specific, named jurist; but it also had many of the characteristics of Hallaq's *doctrinal* schools,[62] in particular its incorporation of legal hermeneutics as an essential element of school doctrine and its critical stance toward the founder's corpus in light of the canonical sources. The preceding analysis of the central features of the emergent school suggests that Shāfiʿism in the third/ninth century could perhaps be described as a *paradigmatic* school: al-Shāfiʿī's intellectual legacy, defined by his canonization of the sacred sources and his reconceptualization of Islamic law as an interpretive venture, produced a paradigm of legal thought that was in essential ways unprecedented and that created a distinctive framework for subsequent inquiry by al-Shāfiʿī's students and their successors. In contrast to the tradition-bound basis of the earlier schools, Shāfiʿism represented from its beginning a scientific discourse, in which the direct and intelligible connection between evidence and outcome was paramount and legal hermeneutics thus occupied a central position.

The shift from tradition to a legal science should, I believe, be understood as part and parcel of a broader process of cultural evolution. As Eyyüp Said Kaya has argued in his study of the Ḥanafī school, the emergence of the legal schools was inextricably tied to the development of Islamic law into a written discipline.[63] This latter step, as I argue in Part I of this book, represents a fundamental transition in the evolution of knowledge. A change in the form of legal discourse did not simply transfer old wine into new skins, but rather transformed its very content by fostering new, more systematic and rationalized patterns of legal thought. The new convention of using fully authored books to address legal topics by means of arguments constructed on evidence and presented in specialized

[61] Schacht, *Introduction to Islamic Law*, 58–59.

[62] Hallaq, "From Regional to Personal Schools," 21–22.

[63] Kaya, "Continuity and Change," 40. I have also benefited from a personal discussion with Dr. Kaya on this subject.

terminology provided Islamic law with the stable memory that is necessary for higher learning. Previously, as seen earlier, law had been developed in the personal encounters of individual scholars and reproduced either aurally or in semiwritten form as personal notes. It was thus dependent on and limited by the discursive memory of the present generation. By fixing cultural memory in a largely unchanging form, writing enabled law to become a cumulative venture, not trapped in the here and now, but rather possessing a distinct and accessible past that preserved shifts and differences of opinion. The existence of such a separate storehouse of memory made it more difficult simply to forget or ignore uncomfortable ideas. Instead, such instances had to be explained, requiring the development and use of further analytical tools and categories.

An analysis of the evolution of Mālikism, Ḥanafism, and Ḥanbalism from regional to personal schools necessarily lies outside the scope of this study. It appears, however, that at least for the first two this process largely coincided with the emergence of Shāfiʿism. Among the Ḥanafīs, a secondary literature began to emerge already before al-Shāfiʿī, with Abū Yūsuf and especially al-Shaybānī composing important works aimed at collecting, classifying, condensing, defending, and modifying Abū Ḥanīfa's legal opinions.[64] As noted in Chapter 2, the inherent dynamic of *raʾy* was progressively drawing Ḥanafism away from its claimed roots in the legal tradition of Kufa. The *raʾy*-based approach was, however, vulnerable to challenges rooted in Hadith that contradicted Ḥanafī positions. Such challenges became increasingly difficult to ignore as the movement to assemble and authenticate the vast body of circulating traditions about the Prophet gathered steam. The Ḥanafīs were consequently forced to theorize their stance on Hadith, a process that gave rise to explicit Ḥanafī legal theories. Al-Shāfiʿī's conceptualization of the role of Hadith in law need not necessarily have played a part in this development, but the cases of ʿĪsā b. Abān (d. 221/836) and Abū Jaʿfar al-Ṭaḥāwī (d. 321/933) discussed in the next chapter indicate that it in fact did do so.

For the Mālikīs, the composition of Mālik's groundbreaking *Muwaṭṭaʾ* counterintuitively represented the first decisive step away from a regional tradition: by encapsulating the tradition of Medina between the covers of a book, Mālik in effect divorced Medinan practice from the actual locality of Medina and rendered it portable. Although Mālikism still claimed

[64] Notably, Abū Yūsuf's *Ikhtilāf Abī Ḥanīfa wa-Ibn Abī Laylā* and *Radd ʿalā Siyar al-Awzāʿī*, and al-Shaybānī's *al-Jāmiʿ al-kabīr*, *al-Jāmiʿ al-ṣaghīr*, *al-Radd ʿalā ahl al-Madīna*, and *al-Aṣl*.

to represent the school of Medina, its connection to the city was henceforth virtual. The appearance of the *Muwaṭṭa'* made possible the emergence of secondary Mālikī writings and indeed necessitated it. Mālik's students, like those of al-Shāfi'ī, wrote works that digested and organized their master's opinions, but they also faced the challenge of responding to the withering critiques of Mālik's thought that the latter's codification in the *Muwaṭṭa'* had provoked.[65] This required a systematic rethinking of Mālik's ideas and especially of his controversial concept of Medinan practice. As with the Ḥanafīs and their inconsistent approach to Hadith, there is evidence (discussed in Chapter 8) that al-Shāfi'ī's attack on and proposed alternative to this concept had a significant influence on at least some important Mālikīs, resulting in the formulation of a Mālikī legal theory with a distinctly Shāfi'ī flavor.

This very brief sketch indicates that although developments under way among both Ḥanafīs and Mālikīs were already propelling the two groups' legal doctrines away from their foundational regional traditions, al-Shāfi'ī's canonization project severed the "umbilical cord" that connected law to such traditions. The need to respond to al-Shāfi'ī's challenge engaged other jurists in a debate that required the justification of school opinions in systematic, universally defensible terms. This emerging methodological consensus led to a reenvisioning of the nature of the law: what had been a mimetic enterprise justified in terms of its connection to a normative past via particular local traditions was transformed into an interpretive project whose parameters within each school were set by the paradigm of a founding jurist (or jurists) and his (or their) followers. The shift from regional traditions to personal legal schools is visible in the marked change in the perception of these schools by subsequent generations of scholars, who abandoned the increasingly procrustean project of identifying the regional connections of jurists who followed the four imams. Both al-Nasā'ī (d. 303/915) and – with the benefit of a century and a half of hindsight – Abū Isḥāq al-Shīrāzī (d. 476/1083) still classified Mālik, Abū Ḥanīfa, Aḥmad b. Ḥanbal, and al-Shāfi'ī as Medinan, Kufan, Baghdadi, and Meccan, respectively, but both omitted such geographical designations for the disciples of these scholars and described them purely in terms of their attachment to one of the imams.[66]

[65] Especially 'Abd Allāh b. 'Abd al-Ḥakam's *al-Mukhtaṣar al-kabīr* and *al-Mukhtaṣar al-ṣaghīr*, Muḥammad b. 'Abd al-Ḥakam's lost refutation of al-Shāfi'ī (see Chap. 8), and various *masā'il* works, of which the best known is Saḥnūn's *Mudawwana*.

[66] Al-Nasā'ī, *Tasmiyat fuqahā' al-amṣār*, 127–28; Abū Isḥāq al-Shīrāzī, *Ṭabaqāt al-fuqahā'*, ed. Iḥsān 'Abbās (Beirut: Dār al-Rā'id al-'Arabī, 1970), 97. See also Éric Chaumont, "Shāfi'iyya," in *EI2*, 9:185–89, at 185.

Al-Shāfiʿī's hermeneutic approach did not, of course, represent the sole theory of the law among subsequent Sunni scholars. In the two centuries that followed al-Shāfiʿī's death, numerous groups of jurists, continuing in the footsteps of the Khārijīs and of Muʿtazilī theologians such as Ibn ʿUlayya and al-Aṣamm, declared adherence to a radical literalism. By insisting on an exclusively literal interpretation of the canonical texts (variously defined), they denied the need for most of the hermeneutic techniques developed in the field of legal theory. However, such literalist approaches did not gain a lasting foothold in mainstream classical Sunni law.[67]

THE QUESTION OF CONFORMISM (*TAQLĪD*)

It might seem reasonable to equate the apparent wholesale acceptance of al-Shāfiʿī's precedent by his followers with *taqlīd*, conformism or "blind following." This, however, creates a paradox. As seen in Chapter 3, al-Shāfiʿī's hermeneutic project – the canonization of the sacred sources as the only authoritative basis of law – was built upon a radical rejection of the practice of *taqlīd*. Éric Chaumont speaks for many modern scholars when he observes that "the very existence of a [Shāfiʿī] school thus appears contradictory from the outset."[68] The apparent paradox, however, rests on the mistaken identification of conformism as the necessary mechanism of authority that binds the followers of a founder-imam into a school of law. The identification of *taqlīd* as an inherent feature of the legal schools originates in polemical arguments leveled against the legal schools,[69] but it has been subsequently accepted as a de facto truism in Western scholarship,[70] in spite of the fact it is entirely at odds with the self-understanding of the majority of Shāfiʿī jurists throughout the ages.[71] For al-Shāfiʿī as for his successors, the term *taqlīd* carried a very specific meaning: it denoted the acceptance of a legal position solely on the authority of its author, without reference to evidence rooted in the normative textual sources. An analysis of the work of al-Shāfiʿī's students

67 Vishanoff, *Formation of Islamic Hermeneutics*, chap. 3.

68 Chaumont, "Shāfiʿiyya," in *EI2*, 9:185.

69 This critique is primarily associated with nineteenth- and early twentieth-century Muslim reformers such as Muḥammad al-Shawkānī (d. 1250/1834) and Muḥammad ʿAbduh (d. 1323/1905), but it was already voiced much earlier by, e.g., Ibn Ḥazm in the fifth/eleventh century. See ʿAlī b. Aḥmad b. Ḥazm, *al-Iḥkām fī uṣūl al-aḥkām*, 8 vols. in 2 (Cairo: Dār al-Ḥadīth, 1984), 5:94.

70 See, for example, the contributions by Norman Calder, Sherman Jackson, and Mohammad Fadel to a special issue on the *madhhab* in *Islamic Law and Society* 3, no. 2 (1996).

71 For a detailed discussion, see El Shamsy, "Rethinking *Taqlīd*."

shows that the way in which they conceptualized their adherence to their teacher's doctrine differed crucially from this understanding of *taqlīd*.

The first indication of this is provided by al-Muzanī's explicit rejection of *taqlīd* in his writings. In the introduction to his compendium, al-Muzanī reminds the reader that although the goal of his work is to make al-Shāfiʿī's ideas accessible to the readers, "I hereby inform such persons that he forbade that one follow him, or any one else, unquestioningly."[72] In a separate work, probably titled "The invalidity of conformism" (*Fasād al-taqlīd*), al-Muzanī developed a *kalām*-style dialectical argument[73] to demonstrate the rational incoherence of *taqlīd*:[74]

A person who arrives at a legal ruling through *taqlīd* is asked: "Do you have evidence (*ḥujja*) for this?" If he answers yes, [his claim of] *taqlīd* becomes void, since it was the evidence that produced the ruling, not *taqlīd*. If he answers, "I arrived at the ruling without evidence," he is asked, "how can you impose physical punishments, make intercourse legal, and confiscate property, when God has forbidden all of these things except by means of evidence?" If he replies, "I know that I am correct, even though I do not know the evidence, because I followed a great scholar whom I consider superior in knowledge and who reached this conclusion through evidence that is inaccessible to me," he is told, "if *taqlīd* of your teacher is permissible, then *taqlīd* of your teacher's teacher is even more permissible, given that he must have formed an opinion based on evidence that was inaccessible to your teacher in the same way that your teacher came to a conclusion through evidence that eluded you." If he says "yes," then he has abandoned *taqlīd* of his teacher and his *taqlīd* has shifted to his teacher's teacher and so on until it reaches a scholar from among the Companions of God's Messenger. If he rejects [this conclusion], his position becomes self-contradictory and he should be told: "How can it be permissible to follow someone who is junior and of lesser knowledge, while it is not permissible to follow one who is senior and more knowledgeable? This is contradictory!" If he replies, "[I do this] because my teacher, though he is junior, unites in himself the knowledge of those who came before him; as a consequence, he has a better overview of the things that he accepts and is more knowledgeable regarding the things that he leaves aside," then he is told, "the same would apply to your teacher's student, as he unites in himself the knowledge

[72] Al-Muzanī, *Mukhtaṣar* (Dār al-Kutub al-ʿIlmiyya ed.), 7 (Introduction).

[73] On the form of *kalām* arguments, see Josef van Ess, "Disputationspraxis in der islamischen Theologie: Eine vorläufige Skizze," *Revue des études islamiques* 44 (1976): 23–60.

[74] The text is quoted in Ibn ʿAbd al-Barr, *Jāmiʿ bayān al-ʿilm*, 2:992–93; al-Khaṭīb al-Baghdādī, *al-Faqīh wa-l-mutafaqqih*, ed. ʿĀdil b. Yūsuf al-ʿAzzāzī, 2 vols. (Dammam: Dār Ibn al-Jawzī, 1996), 2:136–37; and al-Zarkashī, *al-Baḥr al-muḥīṭ*, 6:281–82. Al-Zarkashī attributes this passage to al-Muzanī's *Kitāb Fasād al-taʾwīl* (or, more probably, *Kitāb Fasād al-taqlīd*; ibid., 6:232). I assume that it formed part of the corpus of *masāʾil* transmitted from al-Muzanī that includes *Kitāb al-Amr wa-l-nahy*, for which see Robert Brunschvig, ed. and trans., "'Le livre de l'ordre et de la défense' d'al-Muzani," *Bulletin d'études orientales* 11 (1945–46): 145–93.

of his teacher as well as of those before him, so you would have to follow him and abandon *taqlīd* of your teacher. Therefore, you would have to follow yourself rather than your teacher." ... If he repeats his argument, he ends up declaring more recent scholars as more deserving of *taqlīd* than the Companions of God's Messenger; the Companion would have to follow the Successor (*tābiʿī*), and the Successor would have to follow his successor, so that the predecessor is always inferior to his successor. It is sufficient grounds [to reject this opinion] if it leads to such evil and impiety.[75]

Al-Muzanī's argument is a two-way reductio ad absurdum. If the follower (*muqallid*) defends his *taqlīd* by appealing to the greater knowledge that accompanies precedence, then logic demands that he follow not his teacher but the ultimate predecessors, that is, the Companions. Alternatively, if his position implies that each generation surpasses its predecessors in knowledge, then the person most worthy of the follower's allegiance must be the follower himself.

This argument had a powerful impact both within and outside the Shāfiʿī school. Among the Mālikīs and the Ḥanafīs, al-Muzanī's case against *taqlīd* became incorporated in school-internal debates regarding the permissibility of the practice.[76] These, however, remained inconclusive because of the existence of conflicting opinions on the matter attributed to Mālik, Abū Ḥanīfa, and the latter's students al-Shaybānī and Abū Yūsuf.[77] The Shāfiʿīs, by contrast, enjoyed no such leeway. Al-Shāfiʿī's unequivocal condemnation of *taqlīd* was not softened by any subsequent reinterpretation by his immediate students; to the contrary, al-Muzanī's refutation provided a persuasive reassertion of the rational unacceptability of the practice. The absolute prohibition of conformism consequently became enshrined as an inviolable and enduring premise of Shāfiʿī hermeneutics.

That al-Muzanī's explicit rejection of *taqlīd* did not amount to mere posturing divorced from actual practice is clear from two characteristics of the way in which both al-Buwayṭī and al-Muzanī approached the work of their teacher: their insistence on providing textual evidence for al-Shāfiʿī's positions and their critical stance toward the evidence

[75] This ending is quoted by Ibn ʿAbd al-Barr; the final section is less clear in al-Khaṭīb al-Baghdādī's version and omitted in al-Zarkashī's.

[76] For example, the Mālikī Ibn ʿAbd al-Barr and the Ḥanafī al-Jaṣṣāṣ adopted elements of al-Muzanī's argument in their own refutations of *taqlīd*; see Ibn ʿAbd al-Barr, *Jāmiʿ bayān al-ʿilm*, 2:994, and al-Jaṣṣāṣ, *Uṣūl al-fiqh al-musammā bi-l-Fuṣūl fī al-uṣūl*, ed. ʿUjayl al-Nashamī, 4 vols. (Kuwait: Wizārat al-Awqāf wa-l-Shuʾūn al-Islāmiyya, 1994), 3:373–74.

[77] For the Mālikīs, see Abū al-ʿAbbās al-Qurṭubī's statement as quoted in al-Zarkashī, *al-Baḥr al-muḥīṭ*, 2:286; for the Ḥanafīs, see al-Jaṣṣāṣ, *Fuṣūl fī al-uṣūl*, 2:283–85.

presented by him. The first feature can be seen throughout the compendia in that each quoted opinion is justified with direct reference to the relevant proof texts. For example, on the subject of the manumission contract (*al-mukātaba*), the chapter in al-Buwayṭī's compendium supports al-Shāfiʿī's argument by quoting as evidence six Hadith as well as two Companion reports; al-Muzanī's corresponding chapter cites seven Quranic verses plus one Hadith report.[78] The emphasis on evidence in these works stands in marked contrast to their Mālikī and Ḥanafī equivalents in the compendium (*Mukhtaṣar*) of ʿAbd Allāh b. ʿAbd al-Ḥakam and the *Jāmiʿ al-kabīr* of al-Shaybānī. ʿAbd Allāh's discussion on manumission contracts mentions only a single Quranic verse, which is quoted, epigraph-like, in the beginning of the chapter,[79] while al-Shaybānī gives no evidence at all in support of his position on the matter.[80] This does not mean that Shāfiʿī scholars had solid evidence for their positions whereas the Mālikīs and Ḥanafīs did not. Rather, the comparison demonstrates that the Shāfiʿīs made a point of presenting their evidence even in abridged compendia.

The second feature that distinguishes al-Muzanī's and al-Buwayṭī's adherence to al-Shāfiʿī from simple conformism is the clear contingency of their acceptance of al-Shāfiʿī's positions. The students did not simply passively reproduce al-Shāfiʿī's evidence, but rather actively evaluated the proofs presented by their master and – as seen in previous sections – openly amended his statements and even disagreed with him when his evidence or reasoning failed to convince them. This demonstrates that though al-Buwayṭī and al-Muzanī followed al-Shāfiʿī, in the sense that they accepted prima facie al-Shāfiʿī's legal reasoning and the resulting opinions, this acceptance was always conditional, dependent on their own evaluation of the accuracy and persuasiveness of al-Shāfiʿī's arguments and evidence. In their works, they thus presented al-Shāfiʿī's rulings accompanied in each case by the relevant textual evidence. This provided their readers with the possibility of replicating al-Shāfiʿī's chain of reasoning, should they desire to do so.

This combination of substantive opinions and the hermeneutic principles that gave rise to them rendered the Shāfiʿism of al-Buwayṭī and al-Muzanī transparent: each opinion could be justified as an interpretation

[78] This chapter of ʿAbd Allāh's compendium is reproduced in Brockopp, *Early Mālikī law*, 228–83.

[79] Brockopp, *Early Mālikī Law*, 228.

[80] Al-Shaybānī, *al-Jāmiʿ al-kabīr*, ed. Abū al-Wafāʾ al-Afghānī (Hyderabad: Lajnat Iḥyāʾ al-Maʿārif al-Nuʿmāniyya, 1937 or 1938), 305–7.

of authoritative sources arrived at through the application of explicit rules. This made the process repeatable and, in Karl Popper's phrase, falsifiable,[81] and it contrasts with the opacity inherent in the concept of *taqlīd* defined as "the acceptance of a position without evidence."[82] The formation of a Shāfiʿī school, based on al-Shāfiʿī's work as the paradigm within whose parameters his students would elaborate and extend his legacy, did not, therefore, imply or require conformism on the part of the students. Following al-Shāfiʿī meant that the students were released from the necessity of beginning legal reasoning on each issue from scratch; but it did not mean that they felt free to abandon the essential connection between textual evidence and legal ruling. This connection, and the attendant disavowal of conformism, were maintained by al-Buwayṭī's and al-Muzanī's successors and became a permanent and central feature of the self-image of the Shāfiʿī school.

VARIETIES OF SHĀFIʿISM

Like any paradigm, that of al-Shāfiʿī was open to divergent interpretations. It should be remembered that al-Shāfiʿī lived in Egypt for a mere five or six years before his death, while most of his students survived him by several decades. It would be unrealistic to assume that the students received and circulated their master's teachings as a fully formed and complete package, making no characteristic marks of their own on the body of material that they passed down to their own students. The longest-lived of al-Shāfiʿī's students was al-Rabīʿ, who outlasted him by sixty-four years. However, al-Rabīʿ was not generally considered a distinguished jurist; he specialized in the transmission of al-Shāfiʿī's writings (as well as Hadith), seemingly never composing a work of his own, and his input to the shaping of Shāfiʿī doctrine was thus more limited. Al-Buwayṭī and al-Muzanī, on the other hand, had a keen interest and prior training in jurisprudence, and their particular backgrounds and predilections inevitably influenced the way in which they received and extended al-Shāfiʿī's thought in their respective compendia. It should hardly come as a surprise that the two developed distinctly different interpretations of al-Shāfiʿī's work and that these interpretations correlate strongly with their previous intellectual affiliations.

As seen in Part II of this book, al-Buwayṭī was a former Mālikī. He adhered to a staunchly traditionalist theology and even gave his life to

[81] Karl R. Popper, *The Logic of Scientific Discovery* (London: Routledge, 2002), 18.
[82] "Qabūl qawl bi-lā ḥujja"; see Chap. 3.

its defense during the Inquisition. Al-Buwayṭī's personal affinity with the traditionalists (*ahl al-ḥadīth*) is evident also in his scholarship. His treatment of his teacher's corpus demonstrates a clear tendency toward accentuating the significance of Hadith in accordance with the traditionalist style of addressing legal questions.[83] For example, in abridging al-Shāfiʿī's prose in his compendium, al-Buwayṭī generally omits his teacher's complex legal discussions but retains – and, as mentioned earlier, even adds – evidence from transmitted reports. Consequently, while al-Shāfiʿī's arguments in support of particular legal positions draw on a number of methodological tools, including proof texts as well as argumentative techniques such as analogy (*qiyās*), al-Buwayṭī typically presents al-Shāfiʿī's opinions accompanied simply by the relevant Hadith or Companion reports.

In the realm of legal theory, al-Buwayṭī actively downplays analogy, which was viewed with great suspicion by the Hadith-oriented scholars of his time.[84] He mentions analogy explicitly only to limit its applicability[85] and provides no other discussion of the practice. Indeed, on a number of occasions al-Buwayṭī amends al-Shāfiʿī's wording in his paraphrase in order to excise references to analogy. In a section of the compendium that appears to be based on al-Shāfiʿī's discussion of *istiḥsān* in his *Risāla*, what had in the original text been a list of preconditions for the use of analogy is transformed, in al-Buwayṭī's rendering, into preconditions for the interpretation of scripture in general.[86] On another occasion, al-Buwayṭī reproduces al-Shāfiʿī's known dictum to the effect that in situations where two Companions of the Prophet disagreed on an issue, the opinion that is closer to that supported by analogy is to be preferred.[87] However, the quotation given in the compendium contains a significant change: "analogy" as the criterion of priority is replaced by "Quran and Sunna."[88] Further, of the two positions found in al-Shāfiʿī's corpus

[83] For a detailed discussion of the traditionalist features of al-Buwayṭī's style of jurisprudence, see my "First Shāfiʿī."

[84] See Scott C. Lucas, "The Legal Principles of Muḥammad b. Ismāʿīl al-Bukhārī and Their Relationship to Classical Salafi Islam," *Islamic Law and Society* 13 (2006): 289–324, at 303–35.

[85] Al-Buwayṭī, *Mukhtaṣar*, fols. 173a and 173b (Bāb fī al-Risāla); see also El Shamsy and Aron Zysow, "Al-Buwayṭī's Abridgment of al-Shāfiʿī's *Risāla*: Edition and Translation," *Islamic Law and Society* 19 (2012): 327–55.

[86] Compare al-Shāfiʿī's *Risāla*, in *Umm*, 1:237 (paras. 1472–73), with al-Buwayṭī's *Mukhtaṣar*, fol. 169b (Bāb fī al-Risāla), and El Shamsy and Zysow, "Al-Buwayṭī's Abridgment," 335.

[87] *Umm*, 7:610.

[88] Al-Buwayṭī, *Mukhtaṣar*, fol. 108a (Bāb al-wadīʿa).

regarding the relative hierarchy of analogy and the opinions of prophetic Companions, al-Buwayṭī includes in his work only one – namely, the position that grants greater weight to the Companions, a characteristic of the traditionalist approach.[89] Al-Buwayṭī's traditionalist orientation is also evident in his unabashed use of the Hadith principle to amend al-Shāfiʿī's opinions, in line with the traditionalists' general insistence on acknowledging the prima facie normativity of any Hadith that has been determined to be authentic.[90]

In addition to its strongly traditionalist bent, al-Buwayṭī's compendium displays a distinctly conciliatory attitude toward Mālikism. The breathless polemics of al-Shāfiʿī's *Ikhtilāf Mālik* are toned down significantly in al-Buwayṭī's corresponding chapter, "al-Waḍʿ ʿalā Mālik." Instead of replicating al-Shāfiʿī's aggressive attacks on Mālik's concept of Medinan practice, al-Buwayṭī portrays the differences between Mālik and al-Shāfiʿī in a markedly neutral format: "Mālik holds X, al-Shāfiʿī holds Y, and the latter's evidence consists of Hadith Z."[91] On one occasion, al-Buwayṭī even claims agreement between Mālik and al-Shāfiʿī where there was none. In the case of a pregnant woman breaking her fast out of fear for her unborn child, Mālik believed that the woman would simply have to make up for the missed days of fasting,[92] while al-Shāfiʿī held that she would additionally need to give a specified amount of alms per missed day.[93] In al-Buwayṭī's compendium, Mālik's position is quoted as conforming to that of al-Shāfiʿī.[94] However, Ibn Wahb and Ibn al-Qāsim, the Egyptian students of Mālik, both held the same opinion as al-Shāfiʿī on this matter,[95] so al-Buwayṭī's *qāla Mālik* could be interpreted to refer to the dominant position of Mālikī doctrine as taught in early third-/ninth-century Egypt.

Al-Buwayṭī's peer al-Muzanī, by contrast, sets a very different emphasis in his compendium. Al-Muzanī had been a Ḥanafī before becoming al-Shāfiʿī's disciple,[96] and his scholarship continued to exhibit

[89] Compare *Risāla*, in *Umm*, 1:275 (paras. 1810–11); *Umm*, 8:764; al-Buwayṭī's *Mukhtaṣar*, fols. 172a and 172b (Bāb fī al-Risāla); and El Shamsy and Zysow, "Al-Buwayṭī's Abridgment," 342.

[90] Susan Spectorsky, "Aḥmad ibn Ḥanbal's *Fiqh*," *Journal of the American Oriental Society* 102 (1982): 461–65, at 461.

[91] See al-Buwayṭī, *Mukhtaṣar*, fol. 178a onward (al-Waḍʿ ʿalā Mālik).

[92] Mālik, *Muwaṭṭaʾ*, 1:308.

[93] *Umm*, 8:713–14.

[94] Al-Buwayṭī, *Mukhtaṣar*, fol. 184a (al-Waḍʿ ʿalā Mālik).

[95] For Ibn al-Qāsim, see Saḥnūn, *Mudawwana*, 1:210; for Ibn Wahb, see Ibn Juzayy al-Kalbī, *al-Qawānīn al-fiqhiyya* (Tunis: al-Dār al-ʿArabiyya li-l-Kitāb, 1982), 129 (Bāb fī lawāzim al-ifṭār).

[96] Ibn al-Ṣalāh, *Ṭabaqāt al-fuqahāʾ al-shāfiʿiyya*, 2:683.

characteristics closely associated with Ḥanafī discourse. The traditionist Abū Zurʿa al-Rāzī, who studied with al-Shāfiʿī's students in Egypt, had apparently shunned al-Muzanī's teaching circle with the explanation that he had "no desire for legal reasoning and disputation (*al-kalām wa-l-munāẓara*)."[97] The style of al-Muzanī's compendium displays clear parallels to the Ḥanafī approach. While al-Muzanī, like al-Buwayṭī, uses Hadith extensively as evidence for al-Shāfiʿī's positions, his rearrangement and evaluation of al-Shāfiʿī's arguments are shaped by the primary criterion of consistency. The key feature of al-Muzanī's approach is its prioritization of higher-order principles above individual opinions, a tendency that is evident in his strategy, described earlier, of extracting maxim-like rules (which he calls *uṣūl*) from al-Shāfiʿī's work and using these to overrule or modify al-Shāfiʿī's actual opinions.[98] Another example of al-Muzanī's emphasis on overarching principles is found in his discussion of the *ẓihār* vow, the repudiation of a wife by her husband, which can generally be revoked only through atonement (*kaffāra*) performed by the husband.[99] He reports that al-Shāfiʿī had held conflicting views on the question of whether the divorce and subsequent remarriage of the couple would cancel the need for atonement. Al-Muzanī argues that it would, likening the marriage contract to one involving property rights, which are terminated by the sale or renunciation of the property (analogous to divorce); this position, he claims, is "closer to [al-Shāfiʿī's] principle and more appropriate as his opinion" (*ashbah bi-aṣlihi wa-awlā bi-qawlih*).[100] This strategy also enables al-Muzanī to develop effective critiques of rival doctrines: in his discussion of preemption (*shufʿa*), he notes that the Ḥanafī position to grant preemption even in the absence of the seller contradicts the Ḥanafīs' general principle that no judgment can be entered against an absent defendant.[101]

Al-Muzanī's drive for consistency is reflected in the prominence granted to analogy in his compendium. Al-Muzanī cites al-Shāfiʿī's use of analogy

[97] Ibn Abī Ḥātim al-Rāzī, *al-Jarḥ wa-l-taʿdīl*, 2:204. I translate *kalām* in this instance as legal reasoning; as seen in Chap. 1, it carried this meaning, and had it here referred to engagement in rationalist theological discussions, Ibn Abī Ḥātim would hardly have described al-Muzanī as upright and trustworthy (*ṣadūq*) in the same breath as reporting this anecdote.

[98] This was already noted by John Burton in "Rewriting the Timetable of Early Islam," *Journal of the American Oriental Society* 115 (1995): 453–62, at 459.

[99] On the *ẓihār* vow, see Gerald Hawting, "An Ascetic Vow and an Unseemly Oath? *Īlāʾ* and *Ẓihār* in Muslim Law," *Bulletin of the School of Oriental and African Studies* 57 (1994): 113–25.

[100] Al-Muzanī, *Mukhtaṣar*, 279 (Bāb mā yūjibu ʿalā al-mutaẓāhir al-kaffāra).

[101] Al-Muzanī, *Mukhtaṣar*, 171 (Mukhtaṣar al-shufʿa min al-Jāmiʿ).

and discusses it himself frequently, all in all about a hundred times in his work, in sharp contrast to a mere two references to the subject in al-Buwayṭī's compendium. In further contradistinction to al-Buwayṭī, al-Muzanī states explicitly that it is analogy that constitutes the decisive criterion in cases where the Companions of the Prophet differed. He synthesizes al-Shāfiʿī's complex discussions of this rule into the maxim-like principle, "When they disagree, then our method (lit. our *madhhab*) is analogy" (*wa-idhā ikhtalafū fa-madhhabunā al-qiyās*);[102] or, on another occasion, after outlining two Companions' contradictory positions on an issue, "This constitutes disagreement and its resolution is analogy" (*wa-hādhā ikhtilāf wa-sabīluhu al-qiyās*).[103] This pursuit of consistency through analogical extensions was, as seen in Chapter 1, a characteristic of the *ra'y* method of dialectic debate championed by the Ḥanafīs.

Al-Buwayṭī and al-Muzanī thus developed different interpretations of al-Shāfiʿī's paradigm, shaped by their methodological and perhaps also personal backgrounds and allegiances. These two divergent interpretations gave rise to two distinct strands within the early Shāfiʿī school: one based on al-Buwayṭī's Hadith-oriented approach, the other characterized by al-Muzanī's quest for consistency through sophisticated legal – particularly analogical – reasoning. Furthermore, these two strands do not represent the entire legacy of al-Shāfiʿī's students: other students, such as Ḥarmala, also produced their own interpretations of al-Shāfiʿī's thought, and even scholars such as Muḥammad b. ʿAbd al-Ḥakam, whose primary affiliation was not with the Shāfiʿī school, played a key role in the diffusion of Shāfiʿī doctrine through teaching. Although the works of the latter two scholars are no longer extant, all of these strands of Shāfiʿī thought survived beyond the third/ninth century. The existence of these multiple strands of interpretation, each appealing to a different constituency, played an important part in enabling the Shāfiʿī paradigm and its central canonizing thesis to infiltrate and influence other intellectual factions. This process culminated in the acceptance of canonization by scholars across the Sunni spectrum and the establishment of a common methodological basis in Sunni scholarship. The diffusion and influence of al-Shāfiʿī's thought beyond the Shāfiʿī school are explored in the following chapter.

102 Al-Muzanī, *Mukhtaṣar*, 124 (Bāb al-rajul yabīʿu al-shay' ilā ajal ...).
103 Al-Muzanī, *Mukhtaṣar*, 298 (Bāb ʿiddat al-wafā).

Chapter 8

Canonization beyond the Shāfiʿī School

The suggestion that al-Shāfiʿī's ideas on revelation and its interpretation had a profound impact on the trajectory of Islamic scholarship beyond the Shāfiʿī school is by no means new. The great Muslim thinker Fakhr al-Dīn al-Rāzī (d. 606/1209) compared al-Shāfiʿī's contribution to Islamic law with that of Aristotle to logic: both formulated for the first time abstract principles and definitions to govern processes of reasoning that had previously been carried out in an unreflected and therefore unsystematic way.[1] In the modern study of Islamic law, Joseph Schacht concurred with al-Rāzī, arguing that al-Shāfiʿī's legal-theoretical doctrine, particularly the central role that he granted to Hadith, eventually came to be accepted by all Sunni schools of law.[2] Naṣr Ḥāmid Abū Zayd has gone even further to claim that al-Shāfiʿī's influence transcended law and profoundly shaped the Muslim attitude toward revelation in general.[3]

The following sections sketch the spread and adoption of al-Shāfiʿī's ideas, and in particular his revolutionary project of canonization, across the landscape of third-/ninth-century Muslim thought. They trace the initial impact of Shāfiʿī's theory on other important constituencies in Islamic scholarship: traditionalists (*ahl al-ḥadīth*), Ḥanafīs, and Mālikīs, as well as other jurists, theologians, and Quranic exegetes. Such a venture contains by necessity an element of speculation, given that observable similarity does not necessarily imply influence. In addition, the survey of

[1] Fakhr al-Dīn al-Rāzī, *Manāqib al-Imām al-Shāfiʿī*, ed. Aḥmad Ḥijāzī al-Saqqā (Cairo: Maktabat al-Kulliyyāt al-Azhariyya, 1986), 156.

[2] Schacht, *Introduction to Islamic Law*, 58–59.

[3] Abū Zayd, *Al-Imām al-Shāfiʿī wa-taʾsīs al-aydiyūlūjiyya al-wasaṭiyya* (Cairo: Sīnā, 1992).

third-/ninth-century literature on which this study is based is far from comprehensive. Nonetheless, taken together, the abundant indications provided by this tentative sketch support the conclusion that al-Shāfiʿī's theory of canonization quickly found its way into the broader intellectual discourse of his time and exerted a formative influence on the emerging Islamic sciences.

THE TRADITIONALISTS

A crucial step in the eventual creation of a common methodological basis shared by all Sunni scholars was the gradual convergence of the respective positions of the traditionalists (*ahl al-ḥadīth*) and the rationalists (*ahl al-raʾy*) over the course of the third/ninth century. This development led to the acceptance of juristic reasoning by the former and the integration of the Hadith sciences into jurisprudence by the latter.[4] In this rapprochement, al-Shāfiʿī's legal hermeneutic, mediated by his students, played a central role. This section sketches the influence of al-Shāfiʿī's ideas on traditionalist scholarship in the third/ninth century; the next investigates their reception among the *raʾy*-minded Ḥanafīs.

The primary reason for the appeal of al-Shāfiʿī's theory among the *ahl al-ḥadīth* was most probably its potential for resolving an acute dilemma that confronted traditionalist scholars at this time. This was the seemingly unavoidable choice between, on the one hand, being hopelessly outgunned in debates with the *ahl al-raʾy*, who – as seen in Chapter 1 – could draw on a sophisticated arsenal of argumentative strategies; or, on the other hand, adopting the latter's legal reasoning but thereby transgressing against their own principles by, as the traditionalists saw it, ascribing fallible human opinions to God and His Prophet. This tension, and the resolution offered by the Shāfiʿīs, are well illustrated by a dream that Abū Jaʿfar al-Tirmidhī (d. 295/907) claimed to have had in the Prophet's mosque in Medina. In the dream, Abū Jaʿfar asked Prophet Muḥammad whether he should follow the opinions (*raʾy*) of Mālik or of al-Shāfiʿī. The Prophet replied that while he should follow those opinions of Mālik that were in accordance with the Sunna, the opinions of al-Shāfiʿī were not mere opinions, but rather represented the Sunna itself.[5] Abū Jaʿfar subsequently traveled to Egypt to study al-Shāfiʿī's works with al-Rabīʿ. Irrespective of whether

[4] See Christopher Melchert, "Traditionist-Jurisprudents and the Framing of Islamic Law," *Islamic Law and Society* 8 (2001): 383–406.

[5] Abū Nuʿaym al-Iṣbahānī, *Ḥilyat al-awliyāʾ wa-ṭabaqāt al-aṣfiyāʾ*, 10 vols. (Cairo: Maktabat al-Khānjī, 1932–38; repr., Beirut: Dār al-Kitāb al-ʿArabī, 1967–68), 9:100.

Abū Ja'far did in fact experience such a dream, the report shows that third-/ninth-century Shāfiʿī scholars claimed that they could offer a kind of legal reasoning that was fully compatible with the Sunna and thus free of the intellectual speculation that was causing the mushrooming phenomenon of conflicting personal juristic opinions.

Did traditionalist scholars accept this claim? To a significant extent, it seems that they did. As mentioned in the preceding chapter, the ultimate Hadith scholar Aḥmad b. Ḥanbal is known to have studied legal theory with al-Shāfiʿī; the latter, in turn, relied on Aḥmad's expertise in the evaluation of Hadith. Statements attributed to Aḥmad indicate both his deep suspicions about *ra'y* and his approval, even if reluctant, of al-Shāfiʿī as a jurist. When one of Aḥmad's students[6] sought his advice regarding with whom to study *ra'y*, Aḥmad's reply was "With no one." When the student insisted on an answer, he conceded: "If you must study *ra'y*, then study the *ra'y* of al-Shāfiʿī."[7] According to another report, Aḥmad explicitly acknowledged the indebtedness of the traditionalists to al-Shāfiʿī: "Our napes, as *aṣḥāb al-ḥadīth*, were in the hands of Abū Ḥanīfa and not to be wrested away until we saw al-Shāfiʿī."[8] Numerous other reports attest to Aḥmad's endorsement of al-Shāfiʿī: he recruited the prominent traditionalist al-Ḥumaydī to al-Shāfiʿī's circle,[9] he sent a copy of al-Shāfiʿī's *Risāla* to Isḥāq b. Rāhawayh (d. 238/853),[10] and he is said to have called al-Shāfiʿī a mercy for the entire Muslim community.[11] Aḥmad's son, ʿAbd Allāh, quoted passages of al-Shāfiʿī's writing from notes that his father had written in his own hand.[12] Furthermore, Aḥmad's theorization of the relationship between the Quran and the Sunna bears the imprint of al-Shāfiʿī's influence: when asked whether he considers "the Sunna to determine the [meaning] of the Book," that is, the Quran, Aḥmad replied, "I say: the Sunna indicates the meaning of the Quran (*al-sunna tadullu ʿalā maʿnā al-kitāb*)."[13] Thus when Aḥmad's son asked his father about

[6] This was Muḥammad b. Wārah al-Rāzī (d. between 265 and 270/879 and 884), whose name is given wrongly as Muḥammad b. Fazāra al-Rāzī in most manuscripts of Ibn ʿAbd al-Barr's *Intiqā'*; see the editor's note in *Intiqā'*, 128.

[7] Ibn ʿAbd al-Barr, *Intiqā'*, 128.

[8] Ibn Abī Ḥātim al-Rāzī, *Ādāb al-Shāfiʿī*, 55; translated by Christopher Melchert in "Traditionist-Jurisprudents," 397.

[9] Ibn Abī Ḥātim, *al-Jarḥ wa-l-taʿdīl*, 7:203.

[10] Ibn Abī Ḥātim, *al-Jarḥ wa-l-taʿdīl*, 7:204.

[11] Ibn Abī Ḥātim, *Ādāb al-Shāfiʿī*, 57.

[12] Aḥmad b. Ḥanbal, *al-ʿIlal wa-maʿrifat al-rijāl*, 2:383; cf. *Umm*, 7:322.

[13] Aḥmad b. Ḥanbal, *Masā'il*, 438. Compare to the *Risāla*, in *Umm*, 1:43 (para. 308), and especially *Umm*, 8:44, where al-Shāfiʿī compels his opponent to declare that the Sunna indicates the meaning of the Quran in exactly the words that Aḥmad employed.

Quranic verses that could be either general or particular, Aḥmad recited verse 4:11, which enjoins parents to leave an inheritance for their children, and explained that although on the surface the verse applies to all children, the Sunna indicates that unbelieving children and children who have killed a parent are excluded from the purview of the verse.[14] Both the specific example and the terminology Aḥmad uses to discuss it (*ẓāhir*, *ʿāmm*, and *khāṣṣ*) have clear parallels in al-Shāfiʿī's legal-theoretical discussions as found in his writings.[15]

There is another strand of statements, also attributed to Aḥmad b. Ḥanbal, that discourage traditionalists from studying al-Shāfiʿī's books and brand his work on legal theory a reprehensible innovation.[16] The most likely explanation for the divergence between these statements and those mentioned earlier lies in the events that took place between al-Shāfiʿī's death in 204/820 and Aḥmad's death more than thirty years later. In this period, the Quranic Inquisition in Baghdad had targeted traditionalists such as Aḥmad and led to a split among traditionalists. Aḥmad, as one of the most uncompromising traditionalists, was willing to anathemize anyone who insisted on the createdness of the Quran, including adherents of the compromise position that conceded that the material and audible manifestations of the Quran were created.[17] The extreme traditionalists thus clashed with two of the most prominent Shāfiʿī jurists of the time, al-Muzanī in Egypt and al-Karābīsī in Baghdad.[18] Those of Aḥmad's statements that reject al-Shāfiʿī's work and declare Hadith a sufficient basis for lawmaking appear to be a product of this polarization within Aḥmad's circle. Whether or not the latter group of statements is authentic, Aḥmad's original attachment to al-Shāfiʿī seems too strong to call into serious question.

It is likely that the traditionalists' adoption of al-Shāfiʿī's hermeneutic was significantly facilitated by al-Buwayṭī. As seen earlier, al-Buwayṭī had a close affinity, both intellectual and personal, to the *ahl al-ḥadīth*, and he enjoyed the trust of traditionalist scholars such as Abū Dāwūd al-Sijistānī[19] and al-Ḥumaydī[20] as well as Aḥmad b. Ḥanbal himself,

[14] Aḥmad b. Ḥanbal, *Masāʾil*, 442.

[15] See, e.g., *Umm*, 8:43–51. This section contains both a discussion of the particularization of the inheritance verse and the definition of the Sunna as indicating the meaning of the Quran.

[16] Ibn Abī Yaʿlā, *Ṭabaqāt al-ḥanābila*, 1:139.

[17] Brown, *Canonization of al-Bukhārī and Muslim*, 76–78.

[18] For al-Muzanī, see al-Khalīlī, *Kitāb al-Irshād*, 1:431, and Ibn ʿAbd al-Barr, *Intiqāʾ*, 170; for al-Karābīsī, see al-Dhahabī, *Siyar aʿlām al-nubalāʾ*, 11:289.

[19] Al-Dhahabī, *Tārīkh al-islām*, 14:335.

[20] Al-Khaṭīb al-Baghdādī, *Tārīkh Madīnat al-Salām*, 16:441.

who singled out al-Buwayṭī for recommendation from among al-Shāfiʿī's students.[21] Al-Buwayṭī's interpretation of Shāfiʿism, which placed a primary emphasis on Hadith and subjected individual legal opinions to the test of the "Hadith principle," must have offered reassurance to traditionalists eager to find an acceptable way of responding to the challenge posed by *raʾy* without sacrificing the sovereignty of transmitted reports. Al-Buwayṭī's Shāfiʿism provided a mechanism for harnessing the power of legal reasoning for the systematic analysis and reconciliation of revealed texts, which was necessary to address the myriad hypothetical scenarios generated by the *raʾy* method; but it embedded such techniques, and particularly the tool of analogy, in a methodological hierarchy that guaranteed the primacy of the Quran and Hadith as well as the opinions of prophetic Companions. It is unsurprising, then, that al-Buwayṭī attracted a large number of students with traditionalist backgrounds and that his compendium achieved wide circulation among the *ahl al-ḥadīth*.[22]

The impact of al-Shāfiʿī's ideas on the traditionalists is demonstrated by three related phenomena. The first of these is the widespread adoption by Shāfiʿī-affiliated Hadith scholars (*muḥaddithūn*) of the division of labor suggested by al-Shāfiʿī, involving the authentication of Hadith by the *muḥaddithūn* and the use of this verified material by jurists to derive law.[23] A significant number of third-/ninth-century Hadith scholars who had studied al-Shāfiʿī's works appear to have taken this course: they did not themselves develop legal arguments but rather placed their Hadith expertise in the service of Shāfiʿī teaching by providing textual support for al-Shāfiʿī's arguments. Abū Dāwūd explicitly stated that the Hadith he had collected served this purpose.[24] Abū ʿAwāna al-Isfarāyīnī and Ibn Khuzayma quoted al-Shāfiʿī both as a Hadith transmitter and as a jurist. Abū ʿAwāna appended al-Shāfiʿī's legal reasoning to Hadith reports,[25] while Ibn Khuzayma quoted al-Shāfiʿī's positions to answer legal questions that were not covered by the sources[26] and defended al-Shāfiʿī against the

[21] Ibn ʿAbd al-Barr, *Intiqāʾ*, 128.

[22] See my "First Shāfiʿī," 323–30.

[23] Melchert, "Traditionist-Jurisprudents," 393–94.

[24] Abū Dāwūd al-Sijistānī, *Risālat al-Imām Abī Dāwūd ilā ahl Makka fī waṣf sunanih*, in *Thalāth rasāʾil fī ʿilm muṣṭalaḥ al-ḥadīth*, ed. ʿAbd al-Fattāḥ Abū Ghudda, 27–54 (Aleppo: Maktab al-Maṭbūʿāt al-Islāmiyya, 1997), at 32, 46, and 54.

[25] Abū ʿAwāna al-Isfarāyīnī, *Musnad Abī ʿAwāna*, ed. Ayman b. ʿĀrif al-Dimashqī, 5 vols. (Beirut: Dār al-Maʿrifa, 1998); see, for example, 1:67 and 3:304. On Abū ʿAwāna's traditionalist Shāfiʿism, see also Brown, *Canonization of al-Bukhārī and Muslim*, 113–14.

[26] Ibn Khuzayma quotes al-Shāfiʿī's hardship maxim, "When an issue becomes constricted, it expands" (*al-shayʾ idhā ḍāqa ittasaʿa*); see Ibn Khuzayma [Muḥammad b. Isḥāq

charge that a particular opinion of his had no textual basis by citing a relevant Hadith.[27] Abū al-ʿAbbās al-Aṣamm extracted the Hadith found in al-Shāfiʿī's work and taught them as a separate work of Hadith,[28] thus presenting al-Shāfiʿī as a bona fide Hadith scholar. Abū Bakr b. Ziyād al-Naysābūrī (d. 324/935 or 936) wrote a work that was aimed at providing better chains of transmission for the Hadith used in al-Muzanī's compendium.[29] These scholars thus no longer saw themselves as locked in an adversarial struggle against legal reasoning but rather perceived and pursued a complementary relationship between their efforts and those of the jurists.

Second, it is clear that several traditionalists in this period adopted al-Shāfiʿī's methods of legal reasoning and used his hermeneutic tools in their own work. Muḥammad b. Naṣr al-Marwazī's *Sunna* is a partial commentary on the *Risāla* that contains a lengthy discussion of al-Shāfiʿī's theory of abrogation (*naskh*).[30] Al-Marwazī endorsed the use of abrogation and even argued that the Sunna may abrogate the Quran, a possibility that al-Shāfiʿī had rejected.[31] The staunch traditionalist Abū Bakr al-Athram employed al-Shāfiʿī's hermeneutic concepts, such as *bayān* and the general/specific (*ʿāmm/khāṣṣ*) dichotomy, in his work.[32] His adoption of al-Shāfiʿī's legal theory in order to reconcile conflicting textual sources stands in marked contrast to the approach of the previous generation of traditionalists: these presented seemingly contradictory reports without seeking to reconcile their contents, merely noting the relative strength of the chain of transmission for each report.[33] Ibn Abī Ḥātim al-Rāzī's work on Hadith transmitters (*al-Jarḥ wa-l-taʿdīl*) demonstrates his acceptance of al-Shāfiʿī's two-tier framework of the Quran as divine communication and the Sunna as its clarification. Ibn Abī Ḥātim's exposition of this theory is couched entirely in al-Shāfiʿī's hermeneutic terminology, revealing the extent of his indebtedness to al-Shāfiʿī's legal

al-Sulamī al-Naysābūrī], *Ṣaḥīḥ Ibn Khuzayma*, ed. Muḥammad Muṣṭafā al-Aʿẓamī, 4 vols. (Beirut: al-Maktaba al-Islāmiyya, 1970), 4:157.

[27] *Ṣaḥīḥ Ibn Khuzayma*, 1:23.

[28] Al-Aṣamm, *Musnad al-Shāfiʿī*.

[29] Abū Bakr ʿAbd Allāh b. Ziyād al-Naysābūrī, *al-Ziyādāt ʿalā kitāb al-Muzanī*, ed. Khālid b. Hāyif b. ʿUrayj al-Muṭayrī (Riyadh: Dār Aḍwāʾ al-Salaf; Kuwait: Dār al-Kawthar, 2005).

[30] Muḥammad b. Naṣr al-Marwazī, *al-Sunna*, ed. ʿAbd Allāh al-Buṣayrī (Riyadh: Dār al-ʿĀṣima, 2001).

[31] Al-Marwazī, *Sunna*, 243; cf. *Risāla*, in *Umm*, 1:44 (para. 314).

[32] See his *Nāsikh al-ḥadīth wa-mansūkhuh*, ed. ʿAbd Allāh b. Ḥamad al-Manṣūr (Riyadh: published by the editor, 1420/1999), 33, 42, 48, 52, 69, and 74.

[33] Melchert, "Traditionist-Jurisprudents," 388–89.

theory.[34] Further, at least some traditionalists who studied with al-Shāfiʿī's students are known to have authored books of law or included legal discussions in their Hadith works. The former was done by, for example, ʿUthmān b. Saʿīd al-Dārimī (d. 280/894), best known for his refutation of Jahmī theology,[35] who received his legal education from al-Buwayṭī and his Hadith training from Aḥmad b. Ḥanbal.[36] An example of the latter is Abū ʿĪsā al-Tirmidhī (d. 279/892), who studied al-Buwayṭī's compendium with al-Rabīʿ.[37]

Third, al-Shāfiʿī made significant contributions to the development of the terminology of Hadith criticism. His *Risāla* contains important chapters on the nature of a sound chain of transmission, the different kinds of possible flaws in a chain, and the ramifications of such flaws on the normativity of the Hadith in question.[38] Abū Dāwūd considered al-Shāfiʿī's discussion of broken (*mursal*) chains of transmission to represent a landmark and a formative influence on subsequent Hadith scholars.[39] And al-Shāfiʿī's definition of an "irregular Hadith" (*shādhdh*) as a single report that contradicts other, more reliable reports was adopted by Hadith scholars such as al-Athram and became the dominant definition of the term in the study of Hadith.[40]

These phenomena demonstrate that a significant group of prominent late third-/ninth-century traditionalists adopted important positions championed by al-Shāfiʿī regarding Hadith, namely, the affirmation of the symbiosis of Hadith and jurisprudence in terms of a separation of labor and of a common terminology, as well as the actual use of legal

[34] Ibn Abī Ḥātim writes, for example, that the Prophet "clarified the unambiguous as well as ambiguous verses of His book, its specific and general ones, and its abrogating and abrogated ones" ("bayyana [al-rasūl] min muḥkam kitābihi wa-mutashābihihi, khāṣṣihi wa-ʿāmmihi, nāsikhihi wa-mansūkhih"); *al-Jarḥ wa-l-taʿdīl*, 1:1–2. Ibn Abī Ḥātim knew al-Shāfiʿī's *Risāla* and quotes it in his work; see *al-Jarḥ wa-l-taʿdīl*, 2:29–30, as well as *Kitāb al-Marāsīl*, ed. Shukr Allāh b. Niʿmat Allāh Qūzhānī (Beirut: Muʾassasat al-Risāla, 1977), 7 and 14.

[35] ʿUthmān b. Saʿīd al-Dārimī, *al-Radd ʿalā al-jahmiyya*, ed. Badr b. ʿAbd Allāh al-Badr (Kuwait: Dār Ibn al-Athīr, 1995).

[36] Al-Subkī, *Ṭabaqāt al-shāfiʿiyya al-kubrā*, 2:303–6.

[37] Abū ʿĪsā al-Tirmidhī, *Sunan*; see, e.g., 1:43, 4:119, and 4:122. On al-Tirmidhī's study of al-Buwayṭī's compendium (via correspondence with al-Rabīʿ), see 5:693.

[38] See Shākir's introduction to the *Risāla*, 13, and the *Risāla* itself, paras. 998–1376 (*Umm*, 1:170–227).

[39] Abū Dāwūd, *Risālat al-Imām Abī Dāwūd*, 32–33.

[40] Compare Ibn Abī Ḥātim, *Ādāb al-Shāfiʿī*, 233, with al-Athram, *Nāsikh al-ḥadīth wa-mansūkhuh*, 181. I am grateful to Saud Al-Sarhan for alerting me to al-Athram's definition. For the dominance of al-Shāfiʿī's definition in Hadith scholarship, see Brown, *Canonization of al-Bukhārī and Muslim*, 249.

reasoning, in particular, the application of hermeneutic techniques to reconcile contradictory sources. As a result, the fields of Hadith and law were no longer perceived by the traditionalists as advancing rival claims to knowledge, but rather as two distinct and complementary disciplines, of which an individual scholar could engage in either or both. It is, of course, impossible to prove that al-Shāfiʿī represented the sole source of these propositions, but the fact that many of the first traditionalists to accept them are known to have studied with al-Shāfiʿī and his students strongly suggests such a route of influence.

THE ḤANAFĪS

Parallel to the acceptance of legal reasoning by a significant group of traditionalists, influential Ḥanafī jurists were also moving toward a middle ground by adopting a form of legal reasoning that incorporated complex hermeneutic techniques and consciously justified itself on the basis of revelation – especially Hadith. This methodological integration of the Ḥanafī legal tradition and the available corpus of Hadith began only in the third generation of Ḥanafī jurists, and there is good reason to believe that al-Shāfiʿī's ideas, in particular his critique of the Ḥanafīs' use of Hadith, played a crucial role in it.

According to the judge and historian of the Ḥanafī school al-Ṣaymarī (d. 436/1044 or 1045), the process of reconciliation was triggered by the Abbasid caliph al-Maʾmūn (r. 198–218/813–33). The described incident took place at a time when the methodologies of rationalist theology were increasingly infiltrating Ḥanafī legal thought, introducing new concepts and categories. Abū ʿĪsā b. Hārūn (d. 210/825 or 826),[41] who was most likely al-Maʾmūn's half brother, is reported to have complained to the caliph about the discrepancies between Hadith and Ḥanafī doctrine. Abū ʿĪsā presented al-Maʾmūn with notes from the Hadith lessons that had been given to him, al-Maʾmūn, and the latter's brother al-Amīn by various Hadith experts selected by their father, Hārūn al-Rashīd, and pointed out that the members of al-Maʾmūn's intellectual circle – Ḥanafī scholars who had studied with Abū Yūsuf and/or with al-Shaybānī – were openly contravening many of these Hadith in their legal rulings. "If they are right," he argued, "then al-Rashīd was wrong in choosing [these Hadith teachers] for you; or if he was right, then you must distance yourself from those who are in error,"[42] that is, the Ḥanafī scholars.

[41] See al-Dhahabī, *Tārīkh al-islām*, 14:471–72.
[42] Al-Ṣaymarī, *Akhbār Abī Ḥanīfa*, 147.

Al-Maʾmūn was distressed by the charge and ordered his court jurists to compose a response to it. However, none of the offered responses satisfied the caliph: one scholar authored an unscholarly ad hominem attack, another kept asking for more time, and a third, Bishr al-Marīsī, wrote a work that radically denied the validity of any single-transmitter Hadith. Al-Maʾmūn rejected this thesis, observing (as al-Shāfiʿī had) that the Ḥanafīs do in fact use single-transmitter Hadith in their works and thus cannot claim to reject them wholesale. Eventually, ʿĪsā b. Abān, a Ḥanafī jurist who did not belong to al-Maʾmūn's circle, heard about these discussions and authored a book that won him the caliph's favor.[43] In it he systematically theorized and categorized Hadith in a way that neither rejected all Hadith that fell short of absolute certainty (as Bishr had) nor accepted every single-transmitter Hadith that possessed a reliable chain of transmission, as al-Shāfiʿī had demanded.

The book has been referred to as both "The decisive proof" (*al-Ḥujja*) and "The refutation of Bishr al-Marīsī and al-Shāfiʿī on the subject of reports."[44] Although the work itself appears to have been lost, important fragments of it survive as quotations in later works.[45] What these fragments demonstrate is that while ʿĪsā in principle accepted single-transmitter Hadith reports as carrying some normative weight, he classified their authority with reference to their reception in a way that was similar to, but more systematic than, Mālik's concept of Medinan practice.[46] ʿĪsā distinguished between two basic types of single-transmitter Hadith: those that simply represented historical data that had not been translated into communal acceptance and those that, while still not universally known (and thus representing less than certain knowledge), had become embedded in communal tradition and practice.[47] This distinction appears to be a systematization of elements that were already present in Ḥanafī discourse,[48] and it also underpinned the Ḥanafī defense, discussed in Chapter 2, of the apparently arbitrary practice of sometimes allowing a single-transmitter report to particularize a Quranic rule, while at other times upholding the apparent meaning of the Quran in the face of a

[43] Al-Ṣaymarī, *Akhbār Abī Ḥanīfa*, 147–48.

[44] Bedir, "Early Response to al-Shāfiʿī," 290.

[45] See, in particular, the quotations in al-Jaṣṣāṣ's *Fuṣūl fī al-uṣūl* reproduced in Bedir, "Early Response to al-Shāfiʿī."

[46] Zysow, "Economy of Certainty," 25.

[47] Bedir, "Early Response to al-Shāfiʿī," 297–300.

[48] See, for example, the terminology of Abū Yūsuf in *Siyar al-Awzāʿī*, in *Umm*, 9:208. See also al-Ṭaḥāwī, *Sharḥ maʿānī al-āthār*, 4:22; and al-Sarakhsī, *al-Mabsūṭ*, 3:67, 12:96, and 15:66.

contravening Hadith. In the *Umm*, al-Shāfiʿī's Ḥanafī opponent justified the divergence by arguing that in the former case the Hadith report in question was agreed upon.[49]

However, ʿĪsā did not abandon the category of Hadith that were unsupported by agreement. Instead, he created limited areas within which they could fulfill a role. In the case of an apparently general Quranic rule and a Hadith report purporting to establish an exception to the rule, ʿĪsā held that "simple" single-transmitter Hadith could particularize such a rule as long as there was an agreement among scholars that the Quranic rule in question did in fact apply only to a particular subset of cases, rather than being generally valid.[50] If no such agreement existed, the Hadith was classified as irregular (*shādhdh*) and disregarded.[51] Thus, a Quranic rule could be particularized only if the particularizing Hadith had a higher probability than a "simple" single-transmitter report, or if the Quranic rule was less certain in its import than an ordinary general expression. In both cases it was the agreement of scholars that conferred or denied the crucial level of certainty.[52] By refining the categories of general Quranic rule and of particularizing Hadith, ʿĪsā thus allowed Ḥanafī doctrine to escape the consistency trap set by al-Shāfiʿī.[53]

ʿĪsā also provided an explanation for what al-Shāfiʿī had criticized as one of the fundamental flaws of Ḥanafī doctrine, namely, the fact that the Ḥanafīs used Hadith with discontinuous chains of transmission to ground their legal positions and even sometimes preferred such weak reports to Hadith with sound chains of transmission.[54] His defense consisted of the bold claim that Hadith with broken chains were in fact epistemologically superior to those with continuous chains.[55] Within the frame of reference set by Hadith scholarship this claim seems absurd, and later Ḥanafīs, beginning with al-Jaṣṣāṣ in the fourth/tenth century, moved away from the claim of superiority although they continued to maintain

[49] *Umm*, 8:48.

[50] Abū Bakr al-Bāqillānī, *al-Taqrīb wa-l-irshād*, ed. ʿAbd al-Ḥamīd Abū Zunayd, 3 vols. (Beirut: Muʾassasat al-Risāla, 1998), 3:184–85.

[51] Al-Jaṣṣāṣ, *Fuṣūl fī al-uṣūl*, 1:158.

[52] Al-Jaṣṣāṣ, *Fuṣūl fī al-uṣūl*, 1:156–58.

[53] ʿĪsā reduced the authority of single-transmitter Hadith further by considering Hadith transmitted by certain Companions of the Prophet (particularly Abū Hurayra) to be unreliable; see Bedir, "Early Response to al-Shāfiʿī," 307–8. He also held that such Hadith could be disregarded when they clashed with analogical reasoning; see al-Jaṣṣāṣ, *Fuṣūl fī al-uṣūl*, 3:135.

[54] *Umm*, 7:253 and 10:169–70.

[55] Al-Jaṣṣāṣ, *Fuṣūl fī al-uṣūl*, 3:146.

the acceptability of such reports.[56] However, if we take a step away from the formalism of Hadith scholarship, we can see ʿĪsā's position as possessing its own logic. When a recognized scholar quotes the Prophet directly rather than via a chain of transmitters, this can be seen as a sign of the scholar's unwavering conviction of the veracity of the report. It can also be interpreted as an indication that the report is so widely accepted that specifying a chain of transmission would be not only unnecessary but even frivolous, like providing a footnote today for the observation that the earth is round. Insisting on an unbroken chain of transmission would, from this perspective, constitute an expression of doubt, and its provision would signal either an attempt by a scholar to cover his back or an admission that the report is not widespread enough to make its transmission history irrelevant.

ʿĪsā b. Abān thus set out a theory of Hadith that provided a coherent defense of local legal traditions against the challenge posed by the uncompromising logic of the traditionalist discourse, which isolated Hadith from local contexts and treated them first and foremost as sets of data evaluated in terms of their chains of transmission. If the anecdote regarding the origin of his book is accurate, the work was written between 198/813 and 210/825 or 826.[57] There is a remarkable congruence between, on the one hand, the cases debated by al-Shāfiʿī and the Ḥanafīs during the former's visit to Baghdad and, on the other, the examples discussed by ʿĪsā in his legal-theoretical defense of Ḥanafism.[58] This indicates that ʿĪsā wrote the work, as one of its putative titles suggests, at least partly to counter al-Shāfiʿī's criticisms that must have circulated in written form in Baghdad at the time.[59] The intellectual clash between al-Shāfiʿī and the Ḥanafīs, as revealed in the writings of al-Shāfiʿī and ʿĪsā b. Abān, is thus deeply embedded in a quickly developing written culture. The Abbasid princes' written notes from their itinerant Hadith teachers spurred the production of authored books, written to defend the Ḥanafī legal tradition. Al-Shāfiʿī's notes from his Iraqi debates became part of the work on law that he published through his teaching; this work, in turn, provided the seeds for higher-level thinking about

[56] Al-Jaṣṣāṣ, *Fuṣūl fī al-uṣūl*, 3:146–53.

[57] Al-Maʾmūn became caliph in AH 198; his half brother Abū ʿĪsā died in AH 210.

[58] Compare al-Shāfiʿī's *Umm*, 8:61–62, with al-Jaṣṣāṣ's *Fuṣūl fī al-uṣūl*, 1:158; and *Umm*, 7:253, with *Fuṣūl fī al-uṣūl*, 3:146.

[59] This is also suggested by Ibn al-Nadīm's claim that ʿĪsā accessed al-Shāfiʿī's arguments through the work of Sufyān b. Saḥbān (d. unknown), a Ḥanafī jurist and theologian; Ibn al-Nadīm, *Fihrist*, pt. 1, 2:225.

the law that gave rise to al-Shāfiʿī's and ʿĪsā b. Abān's works on abstract legal theory.

ʿĪsā's theory created and justified a space for Hadith in Ḥanafī legal methodology. However, it did not yet engage with the vast body of Hadith that was being assembled by Hadith scholars. The earliest extant evidence of a Ḥanafī scholar embarking on this task is found in the writings of Abū Jaʿfar al-Ṭaḥāwī (d. 321/933).[60] Al-Ṭaḥāwī's work displays a strikingly close intellectual relationship with Shāfiʿism and features extensive reliance on Hadith, in contrast to the hitherto typical style of Ḥanafī jurisprudence.

Al-Ṭaḥāwī was a product of the intermingling of both Shāfiʿī and Ḥanafī elements. He was the nephew of al-Muzanī and received his initial legal training from al-Shāfiʿī's students, in particular his uncle as well as al-Rabīʿ and Muḥammad b. ʿAbd al-Ḥakam.[61] Later, however, he claimed to have observed how frequently his uncle consulted the works of Abū Ḥanīfa's student al-Shaybānī and consequently developed an interest in Ḥanafism that eventually led him to join that school.[62] Al-Ṭaḥāwī's extant work nonetheless demonstrates that in spite of his overall adherence to Ḥanafī legal positions, he adopted al-Shāfiʿī's justification for the systematic incorporation of Hadith into jurisprudence, employed al-Shāfiʿī's hermeneutic terminology, and concurred with many of al-Shāfiʿī's positions on legal theory.

Al-Ṭaḥāwī's indebtedness to al-Shāfiʿī can be seen clearly in the introduction to his work on the legal implications of Quranic verses, *Aḥkām al-Qurʾān* – a title that, possibly coincidentally, was shared by a now-lost treatise by al-Shāfiʿī.[63] In the introduction, al-Ṭaḥāwī provides a rationale for the integral role of Hadith in jurisprudence via an analysis of the Quranic distinction between clear (*muḥkamāt*) and ambiguous (*mutashābihāt*) verses. This section (like Ibn Abī Ḥātim's work, discussed previously) mirrors closely al-Shāfiʿī's discussion of the issue of *bayān* in the *Risāla* – though al-Ṭaḥāwī at no point acknowledges al-Shāfiʿī by name. Clear verses, argues al-Ṭaḥāwī, are epistemologically self-sufficient

[60] Secondary sources claim that an important force in this development was the work of Ibn Shujāʿ al-Thaljī (d. 266/880), but as none of al-Thaljī's works survive, his theory is impossible to reconstruct. See Melchert, *Formation of the Sunni Schools*, 51–52, and Ibn al-Nadīm, *Fihrist*, pt. 1, 2:29–30.

[61] Al-Ṭaḥāwī, *Sharḥ mushkil al-āthār*, 7:228 and 9:255.

[62] Al-Ṣaymarī, *Akhbār Abī Ḥanīfa*, 168.

[63] Ibn al-Nadīm, *Fihrist*, pt. 1, 2:40. Al-Shāfiʿī also refers to the work in the *Risāla*, in *Umm*, 1:63 (para. 416).

and can thus be understood by anyone; al-Shāfiʿī had called this feature *ghāyat al-bayān*, "total clarity."[64] The meanings of ambiguous verses, in contrast, are not evident and require further elucidation. The role of the prophetic Sunna, then, is to explain the import of such verses (*tibyānan li-mā anzala fī kitābihi mutashābihan*).[65] This function of the Sunna as clarification (*bayān*) of the Quran was, as seen in Chapter 3, a central feature of al-Shāfiʿī's legal theory. Indeed, the way in which al-Ṭaḥāwī conceptualizes revelation as a whole closely parallels al-Shāfiʿī's understanding of revelation as a communicative act taking place through the medium of human language, "clarification for those addressed by it" (*bayān li-man khūṭiba bih*).[66] Using very similar wording, al-Ṭaḥāwī says of revelation that "we are addressed in order to receive clarification" (*khūṭibnā li-yubayyan lanā*).[67]

Al-Ṭaḥāwī goes on to insist that the prophetic Sunna is legally binding and that this obligation is rooted in the Quran itself.[68] Both this argument and the specific evidence offered in its support are found in the work of al-Shāfiʿī, who had made the same claim supported by the Quranic verse "What the Messenger brings you, accept it."[69] It is noteworthy that on both of the two occasions when al-Shāfiʿī makes this point, he does so in the context of a debate with an unnamed Ḥanafī interlocutor.[70] Al-Ṭaḥāwī thus adopts and endorses an argument originally deployed against the Ḥanafīs, without referring to its Shāfiʿī and anti-Ḥanafī origins. Further, al-Ṭaḥāwī appears to have accepted not only al-Shāfiʿī's specific argument but also one of the broader positions in whose defense al-Shāfiʿī originally used it, namely, the rejection of juridical preference (*istiḥsān*). According to Ibn Ḥazm (d. 456/1064), al-Ṭaḥāwī explicitly denied the validity of *istiḥsān* despite its centrality in Ḥanafī legal thought, thereby siding with al-Shāfiʿī against his fellow Ḥanafīs.[71]

64 *Risāla*, in *Umm*, 1:12 (para. 98).

65 Abū Jaʿfar al-Ṭaḥāwī, *Aḥkām al-Qurʾān al-karīm*, ed. Saʿd al-Dīn Ūnāl, 1st vol. in 2 pts. (Istanbul: Türkiye Diyanet Vakfı, İslâm Araştırmaları Merkezi, 1995), vol. 1, pt. 1, 59.

66 *Risāla*, in *Umm*, 1:7 (para. 54).

67 Al-Ṭaḥāwī, *Aḥkām al-Qurʾān*, vol. 1, pt. 1, 64.

68 Al-Ṭaḥāwī, *Aḥkām al-Qurʾān*, vol. 1, pt. 1, 59.

69 Quran 59:7; see *Umm*, 8:36 and 9:69.

70 For the Ḥanafī identity of al-Shāfiʿī's opponent in 8:36, see *Umm*, 8:29, and compare with the typical Ḥanafī position in Muwaffaq al-Dīn b. Qudāma, *al-Mughnī*, ed. ʿAbd Allāh al-Turkī and ʿAbd al-Fattāḥ al-Ḥulw, 15 vols. (Cairo: Hajr, 1986–90), 14:130. The second reference in the *Umm*, at 9:69, is in the context of al-Shāfiʿī's critique of the stereotypically Ḥanafī notion of *istiḥsān*.

71 ʿAlī b. Aḥmad b. Ḥazm, *Mulakhkhaṣ Ibṭāl al-qiyās*, ed. Saʿīd al-Afghānī (Beirut: Dār al-Fikr, 1969), 51.

Al-Ṭaḥāwī was confident in using al-Shāfiʿī's legal-theoretical terminology even when clearly disagreeing with him on the question of whether the Quran could be abrogated by the Sunna, which al-Shāfiʿī considered impossible.[72] As part of the evidence for his position, al-Shāfiʿī quoted a Quranic verse ("Say, 'It is not for me to alter it of my own accord'")[73] and argued that a change in the law regarding bequests and inheritance during the Prophet's lifetime was due to the abrogation of one Quranic verse by another verse, rather than by a prophetic tradition.[74] Al-Ṭaḥāwī refuted each of these positions, introducing al-Shāfiʿī's arguments by means of a hypothetical objection (*fa-in qāla qāʾil*, "if someone were to say ...")[75] without mentioning al-Shāfiʿī, instead only admitting that "some people (*min al-nās*) differed with us on this."[76] In turn, Muḥammad b. Naṣr al-Marwazī, a student of al-Rabīʿ, reproduced the debate on the question of whether the Quran can be abrogated only by the Quran, depicting two camps, one of al-Shāfiʿī and his followers and another, anonymous one.[77] The specific cases and arguments he discussed are the same as in the *Risāla* and in al-Ṭaḥāwī's introduction.

Al-Ṭaḥāwī's adoption of al-Shāfiʿī's legal-theoretical arguments regarding the role and importance of Hadith is reflected in his works on positive law, which employ Hadith and the associated traditionist protocols extensively in the service of Ḥanafī doctrine. In contrast to his legal-theoretical discussions, in this context al-Ṭaḥāwī openly names al-Shāfiʿī wherever he mentions the latter's positions.[78] As the earliest extant full-scale integration of Hadith within Ḥanafī law, al-Ṭaḥāwī's work signals the beginning of this methodological shift in Ḥanafī thought. It had a direct and long-lasting impact on Ḥanafism as a whole: al-Ṭaḥāwī's works on jurisprudence were copied and commented upon by subsequent generations of Ḥanafīs, and many of these commentaries survive, indicating that they became part of the mainstream Ḥanafī canon. Al-Ṭaḥāwī's incorporation of Hadith into Ḥanafī jurisprudence thus represents a significant milestone in the eventual convergence of the traditionalist and rationalist movements.

[72] *Risāla*, in *Umm*, 1:44 (para. 314).
[73] Quran 10:15; *Risāla*, in *Umm*, 1:44 (paras. 315–16).
[74] *Risāla*, in *Umm*, 1:59–63 (paras. 394–407).
[75] Al-Ṭaḥāwī, *Aḥkām al-Qurʾān*, vol. 1, pt. 1, 63–64.
[76] Al-Ṭaḥāwī, *Aḥkām al-Qurʾān*, vol. 1, pt. 1, 62. It is likely that he consciously used this phrase to mirror al-Shāfiʿī's oblique references to al-Shaybānī as *baʿḍ al-nās*; see *Umm*, 7:417.
[77] Al-Marwazī, *Sunna*, 189–99.
[78] See, for example, al-Ṭaḥāwī, *Sharḥ mushkil al-āthār*, 7:228 and 9:255.

THE MĀLIKĪS

Close studies of Mālikī doctrine and individual Mālikī scholars by Yasin Dutton[79] and Sherman Jackson[80] have demonstrated the significant influence that al-Shāfiʿī's canonization project had on Mālikī legal theory. This was reflected particularly in the decline of the concept of Medinan practice (*ʿamal*) and in the narrowing of the definition of Sunna – hitherto understood by the Mālikīs broadly as tradition – to apply specifically and exclusively to the body of Hadith, in accordance with al-Shāfiʿī's understanding of the term. Jackson speculated that the origin of this Shāfiʿī influence within Mālikism, which he termed "crypto-Shāfiʿism," could be traced back to Ibn al-Labbād (d. 333/944), a Mālikī scholar from Qayrawān who wrote a refutation of al-Shāfiʿī. However, the initial point of entry of al-Shāfiʿī's hermeneutic into Mālikī doctrine can, in fact, be found significantly earlier, in the work of al-Shāfiʿī's student Muḥammad b. ʿAbd al-Ḥakam.

As seen in Chapter 5, Muḥammad was one of al-Shāfiʿī's closest followers in Egypt, but he suffered defeat in the struggle over al-Shāfiʿī's succession. Later Shāfiʿīs claimed that Muḥammad subsequently "returned to the *madhhab* of his father,"[81] that is, to Mālikism. This alleged break with Shāfiʿism is claimed to have been sealed by Muḥammad's authoring of a refutation of al-Shāfiʿī (*al-Radd ʿalā al-Shāfiʿī*), which appears to be no longer extant. However, it is clear that Muḥammad did not denounce his former teacher even after his putative return to the Mālikī fold. He continued to acknowledge his intellectual debt to al-Shāfiʿī[82] and to transmit al-Shāfiʿī's works in spite of the disapproval of his fellow Mālikīs.[83] Most significantly, a partial reconstruction of his refutation of al-Shāfiʿī reveals that Muḥammad had adopted his former teacher's legal methodology and was employing it to defend Mālik's positions against al-Shāfiʿī's challenge.

The reconstruction is made possible by a chapter in al-Shāfiʿī's *Umm* titled "Addendum on the Question of Sperm," which contains al-Rabīʿ's explicit counterrefutation of Muḥammad's refutation of al-Shāfiʿī on

[79] Yasin Dutton, "ʿAmal v Ḥadīth in Islamic Law: The Case of Sadl al-Yadayn (Holding One's Hands by One's Sides) When Doing the Prayer," *Islamic Law and Society* 3 (1996): 15–40.

[80] Sherman A. Jackson, "Setting the Record Straight: Ibn al-Labbād's Refutation of al-Shāfiʿī," *Journal of Islamic Studies* 11 (2000): 121–46.

[81] Al-Qāḍī ʿIyāḍ, *Tartīb al-madārik*, 4:160–61.

[82] Al-Qāḍī ʿIyāḍ, *Tartīb al-madārik*, 3:180.

[83] Ibn ʿAsākir, *Tārīkh madīnat Dimashq*, 53:362.

the subject of the purity implications of sperm.[84] Al-Shāfiʿī had argued that sperm is ritually pure and thus that the presence of traces of it on a garment does not constitute an obstacle to prayer. By contrast, the Mālikī position that Muḥammad sought to defend requires such traces to be washed off before the garment can be worn for prayer. Al-Rabīʿ's responses to Muḥammad's arguments demonstrate that Muḥammad's primary strategy to discredit al-Shāfiʿī's position consisted of quoting Hadith that contradicted al-Shāfiʿī. This accords with a description of the aim of Muḥammad's refutation by the fifth-/eleventh-century Mālikī scholar Ibn ʿAbd al-Barr: "There is a work by Muḥammad b. ʿAbd Allāh b. ʿAbd al-Ḥakam that refutes al-Shāfiʿī where the latter transgresses against Hadith with complete chains of transmission (*al-ḥadīth al-musnad*). He thereby defends Mālik against al-Shāfiʿī's criticism that Mālik had abandoned transmitted traditions in favor of [Medinan] practice (*ʿamal*)."[85]

Beyond the first layer of prophetic Hadith, the debate between Muḥammad and al-Rabīʿ as presented in the text of the *Umm* encompasses a number of further elements, including semantic arguments based on the text of the Quran as well as on common knowledge regarding sperm as the origin of life. Conspicuous in its absence is any mention of Medinan practice (*ʿamal*), which formed the centerpiece of Mālik's legal theory but was rejected by al-Shāfiʿī; Muḥammad seems to have made no reference to it in his engagement with al-Shāfiʿī. We can thus detect a hierarchy of arguments both in Muḥammad ʿAbd al-Ḥakam's attack on al-Shāfiʿī and in the arguments made by al-Rabīʿ to defend his master. The first battle is fought over prophetic traditions that specifically address the case of sperm and prayer; al-Rabīʿ makes the primacy of Hadith in the hierarchy clear by stating, "The authoritative basis of our opinion on sperm is the transmitted report" (*aṣl qawlinā fī al-manī al-athar*).[86] Then, the parties call on additional evidence, specifically analogies on the basis of Quranic verses or of general consensus.

What we see in this exchange is that both sides in fact use more or less the same arsenal of arguments and techniques. They begin with the specific (and thus the strongest) traditions from the Prophet, and then support this with indirect reasoning on the basis of general (and thus weaker) verses from the Quran. This debate differs sharply from the

[84] *Umm*, 2:124–27 (Ziyāda fī masʾalat al-manī zādahā al-Rabīʿ b. Sulaymān yaruddu fīhā ʿalā Muḥammad b. ʿAbd Allāh b. ʿAbd al-Ḥakam).

[85] Ibn ʿAbd al-Barr, *Intiqāʾ*, 176.

[86] *Umm*, 2:126.

exchange reproduced in al-Shāfiʿī's *Ikhtilāf Mālik*, in which al-Shāfiʿī attacks Mālik's theory by criticizing an anonymous Mālikī opponent: whereas *Ikhtilāf Mālik* demonstrates fundamental disagreement over the basic propositions of legal hermeneutics, the two sides' arguments in the *Umm*'s chapter on sperm rest on a shared, and highly sophisticated, legal theory. This contains an agreement regarding what the sources are, how they relate to one another hierarchically (traditions over analogy; specific over general), and how complicated arguments, especially legal analogy and the reconciliation of seemingly contradictory traditions, ought to be constructed. It thus seems fair to conclude that Muḥammad ʿAbd al-Ḥakam in fact agreed with al-Shāfiʿī and al-Rabīʿ on legal theory and used this shared legal theory in order to challenge al-Shāfiʿī and to defend Mālik's opinions. He remained a Mālikī in terms of positive law (*fiqh*) but used Shāfiʿī legal theory (*uṣūl al-fiqh*), or at least important elements of it, in service of Mālikī law.

This reading of Muḥammad's legal theory is corroborated by his explicit statement regarding the sources of the law that is preserved in the work of a later Mālikī scholar, Ibn Shās (d. 616/1219):

> The judge rules by that which is in the Book of God. If he does not find [the solution] in the Book of God, then in the Sunna of His Messenger. If it is not in the Sunna of God's Messenger, then he rules by that which his Companions ruled. If there is nothing regarding the case there, and there is no consensus, then he is to apply his individual reasoning after that.[87]

The content of this statement is virtually identical to a parallel section in al-Shāfiʿī's refutation of Mālik, which lists the same hierarchy of sources, as well as to a similar list in al-Buwayṭī's compendium.[88] Muhammad's hierarchy makes no mention of Medinan practice, the centerpiece of Mālik's own hermeneutical approach; rather, it explicitly endorses the contradictory notion that the Sunna can be accessed directly, through Hadith reports.

Muḥammad's legal approach thus stands in sharp contrast to that of his father, the prominent Mālikī scholar ʿAbd Allāh b. ʿAbd al-Ḥakam. As Jonathan Brockopp has shown, ʿAbd Allāh's compendium, written

87 Jalāl al-Dīn b. Shās, *ʿIqd al-jawāhir al-thamīna fī madhhab ʿālim al-Madīna*, ed. Muḥammad Abū al-Ajfān and ʿAbd al-Ḥafīẓ Manṣūr, 3 vols. (Beirut: Dār al-Gharb al-Islāmī, 2003), 3:119. Translated by Mohammad Fadel in "Adjudication in the Mālikī *Madhhab*: A Study of Legal Process in Medieval Islamic Law," 2 vols. (PhD diss., University of Chicago, 1995), 1:231.

88 *Umm*, 8:764; al-Buwayṭī, *Mukhtaṣar*, fols. 172a and 172b (Bāb fī al-Risāla); El Shamsy and Zysow, "Al-Buwayṭī's Abridgment," 342.

sometime before 210/825, is based on the wholesale acceptance of Mālik as a juristic authority in a way that makes legal argumentation obsolete – what Brockopp terms the "Great Shaykh theory of authority."[89] ʿAbd Allāh's work, Brockopp argues, demonstrates that he had "no interest in defending his legal arguments according to the roots of jurisprudence,"[90] that is, *uṣūl al-fiqh*. It seems likely that it was Muḥammad's contact with al-Shāfiʿī that caused the quantum leap in juristic sophistication from the father to the son, giving rise to a new, Shāfiʿī-inspired style of Mālikī jurisprudence in Egypt.

The consequent gulf between Muḥammad's novel approach and the "old-fashioned" Mālikism of his father's generation is further illustrated by an anecdote reported by a certain al-Ḥasan b. ʿAlī b. al-Ashʿath (d. unknown). Muḥammad is said to have met ʿAbd al-Malik b. al-Mājishūn, who was a student of Mālik and the son of Mālik's contemporary and fellow Medinan ʿAbd al-ʿAzīz. Muḥammad questioned ʿAbd al-Malik regarding a point of law and, upon receiving an answer, asked for the evidence (*al-ḥujja*). ʿAbd al-Malik's response was "Because Mālik said such-and-such." Hearing this, Muḥammad is reported to have said to himself, "How absurd! I ask you for your evidence and you say 'my teacher said [so],' even though evidence is incumbent upon you as well as your teacher (*al-ḥujja ʿalayka wa-ʿalā muʿallimik*)."[91]

Muḥammad b. ʿAbd al-Ḥakam's crypto-Shāfiʿism did not remain a mere anomaly. The Andalusian Ibn al-Faraḍī's (d. 403/1013) biographical work, *Tārīkh ʿulamāʾ al-Andalus*, reveals that a substantial minority of third-/ninth-century Andalusian Mālikī scholars visited Egypt during the "golden age" of Shāfiʿī scholarship, studied with al-Shāfiʿī's students, and absorbed al-Shāfiʿī's legal theory, which they took back to Muslim Spain. There they formed a distinct Shāfiʿī-leaning intellectual current within Andalusian Mālikism that Ibn al-Faraḍī defined in terms of adherence to explicit evidence, *ḥujja*, a characteristically Shāfiʿī position that Ibn al-Faraḍī juxtaposed with simple adherence, or *taqlīd*, to Mālik's teaching. His description of a scholar by the name of Qāsim b. Muḥammad b. Sayyār, who had studied in Egypt with Muḥammad b. ʿAbd al-Ḥakam and with al-Muzanī, is typical: "He follows the method of evidence (*ḥujja*) and investigation (*naẓar*) and has abandoned blind following (*taqlīd*), and he tends toward the school of

[89] Brockopp, "Competing Theories of Authority"; see also Brockopp, *Early Mālikī Law*.
[90] Brockopp, *Early Mālikī Law*, 171.
[91] Al-Dhahabī, *Siyar aʿlām al-nubalāʾ*, 10:53–54.

al-Shāfiʿī."[92] This dichotomy of *taqlīd* versus *ḥujja* and *naẓar* is found at least four times in Ibn al-Faraḍī's work, and it always refers to scholars who had traveled abroad in the third/ninth or early fourth/tenth century and absorbed "foreign teachings," particularly Shāfiʿism.[93]

Despite these individual crypto-Shāfiʿīs, the dominant western Mālikī position with regard to legal theory continued to view Medinan practice as more authoritative than single-transmitter Hadith. On the other hand, the embattled minority of Mālikī legal theorists in fourth-/tenth-century Iraq embraced al-Shāfiʿī's and Muḥammad b. ʿAbd al-Ḥakam's hierarchy of sources[94] and denounced blind following (*taqlīd*) as unacceptable.[95] It is likely that this phenomenon is due to the impact of the Egyptian students of al-Shāfiʿī, particularly Muḥammad b. ʿAbd al-Ḥakam, whose implicit or explicit endorsement of the other Shāfiʿī scholars, particularly al-Rabīʿ and al-Muzanī, must have increased their appeal to a Mālikī audience; this is indicated by the frequency with which Mālikīs who visited Egypt listed Muḥammad, al-Rabīʿ, and al-Muzanī as their teachers. Al-Shāfiʿī's abstract legal theory provided a universally accessible language for examining questions of jurisprudence, and it was consequently adopted by Muḥammad and other Mālikīs after him in the service of Mālikism.

THE EXEGETES

The writing of exegetical works on the Quran predated al-Shāfiʿī, but his ideas regarding the relationship between the Quran and Hadith appear to have had a significant influence on the genre. When the great Hadith scholar Ibn Ḥajar al-ʿAsqalānī (d. 852/1449) composed a list of the four most important exegetical works that explain the Quran by means of transmitted material originating in the prophetic and postprophetic age (*al-tafsīr bi-l-maʾthūr*),[96] three of the works he named were written by

[92] Ibn al-Faraḍī, *Tārīkh ʿulamāʾ al-Andalus*, 1:398: "Yadhhabu madhhab al-ḥujja wa-l-naẓar wa-taraka al-taqlīd wa-yamīlu ilā madhhab al-Shāfiʿī."

[93] These references are found in entries on the following scholars: Aḥmad b. Bishr al-Tujībī b. al-Aghbas (d. 327/938 or 939), Abū al-Ḥakam Mundhir b. Saʿīd al-Balūṭī (d. 355/966), Abū ʿAlī Ḥasan b. Saʿd b. Kasīla al-Kattāmī (d. 332/943 or 944), and Qāsim b. Muḥammad b. Sayyār (d. 319/931).

[94] See Abd-Allah, "Mālik's Concept of *ʿAmal*," 1:418, and al-Qāḍī ʿAbd al-Wahhāb al-Baghdādī, *Masāʾil fī uṣūl al-fiqh mustakhraja min kitāb al-Maʿūna ʿalā madhhab ʿālim al-Madīna*, included as an addendum to Ibn al-Qaṣṣār, *Muqaddima fī al-uṣūl*, 235–55, at 254–55.

[95] Ibn ʿAbd al-Barr, *Jāmiʿ bayān al-ʿilm*, 2:993.

[96] Ibn Ḥajar, *al-ʿUjāb fī bayān al-asbāb*, ed. Abū ʿAbd al-Raḥmān Zamarlī (Beirut: Dār Ibn Ḥazm, 2002), 57.

second-generation students of al-Shāfiʿī (that is, students of al-Shāfiʿī's students): Ibn Abī Ḥātim al-Rāzī, Muḥammad b. Jarīr al-Ṭabarī, and Ibn al-Mundhir (d. 318/930). The works written by these scholars differ markedly from the previously common style of Quranic exegesis, and they display clear signs of al-Shāfiʿī's influence.

First, the exegeses of Ibn Abī Ḥātim, al-Ṭabarī, and Ibn al-Mundhir represent deliberately authored books, with introductions in which the authorial voice of the exegete is apparent.[97] In contrast, earlier Quranic commentaries consisted of lecture notes; they included no introductions, and the voice of the author remained obscured. An example of a work of this older type is the commentary of ʿAbd al-Razzāq al-Ṣanʿānī (d. 211/827), which mainly consists of his notes on the exegesis of Maʿmar b. Rāshid (d. 154/770).[98] The work is marked by a univocal and unreflective style of commentary. This style is exemplified by ʿAbd al-Razzāq's statement that according to Maʿmar, the Quranic verse enjoining charity for those "who are poor and who are restricted in the path of God" refers to those taking part in military raids who cannot therefore engage in trade.[99] It is likely that ʿAbd al-Razzāq and/or Maʿmar were aware of other interpretations of the verse but considered this one the most reliable and accurate. Given that other possible interpretations are not mentioned, the reader or hearer of the commentary is confronted with a single, seemingly authoritative explanation, unaccompanied by any justification. This type of commentary thus demands the same kind of unquestioned acceptance as does the type of jurisprudence embodied by Mālik's *Muwaṭṭaʾ*, in which Mālik, like ʿAbd al-Razzāq, discloses neither the full range of the material on which he draws nor the methodology that led him to his stated positions.

By contrast, the commentaries authored by al-Shāfiʿī's second-generation students offer a variety of opinions. On the Quranic verse on charity, Ibn al-Mundhir's work cites the ʿAbd al-Razzāq/Maʿmar position as well as three other opinions, which interpret the verse to refer, respectively, to those maimed in battle, poor Meccan emigrants in general, or specifically those immigrants who lived in the Prophet's

[97] The only known extant copy of Ibn al-Mundhir's commentary is fragmentary and therefore lacks an introduction, but cross-references to his commentary in his other works indicate that his commentary was indeed a fully authored work and therefore must have had an introduction; see Ibn al-Mundhir, *Kitāb Tafsīr al-Qurʾān*, ed. Saʿd b. Muḥammad al-Saʿd, 2 vols. (Medina: Dār al-Maʾāthir, 2002), 1:25.

[98] ʿAbd al-Razzāq al-Ṣanʿānī, *Tafsīr al-Qurʾān*, ed. Muṣṭafā Muḥammad, 3 vols. in 4 (Riyadh: Maktabat al-Rushd, 1989).

[99] ʿAbd al-Razzāq, *Tafsīr*, 1:109.

mosque.[100] Ibn Abī Ḥātim's commentary contains three of the four opinions mentioned by Ibn al-Mundhir (omitting the last one), as well as two further opinions.[101] Finally, al-Ṭabarī reproduces all opinions listed by Ibn Abī Ḥātim but arranges them into two groups, the first containing opinions that interpret the term "restricted" (*uḥṣirū*) to refer to the inability of the Meccan emigrants to engage in trade due to other activities or illness, and the second containing opinions according to which the restriction was imposed by the pagan Meccans. Al-Ṭabarī argues for the former type of interpretation and deploys a linguistic argument to support his opinion.[102]

The variety of opinions presented in these later commentaries is not simply antiquarian in nature. Rather, as the two extant introductions (Ibn Abī Ḥātim's and al-Ṭabarī's) show, their authors had developed self-conscious and explicitly articulated methodological approaches to evaluating and presenting the exegetical material that they had gathered. Ibn Abī Ḥatim's methodology is hierarchical, paralleling al-Shāfiʿī's hermeneutic approach. He argues that if there is a prophetic Hadith that can elucidate the meaning of a particular Quranic verse, this and only this will be used. If no such Hadith is available, the consensus of the Prophet's Companions – if known – regarding the verse is taken to represent the correct interpretation. In the absence of such a consensus, all of the differing opinions of the Companions are laid out. If no Companion's opinion is known, the same procedure is applied to the opinions of the Companions' Successors (*tābiʿūn*), and after that to the opinions of the latter's successors.[103] In its extensive incorporation of postprophetic reports into the process of interpretation, Ibn Abī Ḥātim's exegetical hierarchy differs from al-Shāfiʿī's legal one, but for understandable reasons. Al-Shāfiʿī, too, recognized the value of Companion and Successor reports, but he emphasized that unlike prophetic Hadith they did not constitute independent loci of normativity and thus could not be used as a source in the derivation of law. Quranic exegesis, however, is generally not concerned with the establishment of legal rules but rather simply with the elucidation of the text itself. It is thus natural that exegetes continued to draw on a wider range of material.

[100] Ibn al-Mundhir, *Tafsīr*, 1:42–43.

[101] Ibn Abī Ḥātim al-Rāzī, *Tafsīr al-Qurʾān al-ʿaẓīm*, ed. Asʿad Muḥammad al-Ṭayyib, 14 vols. (Mecca and Riyadh: Maktabat Nizār Muṣṭafā al-Bāz, 1997), 2:540.

[102] Muḥammad b. Jarīr al-Ṭabarī, *Jāmiʿ al-bayān fī taʾwīl al-Qurʾān* [*Tafsīr*], ed. ʿAbd Allāh al-Turkī, 26 vols. (Cairo: Markaz al-Buḥūth wa-l-Dirāsāt al-ʿArabiyya al-Islāmiyya, 2001), 5:22–26.

[103] Ibn Abī Ḥātim, *Tafsīr*, 1:14.

Al-Ṭabarī offers a more complex methodology, clearly inspired by al-Shāfiʿī's conceptualization of revelation as a communicative act. In the lengthy introduction to his exegesis, al-Ṭabarī introduces the term "clarity" (*bayān*), which, as seen earlier, occupies a central position in al-Shāfiʿīs theory of revelation. Al-Ṭabarī's discussion is more extensive than al-Shāfiʿī's, but it closely parallels al-Shāfiʿī's exposition on the clarity and Arabic nature of the Quran.[104] Indeed, al-Ṭabarī's more detailed account serves to elucidate al-Shāfiʿī's original arguments. For example, al-Ṭabarī points out that given the essential clarity of divine speech, the fact that the Quran was in the first instance addressed to Muḥammad, an Arab, necessarily means that the Quran is an Arabic scripture. Rather than representing an unrelated interjection of Arab supremacism, al-Shāfiʿī's and al-Ṭabarī's insistence on the Arabic nature of the Quran is an integral part of the theory of clarity: the existence of non-Arabic elements in revelation to an Arabic prophet and his people would render parts of the divine communicative act futile and thereby create a theological paradox.

Al-Ṭabarī then addresses the ways in which revelation conveys meaning, a section that, according to Claude Gilliot, represents "the epitome of Muslim ideas on the subject and the charter of the exegete."[105] Remarkably, this section follows al-Shāfiʿī's statement on the matter, as it has been translated and discussed in Chapter 3, very closely.[106] In addition, al-Ṭabarī adopts other important hermeneutic terms, including textual inference (*niṣba/naṣaba*) and prudent direction (*irshād*), from al-Shāfiʿī's work.[107] Furthermore, al-Ṭabarī theorizes the relationship between the Quran and the prophetic example in the same way that al-Shāfiʿī did and using the same terminology, by defining the Sunna as an exclusive second-tier clarification of the Quran.[108]

[104] Compare al-Ṭabarī, *Tafsīr*, 1:8–13, with al-Shāfiʿī, *Risāla*, in *Umm*, 1:19 (paras. 152–54).

[105] Claude Gilliot, "Langue et Coran selon Tabari: 1. La Précellence du Coran," *Studia Islamica*, no. 68 (1988): 79–106, at 81–82.

[106] Compare al-Ṭabarī's *Tafsīr*, 1:12–13, with al-Shāfiʿī's *Risāla*, in *Umm*, 1:22 (paras. 173–77).

[107] On textual inference, compare al-Ṭabarī's *Tafsīr*, 1:68, with al-Shāfiʿī's *Risāla*, in *Umm*, 1:15 (para. 66) and 1:234 (para. 1447); see also Lowry, *Early Islamic Legal Theory*, 53–54, on al-Jāḥiẓ's usage of the term. On prudent direction, compare al-Ṭabarī's *Tafsīr*, 1:68, with al-Shāfiʿī's *Risāla*, in *Umm*, 1:161–63 (paras. 946–58); see also *Umm*, 9:344–45. On the application of the concept to an actual case, compare al-Ṭabarī's *Tafsīr*, 5:78 (on Quran 2:282), to *Umm*, 4:181.

[108] Al-Ṭabarī, *Tafsīr*, 1:68.

Like Ibn Abī Ḥātim in the introduction to his exegetical work, al-Ṭabarī emphasizes that the clarification provided by the Prophet is uniquely authoritative and makes the statements and opinions of others superfluous.

The significant novelty in the Quran commentaries by al-Shāfiʿī's second-generation students is thus twofold. First, they exhibit a scientific distance between the author and the subject, which manifests itself in the open presentation of multivocal evidence. Earlier commentaries, such as those by ʿAbd al-Razzāq or Muqātil b. Sulaymān (d. 150/767),[109] present authoritative opinions and coherent narratives, respectively, but do not display such a scientific distance; rather, they project the timeless and unchanging aura of a tradition. Second, this absence of a univocal tradition necessitates a new basis for authority, which is supplied by a hierarchy of sources, in which Hadith function as a complementary part of revelation. Evidence is then weighed using a conscious methodology. Both the scientific attitude and the systematic methodology reveal the influence of al-Shāfiʿī's thought.

OTHER SCHOLARS

Al-Shāfiʿī's ideas appear to have had an impact also on other scholars in the third/ninth and fourth/tenth centuries who are more difficult to characterize.

Al-Jāḥiẓ (d. 255/868 or 869), the celebrated prose writer and theologian, titled one of his most important works on the Arabic language "The Book of Clarity and Clarification" (*Kitāb al-Bayān wa-l-tabyīn*). James Montgomery has argued that al-Jāḥiẓ's treatment of the concept of clarity (*bayān*) in language "is to be understood as an engagement with the jurist al-Shāfiʿī's ... exposition of the same concept."[110] Montgomery's argument gains further support from the fact that al-Jāḥiẓ's central definition of clarity, which he attributes to an anonymous "mighty man of words" (*jahābidhat al-alfāẓ*), is also found in Ibn ʿAsākir's *Tārīkh madīnat Dimashq* as a verbatim quotation attributed to al-Shāfiʿī by the latter's

[109] On Muqātil, see Kees Versteegh, "Grammar and Exegesis: The Origins of Kufan Grammar and the *Tafsīr Muqātil*," *Der Islam* 67 (1990): 206–42, at 210.

[110] James E. Montgomery, "Al-Jāḥiẓ's *Kitāb al-Bayān wa al-Tabyīn*," in *Writing and Representation in Medieval Islam: Muslim Horizons*, ed. Julia Bray, 91–152 (London: Routledge, 2006), 92. Joseph Lowry provides further support for Montgomery's thesis in "Some Preliminary Observations on al-Šāfiʿī and Later *Uṣūl al-Fiqh*: The Case of the Term *Bayān*," *Arabica* 55 (2008): 505–27, at 513.

student Abū Thawr.[111] Al-Jāḥiẓ's failure to name al-Shāfiʿī as his source could be explained by the fact that he dedicated his work to Ibn Abī Duwād, the grand judge of Baghdad, probably at the exact time when the latter's protégé Ibn Abī al-Layth was actively persecuting al-Shāfiʿī's students in Egypt.[112]

Why would someone who is primarily famous as a litterateur and a theologian be interested in a legal-theoretical concept such as *bayān*? As seen previously, al-Shāfiʿī's concept of *bayān*, as elucidated in the *Risāla*, is the key to a comprehensive theory that transcends mere signification and encompasses the entire process of communication; a theory, furthermore, that describes human and divine communication equally. Such a concept must have been attractive both to al-Jāḥiẓ the writer, who sought eloquence and analyzed its nature, and to al-Jāḥiẓ the Muʿtazilī theologian, who was preoccupied with questions of human responsibility and divine justice. These concerns had a strong linguistic dimension: if revelation takes place through language, the question arises how obligations can be imposed in a medium as ambiguous as language. This creates a second problem, namely, how the seemingly deficient nature of language could be reconciled with the rational necessity of God being just as opposed to arbitrary: communicating a message that is necessary for salvation in a medium that precludes full comprehension would imply the imposition of obligations beyond the human capacity to fulfill them. Al-Shāfiʿī's theory of *bayān* offered conceptual tools for addressing these dilemmas, and it possessed an elegance that would have appealed to al-Jāḥiẓ.

A second prominent scholar whose work contains implicit but unacknowledged traces of al-Shāfiʿī's ideas is the already mentioned jurist and Hadith scholar Abū ʿUbayd al-Qāsim b. Sallām. Abū ʿUbayd is reported to have studied al-Shāfiʿī's works with al-Rabīʿ,[113] and al-Shāfiʿī's Baghdadi student al-Karābīsī (d. 248/862) accused him of having plagiarized (*saraqta*) al-Shāfiʿī's writing in his works.[114] An analysis of Abū ʿUbayd's writings strengthens these suspicions. In his book on purity (*al-Ṭahūr*), Abū ʿUbayd uses an explicitly legal-theoretical argument to justify his disagreement with Mālik on the question of the purity of canine saliva.

111 Compare Ibn ʿAsākir, *Tārīkh madīnat Dimashq*, 51:356, with al-Jāḥiẓ, *al-Bayān wa-l-tabyīn*, 7th ed., ed. ʿAbd al-Salām Muḥammad Hārūn, 4 vols. (Cairo: Maktabat al-Khānjī, 1998), 1:75–76.

112 On the dedication and dating of *al-Bayān wa-l-tabyīn*, see Montgomery, "Al-Jāḥiẓ's *Kitāb*," 111–14.

113 Al-Bayhaqī, *Manāqib al-Shāfiʿī*, 2:251.

114 See Ibn Ḥajar al-ʿAsqalānī, *Tahdhīb al-Tahdhīb*, 2:361, and Chap. 6 of this volume.

He claims that Mālik's position – that an explicit Hadith according to which a dog's saliva imparts impurity does not apply to hunting dogs – implies an instance of particularization (*takhṣīṣ*); however, this hermeneutic procedure would require the existence of a contrary Hadith report relating specifically to hunting dogs.[115] Both the identification of Mālik's maneuver as particularization and the hierarchical assumptions underpinning Abū ʿUbayd's criticism of it reflect al-Shāfiʿī's legal theory.[116] Elsewhere, Abū ʿUbayd warns against misconstruing a dispensation (*rukhṣa*), which is by its nature an exception, as an unrestricted general rule (*ʿāmm*). The same warning, using the same terminology, was earlier made by al-Shāfiʿī.[117] These examples suggest not only that Abū ʿUbayd borrowed al-Shāfiʿī's ideas in his work, as suggested by al-Karābīsī, but also that he had begun to see legal problems and debates through the lens of al-Shāfiʿī's theory of revelation.

A third example is provided by a work titled *al-Ḥayda*, which is attributed to ʿAbd al-ʿAzīz al-Kinānī (d. between 221/836 and 240/854 or 855),[118] a student of al-Shāfiʿī. The author of the work (most likely al-Kinānī) claims to reproduce a theological debate between himself and Bishr al-Marīsī (d. 218/833) on the nature of the Quran. In the course of this debate, al-Kinānī lays out the interaction between general and specific expressions in the Arabic language, a distinction that originates in the theory of al-Shāfiʿī as laid out in the *Risāla*.[119] As noted in Chapter 2, al-Shāfiʿī himself had also encountered Bishr al-Marīsī, and it is very possible that Bishr was the first of al-Shāfiʿī's two unnamed interlocutors in the debates that constitute al-Shāfiʿī's *Jimāʿ al-ʿilm*. Interestingly, that part of the *Jimāʿ al-ʿilm* also contains a discussion on the interaction between general and specific expressions in revelation. In it, al-Shāfiʿī cites the Quranic verse "[God is] the creator of everything (*khāliq kulli shayʾ*)" as

[115] Abū ʿUbayd al-Qāsim b. Sallām, *al-Ṭahūr*, ed. Mashhūr Ḥusayn Maḥmūd Sulaymān (Jedda: Maktabat al-Ṣaḥāba, 1994), 270.

[116] Lowry, *Early Islamic Legal Theory*, 71.

[117] Compare Abū ʿUbayd's *Ṭahūr*, 235, with al-Shāfiʿī's *Risāla*, in *Umm*, 1:252 (para. 1608).

[118] On the differing death dates, see van Ess, *Theologie und Gesellschaft*, 3:507–8.

[119] Compare the early sections of the *Risāla* with ʿAbd al-ʿAzīz al-Kinānī, *al-Ḥayda wa-l-iʿtidhār fī al-radd ʿalā man qāla bi-khalq al-Qurʾān*, ed. ʿAlī al-Fiqhī (Medina: Maktabat al-ʿUlūm wa-l-Ḥikam, 2002), 39–40. I am grateful to Rodrigo Adem for pointing out the similarity. Although this work has been called apocryphal (van Ess, *Theologie und Gesellschaft*, 3:507–8), it appears to have been known already by Dāwūd al-Ẓāhirī (d. 270/884), who mentions al-Kinānī's reliance on al-Shāfiʿī's concepts, suggesting that at least this section goes back to al-Kinānī; see al-Bayhaqī, *Manāqib al-Shāfiʿī*, 2:328, where al-Bayhaqī quotes Dāwūd al-Ẓāhirī on al-Kinānī's legal hermeneutic.

an example of a general expression that applies to all its referents.[120] But in the *Ḥayda*, this exact verse, together with al-Shāfiʿī's definition of it as a general expression, is deployed by Bishr to argue for the createdness of the Quran, with al-Kinānī countering that the verse does not refer to the Quran, since God's speech is not a thing.[121] This shows that al-Shāfiʿī's student al-Kinānī had imported his master's hermeneutic theorization to the realm of theology. It also suggests that already al-Shāfiʿī's opponent Bishr al-Marīsī had done so, providing an even more powerful demonstration of the force and appeal of al-Shāfiʿī's ideas.

A final example of the influence of al-Shāfiʿī's ideas can be found in the work of al-Qāḍī al-Nuʿmān (d. 363/974), who laid the foundations of Ismāʿīlī Shiʿi law. In his *Risāla dhāt al-bayān*, within a discussion of the issue of evidence (specifically, the sufficiency of a witness and an oath as evidence in certain types of cases, which al-Shāfiʿī had also addressed), al-Qāḍī al-Nuʿmān explains that the Quran contains statements that are nonspecific (*jumla*) and that God's communicative intention behind such instances of revelation (*murāduhu fī mā anzalahu*) is explicated by the Sunna of the Prophet.[122] This is a clear reference to al-Shāfiʿī's theory, expressed in the latter's specific terminology (*jumla*, *bayān*, *irāda*) and using the same Quranic verse (16:44) in support of the position.[123] Al-Qāḍī al-Nuʿmān then takes the argument further, claiming that the Ismāʿīlī imams fulfill the same clarifying role for the Sunna as the Sunna does for the Quran. As evidence, he cites the Quranic verse "Obey God, and obey the Messenger and those in authority" (Quran 4:59) and identifies "those in authority" as the imams. Again, al-Qāḍī al-Nuʿmān is obviously in close conversation with al-Shāfiʿī, who, in his description of the relationship between the Quran and the Sunna, had also quoted Quran 4:59. Al-Shāfiʿī, however, had understood "those in authority" to refer to political leaders, whose authority he conceived as radically different from and dependent on the first two categories, God and His Messenger.[124] Instead of developing an independent Ismāʿīlī hermeneutic theory, al-Qāḍī al-Nuʿmān thus either adopted or strategically modified al-Shāfiʿī's ideas.

[120] *Umm*, 9:11.

[121] Al-Kinānī, *al-Ḥayda*, 21, 26, 37, and 40.

[122] Al-Qāḍī al-Nuʿmān, *The Epistle of the Eloquent Clarification Concerning the Refutation of Ibn Qutayba*, ed. Avraham Hakim (Leiden: Brill, 2012), 22–23.

[123] For the terminology, see *Risāla*, in *Umm*, 1:41 (para. 298); for the Quranic verse, see 1:7 (para. 50).

[124] *Risāla*, in *Umm*, 1:35 (paras. 260–63).

The last three chapters have demonstrated the multifaceted influence that al-Shāfiʿī exerted on the scholarly world of the third/ninth and fourth/tenth centuries. Thanks to the newly emergent and increasingly sophisticated written culture, al-Shāfiʿī's works were preserved and disseminated throughout the Muslim world and formed the basis of a burgeoning secondary literature. The critical engagement of his followers with his writings gave rise to a distinctive Shāfiʿī school discourse, rooted in al-Shāfiʿī's hermeneutic paradigm and providing the basis for a collective form of authority – the legal school. Beyond the nascent Shāfiʿī school, al-Shāfiʿī's ideas had a transformative influence on the Ḥanafī and Mālikī legal schools as well as other religious sciences. By providing the theoretical foundation for the canonization of Quran and Hadith as well as for the relationship of authority between them, al-Shāfiʿī rendered the sacred sources amenable to the "scientific" application of a systematic interpretive methodology. This step transformed the scholar into a collector and weigher of evidence, rather than an embodiment of an amorphous tradition.

Conclusion

A century after al-Shāfiʿī's last student had died, Abū Hilāl al-ʿAskarī (d. around 400/1010) began one of his books with the observation that "in every branch of the religious sciences as well as of the non-religious disciplines, books have been composed that encompass the subject and organize its subcategories."[1] In the two centuries that had elapsed since the composition of the first proper books of Islamic scholarship, Muslim civilization had developed a sophisticated written culture that covered a wide range of genres and achieved an astounding geographical circulation. The success of this written culture can be seen in al-ʿAskarī's conclusion that by his lifetime the world of ideas had, with few exceptions, been fully mapped.

This immense achievement was not universally or unreservedly celebrated as progress.[2] The shift from a primarily oral scholarly tradition to a culture in which ideas were circulated and reputations made in the form of authored books had its critics, who pointed out the detrimental effects of the medium of writing. As already Plato had Socrates warn his friend Phaedrus:

> The loyalty you feel to writing … has just led you to tell me the opposite of its true effect. It will atrophy people's memories. Trust in writing will make them remember things by relying on marks made by others, from outside themselves,

[1] Abū Hilāl al-ʿAskarī, *al-Furūq al-lughawiyya*, ed. Muḥammad Ibrāhīm Salīm (Cairo: Dār al-ʿIlm wa-l-Thaqāfa, 1418/1997), 21–22.

[2] See Jan Assmann's discussion of the lament of the ancient Egyptian writer who, nearly two millennia before the Common Era, had given up hope of finding "novel untried words, free of repetition," in *Religion and Cultural Memory: Ten Studies*, trans. Rodney Livingstone (Stanford, CA: Stanford University Press, 2006), 83–84.

not on their own inner resources, and so writing will make the things they have learnt disappear from their minds. Your invention is a potion for jogging the memory, not for remembering. You provide your students with the appearance of intelligence, not real intelligence. Because your students will be widely read, though without any contact with a teacher, they will seem to be men of wide knowledge, when they will usually be ignorant.[3]

Writing in the midst of the formative period of the second/eighth and third/ninth centuries, the Iraqi litterateur and poet Muḥammad b. Yasīr al-Riyāshī (d. around 210/825) lamented the influence of writing in very similar terms:

Were I to remember all that I hear
And memorize all that I record of that
And only benefit from what I have thus collected –
They would call me an erudite scholar
But restlessly I am drawn to every field of study I encounter
So I neither memorize what I have recorded,
Nor tire of recording
So I sit in the company of ignorance,
While my knowledge lies deposited in books
Whoever finds his learning thus,
Will never progress
If you neither retain nor remember,
Then collecting books is futile indeed![4]

Plato and Ibn Yasīr find themselves trapped in a paradox. Both decry written knowledge as a barren imitation of the real, embodied knowledge that resides in the individual, but neither is able to resist the power of writing as a medium for gathering and disseminating ideas.[5] The conundrum faced by Plato and Ibn Yasīr is an outcome of the impact of writing on scholarship: the ineluctable logic of the written mode of scholarly discourse quickly made writing indispensable, while exerting a profound influence on the nature of the knowledge that it was merely meant to record. When Mālik wrote his *Muwaṭṭaʾ*, his aim was to produce a stable and unchanging intellectual edifice that could withstand the dialectic momentum of *raʾy*. But as Aḥmad b. Ḥanbal noted a century later

[3] Plato, *Phaedrus*, trans. Robin Waterfield (Oxford: Oxford University Press, 2002), 274e–275b.

[4] Al-Jāḥiẓ, *Kitāb al-Ḥayawān*, 2nd ed., ed. ʿAbd al-Salām Muḥammad Hārūn, 8 vols. (Cairo: Muṣṭafā al-Bābī al-Ḥalabī, 1965–69), 1:59. The poem is also attributed to al-Aṣmaʿī (d. 213/826); see (Pseudo-)al-Jāḥiẓ, *al-Maḥāsin wa-l-aḍdād* (Cairo: Maktabat al-Khānjī, 1994), 9.

[5] Jacques Derrida has shown how widespread this trope is in the Western intellectual tradition; see his *De la grammatologie* (Paris: Éditions de Minuit, 1967).

when cautioning his students not to write books, written discourse possesses its own momentum, which mirrors that of *ra'y*: one book, such as Mālik's, invites another, such as al-Shāfiʿī's, which in turn prompts further responses, refutations, and counterrefutations in an endless sequence.[6]

The connection between the revolution of writing and the transformation of legal discourse in Islamic societies did not go unnoticed. The Iraqi scholar Abū Ṭālib al-Makkī (d. 386/998) noted that

> books and compilations are all later developments, as is holding to the statements that people have made, giving legal opinions based on the school of a single individual, holding to his opinion, emulating him in everything, and conducting jurisprudence according to his school. This was not the way of the people who preceded us in the first and the second centuries.[7]

Al-Makkī was right: these concurrent developments – the emergence of legal literature and the formation of personal legal schools – did indeed represent a novel stage in the evolution of the Muslim normative discourse. This book has sought to demonstrate and explain what already al-Makkī implied, namely, that these two innovations were intimately connected. The spread of purposefully composed works enabled the preservation and unambiguous attribution of legal opinions and their justifications, and it initiated a metadiscourse on questions of interpretation and consistency. Writing also rendered change and inconsistency easily discernible and thereby undermined the perception of tradition as an unchanging monolith. The canonization project of al-Shāfiʿī was thus an attempt to extricate tradition from revelation, to delegitimize the former as the primary mediator of the revealed message, and to enshrine the latter as a fixed, clearly demarcated category.

While writing changed thought, the opposite was also true. Al-Shāfiʿī's radical reconceptualization of revelation as an act of direct divine communication, grounded in the Arabic language and explicable through the prophetic Sunna, spawned new genres of writing, creating new literatures. The collection and recording of prophetic Hadith with the aim of producing an exhaustive inventory of authentic reports took place only after these reports had been canonized *in theory*.[8] Likewise, the movement of

[6] Aḥmad, *Masāʾil*, 437.

[7] Abū Ṭālib al-Makkī, *Qūt al-qulūb*, 2:127; quoted and translated in Shāh Walī Allāh al-Dihlawī, *The Conclusive Argument from God: Shāh Walī Allāh of Delhi's "Ḥujjat Allāh al-bāligha,"* trans. Marcia K. Hermansen (Leiden: E. J. Brill, 1996), 451. Kaya also refers to this passage and notes its significance in "Continuity and Change," 40.

[8] Wheeler, *Applying the Canon in Islam*, 59; Brown, *Canonization of al-Bukhārī and Muslim*, chap. 3. Brown notes (on p. 135) that the quest to canonize definitive collections of prophetic Hadith in the fourth/tenth century was "an exclusively Shāfiʿī endeavor."

writing substantive exegetical works that interpret the Quran in light of prophetic Hadith began once the hermeneutic symbiosis of Hadith and Quran had been theorized by al-Shāfiʿī and popularized by his followers – most famously by his second-generation students al-Ṭabarī, Ibn Abī Ḥātim, and Ibn al-Mundhir. Canonization and writing thus constitute a mutually generating complex in the history of early Islamic law: the former endows the revelatory sources with authority and meaning, and the latter encases them in a stable form that lends itself to systematic analysis.

Viewing this transformation of Islamic scholarship and its literatures through the lens of canonization is useful, because it allows us to appreciate the broader cultural significance of texts in relation to historical circumstances and invites comparative insights from and on other cultures and religions. But given the connotations of the term "canon," it is important to bear in mind that Islamic law was not canonized in the same sense in which the so-called ʿUthmanic codex of the Quran was canonized – that is, established once and for all in a fixed, unchanging form. Islamic law after canonization was a project, not a product; it was constituted by a continuing, open-ended process of interpretation and debate taking place within the disciplinary realm of legal theory. This could rightfully be called a canonizing discourse, because its core purpose was to establish rules for connecting lawmaking rigorously to the sacred sources. Rather than eventually leading to the emergence of a single school of law, it provided a common methodological framework that was based on a shared understanding of what the sources of religious normativity are and thus forced jurists to justify their views in commensurate terms.

Al-Shāfiʿī's model, which clearly separated the canonical age of revelation from the subsequent span of profane, nonnormative history, stood in sharp contrast to the alternative theory proposed by Ibn ʿUlayya. As seen in Chapter 2, the latter defended the primacy of consensus as the criterion of normativity, an approach that rendered continuity over time largely irrelevant. It is only in al-Shāfiʿī's model that the connection back in time through the channel of Hadith could come to play the central role that it eventually did in Islamic thought. Through the delineation of a certain sacralized past as the sole fount of normativity, religious authority shifted to those who could access and recapture this past: the verifiers of Hadith, the exegetes of the Quran, and the jurists whose expertise permitted them to extract the normative implications of both sources. The scholars thus came to occupy a powerful position from which to critique state policies, societal customs, and established orthodoxies and orthopraxies. By contrast, in theories that proposed the continued generation of normative values through communal practice (Mālikism), consensus (Ibn ʿUlayya), or the living imam and his deputies (several Shiʿi groups at various points in time), communal leadership and, by extension, politics held much greater importance.

Nevertheless, canonization of the sacred sources did not turn Islamic legal reasoning into a purely solipsistic process, with individual jurists interpreting the sacred sources unconstrained by the opinions of their predecessors or peers. There can be neither private religions nor private legal systems.[9] Al-Shāfiʿī's students and their successors created a school that was based on al-Shāfiʿī's canonization project but that also furnished the basis for a communal venture of interpretation by establishing a shared methodology for the elucidation and extension of al-Shāfiʿī's paradigm. Among later generations of Shāfiʿīs, the founder's works would experience something akin to a secondary canonization, significantly limiting the ability of later scholars to disagree overtly with al-Shāfiʿī; I have explored this development elsewhere.[10] However, Shāfiʿī scholars continued to maintain the crucial theoretical distinction between revelatory evidence and al-Shāfiʿī's opinions, justifying the latter in terms of the former and thus claiming to honor the founder's prohibition of *taqlīd*.

Al-Shāfiʿī can be said to have founded the Shāfiʿī school because he established a paradigm that both *could* and *would* be followed by subsequent generations of students. It *could* be followed because of its "scientific" structure, incorporating a canon of sacred sources and a set of interpretive rules. The fact that it *was* followed was a matter of historical contingency, influenced by the crumbling of the old social order, the longevity of al-Shāfiʿī's students, and the opportunities created by periods of toleration and patronage. The Shāfiʿī school that grew around al-Shāfiʿī's paradigm of law in the third/ninth century was thus primarily a discursive institution, rooted in a central corpus of texts and shared techniques for its analysis. These were transmitted and developed in a burgeoning secondary literature and spread rapidly to other legal schools, inaugurating a process of convergence that would eventually culminate in the creation of a common terminological and methodological basis in Sunni thought.

In the broader scheme of Islamic history, al-Shāfiʿī's theory of canonization emerged against the background of a society undergoing a profound

[9] The legal schools were, of course, never complete legal systems, given that they relied on the state for enforcement.

[10] See my "Rethinking *Taqlīd*."

transition: the dissolution of the conquest identity that had fused Islam, Arabness, and loyalty to the Islamic empire into a unitary whole. In the Egyptian context, characterized by the gradual replacement of the Arab ruling elite by non-Arabs and the presence of a sedentary non-Muslim majority population, this process of dissolution took two seemingly contradictory directions. On the one hand, it led to a *localization* of political and economic interests and loyalties, as we saw, for example, in the case of the Arabs turned farmers who found themselves rebelling against the central government in alliance with Coptic Egyptians. On the other hand, it promoted a *universalization* and *deethnicization* of Islam: given the growing numbers of new converts to Islam and their increasing prominence in the fields of politics and scholarship, there was rising pressure toward the discovery and legitimation of a new, non–ethnically defined framework for religious norms.

Al-Shāfiʿī's paradigm found its niche within this wider movement. The solution that it offered to the crisis of normative tradition consisted of an elitist scripturalism. This was based on the revolutionary assertion that the message of revelation was intelligible by itself and that its comprehension required no mediation by tradition. But the challenges posed by the medium and the transmission of the message also meant that the task of interpreting revelation had to be carried out by specialists, who could weigh the relevant evidence and identify the most probable conclusion. As a result, Islamic law was transformed from a communal venture, based on an organic link to revelation through shared tradition, to a science of interpretation that soon became embedded in a discursive community of scholars. The cohesion that was undermined in the *umma*, or community of Muslims, as a whole through its increasing diversity was thus recreated in the institution of the legal school.

Bibliography

Abd-Allah, Umar Faruq. "Mālik's Concept of *ʿAmal* in Light of Mālikī Legal Theory." 2 vols. PhD diss., University of Chicago, 1978.

ʿAbd al-Razzāq al-Ṣanʿānī. *Tafsīr al-Qurʾān*. Edited by Muṣṭafā Muḥammad. 3 vols. in 4. Riyadh: Maktabat al-Rushd, 1989.

Abū ʿAwāna al-Isfarāyīnī. *Musnad Abī ʿAwāna*. Edited by Ayman b. ʿĀrif al-Dimashqī. 5 vols. Beirut: Dār al-Maʿrifa, 1998.

Abū Dāwūd al-Sijistānī. *Risālat al-Imām Abī Dāwūd ilā ahl Makka fī waṣf sunanih*. In *Thalāth rasāʾil fī ʿilm muṣṭalaḥ al-ḥadīth*, edited by ʿAbd al-Fattāḥ Abū Ghudda, 27–54. Aleppo: Maktab al-Maṭbūʿāt al-Islāmiyya, 1997.

Abū Ghudda, ʿAbd al-Fattāḥ, ed. *Namādhij min rasāʾil al-aʾimma al-salaf*. Aleppo: Maktab al-Maṭbūʿāt al-Islāmiyya, 1996.

Abū ʿUbayd al-Qāsim b. Sallām. *Al-Ṭahūr*. Edited by Mashhūr Ḥusayn Maḥmūd Sulaymān. Jedda: Maktabat al-Ṣaḥāba, 1994.

Abū Yūsuf. *Ikhtilāf Abī Ḥanīfa wa-Ibn Abī Laylā*. Edited by Abū al-Wafāʾ al-Afghānī. Hyderabad: Lajnat Iḥyāʾ al-Maʿārif al-Nuʿmāniyya, 1938 or 1939.

Kitāb al-Āthār. Edited by Abū al-Wafāʾ al-Afghānī. Hyderabad: Lajnat Iḥyāʾ al-Maʿārif al-Nuʿmāniyya, 1936.

Abū Zahra, Muḥammad. *Mālik: Ḥayātuhu wa-ʿaṣruhu, ārāʾuhu wa-fiqhuh*. Cairo: Maktabat al-Anjilū al-Miṣriyya, 1952.

Al-Shāfiʿī: Ḥayātuhu wa-ʿaṣruhu, ārāʾuhu wa-fiqhuh. Cairo: Dār al-Fikr al-ʿArabī, 1948.

Abū Zayd, Naṣr Ḥāmid. *Al-Imām al-Shāfiʿī wa-taʾsīs al-aydiyūlūjiyya al-wasaṭiyya*. Cairo: Sīnā, 1992.

Ahmad, Ahmad Atif. *Structural Interrelations of Theory and Practice in Islamic Law: A Study of Six Works of Medieval Islamic Jurisprudence*. Leiden: Brill, 2006.

Al-Ājurrī, Abū Bakr. *Kitāb al-Sharīʿa*. Edited by al-Walīd b. Muḥammad b. Nabīḥ Sayf al-Naṣr. 3 vols. Cairo: Muʾassasat Qurṭuba, 1996.

Al-Akfānī, Hibat Allāh. *Tasmiyat man rawā ʿan al-Muzanī al-Mukhtaṣar al-ṣaghīr min ʿilm al-Shāfiʿī*. Manuscript. Damascus: al-Ẓāhiriyya, MS Majmūʿ 94, fol. 85b. 1 fol., copied 701/1301.

Al-ʿAlāʾī, Ṣalāḥ al-Dīn Khalīl b. Kaykaldī. *Ithārat al-fawāʾid al-majmūʿa fī al-ishāra ilā al-farāʾid al-masmūʿa*. Edited by Marzūq b. Hayyās Āl Marzūq al-Zahrānī. 2 vols. Medina: Maktabat al-ʿUlūm wa-l-Ḥikam; Damascus: Dār al-ʿUlūm wa-l-Ḥikam, 2004.

Ali, Mohamed Mohamed Yunis. *Medieval Islamic Pragmatics: Sunni Legal Theorists' Models of Textual Communication*. Richmond: Curzon, 2000.

Al-Aṣamm, Abū al-ʿAbbās. *Musnad al-Imām Muḥammad b. Idrīs al-Shāfiʿī*. Edited by Rifʿat Fawzī ʿAbd al-Muṭṭalib. 3 vols. Beirut: Dār al-Bashāʾir al-Islāmiyya, 2005.

Al-Ashʿarī, Abū al-Ḥasan. *Maqālāt al-islāmiyyīn*. Edited by Muḥammad al-Dīn ʿAbd al-Ḥamīd. 2 vols. Cairo: Maktabat al-Nahḍa al-Miṣriyya, 1950–54.

Al-ʿAskarī, Abū Hilāl. *Al-Furūq al-lughawiyya*. Edited by Muḥammad Ibrāhīm Salīm. Cairo: Dār al-ʿIlm wa-l-Thaqāfa, 1418/1997.

Assmann, Aleida, and Jan Assmann, eds. *Kanon und Zensur*. Munich: W. Fink, 1987.

Assmann, Jan. *Das kulturelle Gedächtnis: Schrift, Erinnerung und politischer Identität in frühen Hochkulturen*. Munich: C. H. Beck, 1992.

Religion and Cultural Memory: Ten Studies. Translated by Rodney Livingstone. Stanford, CA: Stanford University Press, 2006.

Religion und kulturelles Gedächtnis. Munich: C. H. Beck, 2000.

Al-Athram, Abū Bakr. *Nāsikh al-ḥadīth wa-mansūkhuh*. Edited by ʿAbd Allāh b. Ḥamad al-Manṣūr. Riyadh: published by the editor, 1420/1999.

Aybakan, Bilal. *İmam Şâfiî ve Fıkıh Düşüncesinin Mezhepleşmesi*. Istanbul: İz Yayıncılık, 2007.

Al-Azmeh, A. "The Muslim Canon from Late Antiquity to the Era of Modernism." In *Canonization and Decanonization*, edited by A. van der Kooij and K. van der Toorn, 191–228. Leiden: Brill, 1998.

Al-Bāqillānī, Abū Bakr. *Al-Taqrīb wa-l-irshād*. Edited by ʿAbd al-Ḥamīd Abū Zunayd. 3 vols. Beirut: Muʾassasat al-Risāla, 1998.

Al-Bayhaqī, Abū Bakr. *Manāqib al-Shāfiʿī*. Edited by al-Sayyid Aḥmad Ṣaqr. 2 vols. Cairo: Maktabat Dār al-Turāth, 1971.

Al-Sunan al-kubrā. 10 vols. Hyderabad: Majlis Dāʾirat al-Maʿārif al-Niẓāmiyya, 1925–37.

Bedir, Murteza. "An Early Response to al-Shāfiʿī: ʿĪsā b. Abān on the Prophetic Report (*khabar*)." *Islamic Law and Society* 9 (2002): 285–311.

Bloom, Jonathan M. *Paper before Print: The History and Impact of Paper in the Islamic World*. New Haven, CT: Yale University Press, 2001.

Bosworth, C. E. "Al-Ṭabarī." In *Encyclopaedia of Islam*, 2nd ed., 10:11–15.

Brockopp, Jonathan E. "Competing Theories of Authority in Early Mālikī Texts." In *Studies in Islamic Legal Theory*, edited by Bernard G. Weiss, 3–22. Leiden: Brill, 2002.

Early Mālikī Law: Ibn ʿAbd al-Ḥakam and His Major Compendium of Jurisprudence. Leiden: Brill, 2000.

Brown, Jonathan A. C. *The Canonization of al-Bukhārī and Muslim: The Formation and Function of the Sunnī Ḥadīth Canon*. Leiden: Brill, 2007.

Brunschvig, Robert, ed. and trans. "'Le livre de l'ordre et de la défense' d'al-Muzani." *Bulletin d'études orientales* 11 (1945–46): 145–93.

Burton, John. "Rewriting the Timetable of Early Islam." *Journal of the American Oriental Society* 115 (1995): 453–62.

Al-Bustī, Abū Ḥātim. *Al-Majrūḥīn*. Edited by Maḥmūd Ibrāhīm Zāyid. 3 vols. Aleppo: Dār al-Waʿī, 1976.

Al-Buwayṭī, Abū Yaʿqūb. *Mukhtaṣar al-Buwayṭī*. Manuscript. Cairo: Dār al-Kutub al-Miṣriyya, Fiqh Ṭalaʿat, MS 208. 430 pp., copied 1325/1907.

Mukhtaṣar al-Buwayṭī. Manuscript. Istanbul: Süleymaniye, Murad Molla, MS 1189. 196 fols., copied 625/1228.

Mukhtaṣar al-Buwayṭī. Manuscript. Istanbul: Topkapı Sarayı, Ahmet III, MS 1078. 107 fols., copied 868/1464.

Calder, Norman. "Al-Nawawī's Typology of *Muftīs* and Its Significance for a General Theory of Islamic Law." *Islamic Law and Society* 3 (1996): 137–64.

Studies in Early Muslim Jurisprudence. Oxford: Clarendon, 1993.

Carter, Michael. "Foreign Vocabulary." In *The Blackwell Companion to the Qurʾān*, edited by Andrew Rippin, 120–39. Malden, MA: Blackwell, 2006.

"Pragmatics and Contractual Language in Early Arabic Grammar and Legal Theory." In *Approaches to Arabic Linguistics: Presented to Kees Versteegh on the Occasion of His Sixtieth Birthday*, edited by Everhard Ditters and Harald Motzki, 25–44. Leiden: Brill, 2007.

Chaumont, Éric. "Le 'dire d'un Compagnon unique' (*qawl al-wāḥid min l-ṣaḥāba*) entre la *sunna* et l'*iǧmāʿ* dans les *uṣūl al-fiqh* šāfiʿites classiques." *Studia Islamica*, no. 93 (2001): 59–76.

"Al-Shāfiʿī." In *Encyclopaedia of Islam*, 2nd ed., 9:181–85.

"Shāfiʿiyya." In *Encyclopaedia of Islam*, 2nd ed., 9:185–89.

"Al-Shaybānī." In *Encyclopaedia of Islam*, 2nd ed., 9:392–94.

Conrad, Gerhard. *Die quḍāt Dimašq und der maḏhab al-Auzāʿī: Materialien zur syrischen Rechtsgeschichte*. Beirut and Stuttgart: F. Steiner, 1994.

Cook, Michael. "ʿAnan and Islam: The Origins of Karaite Scripturalism." *Jerusalem Studies in Arabic and Islam* 9 (1987): 161–82.

Coulson, Noel J. *A History of Islamic Law*. Edinburgh: Edinburgh University Press, 1964.

Crone, Patricia. "Islam and Religious Freedom." Keynote speech, 30th Deutscher Orientalistentag, Freiburg im Breisgau, Germany, Sept. 24, 2007. Available online at http://orient.ruf.uni-freiburg.de/dotpub/crone.pdf.

Roman, Provincial, and Islamic Law: The Origins of the Islamic Patronate. Cambridge: Cambridge University Press, 1987.

"Walāʾ." In *Encyclopaedia of Islam*, 2nd ed., 6:874.

Crone, Patricia, and Martin Hinds. *God's Caliph: Religious Authority in the First Centuries of Islam*. Cambridge: Cambridge University Press, 1986.

Al-Dānī, Abū ʿAmr. *Al-Muqniʿ fī rasm maṣāḥif al-amṣār*. Edited by Ḥasan Sirrī. Alexandria: Markaz al-Iskandariyya li-l-Kitāb, 2005.

Al-Dāraquṭnī, Abū al-Ḥasan. *Mawsūʿat aqwāl Abī al-Ḥasan al-Dāraquṭnī*. Edited by Muḥammad al-Muslimī, ʿIṣām Maḥmūd, Ayman al-Zāmilī, et al. 2 vols. Beirut: ʿĀlam al-Kutub, 2001.

Al-Muʾtalif wa-l-mukhtalif. Edited by Muwaffaq b. ʿAbd Allāh b. ʿAbd al-Qādir. 5 vols. Beirut: Dār al-Gharb al-Islāmī, 1986.

Al-Dārimī, ʿUthmān b. Saʿīd. *Al-Radd ʿalā al-jahmiyya*. Edited by Badr b. ʿAbd Allāh al-Badr. Kuwait: Dār Ibn al-Athīr, 1995.

Davis, Steven. Introduction to *Pragmatics: A Reader*, edited by Steven Davis, 3–15. New York: Oxford University Press, 1991.

Al-Dhahabī, Shams al-Dīn Abū ʿAbd Allāh. *Al-Kāshif fī maʿrifat man lahu riwāya fī al-kutub al-sitta*. Edited by Muḥammad ʿAwwāma and Aḥmad Muḥammad Nimr al-Khaṭīb. 2 vols. Jedda: Dār al-Qibla, 1992.

Siyar aʿlām al-nubalāʾ. Edited by Shuʿayb al-Arnāʾūṭ and Muḥammad Nuʿaym al-ʿArqasūsī. 25 vols. Beirut: Muʾassasat al-Risāla, 1401–9/1981–88.

Tadhkirat al-ḥuffāẓ. Edited by Zakariyyā ʿUmayrāt. 5 vols. Beirut: Dār al-Kutub al-ʿIlmiyya, 1998.

Tārīkh al-islām wa-wafayāt al-mashāhīr wa-l-aʿlām. Edited by ʿUmar ʿAbd al-Salām Tadmurī. 52 vols. Beirut: Dār al-Kitāb al-ʿArabī, 1987.

Dietrich, Albert. "Zwei arabisch beschriftete Knochenstücke aus dem mittelalterlichen Ägypten." *Le Muséon* 65 (1952): 259–70.

Al-Dūrī, ʿAbd al-ʿAzīz. *Al-Judhūr al-tārīkhiyya li-l-shuʿūbiyya*. Beirut: Dār al-Ṭalīʿa, 1962.

Dutton, Yasin. "ʿAmal v Ḥadīth in Islamic Law: The Case of Sadl al-Yadayn (Holding One's Hands by One's Sides) When Doing the Prayer." *Islamic Law and Society* 3 (1996): 15–40.

Review of *Early Mālikī Law: Ibn ʿAbd al-Ḥakam and His Major Compendium of Islamic Jurisprudence*, by Jonathan Brockopp. *Journal of Islamic Studies* 13 (2002): 42–49.

Eckberg, Douglas E., and Lester Hill. "The Paradigm Concept and Sociology: A Critical Review." *American Sociological Review* 44 (1979): 925–37.

El Shamsy, Ahmed. "The First Shāfiʿī: The Traditionalist Legal Thought of Abū Yaʿqūb al-Buwayṭī (d. 231/846)." *Islamic Law and Society* 14 (2007): 301–41.

"Rethinking *Taqlīd* in the Early Shāfiʿī School." *Journal of the American Oriental Society* 128 (2008): 1–24.

Review of *The Formation of Islamic Hermeneutics: How Sunni Legal Theorists Imagined a Revealed Law*, by David Vishanoff. *Journal of the American Oriental Society* (forthcoming).

"Al-Shāfiʿī's Written Corpus: A Source-Critical Study." *Journal of the American Oriental Society* 132 (2012): 199–220.

El Shamsy, Ahmed, and Aron Zysow. "Al-Buwayṭī's Abridgment of al-Shāfiʿī's *Risāla*: Edition and Translation." *Islamic Law and Society* 19 (2012): 327–55.

Encyclopaedia of Islam. 2nd ed. Edited by P. J. Bearman et al. 12 vols. Leiden: E. J. Brill, 1960–2004.

Ess, Josef van. "Al-Aṣamm." In *Encyclopaedia of Islam*, 2nd ed., 12:88–90.

"Disputationspraxis in der islamischen Theologie: Eine vorläufige Skizze." *Revue des études islamiques* 44 (1976): 23–60.

The Flowering of Muslim Theology. Translated by Jane Marie Todd. Cambridge, MA: Harvard University Press, 2006.

Review of *Die Festung des Glaubens*, by Tilman Nagel. *Der Islam* 67 (1990): 366–74.

Theologie und Gesellschaft im 2. und 3. Jahrhundert Hidschra: Eine Geschichte des religiösen Denkens im frühen Islam. 6 vols. Berlin: W. de Gruyter, 1991–97.

Fadel, Mohammad. "Adjudication in the Mālikī *Madhhab*: A Study of Legal Process in Medieval Islamic Law." 2 vols. PhD diss., University of Chicago, 1995.

"The Social Logic of *Taqlīd* and the Rise of the *Mukhtaṣar*." *Islamic Law and Society* 3 (1996): 193–233.

Al-Fasāwī, Abū Yūsuf Yaʿqūb b. Sufyān. *Al-Maʿrifa wa-l-tārīkh*. Edited by Khalīl al-Manṣūr. 3 vols. Beirut: Dār al-Kutub al-ʿIlmiyya, 1999.

Al-Fāsī, Ibn al-Qaṭṭān. *Bayān al-wahm wa-l-īhām al-wāqiʿayn fī kitāb al-Aḥkām*. Edited by al-Ḥusayn Saʿīd. 6 vols. Riyadh: Dār Ṭayyiba, 1997.

Fleischer, Heinrich L. *Kleinere Schriften*. Edited by Anton Huber, Heinrich Thorbecke, and Ferdinand Mühlau. 3 vols. Leipzig: S. Hirzel, 1885–88.

Fück, Johann. "Isḥāq al-Mawsilī." In *Encyclopaedia of Islam*, 2nd ed., 4:110–11.

Gacek, Adam. *Arabic Manuscripts: A Vademecum for Readers*. Leiden: Brill, 2009.

Ghanāyim, Muḥammad Nabīl. *Al-Muzanī wa-atharuhu fī al-fiqh al-shāfiʿī*. Cairo: Dār al-Hidāya, 1998.

Gilliot, Claude. "Langue et Coran selon Tabari: 1. La Précellence du Coran." *Studia Islamica*, no. 68 (1988): 79–106.

Goldziher, Ignaz. *Introduction to Islamic Theology and Law*. Translated by Andras and Ruth Hamori. Princeton, NJ: Princeton University Press, 1981.

The Ẓāhirīs: Their Doctrine and Their History. Translated by Wolfgang Behn. Leiden: E. J. Brill, 1971.

Goody, Jack. *The Logic of Writing and the Organization of Society*. Cambridge: Cambridge University Press, 1986.

Görke, Andreas. *Das Kitāb al-Amwāl des Abū ʿUbaid al-Qāsim b. Sallām: Entstehung und Überlieferung eines frühislamischen Rechtswerkes*. Princeton, NJ: Darwin Press, 2003.

Gottschalk, Hans. "Abū ʿUbayd al-Qāsim b. Sallām: Studie zur Geschichte der arabischen Biographie." *Der Islam* 23 (1936): 245–89.

Grice, Paul. "Logic and Conversation." In *Pragmatics: A Reader*, edited by Steven Davis, 305–15. New York: Oxford University Press, 1991.

"Utterer's Meaning, Sentence-Meaning, and Word-Meaning." In *Pragmatics: A Reader*, edited by Steven Davis, 65–76. New York: Oxford University Press, 1991.

Haack, Susan. "A Foundherentist Theory of Empirical Justification." In *Epistemology: Contemporary Readings*, edited by Michael Huemer, 417–30. London: Routledge, 2002.

Hallaq, Wael B. *Authority, Continuity and Change*. Cambridge: Cambridge University Press, 2001.

"From Regional to Personal Schools of Law? A Reevaluation." *Islamic Law and Society* 8 (2001): 1–26.

The Origins and Evolution of Islamic Law. Cambridge: Cambridge University Press, 2005.

Halm, Heinz. "Der Wesir al-Kundurī und die Fitna von Nīšāpūr." *Die Welt des Orients* 6 (1971): 205–33.

Hamlyn, D. W. "Aristotle on Dialectic." *Philosophy* 65 (1990): 465–76.

Hansu, Hüseyin. *Mutezile ve Hadis*. Ankara: Kitâbiyât, 2004.

Hardy, Paul. "Epistemology and Divine Discourse." In *The Cambridge Companion to Classical Islamic Theology*, edited by T. J. Winter, 288–307. Cambridge: Cambridge University Press, 2008.

Ḥasan, Khalīfa Bā Bakr. *Al-Ijtihād bi-l-ra'y fī madrasat al-Ḥijāz al-fiqhiyya*. Cairo: Maktabat al-Zahrā', 1997.

Hawting, Gerald. "An Ascetic Vow and an Unseemly Oath? *Īlā'* and *Ẓihār* in Muslim Law." *Bulletin of the School of Oriental and African Studies* 57 (1994): 113–25.

Heidemann, Stefan. "Die Geschichte von ar-Raqqa/ar-Rāfiqa: Ein Überblick." In *Raqqa II: Die islamische Stadt*, edited by Stefan Heidemann and Andrea Becker, 9–56. Mainz: P. von Zabern, 2003.

Hilloowala, Yasmin. "The History of the Conquest of Egypt." PhD diss., University of Arizona, 1998.

Hurvitz, Nimrod. *The Formation of Ḥanbalism: Piety into Power*. London: RoutledgeCurzon, 2002.

Ibn ʿAbd al-Barr, Abū ʿUmar Yūsuf. *Al-Intiqā' fī faḍā'il al-a'imma al-thalātha al-fuqahā'*. Edited by ʿAbd al-Fattāḥ Abū Ghudda. Aleppo: Maktab al-Maṭbūʿāt al-Islāmiyya, 1997.

Jāmiʿ bayān al-ʿilm. Edited by Abū al-Ashbāl al-Zuhayrī. 2 vols. Dammam: Dār Ibn al-Jawzī, 1994.

Ibn ʿAbd al-Ḥakam, ʿAbd al-Raḥmān. *The History of the Conquest of Egypt, North Africa and Spain* (*Futūḥ Miṣr wa-akhbāruhā*). Edited by Charles Torrey. New Haven, CT: Yale University Press, 1922.

Ibn Abī Ḥātim al-Rāzī. *Ādāb al-Shāfiʿī wa-manāqibuh*. Edited by ʿAbd al-Ghanī ʿAbd al-Khāliq. Cairo: Maktabat al-Khānjī, 1953.

Al-Jarḥ wa-l-taʿdīl. 4 vols. in 9. Beirut: Dār Iḥyā' al-Turāth al-ʿArabī, 1952–53.

Kitāb al-Marāsīl. Edited by Shukr Allāh b. Niʿmat Allāh Qūzhānī. Beirut: Mu'assasat al-Risāla, 1977.

Tafsīr al-Qur'ān al-ʿaẓīm. Edited by Asʿad Muḥammad al-Ṭayyib. 14 vols. Mecca and Riyadh: Maktabat Nizār Muṣṭafā al-Bāz, 1997.

Ibn Abī al-Wafā' al-Qurashī. *al-Jawāhir al-muḍiyya fī ṭabaqāt al-ḥanafiyya*. Edited by ʿAbd al-Fattāḥ al-Ḥulw. 5 vols. Cairo: Dār Iḥyā' al-Kutub al-ʿArabiyya, 1978–88. Reprint, Giza: Hajr, 1993.

Ibn Abī Yaʿlā al-Farrā', Abū al-Ḥusayn. *Ṭabaqāt al-ḥanābila*. Edited by ʿAbd al-Raḥmān al-ʿUthaymīn. 3 vols. Riyadh: al-Amāna al-ʿĀmma li-l-Iḥtifāl bi-Murūr Mi'at ʿĀm ʿalā Ta'sīs al-Mamlaka, 1999.

Ibn ʿAsākir. *Tārīkh madīnat Dimashq*. Edited by Muḥī al-Dīn al-ʿAmrawī. 70 vols. Beirut: Dār al-Fikr, 1995–2001.

Ibn al-Faraḍī, ʿAbd Allāh b. Muḥammad. *Tārīkh al-ʿulamā' wa-l-ruwāt li-l-ʿilm bi-l-Andalus*. Edited by ʿIzzat al-ʿAṭṭār al-Ḥusaynī. 2 vols. Cairo: Maktabat al-Khānjī, 1954.

Ibn Ḥajar al-ʿAsqalānī. *Fatḥ al-bārī.* 13 vols. Beirut: Dār al-Maʿrifa, n.d.
Al-Imtāʿ bi-l-arbaʿīn al-mutabāyina al-samāʿ. Edited by Abū ʿAbd Allāh Muḥammad Ismāʿīl. Beirut: Dār al-Kutub al-ʿIlmiyya, 1997.
Rafʿ al-iṣr ʿan quḍāt Miṣr. Edited by Ḥāmid ʿAbd al-Majīd, Muḥammad al-Mahdī Abū Sinna, and Muḥammad Ismāʿīl al-Sāwī. 2 vols. Cairo: Maṭbaʿat al-Amīriyya, 1957–61.
Tahdhīb al-Tahdhīb. 12 vols. Hyderabad: Dār al-Maʿārif al-ʿUthmāniyya, 1907–9.
Tawālī al-taʾnīs bi-maʿālī Ibn Idrīs. Edited by ʿAbd Allāh al-Kandarī. Beirut: Dār Ibn Ḥazm, 2008.
Al-ʿUjāb fī bayān al-asbāb. Edited by Abū ʿAbd al-Raḥmān Zamarlī. Beirut: Dār Ibn Ḥazm, 2002.
Ibn Ḥanbal, Aḥmad. *Al-ʿIlal wa-maʿrifat al-rijāl.* Edited by Waṣī Allāh ʿAbbās. 4 vols. Riyadh: Dār al-Khānī, 1988.
Masāʾil al-Imām Aḥmad b. Hanbal: Riwāyat ibnihi ʿAbd Allāh b. Aḥmad. Edited by Zuhayr al-Shāwīsh. Beirut: al-Maktab al-Islāmī, 1981.
Ibn Ḥazm, ʿAlī b. Aḥmad. *Mulakhkhaṣ Ibṭāl al-qiyās.* Edited by Saʿīd al-Afghānī. Beirut: Dār al-Fikr, 1969.
Al-Iḥkām fī uṣūl al-aḥkām. 8 vols. in 2. Cairo: Dār al-Ḥadīth, 1984.
Ibn Hishām. *Sīrat Ibn Hishām.* Edited by Majdī Fatḥī al-Sayyin. 5 vols. Cairo: Dār al-Ṣaḥāba, 1995.
Ibn al-Humām. *Sharḥ Fatḥ al-qadīr.* 7 vols. Damascus: Dār al-Fikr, n.d.
Ibn Juzayy al-Kalbī. *Al-Qawanīn al-fiqhiyya.* Tunis: al-Dār al-ʿArabiyya li-l-Kitāb, 1982.
Ibn Khallikān. *Wafayāt al-aʿyān wa-anbāʾ abnāʾ al-zamān.* Edited by Iḥsān ʿAbbās. 8 vols. Beirut: Dār Ṣādir, 1398/1978.
Ibn Khuzayma [Muḥammad b. Isḥāq al-Sulamī al-Naysābūrī]. *Ṣaḥīḥ Ibn Khuzayma.* Edited by Muḥammad Muṣṭafā al-Aʿẓamī. 4 vols. Beirut: al-Maktaba al-Islāmiyya, 1970.
Ibn Maʿīn, Yaḥyā. *Tārīkh Yaḥyā b. Maʿīn.* Edited by ʿAbd Allāh Aḥmad Ḥasan. Beirut: Dār al-Qalam, 1990.
Ibn Mākūlā, ʿAlī b. Hibat Allāh. *Al-Ikmāl fī rafʿ al-irtiyāb ʿan al-muʾtalif wa-l-mukhtalif min al-asmāʾ wa-l-kunā wa-l-ansāb.* 7 vols. Hyderabad: Dāʾirat al-Maʿārif al-ʿUthmāniyya, 1962–.
Ibn al-Mundhir, Abū Bakr Muḥammad b. Ibrāhīm. *Al-Awsaṭ fī al-sunan wa-l-ijmāʿ wa-l-ikhtilāf.* Edited by Ṣaghīr Aḥmad Muḥammad Ḥanīf. 11 vols. Riyadh: Dār Ṭayyiba, 1985–99.
Kitāb Tafsīr al-Qurʾān. Edited by Saʿd b. Muḥammad al-Saʿd. 2 vols. Medina: Dār al-Maʾāthir, 2002.
Ibn al-Muqaffaʿ. *Risālat al-ṣaḥāba.* In *Rasāʾil al-bulaghāʾ*, edited by Muḥammad Kurd ʿAlī, 120–31. Cairo: Dār al-Kutub al-ʿArabiyya al-Kubrā, 1913.
Ibn al-Nadīm, Muḥammad b. Isḥāq. *Kitāb al-Fihrist.* Edited by Ayman Fuʾād Sayyid. 2 pts. with 2 vols. each. London: Al-Furqan Islamic Heritage Foundation, 2009.
Ibn Nujaym, Zayn al-Dīn. *Al-Ashbāh wa-l-naẓāʾir.* Edited by Muḥammad Muṭīʿ al-Ḥāfiẓ. Damascus: Dār al-Fikr, 2005.
Ibn al-Qāṣṣ. *Adab al-qāḍī.* Edited by Ḥusayn al-Jubūrī. 2 vols. Taʾif: Maktabat al-Ṣiddīq, 1409/1989.

Al-Talkhīṣ. Edited by ʿĀdil Aḥmad ʿAbd al-Mawjūd and ʿAlī Muḥammad Muʿawwaḍ. Mecca: Maktabat Nizār Muṣṭafā al-Bāz, 1999.
Ibn al-Qaṣṣār, Abū al-Ḥasan. *Al-Muqaddima fī al-uṣūl*. Edited by Muḥammad b. al-Ḥusayn al-Sulaymānī. Beirut: Dār al-Gharb al-Islāmī, 1996.
Ibn Qayyim al-Jawziyya. *Ijtimāʿ al-juyūsh*. Edited by Bashīr Muḥammad ʿUyūn. Damascus: Maktabat Dār al-Īmān, 2000.
Iʿlām al-muwaqqiʿīn. Edited by Hānī al-Ḥājj. 4 vols. in 2. Cairo: al-Maktaba al-Tawfīqiyya, 2013.
Ibn Qudāma, Muwaffaq al-Dīn. *Al-Mughnī*. Edited by ʿAbd Allāh al-Turkī and ʿAbd al-Fattāḥ al-Ḥulw. 15 vols. Cairo: Hajr, 1986–90.
Ibn Qutayba. *Gharīb al-ḥadīth*. Edited by ʿAbd Allāh al-Jubūrī. 3 vols. Baghdad: Maṭbaʿat al-ʿĀnī, 1397/1997.
Taʾwīl mukhtalif al-ḥadīth. Edited by Muḥammad Zuhrī al-Najjār. Beirut: Dār al-Jīl, 1393/1972.
Ibn Saʿd, Muḥammad. *Al-Ṭabaqāt al-kubrā*. 8 vols. Beirut: Dār Ṣādir, 1957–68.
Al-Ṭabaqāt al-kubrā. Edited by Ziyād Muḥammad Manṣūr. Medina: Maktabat al-ʿUlūm wa-l-Ḥikam, 1987.
Al-Ṭabaqāt al-kubrā. Edited by ʿAlī Muḥammad ʿUmar. 11 vols. Cairo: Maktabat al-Khānjī, 2001.
Ibn al-Ṣalāḥ al-Shahrazūrī. *Adab al-muftī wa-l-mustaftī*. Edited by Muwaffaq ʿAbd Allāh ʿAbd al-Qādir. Beirut: Maktabat al-ʿUlūm wa-l-Ḥikam, 1407/1986 or 1987.
An Introduction to the Science of the Ḥadīth (Kitāb Maʿrifat anwāʿ ʿilm al-ḥadīth). Translated by Eerik Dickinson. Reading: Garnet, 2006.
Ṭabaqāt al-fuqahāʾ al-shāfiʿiyya. Edited by Muḥī al-Dīn ʿAlī Najīb. 2 vols. Beirut: Dār al-Bashāʾir al-Islāmiyya, 1992.
Ibn Shās, Jalāl al-Dīn. *ʿIqd al-jawāhir al-thamīna fī madhhab ʿālim al-Madīna*. Edited by Muḥammad Abū al-Ajfān and ʿAbd al-Ḥafīẓ Manṣūr. 3 vols. Beirut: Dār al-Gharb al-Islāmī, 2003.
Ibn Taymiyya, Abū al-ʿAbbās Aḥmad. *Iqāmat al-dalīl ʿalā ibṭāl al-taḥlīl*. In *al-Fatāwā al-kubrā*, edited by Muḥammad ʿAṭā and Muṣṭafā ʿAṭā, 6 vols., 6:5–320. Beirut: Dār al-Kutub al-ʿIlmiyya, 1987.
Al-Istiqāma. Edited by Muḥammad Rashshād Sālim. 2 vols. Medina: Jāmiʿat Muḥammad b. Saʿūd, 1983.
Majmūʿat al-fatāwā. Edited by ʿĀmir al-Jazzār and Anwar al-Bāz. 20 vols. Mansura: Dār al-Wafāʾ, 1997.
Ṣiḥḥat uṣūl ahl al-Madīna. In *Majmūʿat al-fatāwā*, edited by ʿĀmir al-Jazzār and Anwar al-Bāz, 20 vols., 20:163–219. Mansura: Dār al-Wafāʾ, 1997.
Ibn Yūnus, ʿAlī b. ʿAbd al-Raḥmān. *Tārīkh Ibn Yūnus al-Ṣadafī*. Compiled by ʿAbd al-Fattāḥ Fatḥī ʿAbd al-Fattāḥ. 2 vols. Beirut: Dār al-Kutub al-ʿIlmiyya, 2000.
Al-Iṣbahānī, Abū Nuʿaym. *Ḥilyat al-awliyāʾ wa-ṭabaqāt al-aṣfiyāʾ*. 10 vols. Cairo: Maktabat al-Khānjī, 1932–38. Reprint, Beirut: Dār al-Kitāb al-ʿArabī, 1967–68.
Jackson, Sherman A. "Fiction and Formalism: Toward a Functional Analysis of *Uṣūl al-Fiqh*." In *Studies in Islamic Legal Theory*, edited by Bernard G. Weiss, 177–201. Leiden: Brill, 2002.

"Setting the Record Straight: Ibn al-Labbād's Refutation of al-Shāfiʿī." *Journal of Islamic Studies* 11 (2000): 121–46.

"*Taqlīd*, Legal Scaffolding and the Scope of Legal Injunctions in Post-Formative Theory: *Muṭlaq* and *ʿĀmm* in the Jurisprudence of Shihāb al-Dīn al-Qarāfī." *Islamic Law and Society* 3 (1996): 165–92.

Al-Jāḥiẓ, Abū ʿUthmān. *Al-Bayān wa-l-tabyīn*. 7th ed. Edited by ʿAbd al-Salām Muḥammad Hārūn. 4 vols. Cairo: Maktabat al-Khānjī, 1998.

Kitāb al-Ḥayawān. 2nd ed. Edited by ʿAbd al-Salām Muḥammad Hārūn. 8 vols. Cairo: Muṣṭafā al-Bābī al-Ḥalabī, 1965–69.

(Pseudo-)al-Jāḥiẓ. *Al-Maḥāsin wa-l-aḍdād*. Cairo: Maktabat al-Khānjī, 1994.

Jaques, R. Kevin. "The Other Rabīʿ: Biographical Traditions and the Development of Early Shāfiʿī Authority." *Islamic Law and Society* 14 (2007): 143–79.

Al-Jaṣṣāṣ, Abū Bakr al-Rāzī. *Uṣūl al-fiqh al-musammā bi-l-Fuṣūl fī al-uṣūl*. Edited by ʿUjayl al-Nashamī. 4 vols. Kuwait: Wizārat al-Awqāf wa-l-Shuʾūn al-Islāmiyya, 1994.

Johansen, Baber. "The All-Embracing Town and Its Mosques: Al-Misr al-Jami." *Revue de l'Occident Musulman et de la Méditerranée* 12 (1981–82): 139–61.

"Casuistry: Between Legal Concept and Social Praxis." *Islamic Law and Society* 2 (1995): 135–56.

Jokisch, Benjamin. *Islamic Imperial Law: Harun-al-Rashid's Codification Project*. Berlin and New York: W. de Gruyter, 2007.

Juynboll, G. H. A. *Muslim Tradition: Studies in Chronology, Provenance, and Authorship of Early Ḥadīth*. Cambridge: Cambridge University Press, 1983.

Al-Kāsānī, ʿAlāʾ al-Dīn Abū Bakr b. Masʿūd. *Badāʾiʿ al-ṣanāʾiʿ fī tartīb al-sharāʾiʿ*. Edited by Aḥmad ʿAbd al-Mawjūd and ʿAlī Muʿawwaḍ. 10 vols. Beirut: Dār al-Kutub al-ʿIlmiyya, 1997.

Al-Kawtharī, Muḥammad Zāhid. *Fiqh ahl al-ʿIrāq wa-ḥadīthuhum*. Edited by ʿAbd al-Fattāḥ Abū Ghudda. Cairo: Maktab al-Maṭbūʿāt al-Islāmiyya, 1970.

Kaya, Eyyüp Said. "Continuity and Change in Islamic Law: The Concept of Madhhab and the Dimensions of Legal Disagreement in Hanafi Scholarship of the Tenth Century." In *The Islamic School of Law: Evolution, Devolution, and Progress*, edited by Peri Bearman, Rudolph Peters, and Frank Vogel, 26–40. Cambridge, MA: Islamic Legal Studies Program, 2005.

Kennedy, Hugh. "Central Government and Provincial Elites in the Early ʿAbbasid Caliphate." *Bulletin of the School of Oriental and African Studies* 44 (1981): 26–38.

"Egypt as a Province in the Islamic Caliphate, 641–868." In *The Cambridge History of Egypt*, vol. 1, *Islamic Egypt, 640–1517*, edited by Carl Petry, 62–85. Cambridge: Cambridge University Press, 1998.

"Miṣr." In *Encyclopaedia of Islam*, 2nd ed., 7:146.

"Al-Muwaffaḳ." In *Encyclopaedia of Islam*, 2nd ed., 7:801.

Kern, Friedrich. "Zwei Urkunden vom Imām Šāfiʿī." *Mitteilungen des Seminars für Orientalische Sprachen* 7 (1904): 53–68.

[Al-Khaffāf, Abū Bakr]. *Al-Aqsām wa-l-khiṣāl*. Manuscript. Dublin: Chester Beatty, MS Arabic 5115. 43 fols., copied 660/1262.

Al-Khalīlī, Abū Ya'lā al-Qazwīnī. *Kitāb al-Irshād fī ma'rifat 'ulamā' al-ḥadīth*. Edited by Muḥammad Sa'īd b. 'Umar Idrīs. 3 vols. Riyadh: Maktabat al-Rushd, 1989.

Al-Khaṭīb al-Baghdādī. *Al-Faqīh wa-l-mutafaqqih*. Edited by 'Ādil b. Yūsuf al-'Azzāzī. 2 vols. Dammam: Dār Ibn al-Jawzī, 1996.

Al-Kifāya fī 'ilm al-riwāya. Edited by Abū 'Abd Allāh al-Sawraqī and Ibrāhīm Ḥamdī al-Madanī. Medina: al-Maktaba al-'Ilmiyya, 1980.

Tārīkh Madīnat al-Salām. Edited by Bashshār 'Awwād Ma'rūf. 17 vols. Beirut: Dār al-Gharb al-Islāmī, 2001.

Al-Khuḍarī, Muḥammad. *Tārīkh al-tashrī' al-islāmī*. Cairo: Dār al-Istiqāma, 1967.

Al-Kindī, Muḥammad b. Yūsuf. *The Governors and Judges of Egypt, or Kitāb el 'umarā' (el wulāh) wa Kitāb el quḍāh of el Kindī*. Edited by Rhuvon Guest. Leiden: E. J. Brill, 1912.

Kuhn, Thomas. *The Structure of Scientific Revolutions*. 3rd ed. Chicago: University of Chicago Press, 1996.

Al-Lālakā'ī, Abū al-Qāsim. *Sharḥ uṣūl i'tiqād ahl al-sunna wa-l-jamā'a*. Edited by Aḥmad b. Sa'd al-Ghāmidī. 4 vols. Riyadh: Dār Ṭayyiba, 1402/1981 or 1982.

Lane, Edward W. *Arabic-English Lexicon*. 2 vols. Cambridge: Islamic Texts Society, 1984.

Lapidus, Ira M. "The Separation of State and Religion in the Development of Early Islamic Society." *International Journal of Middle East Studies* 6 (1975): 363–85.

Lassner, Jacob. *The Topography of Baghdad in the Early Middle Ages*. Detroit: Wayne State University Press, 1970.

Lecker, Michael. "Biographical Notes on Ibn Shihāb al-Zuhrī." *Journal of Semitic Studies* 41 (1996): 21–63.

The "Constitution of Medina": Muḥammad's First Legal Document. Princeton, NJ: Darwin Press, 2004.

"Taym b. Murra." In *Encyclopaedia of Islam*, 2nd ed., 10:401.

Lim, Richard. "Christian Triumph and Controversy." In *Interpreting Late Antiquity: Essays on the Postclassical World*, ed. G. W. Bowersock, Peter Brown, and Oleg Grabar, 196–218. Cambridge, MA: Belknap Press of Harvard University Press, 2001.

Lowry, Joseph E. *Early Islamic Legal Theory: The Risāla of Muḥammad ibn Idrīs al-Shāfi'ī*. Leiden: Brill, 2007.

"The First Islamic Legal Theory: Ibn al-Muqaffa' on Interpretation, Authority, and the Structure of the Law." *Journal of the American Oriental Society* 128 (2008): 25–40.

"Ibn Qutayba: The Earliest Witness to al-Shāfi'ī and His Legal Doctrines." In *'Abbasid Studies*, edited by James E. Montgomery, 303–19. Leuven: Peeters, 2004.

"The Reception of al-Shāfi'ī's Concept of *Amr* and *Nahy* in the Thought of His Student al-Muzanī." In *Law and Education in Medieval Islam*, edited by Joseph E. Lowry, Devin J. Stewart, and Shawkat M. Toorawa, 128–49. Cambridge: E. J. W. Gibb Memorial Trust, 2004.

Review of *Das Kitāb al-Amwāl des Abū ʿUbaid al-Qāsim b. Sallām: Entstehung und Überlieferung eines frühislamischen Rechtswerkes*, by Andreas Görke. *Journal of the American Oriental Society* 126 (2006): 114–16.

"Some Preliminary Observations on al-Šāfiʿī and Later *Uṣūl al-Fiqh*: The Case of the Term *Bayān*." *Arabica* 55 (2008): 505–27.

Lucas, Scott C. *Constructive Critics, Ḥadīth Literature, and the Articulation of Sunnī Islam: The Legacy of the Generation of Ibn Saʿd, Ibn Maʿīn, and Ibn Ḥanbal*. Leiden: Brill, 2004.

"The Legal Principles of Muḥammad b. Ismāʿīl al-Bukhārī and Their Relationship to Classical Salafi Islam." *Islamic Law and Society* 13 (2006): 289–324.

Madelung, Wilferd. *Arabic Texts Concerning the History of the Zaydī Imāms of Tabaristān, Daylamān and Gīlān*. Beirut: Deutsches Orient-Institut, 1987.

"The Origins of the Controversy Concerning the Creation of the Koran." In *Orientalia Hispanica*, vol. 1, edited by J. M. Barral, 504–25. Leiden: E. J. Brill, 1974.

Makdisi, George. "Ashʿarī and the Ashʿarites in Islamic Religious History I." *Studia Islamica*, no. 17 (1962): 37–80.

The Rise of Colleges: Institutions of Learning in Islam and the West. Edinburgh: Edinburgh University Press, 1981.

Al-Makkī, Abū Ṭālib. *Qūt al-qulūb*. Edited by ʿAbd al-Munʿim al-Ḥifnī. 3 vols. Cairo: Dār al-Rashād, 1991.

Mālik b. Anas. *Al-Muwaṭṭaʾ* [Yaḥyā al-Laythī's recension]. Edited by Muḥammad Fuʾād ʿAbd al-Bāqī. 2 vols. Cairo: Dār Iḥyāʾ al-Turāth al-ʿArabī, 1951.

Muwaṭṭaʾ al-Imām Mālik. Edited by Muḥammad Muṣṭafā al-Aʿẓamī. 8 vols. Abu Dhabi: Muʾassasat Zāyid b. Sulṭān, 2004.

Al-Maqrīzī, Taqī al-Dīn. *Al-Mawāʿiẓ wa-l-iʿtibār bi-dhikr al-khiṭaṭ wa-l-āthār* [*al-Khiṭaṭ*]. 2 vols. Bulaq: Dār al-Ṭibāʿa al-Miṣriyya, 1853.

Al-Muqaffā al-kabīr. Edited by Muḥammad al-Yaʿlāwī. 8 vols. Beirut: Dār al-Gharb al-Islāmī, 1990.

Maraqten, Mohammed. "Writing Materials in Pre-Islamic Arabia." *Journal of Semitic Studies* 43 (1998): 287–310.

Al-Marwazī, Muḥammad b. Naṣr. *Al-Sunna*. Edited by ʿAbd Allāh al-Buṣayrī. Riyadh: Dār al-ʿĀṣima, 2001.

Maydānī, ʿAbd al-Ghanī. *Kashf al-iltibās ʿammā awradahu al-Imām al-Bukhārī ʿalā baʿḍ al-nās*. Edited by ʿAbd al-Fattāḥ Abū Ghudda. Aleppo: Maktab al-Maṭbūʿāt al-Islāmiyya, 1993.

Melchert, Christopher. *Ahmad ibn Hanbal*. Oxford: Oneworld, 2006.

"The Early History of Islamic Law." In *Method and Theory in the Study of Islamic Origins*, edited by Herbert Berg, 293–324. Leiden: Brill, 2003.

The Formation of the Sunni Schools of Law, 9th–10th Centuries C.E. Leiden: Brill, 1997.

"The Meaning of *Qāla 'l-Shāfiʿī* in Ninth Century Sources." In *ʿAbbasid Studies*, edited by James E. Montgomery, 277–301. Leuven: Peeters, 2004.

"The Piety of the Hadith Folk." *International Journal of Middle East Studies* 34 (2002): 425–39.
"Traditionist-Jurisprudents and the Framing of Islamic Law." *Islamic Law and Society* 8 (2001): 383–406.
Mikhail, Maged S. A. "Egypt from Late Antiquity to Early Islam: Copts, Melkites, and Muslims Shaping a New Society." PhD diss., University of California, Los Angeles, 2004.
Miles, G. C. "Dirham." In *Encyclopaedia of Islam*, 2nd ed., 3:319.
Miller, Larry B. "Islamic Disputation Theory: A Study of the Development of Dialectic in Islam from the Tenth through Fourteenth Centuries." PhD diss., Princeton University, 1984.
Modarressi, Hossein. *Kharāj in Islamic Law*. London: Anchor Press, 1983.
Tradition and Survival: A Bibliographical Survey of Early Shīʿite Literature. Oxford: Oneworld, 2003.
Montgomery, James E. "Al-Jāḥiẓ's *Kitāb al-Bayān wa al-Tabyīn*." In *Writing and Representation in Medieval Islam: Muslim Horizons*, edited by Julia Bray, 91–152. London: Routledge, 2006.
Morimoto, Kosei. *The Fiscal Administration of Egypt in the Early Islamic Period*. Kyoto: Dohosha, 1981.
Morris, Charles W. "Foundations of the Theory of Signs." In *Writings on the General Theory of Signs*. The Hague: Mouton, 1971.
Mottahedeh, Roy P. *Loyalty and Leadership in an Early Islamic Society*. 2nd ed. London: I. B. Tauris, 2001.
Motzki, Harald. *Die Anfänge der islamischen Jurisprudenz: Ihre Entwicklung in Mekka bis zur Mitte des 2./8. Jahrhunderts*. Stuttgart: Deutsche Morgenländische Gesellschaft and F. Steiner, 1991.
"The Role of Non-Arab Converts in the Development of Early Islamic Law." *Islamic Law and Society* 6 (1999): 293–317.
Motzki, Harald, with Nicolet Boekhoff-Van der Voort and Sean W. Anthony. *Analysing Muslim Traditions: Studies in Legal, Exegetical and Maghāzī Ḥadīth*. Leiden: Brill, 2010.
Al-Muʿallimī, ʿAbd al-Raḥmān. *Al-Tankīl bi-mā fī taʾnīb al-Kawtharī min al-abāṭīl*. 2nd ed. Edited by Muḥammad Nāṣir al-Albānī and ʿAbd al-Razzāq Ḥamza. 2 vols. Riyadh: Maktabat al-Maʿārif, 1406/1985 or 1986.
Mubārak, Zakī. *Iṣlāḥ ashnaʿ khaṭaʾ fī tārīkh al-tashrīʿ al-islāmī*. Cairo: al-Maktaba al-Tijāriyya al-Kubrā, 1352/1934.
Al-Mufīd, Abū ʿAbd Allāh Muḥammad, al-Shaykh. *Al-Masāʾil al-ṣāghāniyya*. Vol. 3 of *Muṣannafāt Abī ʿAbd Allāh Muḥammad b. Muḥammad b. al-Nuʿmān b. al-Muʿallim al-ʿUkbarī al-Baghdādī*. 14 vols. Qum: al-Muʾtamar al-ʿĀlamī li-Alfiyyat al-Shaykh al-Mufīd, 1993.
Al-Munāwī, Shams al-Dīn. *Farāʾid al-fawāʾid*. Edited by Abū ʿAbd Allāh Ismāʿīl. Beirut: Dār al-Kutub al-ʿIlmiyya, 1995.
Muranyi, Miklos. *Ein altes Fragment medinensischer Jurisprudenz aus Qairawān*. Stuttgart: F. Steiner, 1985.
"Die frühe Rechtsliteratur zwischen Quellenanalyse und Fiktion." *Islamic Law and Society* 4 (1997): 224–41.

Musa, Aisha Y. *Ḥadīth as Scripture: Discussions on the Authority of Prophetic Traditions in Islam*. New York: Palgrave Macmillan, 2008.

Al-Muzanī, Ismāʿīl b. Yaḥyā. *Mukhtaṣar kitāb al-Umm li-l-Shāfiʿī* [*Mukhtaṣar al-Muzanī*]. Edited by Khalīl Shīḥā. Beirut: Dār al-Maʿrifa, 2004.

Mukhtaṣar al-Muzanī fī furūʿ al-shāfiʿiyya. Beirut: Dār al-Kutub al-ʿIlmiyya, 1998.

Mukhtaṣar al-Muzanī. Manuscript. Cairo: Dār al-Kutub al-Misriyya, MS Fiqh Shāfiʿī 268. 234 fols., copied 798/1395 or 1396.

Mukhtaṣar al-Muzanī. Manuscript. Cairo: Dār al-Kutub al-Misriyya, MS Fiqh Shāfiʿī 242. 211 fols., copied 698/1298 or 1299.

Sharḥ al-sunna. Edited by Jamāl ʿAzzūn. Riyadh: Dār al-Minhāj, 2009.

Al-Nasāʾī, Abū ʿAbd al-Raḥmān Aḥmad b. Shuʿayb. *Tasmiyat fuqahāʾ al-amṣār min aṣḥāb rasūl Allāh wa-man baʿdahum*. Edited by Muḥammad Ibrāhīm Zāyid. Aleppo: Dār al-Waʿī, 1950.

Nawas, John A. "The Emergence of *Fiqh* as a Distinct Discipline and the Ethnic Identity of the *Fuqahāʾ* in Early and Classical Islam." In *Studies in Arabic and Islam: Proceedings of the 19th Congress, Halle 1998*, edited by S. Leder, H. Kilpatrick, B. Martel-Thoumian, and H. Schönig, 491–99. Sterling, VA: Peeters, 2002.

"A Reexamination of Three Current Explanations for al-Maʾmun's Introduction of the *Miḥna*." *International Journal of Middle East Studies* **26** (1994): 615–29.

Al-Nawawī, Abū Zakariyyā Muḥī al-Dīn. *Tahdhīb al-asmāʾ wa-l-lughāt*. 4 vols. Cairo: Idārat al-Ṭibāʿa al-Munīriyya, 1927.

Al-Naysābūrī, Abū Bakr ʿAbd Allāh b. Ziyād. *Al-Ziyādāt ʿalā kitāb al-Muzanī*. Edited by Khālid b. Hāyif b. ʿUrayj al-Muṭayrī. Riyadh: Dār Aḍwāʾ al-Salaf; Kuwait: Dār al-Kawthar, 2005.

Nye, Joseph. *Bound to Lead: The Changing Nature of American Power*. New York: Basic Books, 1990.

O'Brian, Patrick. *Master and Commander*. New York: W. W. Norton, 1990.

Ong, Walter J. *Orality and Literacy: The Technologizing of the Word*. London: Methuen, 1982.

Patton, Walter. *Aḥmed ibn Ḥanbal and the Miḥna: A Biography of the Imâm Including an Account of the Mohammedan Inquisition Called the Miḥna, 218–234 A. H.* Leiden: E. J. Brill, 1897.

Pedersen, Johannes. *The Arabic Book*. Edited by Robert Hillenbrand. Translated by Geoffrey French. Princeton, NJ: Princeton University Press, 1984.

Plato. *Phaedrus*. Translated by Robin Waterfield. Oxford: Oxford University Press, 2002.

Popper, Karl R. *The Logic of Scientific Discovery*. London: Routledge, 2002.

Al-Qāḍī ʿAbd al-Wahhāb al-Baghdādī. *Masāʾil fī uṣūl al-fiqh mustakhraja min kitāb al-Maʿūna ʿalā madhhab ʿālim al-Madīna*, included as an addendum to Ibn al-Qaṣṣār, *al-Muqaddima fī al-uṣūl*, edited by Muḥammad b. al-Ḥusayn al-Sulaymānī, 235–255. Beirut: Dār al-Gharb al-Islāmī, 1996.

Al-Qāḍī ʿIyāḍ b. Mūsā al-Yaḥṣūbī. *Tartīb al-madārik wa-taqrīb al-masālik li-maʿrifat aʿlām madhhab Mālik*. Edited by Aḥmad Bakīr Maḥmūd. 8 vols. Rabat: Wizārat al-Awqāf wa-l-Shuʾūn al-Islāmiyya, 1965–83.

Al-Qāḍī al-Nuʿmān. *The Epistle of the Eloquent Clarification Concerning the Refutation of Ibn Qutayba*. Edited by Avraham Hakim. Leiden: Brill, 2012.

Al-Qarāfī, Shihāb al-Dīn. *Al-Furūq aw Anwār al-burūq fī anwāʾ al-furūq*. Edited by Khalīl al-Manṣūr. 4 vols. Beirut: Dār al-Kutub al-ʿIlmiyya, 1998.

Raddatz, H. P. "Sufyān al-Thawrī." In *Encyclopaedia of Islam*, 2nd ed., 9:770.

Al-Rāzī, Fakhr al-Dīn. *Manāqib al-Imām al-Shāfiʿī*. Edited by Aḥmad Ḥijāzī al-Saqqā. Cairo: Maktabat al-Kulliyyāt al-Azhariyya, 1986.

Rebstock, Ulrich. "Vom Abwägen (*tarǧīḥ*): Stationen einer Begriffskarriere." Paper presented at the 30th Deutscher Orientalistentag, Freiburg im Breisgau, Germany, Sept. 25, 2007. Available online at http://orient.ruf.uni-freiburg.de/dotpub/rebstock.pdf.

Rosenthal, Franz. "The Technique and Approach of Muslim Scholarship." *Analecta Orientalia* 24 (1947): 1–74.

Sadeghi, Behnam. "The Authenticity of Two 2nd/8th Century Ḥanafī Legal Texts: The *Kitāb al-āthār* and *al-Muwaṭṭaʾ* of Muḥammad b. al-Ḥasan al-Shaybānī." *Islamic Law and Society* 17 (2010): 291–319.

Al-Sahmī, Ḥamza b. Yūsuf. *Tārīkh Jurjān*. Edited by Muḥammad ʿAbd al-Muʿīd Khān. Beirut: ʿĀlam al-Kutub, 1981.

Saḥnūn [ʿAbd al-Salām b. Saʿīd al-Tanūkhī]. *Al-Mudawwana al-kubrā*. 16 vols. in 6. Cairo: Maṭbaʿat al-Saʿāda, 1322/1905 or 1906. Reprint, Beirut: Dār Ṣādir, n.d.

Al-Samʿānī, ʿAbd al-Karīm b. Muḥammad. *Al-Ansāb*. Edited by ʿAbd Allāh al-Bārūdī. 5 vols. Beirut: Dār al-Janān, 1988.

Al-Sarakhsī, Shams al-Dīn. *Al-Mabsūṭ*. Edited by Khalīl al-Mays. 31 vols. Beirut: Dār al-Fikr, 2000.

Saussure, Ferdinand de. *Saussure's Third Course of Lectures on General Linguistics (1910–1911): From the Notebooks of Emile Constantin*. Edited by Eisuke Komatsu. Translated by Roy Harris. Oxford: Pergamon, 1993.

Al-Ṣaymarī, Abū ʿAbd Allāh. *Akhbār Abī Ḥanīfa wa-aṣḥābih*. Edited by Abū al-Wafāʾ al-Afghānī. Hyderabad: Lajnat Iḥyāʾ al-Maʿārif al-Nuʿmāniyya, 1974. Reprint, Beirut: ʿĀlam al-Kutub, 1985.

Schacht, Joseph. "Abū Ḥanīfa al-Nuʿmān." In *Encyclopaedia of Islam*, 2nd ed., 1:123–24.

"Aghlabids." In *Encyclopaedia of Islam*, 2nd ed., 1:247.

An Introduction to Islamic Law. Oxford: Clarendon, 1964.

The Origins of Muhammadan Jurisprudence. Oxford: Clarendon, 1950.

Schöck, Cornelia. *Koranexegese, Grammatik und Logik: Zum Verhältnis von arabischer und aristotelischer Urteils-, Konsequenz- und Schlusslehre*. Leiden: Brill, 2006.

Schoeler, Gregor. *The Genesis of Literature in Islam: From the Aural to the Read*. Translated by Shawkat M. Toorawa. Edinburgh: Edinburgh University Press, 2009.

The Oral and the Written in Early Islam. Edited by James Montgomery. Translated by Uwe Vagelpohl. London: Routledge, 2006.

Scribner, Sylvia, and Michael Cole. *The Psychology of Literacy*. Cambridge, MA: Harvard University Press, 1981.

Sellheim, Rudolf. "Al-Kisāʾī." In *Encyclopaedia of Islam*, 2nd ed., 5:174–75.
Sezgin, Fuat. *Geschichte des arabischen Schrifttums*. 15 vols. Leiden: E. J. Brill, 1967–.
Al-Shāfiʿī, Muḥammad b. Idrīs. *Dīwān al-Imām al-Shāfiʿī*. Edited by ʿUmar Fārūq al-Ṭabbāʿ. Beirut: Dār al-Arqam, n.d.
Dīwān al-Shāfiʿī. Edited by Mujāhid Bahjat. Damascus: Dār al-Qalam, 1999.
The Epistle on Legal Theory. Translated by Joseph E. Lowry. New York: New York University Press, 2013.
Al-Risāla. Edited by Aḥmad Muḥammad Shākir. Cairo: al-Bābī al-Ḥalabī, 1940.
Al-Risāla, in *al-Umm*, edited by Rifʿat Fawzī ʿAbd al-Muṭṭalib, vol. 1. Mansura: Dār al-Wafāʾ, 2001.
Al-Shāfiʿī's Risāla: Treatise on the Foundations of Islamic Jurisprudence. Translated by Majid Khadduri. Cambridge: Islamic Texts Society, 1987.
Al-Sunan al-maʾthūra [al-Ṭaḥāwī's transmission through al-Muzanī]. Edited by ʿAbd al-Muʿṭī Qalʿajī. Beirut: Dār al-Maʿrifa, 1986.
Al-Umm. Edited by Rifʿat Fawzī ʿAbd al-Muṭṭalib. 11 vols. Mansura: Dār al-Wafāʾ, 2001.
Shāh Walī Allāh al-Dihlawī. *The Conclusive Argument from God: Shāh Walī Allāh of Delhi's "Ḥujjat Allāh al-Bāligha."* Translated by Marcia K. Hermansen. Leiden: E. J. Brill, 1996.
Shākir, Maḥmūd Muḥammad. *Qaḍiyyat al-shiʿr al-jāhilī fī kitāb Ibn Sallām*. Cairo: Maṭbaʿat al-Madanī, 1997.
Al-Shaybānī, Muḥammad b. al-Ḥasan. *Al-Ḥujja ʿalā ahl al-Madīna*. Edited by Mahdī Ḥasan al-Kīlānī al-Qādirī. 5 vols. Hyderabad: Lajnat Iḥyāʾ al-Maʿārif al-Nuʿmāniyya, 1965–71. Reprint, Beirut: ʿĀlam al-Kutub, 1983.
Al-Jāmiʿ al-kabīr. Edited by Abū al-Wafāʾ al-Afghānī. Hyderabad: Lajnat Iḥyāʾ al-Maʿārif al-Nuʿmāniyya, 1937 or 1938.
Kitāb al-Āthār. Edited by Khālid ʿAwwād. Damascus: Dār al-Nawādir, 2008.
Muwaṭṭaʾ al-Imām Mālik. Edited by ʿAbd al-Wahhāb ʿAbd al-Laṭīf. Cairo: al-Majlis al-Aʿlā li-l-Shuʾūn al-Islāmiyya, 1962.
Al-Shīrāzī, Abū Isḥāq. *Ṭabaqāt al-fuqahāʾ*. Edited by Iḥsān ʿAbbās. Beirut: Dār al-Rāʾid al-ʿArabī, 1970.
Sourdel, Dominique. "Ibn Māsawayh." In *Encyclopaedia of Islam*, 2nd ed., 3:872–73.
Spectorsky, Susan. "Aḥmad ibn Ḥanbal's *Fiqh*." *Journal of the American Oriental Society* 102 (1982): 461–65.
Sperber, Dan, and Deirdre Wilson. *Relevance: Communication and Cognition*. Cambridge, MA: Harvard University Press, 1986.
Stewart, Devin. "The Structure of the *Fihrist*: Ibn al-Nadim as Historian of Islamic Legal and Theological Schools." *International Journal of Middle East Studies* 39 (2007): 369–87.
Street, Brian V. *Literacy in Theory and Practice*. Cambridge: Cambridge University Press, 1984.
Al-Subkī, Tāj al-Dīn. *Ṭabaqāt al-shāfiʿiyya al-kubrā*. Edited by Maḥmūd Muḥammad al-Ṭanāḥī and ʿAbd al-Fattāḥ Muḥammad al-Ḥulw. 10 vols. Cairo: ʿĪsā al-Bābī al-Ḥalabī, 1964–76. Reprint, Cairo: Dār Iḥyāʾ al-Kutub al-ʿArabiyya, 1413/1992 or 1993.

Al-Suyūṭī, Jalāl al-Dīn. *Al-Ḥujaj al-mubīna fī al-tafḍīl bayna Makka wa-l-Madīna*. Edited by ʿAbd Allāh al-Darwīsh. Damascus: al-Yamāma, 1985.

Ḥusn al-muḥāḍara. Edited by Muḥammad Abū al-Faḍl Ibrāhīm. 2 vols. Cairo: ʿĪsā al-Bābī al-Ḥalabī, 1967–68.

Al-Ṭabarī, Muḥammad b. Jarīr. *Ikhtilāf al-fuqahāʾ*. Edited by Friedrich Kern. Beirut: Dār al-Kutub al-ʿIlmiyya, 1990.

Jāmiʿ al-bayān fī taʾwīl al-Qurʾān [*Tafsīr*]. Edited by ʿAbd Allāh al-Turkī. 26 vols. Cairo: Markaz al-Buḥūth wa-l-Dirāsāt al-ʿArabiyya al-Islāmiyya, 2001.

Al-Ṭaḥāwī, Abū Jaʿfar. *Aḥkām al-Qurʾān al-karīm*. Edited by Saʿd al-Dīn Ūnāl. 1st vol. in 2 parts. Istanbul: Türkiye Diyanet Vakfı, İslâm Araştırmaları Merkezi, 1995.

Mukhtaṣar al-Ṭaḥāwī. Edited by Abū al-Wafāʾ al-Afghānī. Hyderabad: Lajnat Iḥyāʾ al-Maʿārif al-Nuʿmāniyya, n.d. Reprint, Cairo: Dār al-Kitāb al-ʿArabī, 1370/1950 or 1951.

Sharḥ maʿānī al-āthār. Edited by Muḥammad Zuhrī al-Najjār and Muḥammad Jād al-Ḥaqq. 4 vols. Beirut: ʿĀlam al-Kutub, 1994.

Sharḥ mushkil al-āthār. Edited by Shuʿayb al-Arnaʾūṭ. 16 vols. Beirut: Muʾassasat al-Risāla, 1994.

Tallis, Raymond. *The Enduring Significance of Parmenides*. London: Continuum, 2008.

Al-Tamīmī, Muḥammad b. Aḥmad Abū al-ʿArab. *Al-Miḥan*. Edited by ʿUmar b. Sulaymān al-ʿUqaylī. Riyadh: Dār al-ʿUlūm, 1983.

Al-Taymī al-Iṣbahānī, Abū al-Qāsim Ismāʿīl b. Muḥammad. *Al-Ḥujja fī bayān al-maḥajja*. 2nd ed. Edited by Muḥammad al-Madkhalī. 2 vols. Riyadh: Dār al-Rāya, 1999.

Tillschneider, Hans-Thomas. *Die Entstehung der juristischen Hermeneutik (*uṣūl al-fiqh*) im frühen Islam*. Würzburg: Ergon, 2006.

"Typen historisch-exegetischer Überlieferung: Formen, Funktionen und Genese des Asbāb al-Nuzūl Materials." PhD diss., University of Freiburg, Germany, 2009.

Al-Tirmidhī, Abū ʿĪsā. *Al-Jāmiʿ al-ṣaḥīḥ* [*al-Sunan*]. Edited by Aḥmad Muḥammad Shākir, Muḥammad Fuʾād ʿAbd al-Bāqī, and Ibrāhīm ʿAṭwa ʿAwaḍ. 5 vols. Cairo: Muṣṭafā al-Bābī al-Ḥalabī, 1937–62.

Torrey, Charles. "Medina and ΠΟΛΙΣ, and Luke i. 39." *Harvard Theological Review* 17 (1924): 83–91.

Tsafrir, Nurit. *The History of an Islamic School of Law: The Early Spread of Hanafism*. Cambridge, MA: Islamic Legal Studies Program at Harvard Law School, 2004.

Versteegh, Kees. "Grammar and Exegesis: The Origins of Kufan Grammar and the *Tafsīr Muqātil*." *Der Islam* 67 (1990): 206–42.

Vikør, Knut. *Between God and the Sultan: A History of Islamic Law*. Oxford: Oxford University Press, 2005.

Vishanoff, David. *The Formation of Islamic Hermeneutics: How Sunni Legal Theorists Imagined a Revealed Law*. New Haven, CT: American Oriental Society, 2011.

Wakīʿ, Muḥammad b. Khalaf. *Akhbār al-quḍāt*. Edited by ʿAbd al-ʿAzīz Muṣṭafā al-Marāghī. 3 vols. Cairo: al-Maktaba al-Tijāriyya al-Kubrā, 1947–50.

Wakin, Jeanette, and Aron Zysow. "Ra'y." In *Encyclopaedia of Islam*, 2nd ed., 12:687.

Wālī, Ḥusayn. "Kitāb al-Umm wa-mā yuḥīṭu bih." *Majallat nūr al-islām* 4 (1352/1933 and 1934): 656–88.

Weiss, Bernard G. *The Spirit of Islamic Law*. Athens: University of Georgia Press, 1998.

Wheeler, Brannon. *Applying the Canon in Islam: The Authorization and Maintenance of Interpretive Reasoning in Ḥanafī Scholarship*. Albany: State University of New York Press, 1996.

Wheeler, Samuel C., III. *Deconstruction as Analytic Philosophy*. Stanford, CA: Stanford University Press, 2000.

Yahia, Mohyddin. *Šāfiʿī et les deux sources de la loi islamique*. Turnhout, Belgium: Brepols, 2009.

Yāqūt al-Ḥamawī. *Irshād al-arīb ilā maʿrifat al-adīb* [*Muʿjam al-udabāʾ*]. Edited by Iḥsān ʿAbbās. 9 vols. Beirut: Dār al-Gharb al-Islāmī, 1993.

Muʿjam al-buldān. 5 vols. Beirut: Dār Iḥyāʾ al-turāth al-ʿArabī, 1979.

Zaman, Muhammad Qasim. *Religion and Politics under the Early ʿAbbāsids: The Emergence of the Proto-Sunnī Elite*. Leiden: Brill, 1997.

Al-Zarkashī, Badr al-Dīn. *Al-Baḥr al-muḥīṭ*. Edited by ʿAbd al-Qādir ʿAbd Allāh al-ʿĀnī, ʿUmar Sulaymān al-Ashqar, et al. 6 vols. Kuwait: Wizārat al-Awqāf wa-l-Shuʾūn al-Islāmiyya, 1992.

Al-Nukat ʿalā Muqaddimat Ibn al-Ṣalāḥ. Edited by Zayn al-ʿĀbidīn b. Muḥammad Bilā Farīj. 4 vols. Riyadh: Maktabat Aḍwāʾ al-Salaf, 1998.

Al-Ziriklī, Khayr al-Dīn. *Al-Aʿlām*. 8 vols. Beirut: Dār al-ʿIlm li-l-Malāyīn, 1979.

Zysow, Aron. "The Economy of Certainty: An Introduction to the Typology of Islamic Legal Theory." PhD diss., Harvard University, 1984.

Index

Note that the letters *'ayn* (') and *hamza* ('), the lowercase prefix *al-*, and the abbreviation *b.* (*ibn*) are ignored in alphabetization.

militia (*jund*), 93, 111
misappropriation (*ghaṣb*), 23, 25
Modarressi, Hossein, 37n83
Montgomery, James, 216
mosques
  as arena of scholarship, 18, 56, 113, 120, 128, 129, 135, 139
  as public space, 109–110, 128, 129, 132
Mottahedeh, Roy P., 98n23
Motzki, Harald, 8n14, 9, 52n39, 99n27
Muʿallā al-Ṭāʾ ī, 98
Muʿallimī, ʿAbd al-Raḥmān al-, 129n44
Muʿāwiya b. Ḥudayj, 101
Mubārak, Zakī, 163
Mufaḍḍal b. Faḍāla (judge), 104, 106, 107, 109n62
muḥaddithūn. *See* Hadith scholars
Mukhtaṣar. *See* Buwayṭī, Abū Yaʿqūb al-: *Mukhtaṣar*; Ḥarmala b. Yaḥyā: *Mukhtaṣar*; Ibn ʿAbd al-Ḥakam, ʿAbd Allāh: *Mukhtaṣar*; Muzanī, Ismāʿīl b. Yaḥyā al-: *Mukhtaṣar*
Muqātil b. Sulaymān, 216
Musa, Aisha Y., 55n51, 58n69, 59n71
Muʿtaḍid, al- (caliph), 141
Muʿtamid, al- (caliph), 140
Muʿtaṣim, al- (caliph), 125, 127, 132
Mutawakkil, al- (caliph), 131
Muʿtazilism, 22, 56, 124, 185, 217
Muwaffaq, al-, 140
Muzanī, Ismāʿīl b. Yaḥyā al-
  engagement with al-Shāfiʿī's thought, 177–182, 187–188, 191–193
  and Ḥanafism, 191–193, 205
  legal argumentation, 138, 186–187
  life and career, 114, 130, 135, 136, 170, 172
  Mukhtaṣar, 136, 137, 139n92, 141, 143, 174–175, 199
  and rationalism, 135, 136, 197
  as transmitter, 153n30, 163

Nāfiʿ, 20
Nakhaʿī, al-, 47
Nasafī, Abū al-Barakāt al-, 62n83
Nasāʾī, Aḥmad b. Shuʿayb al-, 170, 184
Nawas, John, 99n27
Naysābūrī, Abū Bakr b. Ziyād al-, 199
non-Arabs, 31, 97–102, 116
non-Muslims, 109
normal science, 175–176
notables. *See* aristocratic class in Egypt
notes
  as form of writing, 27, 36–37, 38, 148, 183, 204, 213
  in al-Shāfiʿī's writing, 149–151, 152
  in textual transmission, 19, 156–157, 158, 159
Nuʿaym b. Ḥammād, 131n54
Nūh b. Mirdās Abū Muslim al-Sulamī, 143

orality. *See* writing and orality
orphans' property, 104, 105

paper, 157
paradigm, 175–177, 225
particularization (*takhṣīṣ*), 69, 80, 197, 202, 203, 218
pension (*ʿaṭāʾ*), 93, 97, 100, 110–111
pilgrimage, 181
plagiarism, 164–165, 217
Plato, 221
political authority in religion, 86, 126, 144, 219, 225
Popper, Karl, 189
Powell, Jon, 110n71
pragmatic context, 38, 71, 77
pragmatics, 75
prayer, 54, 132, 180, 209
preemption (*shufʿa*), 138–139, 192
probability, 50n26, 58, 62, 81, 83, 203
prudent direction (*irshād*), 57, 215
punishment, 32–33, 64
purity (*ṭahāra*), 109, 209, 217

Qāḍī al-Nuʿmān, al-, 219
Qallās, Ḥusayn al-, 170
Qarāṭīsī, Idrīs b. Yūsuf al-, 164
Qarāṭīsī, Yūsuf b. Yazīd al-, 113, 163–164
Qārī, Ibrāhīm b. Isḥāq al-, 121
Qaṭṭān, Yaḥyā b. Saʿīd al-, 30
qibla, as metaphor, 81, 85–86
qirāʾa, 19, 155, 161
Quran
  Arabic nature of, 72–73, 215
  createdness of, 122, 126, 128, 131, 197, 219
  occasions of (*asbāb al-nuzūl*), 79
  role in law of, 4, 40, 69–70
Quranic exegesis (*tafsīr*), 212–216, 224
Quranic Inquisition (*miḥnat al-Qurʾān*), 126–131, 197
  legal dimension of, 128–129
Qurṭubī, Abū al-ʿAbbās al-, 187n77

Made in the USA
Monee, IL
06 January 2021

56427532R00149